Art and Archaeology of Ancient Rome: An Introduction
by David Soren and Archer Martin

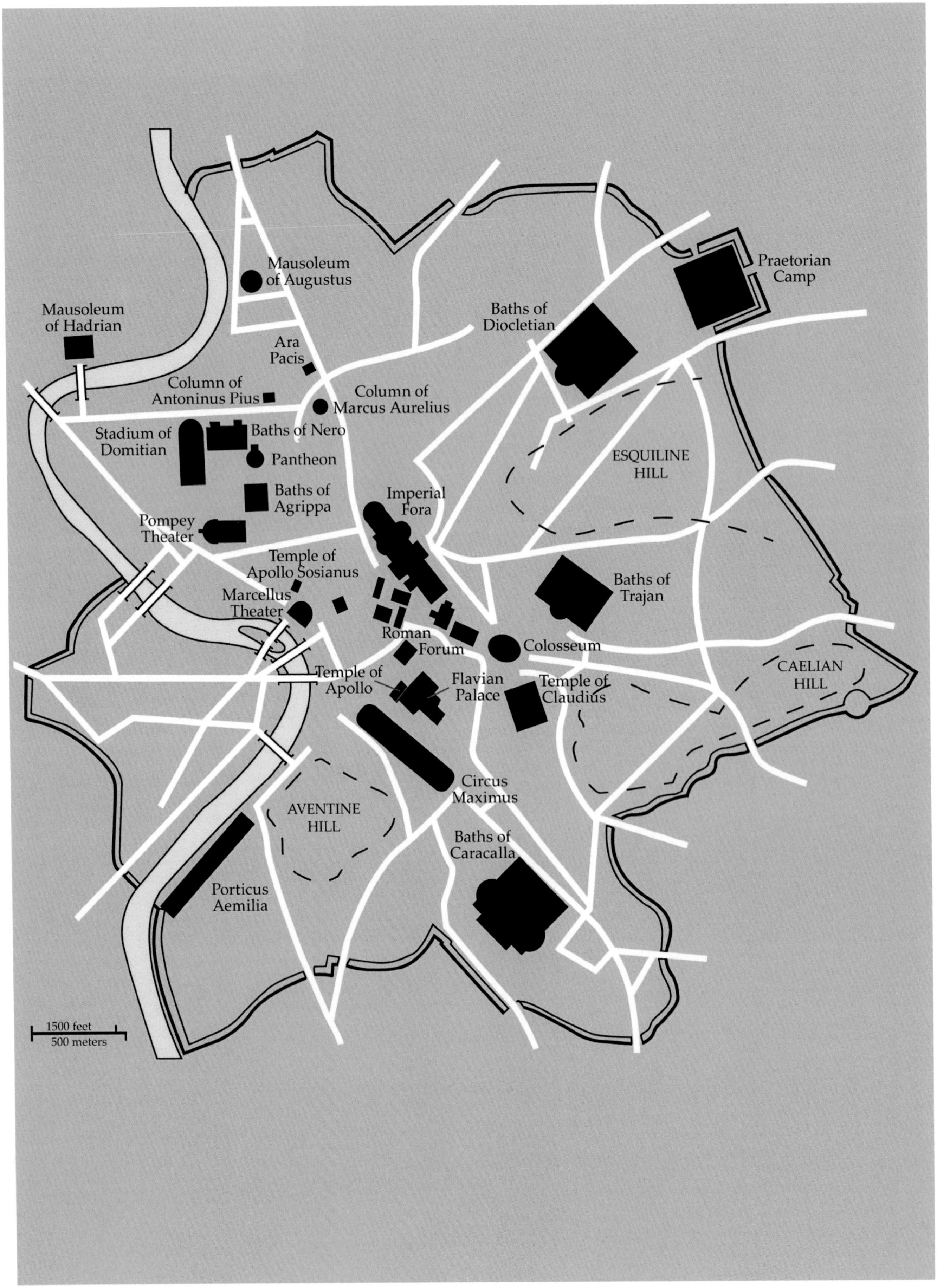

Mausoleum of Augustus
Mausoleum of Hadrian
Ara Pacis
Column of Antoninus Pius
Column of Marcus Aurelius
Stadium of Domitian
Baths of Nero
Pantheon
Baths of Agrippa
Pompey Theater
Temple of Apollo Sosianus
Marcellus Theater
Imperial Fora
Roman Forum
Temple of Apollo
Flavian Palace
Circus Maximus
AVENTINE HILL
Porticus Aemilia
Baths of Caracalla
Colosseum
Temple of Claudius
CAELIAN HILL
Baths of Trajan
ESQUILINE HILL
Baths of Diocletian
Praetorian Camp
1500 feet
500 meters

Art and Archaeology of Ancient Rome: An Introduction Volume II

by David Soren and Archer Martin

A Publication of the Joseph and Mary Cacioppo Foundation

Midnight Marquee Press, Inc.
Baltimore, Maryland, USA and London, UK

About the Authors

Archer Martin specializes in the study of Roman pottery and related socio-economic questions. He studied at Vanderbilt University and the Universität Regensburg in Bavaria, before doing his graduate studies in classical archaeology at the Università degli Studi di Roma "La Sapienza" and the Scuola Archeologica Italiana di Atene. He has taught at the Universities of Fribourg, Trento and Suor Orsola Benincasa (Naples) and served as the Andrew W. Mellon Professor-in-Charge of the School of Classical Studies at the American Academy in Rome. He also founded and directs the Howard Comfort FAAR '29 Summer School in Roman Pottery at the AAR. He has worked on many archaeological projects in Italy (in particular at Rome, Ostia and Pompeii, as well as in Tuscany, Umbria and Abruzzo), Greece (Olympia and Gortyna), Turkey (Ephesos) and Egypt (Schedia in the western Delta near Alexandria). He is the treasurer of the Rei Cretariae Romanae Fautores, the leading association for the promotion of Roman pottery studies.

David Soren is the Regents Professor of Anthropology and Classics and Adjunct Regents Professor of Art History at the University of Arizona. He received his B.A. from Dartmouth College in Greek and Roman Studies, his M.A. from Harvard in Fine Arts and his Ph.D. from Harvard in Classical Archaeology. He is a Fellow of Great Britain's Royal Institute of International Affairs and the Johns Hopkins School of Advanced International Studies. He has published 10 books and more than 100 articles on archaeology, art history, film, vaudeville and dance and has directed excavations in Tunisia, Portugal, Cyprus and Italy. He has won the Ciné Golden Eagle Award for documentary filmmaking and has worked extensively as a producer, director, screenwriter and consultant for NBC, PBS, A & E, BBC, RAI 1 (Italy), Discovery, National Geographic and the Learning Channel. For his contributions to Italian archaeology, he has been named an honorary Italian citizen.

Front Cover: Reconstruction of the Barracks of the Vigils at Ostia. Reconstruction by Angelo Coccettini and Marzia Vinci.
Back Cover: Arch of the Argentarii in Rome, including detail of the Severan family sacrificing. Photo Credit: Noelle Soren. University of Arizona School of Anthropology Archive.

Interior layout and cover design by Susan Svehla

Volume II paperback: ISBN 978-1-936168-52-1
Library of Congress Catalog Card Number 2014938438
Manufactured in the United States of America
First Printing December 2014
First Paperback Printing May 2015

This volume is dedicated to Charles R. "Chuck" Young

Charles R. "Chuck" Young

Born in Forest Hills, New York in 1931, the son of a Sicilian father and German mother, young Chuck wanted to be a cowboy.

He witnessed the hard day's work of his immigrant Grandfather, Giuseppe, that began in 1898 when Giuseppe brought his family to America to fulfill their dreams. And they did.

For him, there was art in nearly everything. Some call it having 'a knack for something'—he called it art. He studied the light, the carving, the brush strokes, the scene's integrity and he was a master at getting you to see what he saw and to take pleasure in it. He was also a master storyteller.

The Navy, forest service and horses were his interests as a young man. A professional career in Real Estate spanned 6 decades. Today, The Joseph and Mary Cacioppo Foundation benefits tremendously from his 30 years of dedication. His legacy is one of compassionate giving with an expanded view of philanthropy.

He taught about the significance of the past, loyalty to what is true in the present and the possibilities of the future.

He loved his country and may very well have continued to 'serve', had a cowboy hat & pair of riding boots been standard issue. Chuck (Dad), you lived authentic.

Michael-Anne Young
President, The Joseph and Mary Cacioppo Foundation.

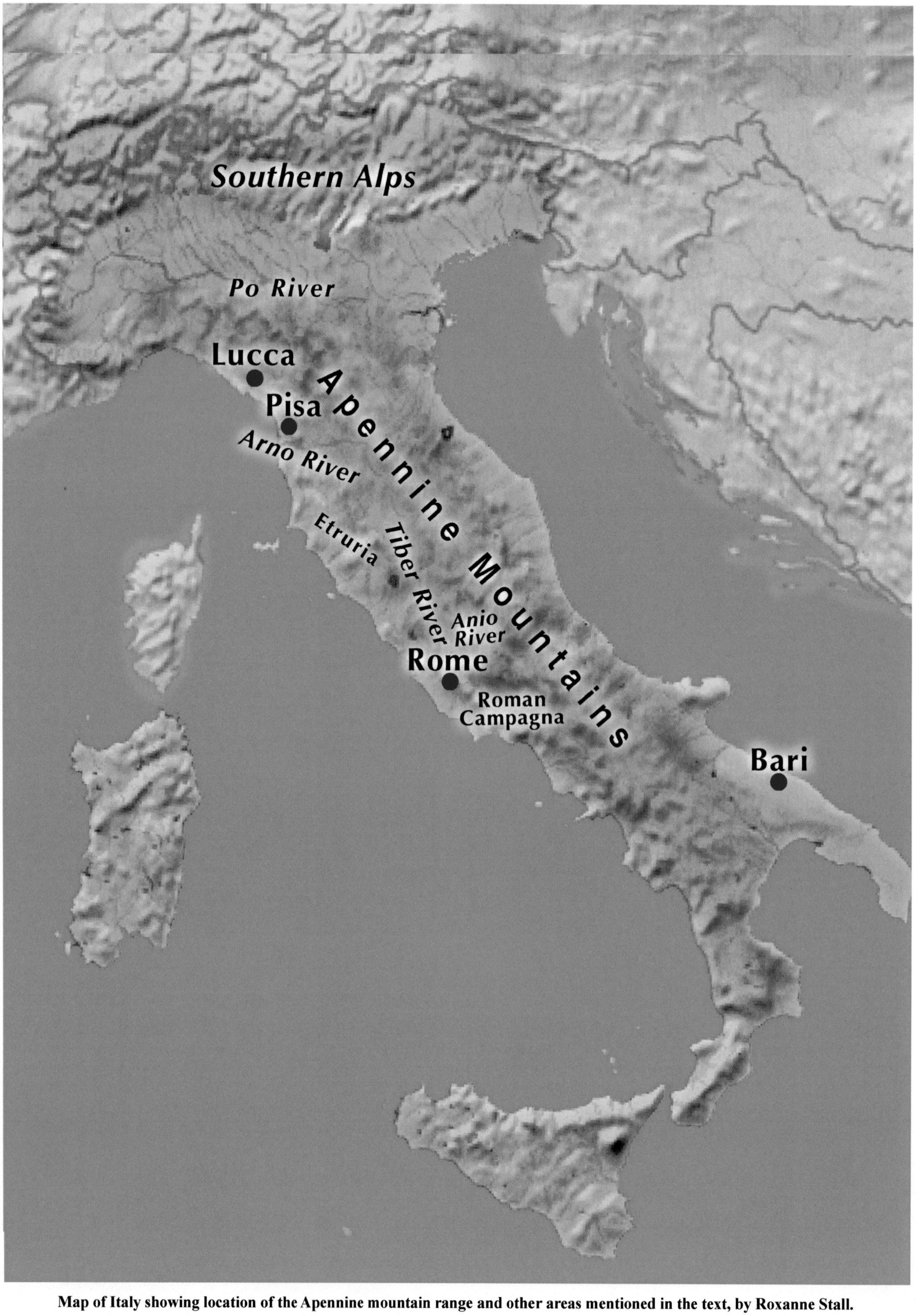

Map of Italy showing location of the Apennine mountain range and other areas mentioned in the text, by Roxanne Stall.

TABLE OF CONTENTS: VOLUME I

Films that enhance this text can be found at: http://www.midmar.com/SOREN.html

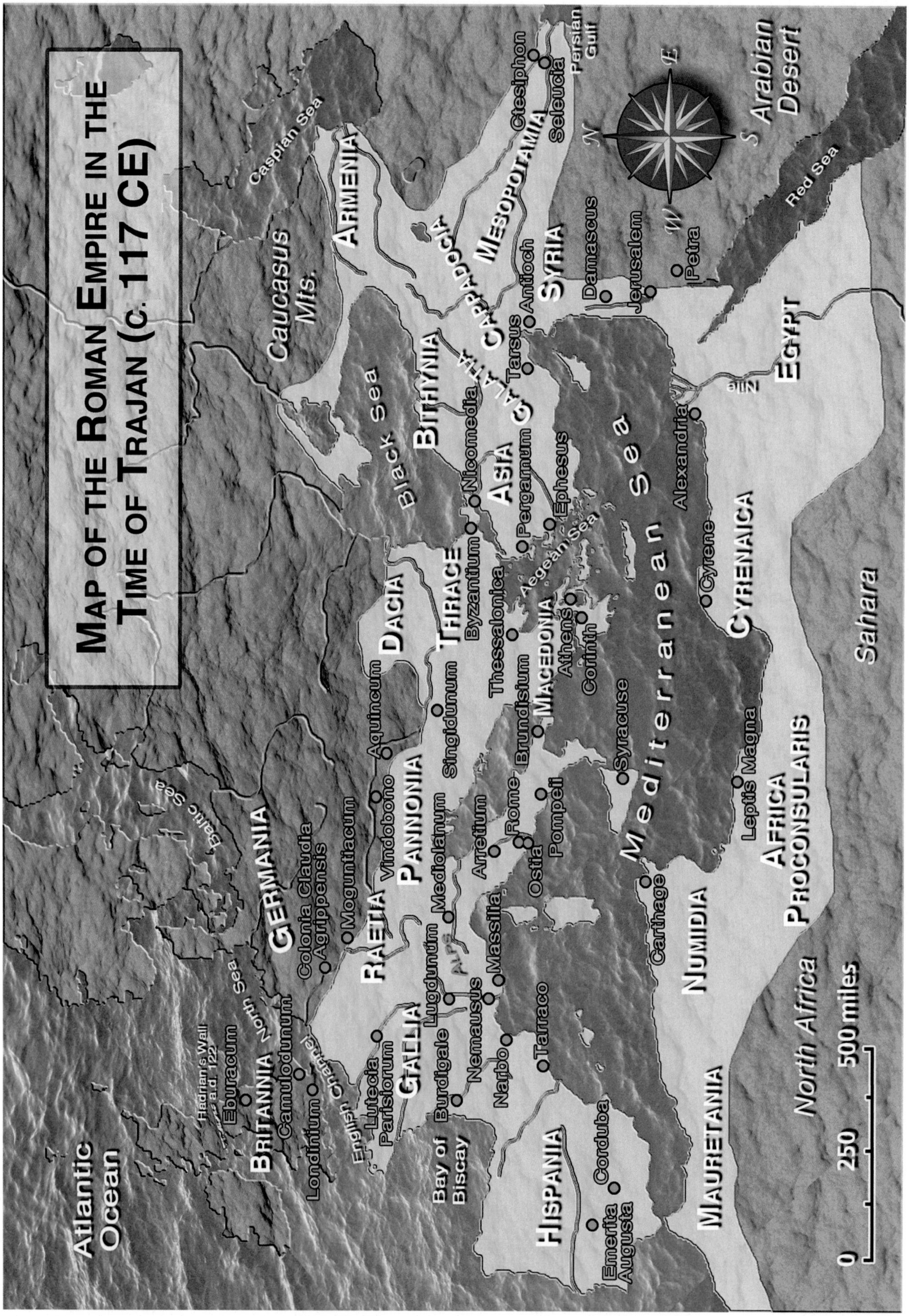

Fig. X-2 Map of the Roman Empire in the time of Trajan by Cherylee Francis.

Chapter X

Trajan and Hadrian—The Empire at its Zenith

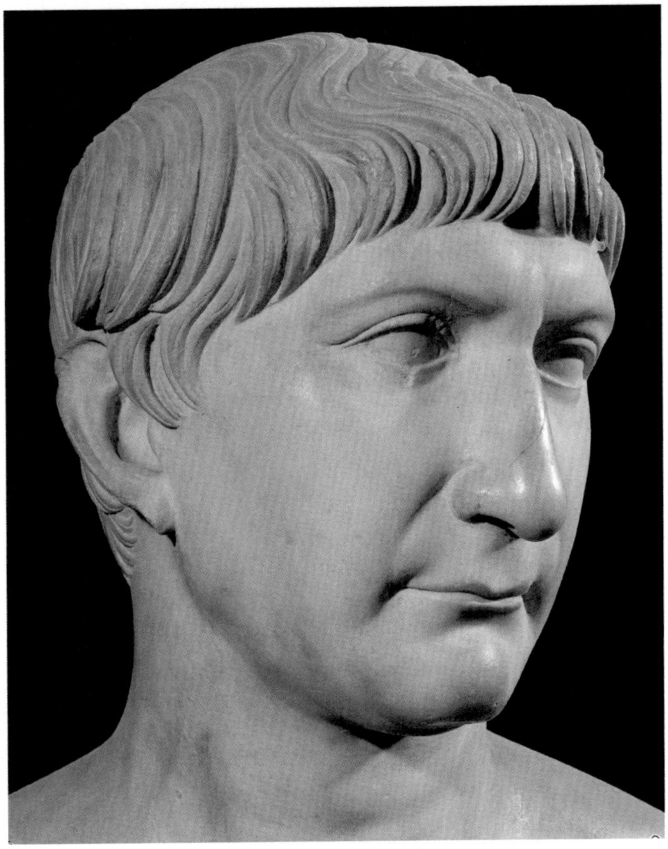

Fig. X-1 Emperor Trajan (98-117 CE). Marble bust. h. 55 cm. Location: Louvre Museum, Paris, France. Photo Credit: Erich Lessing / Art Resource, N.Y.

After the murder of Domitian, the empire plunged into another period of chaos, but the situation was quickly resolved when the Senate put forth a new emperor, Marcus Cocceius Nerva, a Senator from Umbria well into his 70s. During his two-year reign, Rome became stable once again. He oversaw a smooth transition to Marcus Ulpius Traianus (Fig. X-1) or Trajan, as he is commonly known now. A popular troop commander in Upper Germany, Trajan was from an Italian family but grew up in Italica, near modern Seville, in Spain. With Trajan, the empire undoubtedly reached its greatest expansion (Fig. X-2). Some of Trajan's conquests were ephemeral, however. Those in the East were abandoned as untenable by his successor Hadrian while those in the Balkans were longer lasting. The new province of Dacia remained in the empire for a century-and-a-half and is seen by the Romanians as the antecedent of their country today.

With Trajan's campaigns, Rome renewed its military reputation with emphasis on order and discipline in the troops. Trajan also restored confidence in the emperor after Domitian's program of military appeasement. In his dazzling architectural program he combined self-glorification with complexes useful to the general populace, thus insuring the perpetuation of his memory. The Empire was prosperous, as Edward Gibbon's *Decline and Fall of the Roman Empire* in the 18th century famously suggested for the period from Trajan to the Antonines, but there were signs of the crisis to come. For the first time the emperor was a provincial rather than an Italian. The first half of the second century was the last time Italian products (from wine to pottery) found a market outside the peninsula. The Italian heartland with its slave mode of production was entering into decline, and the formerly underdeveloped areas were beginning to assert themselves.

Trajan believed it was necessary to expand the limits of the empire and, particularly, to reduce the potential threat to the north. His attempts to maintain the Danube area and the provinces of Moesia and Pannonia led to several wars with the native peoples of Romania known as the Dacians, who were commanded by a brave warrior named Decebalus and whose capital city was Sarmezagethusa. The Dacian Wars raged from 101 to 102 CE, then after a brief truce, resumed in 106 and 107. As a result the Dacian capital was taken and their king committed suicide while being hunted down by a Roman legion. The Romans perceived the Dacians as a threat to their Danubian provinces. The Dacians were developing a powerful state on the strength of the gold mines they controlled, which was a situation the Romans never willingly tolerated in their neighbors, and there had been conflict with them before this.

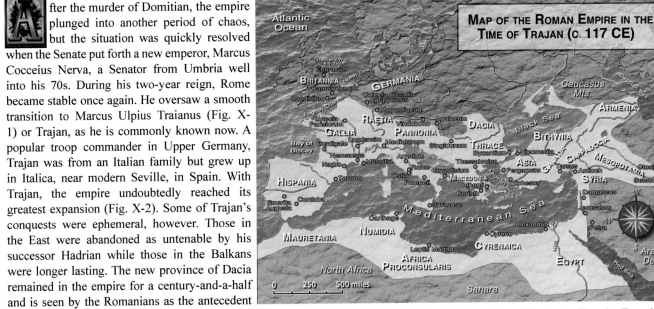

Fig. X-2 Map of the Roman Empire in the time of Trajan by Cherylee Francis.

Fig. X-3 Traditional reconstruction of the Forum of Trajan plaza, Rome. Photo Credit: © DeA Picture Library / Art Resource, N.Y.

Trajan celebrated a triumph, and his spoils were considerable. The image of the brave Dacian captive was promoted substantially at the time, something akin to the noble savage in American Western art. This notion was developed by Imperial chroniclers such as Tacitus, the foremost historian of the era. In art and architecture, the triumph was celebrated in one of the wonders of ancient Rome, the Forum of Trajan.

THE FORUM OF TRAJAN

For his major building project in Rome, Trajan appropriated a significant portion of the Quirinal Hill and slowly razed it to the ground. In this artificially flattened area, the engineer Apollodorus of Damascus, who had constructed the great bridge over the Danube River for Trajan's army in the Dacian campaigns, installed a wondrous Forum dedicated in 112 CE. The design of Trajan's Forum is currently the subject of major controversy (Figs. VII-11, 12, Figs. X-3, 4), because the most recent work in the Forum has cast doubt on the interpretation of its organization that has long been presented in textbooks and architectural surveys.

Ancient sources agree that Trajan's Forum, the last and most complicated of the Imperial Fora, was one of the most impressive structures in Rome. Inscriptions and literary sources provide various pieces of information about its history, such as the fact that Trajan was buried in a chamber in the base of his enormous column in the Forum in 117, and that Hadrian built a temple to the deified Trajan, perhaps also in this Forum. In spite of its renown, the complex's archaeological fate has been unfortunate until recently. The western end of the Forum was long hidden under later constructions and the eastern end was dismantled and hidden under a Renaissance neighborhood known as the Quartiere Alessandrino.

The first excavations go back to Napoleonic times, but much of the documentation was published only in the late 20th century. Although there was some limited work during the rest of the 19th century, the second great period of excavation in Trajan's Forum was in the 1920s and 1930s, supervised by the Italian archaeologist Corrado Ricci, with the clearances for Benito Mussolini's processional route now known as Via dei Fori Imperiali (in Mussolini's day Via dell'Impero) (Fig. X-5). However, the results were left practically unpublished until the late 20th century.

Finally, in the late 1990s an American scholar, James Packer of Northwestern University, published a detailed work, the fruit of decades of labor, bringing together everything that was known about the complex or could be deduced from what was visible at the time. Packer, in accord with his predecessors, envisioned the complex from east to west. In this conception, the main entrance was through three arches in a curved wall on the side by the Forum of Augustus. The principal element was the open area of the Forum, planted with four rows of trees, at the center of which Packer located the equestrian statue of Trajan recalled by the sources. The Forum area was flanked by a colonnade and a hemicycle on either side. The majestic Basilica Ulpia stood across the west end of the Forum area. Beyond the Basilica Ulpia was Trajan's Column in a small peristyle or colonnaded open space between two buildings identified as the Greek and Latin libraries, which were known to

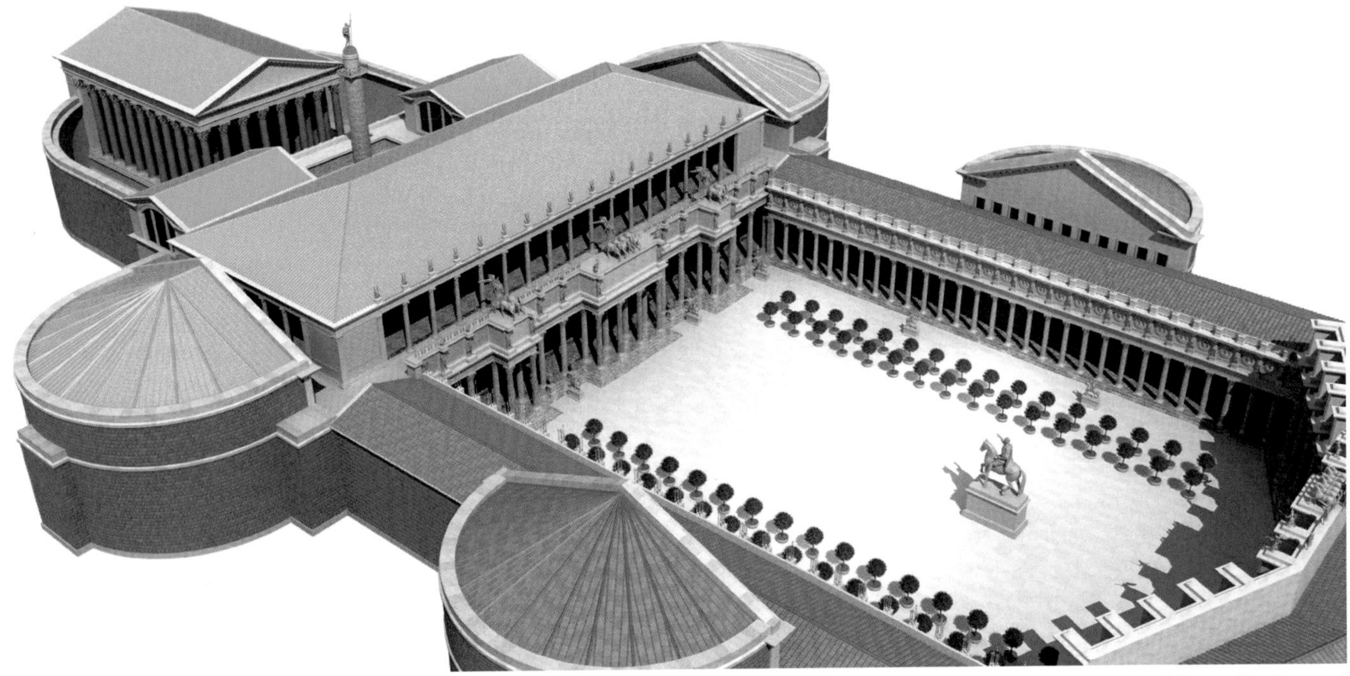

Fig. X-4 Reconstruction of the Forum of Trajan by James Packer and John Burge. Aerial view from the south. Courtesy of James Packer and John Burge.

have been part of the complex. In this scheme the complex ended in the west with a perimeter in which was the Temple to Trajan, known archaeologically through some grandiose columns. The presence today in the alleged temple area of a giant column of grey Egyptian granite 6 1/2 feet in diameter suggests that something large was there. The column is estimated to weigh 117 tons, more than twice the weight of the drums composing Trajan's Column.

At the same time Packer's work was published the archaeological service of the city of Rome began a third major series of excavations, bringing to light new evidence. The archaeologist responsible for the excavations, Roberto Meneghini, proposed a radical rethinking of the complex, very much at odds with the Packer thesis. In his conception the complex is to be seen from west to east instead of east to west. There is no perimeter or temple to the west of the Column and its flanking buildings, since only remains of *insulae* have been found where they were supposed to be. Instead of supposing a temple, Meneghini uses the columns to reconstruct a monumental temple-like façade constituting the main entrance or *propylon* to the complex. In his scheme the visitor would proceed past the Column and through the Basilica Ulpia to the Forum area. In the square continuous paving makes Packer's idea of rows of trees implausible. More tellingly, the base of the equestrian statue was actually discovered in new excavations not at the center of the piazza but rather along the main longitudinal axis much closer to the eastern end, indicating that its preferential viewpoint was from the west. The eastern end of the complex thus mirrors to some extent the western. Instead of a curved wall, the excavation revealed a wall in three segments, in the central one of which Meneghini reconstructs another temple-like façade. Beyond that is an open area similar to the courtyard of the Column. It is flanked by corridors, from which the Forum of Augustus is accessible. According to Meneghini, this can hardly be the main entrance because it is such an awkward space. Further excavations southeast of the Forum of Trajan produced an unexpected courtyard just south of the Forum of Augustus,

Fig. X-5 Achille Beltrame (1871- 1945). Portrait of Benito Mussolini, 1883-1945 Italian fascist leader, visiting the building yards for the Via dei Fori Imperiali as part of the restoration of Rome which he ordered, published in the newspaper *La Domenica del Corriere*, 1932 Photo Credit: Alfredo Dagli Orti / The Art Archive at Art Resource, N.Y.

making it even more uncertain how crowds of people could have entered the Forum of Trajan from this side and even more difficult to know how the area functioned. The purpose of this zone in the middle of the Imperial Fora is still unclear; it may have been a small *nymphaeum* with gurgling flowing water.

The scholarly discussion about the merits of the two proposals is still ongoing. Meneghini's conception leaves one wondering where the temple was. He has proposed that there is no firm evidence that the temple ever existed within the Forum, while Packer believes it must be situated within the Forum. On the other hand, before the invention of dynamite it would have been practically impossible to eliminate the massive base of a Roman temple, which casts very serious doubt on the traditional reconstruction as Packer envisions it, although he feels that some recently discovered blocks support his hypothesis. A new twist comes in the atlas of ancient Rome published in 2012 by Andrea Carandini and his collaborators—there the west-east orientation is accepted for Trajan's building program, but with the temple dedicated to Trajan by Hadrian located in front of (and west of) the entrance, in the area that would have remained unencumbered during the building operations for the Forum. The placement of the Equestrian Statue and the configuration of the eastern end of the complex give strong indications for a west-east orientation. Packer's reconstruction may prove correct on some points, such as the development of the upper stories and roofs, where he also differs from Meneghini, but the traditional conception of Trajan's Forum cannot prevail unless some very serious questions are answered.

Nonetheless, Packer's efforts at pulling together the entire history of the complex have made it possible to bring the discussion to the advanced level it has arrived at today. Thus, we can say that the complex contains three certain elements: the square, the Basilica Ulpia and the courtyard with the Column, whether the visitor experienced them in that order or in the reverse. On the long sides of the courtyard, paved with huge slabs, were corridors lined with columns and above them an attic story with caryatid-like images of conquered Dacians produced in brilliant colored marble. At the western end of the court loomed the fabulous Basilica Ulpia, one of the largest such halls in Rome and equipped with a large apse at each end and three entrances from the east. It is still not certain whether the enormous Basilica had a barrel vaulted roof or was roofed with huge wooden crossbeams. The columns were made of thick Egyptian granite on the ground floor in the nave and of *cipollino* marble from Euboea above them. White marbles were used for decorative details, either Carrara from northern Italy or Pentelic marble from Athens. In the northern apse manumission or freeing of slaves was practiced, but the purpose of the southern apse is not known. The strongly projecting apses mirrored and were inspired by the hemicycles of the Forum of Augustus to the east (Fig. VII-11).

COLUMN OF TRAJAN

On the other side of the Basilica rose one of the most famous surviving monuments from antiquity, the Column of Trajan (Figs. X-4, 6, 7), dedicated in 113 CE. Celebrating both Dacian Wars and dividing the First from the Second, the Column resembled a book scroll (*rotulus*), relating the story of the Roman army advancing into Dacian territory, led by Trajan and his staff. The Column was made of 18 blocks of Carrara marble put into place by giant cranes. Its interior contains a flight of steps that spiral up to the top. Occasional windows unobtrusively set into the design provided minimal light inside the staircase. The column was intended to house the cremated remains of Trajan, since it was located just outside the official city limit, where burials were permitted. A statue of the deified emperor graced the top of the column.

Huge dedicatory columns were hardly anything new to Rome since the tradition dates back there to at least the later fourth century BCE. Greek examples such as the Column of the Naxians at Delphi, which was topped with a large sphinx, were known from as early as 570 BCE. Columns with sculpted images on their sides were also known, as a famous Neronian example, the Jupiter Column from Mainz in Germany has already shown us (see Chapter VIII; Fig. VIII-10). However, the concept of transforming a column into a winding scroll of carved images is unprecedented and represents an inventive departure in Roman architecture and relief sculpture. Some 625 feet of sculptured relief on the Column of Trajan comprise more than 2,500 figures and feature the same peculiar continuous style of narrative that we first noted on the *Ficoroni Cista* in the fourth century BCE (see Chapter IV). This design was repeated in antiquity in the still-surviving Column of Marcus Aurelius, located today in its own square in the Piazza

Fig. X-6 View over the Forum of Trajan showing the Basilica Ulpia and the Column of Trajan. Photo Credit: Noelle Soren. University of Arizona School of Anthropology Archive.

Fig. X-7 Relief from the Column of Trajan: Soldiers building a fort, sculpture showing multiple perspectives and overlarge figure size. Rome. Photo Credit: Alinari / Art Resource, N.Y.

Colonna. Post-Antique rulers, including Napoleon have also found the concept irresistible for giving their own reigns that special Roman Imperial stamp.

The style of the relief sculpture on the Column of Trajan is far from Classical. Faced with a broad area to cover and the fact that most of the upper register could not be seen well from the Forum or Basilica, the sculptors used an approach that drew inspiration from Italian popular art. It may have been a style used in military paintings of the time in order to provide clarity and emphasize specific actions and gestures. Major figures were made larger than other figures. Crowds were depicted as small clusters of people. Several different vantage points or views could be employed in a single scene, including a sideways view and a tilted-up perspective that allowed the viewer to look inside a camp or within walls. True perspective was disregarded in favor of giving each scene its own best viewpoint to convey its message. This was a way of reordering reality with objects and figures arranged in a selective hierarchy of importance, a traditional folk art approach used occasionally even in Roman Imperial sculpture from at least the Augustan Period. Figures were stylized into simple, repetitive forms that lacked Classical grace (Figs. X-8, 9). Figures standing behind each other were stacked in tiers rather than blended into the background in lighter relief as was the case on the *Ara Pacis*

Fig. X-8 Trajan's Column, lower register detail: Two soldiers show the decapitated heads of their enemies to the Imperial officials at the battle of Tapa in 101 CE. Upper register detail: military operations following the campaign of 101 in which Dacian women and children are repatriated to Rome (to the upper left of the dividing tree trunk) Location: Column of Trajan, Rome, Italy. Photo Credit: Dan Duncan.

Fig. X-9 Reliefs from the base of the Trajan Column showing the River God Danube preceded by structures along the river bank and followed by marching Roman troops in the lower register. Location: Column of Trajan, Rome, Italy. Photo Credit: Alinari / Art Resource, N.Y.

Augustae (see Chapter VII). Gestures of figures were also simple and repetitive. Heads, hands and feet were often overlarge with respect to their bodies.

Viewing the Column makes the modern visitor feel as if he is watching a film. The story unfolds gradually from the base with an establishing shot or scene on the banks of the Danube as buildings gradually come into view, including the reserves for grain and fodder (Fig. X-9). Continuing along the coast, we see a few Roman soldiers keeping watch and others at the next port working along the docks unloading military parcels from ships and creating a supply chain for the army. These overlarge forms take the place of movie close-ups and show us what the sculptor seeks to emphasize: the matter-of-fact efficiency of the Roman army. A personification of the Danube River, the critical border between Romans and Dacians and one of the prizes of this campaign, looks on. His form is a stylized version of the muscular, dramatic sculpture developed in the Hellenistic east in Pergamum or Rhodes and known as Pergamene or Rhodian Baroque, but the massive rippling back muscles have been simplified into the popular art style. Suddenly Roman soldiers burst through an arch, and one can almost hear them marching this spring day of 101 CE, breaking the tranquility of the opening scenes with a loud tumult of stomping feet and music. Proceeding to the front of the group, we see the cavalry and their horses, musicians setting the pace, and the emperor appearing with his men. It may not be high Classical art, but it is highly effective storytelling.

In the beginning of the narrative the essential elements of the story to be told are here. Trajan is portrayed as a soldier emperor, as active with his men as his predecessor Domitian was not. Figures are massed together, tiered above each other, stylized and patterned. The high sky above them helps to generate the same epic feel that appears in the interior panels of the Arch of Titus (See Chapter IX). When all the scenes are completely viewed—something a Roman actually visiting it could scarcely do—the Column reveals itself to be a documentary account of how Romans marched, fought, besieged towns, and built camps and forts. The matter-of-factness of the presentation and the concept of never showing a Roman in grave danger or fearful is a part of the panegyric to Trajan and to Roman Imperialism, the glory of the troops (*gloria exercitus*). The sculptor is conveying the dedication and perseverance of the soldiers. There is also respect for the enemy, who is fiercely combative and powerful, but the Dacians are nonetheless barbarians who are defeated by the Romans' methodical planning and technical superiority in siege weapons and engineering projects such as the famous Danube pontoon bridge built by Apollodorus, the engineer architect. The art is stylized and simplified, and yet the exactitude in the detail of important objects is striking. Military emblems can be readily recognized. Shields are rendered with detail specific enough to allow them to be attributed to their particular military association.

The analogy made above between the relief decoration of the Column of Trajan and the viewing of a film may be pursued to understand the intent of the designer. The designer of the Column of Trajan was not showing a moment in time or an image of a god. He was really functioning as a director/screenwriter who must pre-plan a complete narrative. Just like a television director preparing for a time slot infused with commercials, he must finish his tale at a precise point and divide it up into key segments. To accomplish this he must first have produced detailed storyboards of each scene, carefully planning the relationship of each scene to the next. He must select highlights, for it is not possible to tell the story in real time. Perhaps he was working from an actual account of the war by Licinius Sura (who wrote the *Dacica*) or Appian of Alexandria, who offered his own account. The column may thus be an adaptation from an original work, departing from the text or excerpting from it to suit the medium of stone relief sculpture. Its designer edited scenes together to contrast total calm with shocking violence or vigorous activity, in just the same manner that a modern film director manipulates his screen audience.

In order to fade out a scene and begin a completely new one, the sculptor often used trees as dividers. Montage or creative juxtaposition is also used to contrast images dramatically. The clemency shown to the Romans' prisoners is, for example, contrasted with the massacre of Roman prisoners by the Dacian women. Linkage devices are employed also. In one scene the emperor is in a boat on the river. The boat appears at port, and we assume he is on board, but he then appears instead at the right already on his horse. In this sequence the boat is used to make us think he is still on board arriving at the port, and at the same time it leads us to the next narrative sequence. This is a linking device commonly used in narrative filmmaking and known as progressive linkage or a jump cut. The sculptor here is keenly aware of the visual tricks necessary to involve his audience and to move the action narrative along from one time and place to another. It is possible that there may have been an accompanying text that visitors could receive that explained the progressing scenes of the columns, or there may have been guides available to illustrate the highlights to tourists of the time. Even into the fourth century CE this Forum was considered a special wonder that should be experienced when in Rome.

One final characteristic of the Column of Trajan is the use of the *leitmotiv*, just as one would use it in film or music. An image is repeated throughout for emphasis, such as the emperor surrounded by his staff, delivering an *adlocutio* or formal address to his troops. The *submissio* of the barbarians to the emperor is another repeated concept. Both the *adlocutio* and the *submissio* are commonly found on Roman coins and were instantly recognizable indicators to the public of the might and majesty of the emperor. It was a way of getting a propaganda message across succinctly.

The director, writer and sculptors of the project remain unknown, but, following the cinematic analogy, the "producer" was surely Apollodorus of Damascus with Trajan as the executive producer overseeing everything. The Column had the themes of *gloria exercitus* and the emperor following the Augustan tradition of being *primus inter pares* (first among equals), as well as the theme of the civilized Roman versus the barbarian, who lives in a primitive village or is shown in the forest. Like a film or television program, scenes were composed of long establishing shots and intermediate shots with considerable depth of field. There were no close-ups but this was compensated for by the exaggerated emphasis on the various essential parts of each scene.

It may seem odd that the Column of Trajan rarely used sculptural forms of the Classical tradition, but it must be remembered that Classical art was not native to Rome and had been imported from the Greek world. Native Italic art—that is, art not done by imported artists or those formally trained in Classical values of idealized forms and smooth catenaries of drapery—always remained ready to come into the mainstream. At times it could be suppressed, as in the reign of Augustus to a large extent and also in the reign of Trajan's successor Hadrian, but many surviving Imperial monuments reflect the popular approach rather than the Classical.

Flanking the Column were two controversial buildings often described as libraries, which perhaps contained the official records of Trajan's administration, much like a United States Presidential Library of today. Niches in the walls are plainly visible, but the buildings were remodeled at some point and the access steps narrowed. Although they are usually considered libraries, the attribution is by no means certain, and Robert Meneghini believes that the use as libraries may be secondary. Still it is tempting to see the Column of Trajan as a giant *rotulus* symbolizing the works contained within the archives of these two buildings.

By Later antiquity, the Forum of Trajan was considered the one thing everyone had to experience in Rome. When the emperor Constantius II visited Rome in 357 CE he admired this most. Today one can still appreciate its sheer size, but except for the columns of the Basilica Ulpia and the Column of Trajan there is little left at which the casual tourist can marvel. The overall plan reflects a fascination for drawing-board symmetry, that is, the presentation of a clearly emphasized axis that cannot directly be experienced. One can see one's goal straight ahead but cannot get there by going in a straight line. For example, if a visitor enters from the west through a gateway, the path is interrupted by the Column of Trajan. If one desires to view the Column, the Basilica prevents one from getting any distance (Fig. X-4). The visitor goes through the Basilica and out the other side of it only to find the path straight ahead blocked by the placing of the Equestrian Statue of Trajan. This constant placing of detours is caused by the desire to interrupt the natural progression of the visitor by placing key objects in his path for him to focus on and appreciate, a sophisticated approach to architectural planning. The propaganda items are literally stuck in the viewer's way so he cannot miss them.

Another innovative aspect of the plan is the placing of the Basilica in the middle of everything, using it as a giant architectural backdrop and marker of two distinct spaces: the main area to the east and the smaller square of the column and libraries to the west. The Basilica thus divides the Forum into two distinct complexes, one for massive ceremonies (such as canceling public debts) and one for more personal reflection about the life, times and accomplishments of the emperor. It has been suggested that the placing of the Basilica and the buildings interpreted as libraries behind it reflects the typical plan of a military camp, thus underlining Trajan's role as a military man who came up through the army.

Fig. X- 10 Reconstruction of the Markets of Trajan constructed by Apollodorus of Damascus. Watercolor by Peter Connolly.

THE MARKETS OF TRAJAN

Trajan's military engineer architect Apollodorus of Damascus also produced another extraordinary (and quite different) monument immediately to the north of the Forum on the Quirinal Hill: the Markets of Trajan (Fig. X-10). The structure stepped up the hill reaching a height of perhaps seven stories and opened above onto an angled, paved street, which still exists. The upper level street was known as the Via Biberatica. The Italian scholar Filippo Coarelli derives *Biberatica* from *biber* (drink) referring to the abundance of bars in the *tabernae* or shops there (Fig. X-11). Giuseppe Lugli also offered that derivation but suggested that the connection could be with *piper* or *biper* (spice) as a main product sold in the *tabernae*.

There was a myriad of offices and shops that probably sold food and helped to run the market area. Several suites of offices were grouped around half domes, one of them featuring proto-flying buttresses resembling those of the *Domus Aurea*, but the *pièce de rèsistance* was the enormous *aula* or market hall with a long nave-like central space and shops on two stories (Fig. X-12, 13). The complex houses the Museo Nazionale dei Fori Romani and is also used for diverse national exhibitions featuring a wide variety of subjects. The *aula* contains groin vaults, and the upstairs offices are separated from the main block by small horizontal proto-flying buttresses. That the hall is still standing today with little remodeling is a tribute to the skill of Apollodorus.

During Trajan's reign a subtle shift in the treatment of building facades can be noted. In the earlier Empire buildings might be covered with stucco or given trimmings of Classical ornament, but with Trajan increasing emphasis was given to

Fig. X-11 View over Via Biberatica and Trajan's Market. Photo Credit: Noelle Soren. University of Arizona School of Anthropology Archive.

Fig. X-12 View of the *Aula* of the Markets of Trajan showing the proto-flying buttresses. Photo Credit: Noelle Soren. University of Arizona School of Anthropology Archive.

Fig. X- 13 Detail of the flying buttresses of the *Aula*. Photo credit: Noelle Soren. University of Arizona School of Anthropology Archive

the use of decorative brickwork that was allowed to stand on its own. In the Roman port town of Ostia at the mouth of the Tiber, even functional warehouses were given such treatment and the Markets of Trajan were no exception. The façade of the markets, viewed from the street just north of the Forum of Trajan, reveal a *tour de force* of decorative brickwork, including carefully juxtaposed broken pediments, lunette pediments (with curved upper borders), engaged pilasters with travertine capitals and bases, and relieving arches. It is probably in this period that the finest Roman decorative brickwork was done (Fig. X-14).

Fig. X-14 (right) Decorative brickwork on the façade of the Market of Trajan. University of Arizona School of Anthropology Archive.

THE *ANAGLYPHAE TRAIANI* OR *HADRIANI*

The reigns of Trajan and Hadrian saw several initiatives in favor of the poor. A particularly dramatic example was the cancellation of debts for the Roman people held in the Roman Forum by Hadrian in the year 118. The occasion was marked by a gathering up of debt records that were kept on rectangular wooden tablets. They were brought to the forum in groups that were tied together, heaped up in a mound, and burned.

An extraordinary monument of the period known as an *anaglypha* or relief decorated stone panel was discovered in 1872 in the Roman Forum (Figs. X- 15, 16). It had sculptures on both sides and might have been the balustrade visible at the entry to a tribunal or even for the *rostra* itself. One side shows a procession of Roman soldiers carrying in the tablets for burning by a lictor to the right (Fig. X-15). The emperor Hadrian may be the individual seated prominently on the *rostra* at the end of the panel but the figure is too damaged to identify.

Quite remarkable is the representation of the Roman Forum where the event took place. At the extreme left is the fig tree and statue of Marsyas long associated with the central area of the Forum to the west of the *rostra* while the long low building that appears next may be the *Basilica Iulia* and other structures associated with the south side of the Forum, but scholars are not sure what structures are being shown. They may include the Temples of Vespasian and Concord with a building traditionally identified as the Tabularium located behind, but that would mean that the Temple of Saturn was left out. There may be multiple perspectives at work so that we are expected to view the south and east sides of the Forum at the same time all along one line, a special collapsed or multiple perspective designed to show the burning of the debt tablets and the approving emperor on the *rostra*. There seems no way to equate the images on the relief with the actual ruins of the Forum in a manner that will satisfy all scholars.

Furthermore, the style of the figures and the odd multiple viewpoints of the relief seem closer to Trajan's Column than to Hadrianic monuments we know, and this has led many Italian scholars to proclaim that the lost emperor shown was intended to be Trajan and not Hadrian at all!

On the second side of the balustrade was illustrated the *suovetaurilia*, a scene of typical Roman sacrifice of a sheep, pig and goat that accompanied many important ceremonies of state.

A second slab or anaglyph, found with the first, commemorates a ceremony that might be establishing *alimenta* (Fig. X-16). Trajan is known to have endowed a fund, initially with proceeds from the Dacian Wars, to help feed poor children in Italy. This is undoubtedly to be seen in the context of the looming crisis of the economy of central Italy and the decline of that region's exports.

Fig. X-15 So-called *Anagylpha Traiani* showing burning of debt records. *Anaglypha Traiani/Hadriani*. 118-19 CE. Marble relief. Location: *Curia, Forum Romanum*, Rome, Italy. Photo Credit: Scala / Art Resource, N.Y.

On the front of the *alimenta* relief, an emperor with head defaced stands on the *rostra* surrounded by lictors who carry beech rods, symbols of his authority. A variety of classes of people look on. The rich wear their togas but the poor wear the *paenula,* a heavy wool poncho often used by travelers. To the right is a figure sitting on a platform benignly regarding a woman with two small children while four more individuals dressed in a *paenula* appear to the right.

Considerable scholarly debate has arisen over this scene. Is Hadrian the emperor at the left with the figure on the podium at the right being a statue of Trajan? Was the figure on the podium mother Italia looking after the poor? Could Trajan be at the left and his predecessor Nerva honored at the right? Could Trajan be shown twice celebrating an *alimenta* at the left and a *congiarium* (or distribution of money or food directly to the people) at the right? There is no way to know for sure but the ceremony was apparently also accompanied by the *suovetaurilia* that appears on the back of the slabs. Sometimes archaeologists and art historians can only provide possible answers or scenarios to scenes such as those on the *Anaglypha Traiani* or *Hadriani*. Therefore it is best to read as much as possible about the various hypotheses of identification and decide which seems most reasonable until more evidence tilts the scales toward one solution or another.

Fig. X-16 So-called *Anaglypha Traiani* from the Roman forum, showing an *adlocutio* with Hadrian (?) addressing the people, and an *alimenta*, perhaps showing Trajan's charity for poor children. *Anaglypha Traiani/Hadriani.* 118-119 CE. Location: *Curia, Forum Romanum,* Rome, Italy. Photo Credit:Scala / Art Resource, N.Y.

CHIANCIANO TERME: AN ANCIENT SPA

Fig. X-17 (below) View of the large pool (*vasca*) in the spa complex of Chianciano Terme, Tuscany. Photo by Noelle Soren. University of Arizona School of Anthropology Archive.

Over the course of his 19-year reign Trajan promoted investment in Italian land and business and sought to improve the roadways throughout Italy. One of the most unusual building projects of his time is found about two hours' drive north of Rome, in the modern spa town of Chianciano Terme, Tuscany. In this region, near the major Etruscan center of Chiusi, a rustic cold water spring and spa had existed for hundreds of years and gradually had gained considerable attention (Fig. X-17). The *fontes clusinii* or springs of Chiusi became renowned as a healing site where the emperor Augustus was "miraculously" cured of problems with his stomach or liver. Feeling near death and desperate, the emperor had consulted his chief physician Antonius

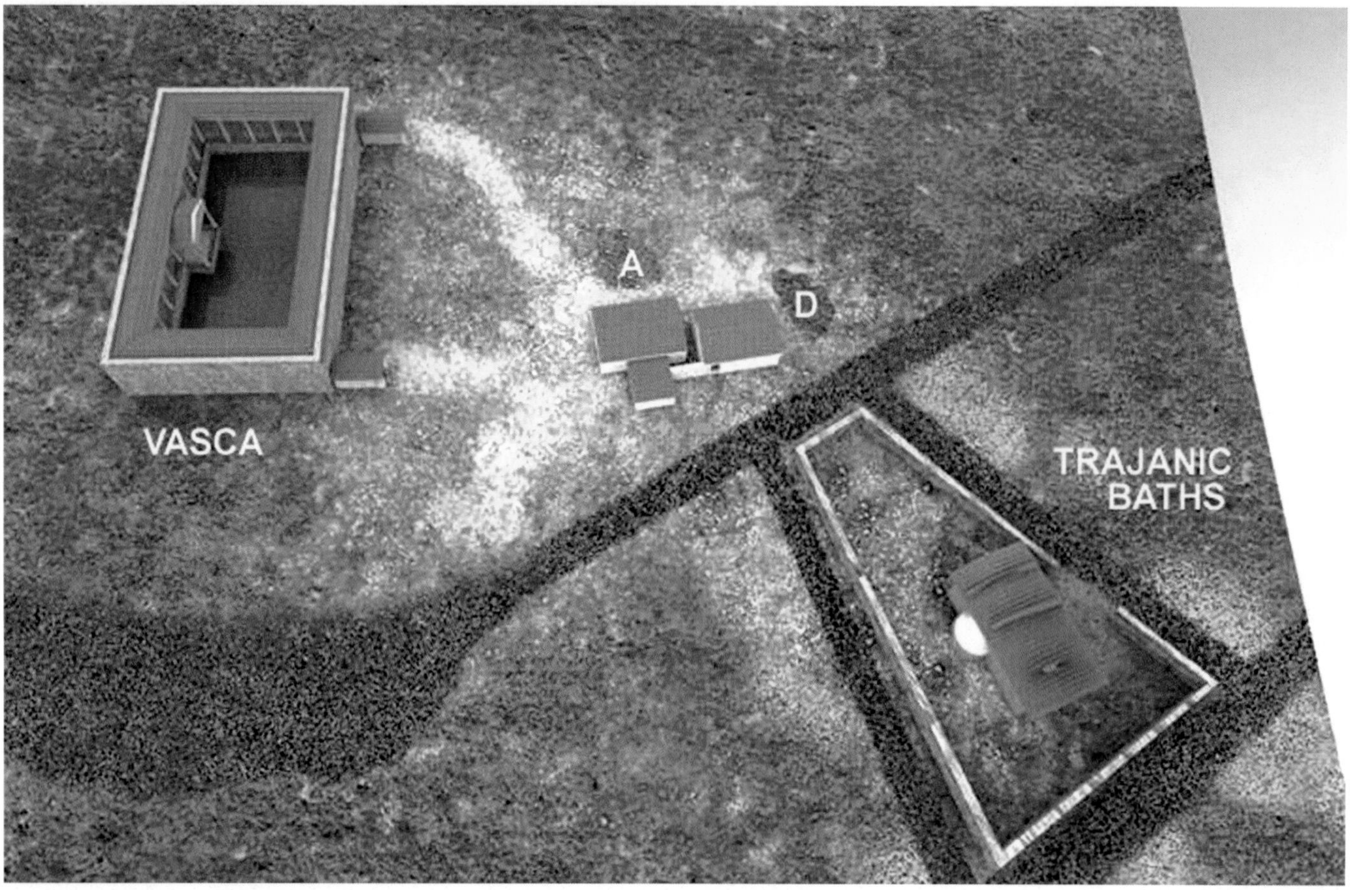

Fig. X-18 Reconstruction of the spa complex of the Trajanic Period at Chianciano Terme locality Mezzomiglio in Tuscany. Reconstruction by Michael Martelle, Marvin Landis, Jose Olivas.

Musa, who urged him to make a visit there rather than to go to the more famous hot water spa of Baiae on the Bay of Naples. Following a regimen of immersion and probably also drinking the water in conjunction with a special diet, the emperor was soon feeling better, and Musa became a hero, receiving freedom from taxation for himself and for all Roman doctors for all time. The Augustan poet Horace also came to the *fontes*, suffering from sore eyes. He described the experience of how he waded into the water and ducked his shoulder down to immerse himself more fully.

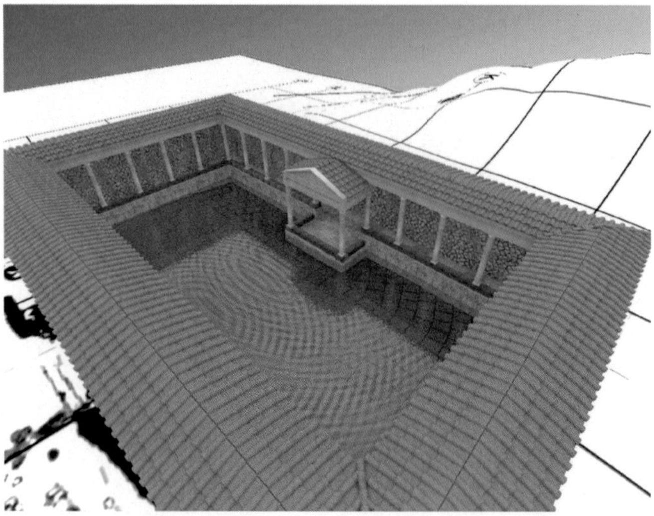

Fig. X- 19 The large wading pool of Chianciano Terme. Reconstruction by Michael Martelle, Marvin Landis, Jose Olivas, showing ancient topography of the land around the vasca.

The site of the *fontes clusinii* with its alleged magic healing powers has been sought for hundreds of years and in a small way is like the search for the Holy Grail of Jesus. Many theories have been put forth about its location, but nothing concrete was ever found. However, recent excavations in the town of Chianciano Terme have unearthed the largest ancient cold water spa in Italy right in the area where the mysterious *fontes* were thought to have existed (Figs. X-17 through 20). A series of major buildings has been uncovered, which were still functioning well into the second century CE. Chief among them is the large colonnaded wading and immersion pool, which was remodeled and repaved in the Trajanic Period but which had a long life going back perhaps to the later second century BCE.

At Chianciano the pool was entered from the east side, where old and infirm visitors could walk gently down into the water by following the terracotta tile paved interior floor until they found themselves fully immersed in front of a mini-temple (*sacellum*) to an as yet unidentified divinity. Only part of a marble horse leg two-thirds life-size has been found in the area of the little shrine. Amazingly, the spring that brought water at 59.6 degrees Fahrenheit into the complex was rediscovered and still flows into the complex. Unable to remain in the water for very long, the visitor would exit, probably through another route at the north limit of the east side.

The wall construction in *opus incertum* and *quasi-reticulatum* is held together by clay and sand instead of mortar, and the pool itself is dug into natural kaolinitic clay, which holds the water perfectly and does not require mortar. If the pool were indeed originally built in the later second century to early first century BCE, as seems

Fig. X- 20 Grotto entry to the large wading pool at Chianciano. Reconstruction by Michael Martelle, Marvin Landis, Jose Olivas.

likely, it shows a fascinating relationship between Etruscan and Roman technology. Its walls are later Roman Republican in style, but the lack of mortar in the walls, with clay substituted, is Etruscan. The concept of a giant pool with colonnades and mini-temple is not otherwise known in Etruscan architecture but might fit well with Roman experimentation of the Sullan Period. However, the lack of a concrete bottom for the pool and the use of the natural clay of the area to contain the natural spring derive from Etruscan technology and hydraulics.

Under Trajan the complex upgraded and may have added several administrative buildings, a water distributor, and a small but typical Roman bath building nearby, but the site remained rustic. One of the most unusual aspects of the pool is that its entrances appear to have been transformed into small grottos with rusticated boulders placed in the position of door jambs with a large rock garden surrounding them (Fig. X-20).

What was the secret of the therapeutic water of Chianciano, which is still used today in the four major spas thriving in the city? One element is a high quantity of calcium sulfate, which functions as a strong laxative. It may be that the emperor Augustus was suffering from severe constipation. If that were the case, consuming large quantities of the spring water of the *fontes clusinii* would have solved his problem quickly.

TIMGAD: A TRAJANIC CASTRUM IN NUMIDIA

As a part of Trajan's effort to stabilize the Roman world, he established the colony of Timgad in Algeria (Figs. X-21, 22, 23). Much earlier, Augustus had sought to reorganize the supervision of the area of Numidia under a *legatus* or governor looking after the region between what are now the towns of Cirta and Setif. The Legion installed its headquarters at Haidra in what is now western Tunisia, which was initially easier to control, and then expanded gradually westward, first to Tebessa under Vespasian and then Lambaesis in 81 CE. Forging alliances with local tribes in the zone of the Aurès Mountains, the emperor assigned the legate Munatius Gallus to set up Thamugadi, now known as Timgad, as a Roman camp and town at the foot of

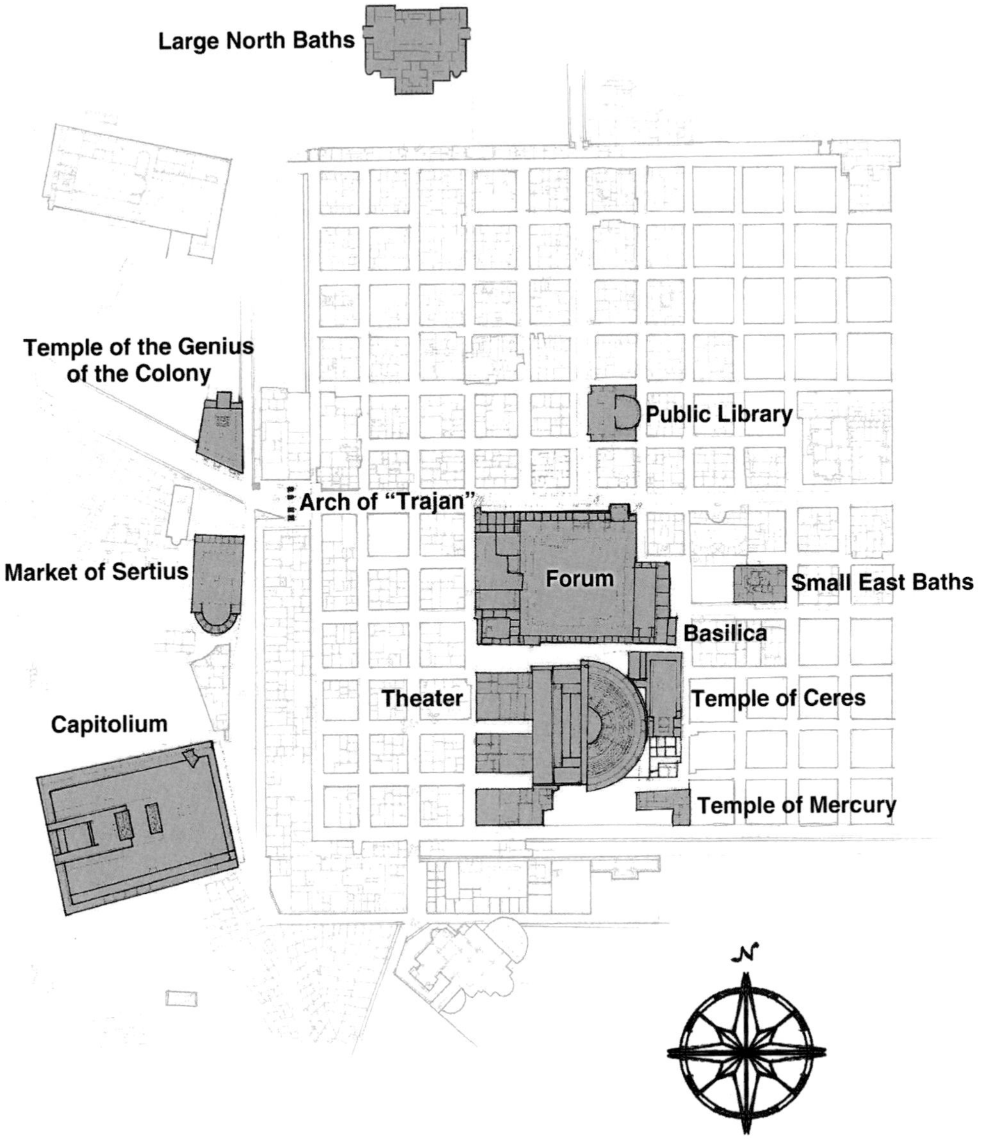

Fig. X-21 Plan of the the Roman *castrum* of Timgad in Algeria (founded 100 CE by Trajan, Roman Emperor, as a bastion against Berber incursions from the Aurès mountains), Algeria, North Africa. Drawing by Joshua Meehan.

Fig. X-22 View over Timgad, a Roman *castrum.* Photo Credit: Gianni Dagli Orti / The Art Archive at Art Resource, N.Y.

the Aurès, dominating one of the principal access routes to the hinterland of today's Algeria.

Trajan placed about 300 Legionary veterans here in this starkly picturesque but dangerous location, which required a fortification wall around it and constant vigilance to maintain the road from the Aurès through old Africa (now Tunisia) on to the metropolitan center of Carthage. At first glance it looked like a temporary camp, a giant square 350 meters on a side. The settlement was actually a *colonia* or colony rather than a temporary camp. Instead of a general's tent and *quaestorium* for paying and meeting of troops in the center of the town, a permanent Forum was built. Timgad has a principal north-to-south street, the *cardo,* and a *decumanus* leading to the Forum, with all the major roads paved in blue limestone to add to the uniformity of the place. The colony was so successful in both bringing peace and offering a viable life for veterans that the town grew rapidly and expanded beyond its borders, although it was still possible to withdraw behind the city walls for protection.

Today scholars admire the extraordinary groups of elegant geometric color mosaics that were used to decorate the numerous homes and especially the public baths of Timgad. More than 100 major floors have been recovered, beginning in the Trajanic Period and continuing into Late Antiquity; these form the major holdings of the Musée de Timgad. The most sumptuous floral mosaics of Timgad, about 40 of them, may date to the Trajanic Period and be contemporary with the layout of the colony. The decorative style is full of complex interrelated repeated designs including the *rinceau* or decorated scroll pattern, acanthus leaves, the ace of spades, vases with emerging volutes, and squares with curved

Fig. X-23 Bread and cakes, mosaic from an inn near Sertius market, Roman, Timgad, Algeria, North Africa. Location: Musée Archéologique de Timgad, Algeria. Photo Credit: Gianni Dagli Orti / The Art Archive at Art Resource, N.Y.

sides. The impression is that of a floor teeming with rich, weighty vegetal ornament and color (Fig. X-23). Colored mosaics remained popular at this time in provincial areas such as North Africa, while the fashion in Italy was for black-and-white mosaics, even in locations such as Imperial structures, where colored mosaics would have been installed if they were desired.

HADRIAN

Publius Aelius Hadrianus, known to us as Hadrian, succeeded Trajan in 117 CE and ruled until his death in 138 (Fig. X-24). Hadrian was no ordinary man. He has captured the imagination of scholars and writers over the years, not least among them

Fig. X-24 Emperor Hadrian. Marble bust. From his villa near Tibur (Tivoli). Location: British Museum, London. Photo Credit: Werner Forman / Art Resource, N.Y.

Marguérite Yourcenar (the first woman elected to the Académie Française), whose *Mémoires d'Hadrien* (*Memoirs of Hadrian*) is her most widely read novel.

Hadrian was an accomplished administrator and capable commander-in-chief. He traveled widely throughout the Empire on trips that sometimes lasted for years, and he took an active interest in regions as far apart as northern England, Greece, and Egypt. He was also interested in architecture, building in a style combining Classical imagery and experimental Baroque forms.

Hadrian had little time for his arranged marriage to Trajan's grandniece Sabina. He preferred his young favorite Antinous, a Greek youth from Bithynia, a province on the Black Sea. Their relationship has been scandalous and controversial from their day to ours, with many modern scholars denying the evidence of anything untoward and early Christian authors emphasizing its impure nature. Aristocratic Romans of the Imperial Period before Hadrian, including Trajan, had had homosexual affairs, but no emperor had given them such public prominence as Hadrian did with Antinous. The basis for the relationship between the philhellene Hadrian and the Greek Antinous appears to be in the ancient Greek concept, not shared by Romans, of an older man acting as a mentor in the education of an adolescent in exchange for love and sexual favors—it must be remembered that Antinous must have been about 16-20 years old at the time of his story with Hadrian. When the young man died mysteriously by falling out of a boat and drowning in the Nile, Hadrian was overcome with grief. The emperor founded a town named after his beloved boy on the spot of his death. He declared Antinous a god, perhaps aided by an Egyptian belief that those drowned in the Nile became immortal. Many places, mostly in the East but also in Italy, established his worship or added Antinous to existing cults, including the Sanctuary of Apollo at Kourion on Cyprus (see Chapter VIII). Even his critics conceded that Antinous possessed an extraordinary beauty, which played a part in his acceptance as a god according to the ancient Greek ideal of the beautiful partaking of the divine. Certainly, his images with their massively curly and wavy mop of hair (Fig. X-25) are instantly recognizable in the many museums in which they are preserved. The cult of Antinous continued to have followers even after Hadrian's death. Apparently, it answered the need for an approachable deity, a man who had become a god, in an age that was growing disenchanted with the state religion and sought something more personal. From our point of view, it was not obviously necessary to draw a line between Christ the Savior and Antinous, but some early Christian writers took the trouble

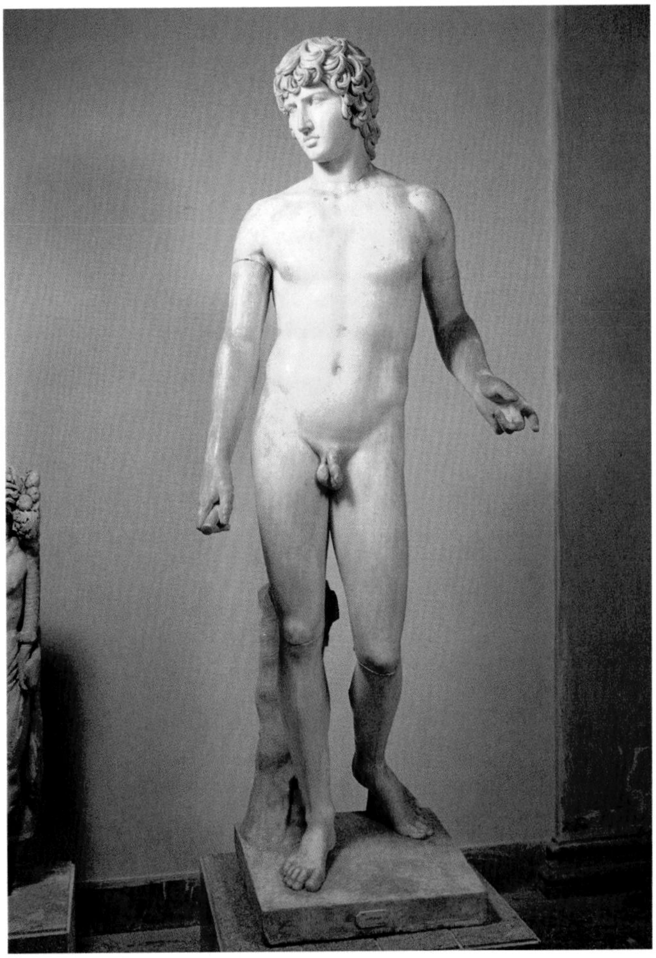

Fig. X-25 Sculpture of Antinous. Location: Museo Archeologico Nazionale, Naples, Italy. Photo Credit: Scala / Art Resource, N.Y.

to do so. Such is the strange fate of a boy from obscure provincial origins who lived for barely two decades in the first half of the second century CE.

HADRIANIC SCULPTURE

Hadrianic sculpture is easy to recognize because of its fondness for polished white marble surfaces and emphasis on precise detail. Because Hadrian had a birth defect on his chin, he wore a beard, and this became a vogue for Roman men of the time except of course for Antinous. In sculpture generally smooth polished skin was contrasted with wavy hair that was often punctuated with butter-curl effects rendered with increased use of the running drill, which was developed by the Greeks perhaps as early as 400 BCE. It could be rotated swiftly by wrapping string around it and affixing it to a bow. The contrast of the ultra-smooth polished surface of the skin with the restless drilled hair is particularly evident on many of the Antinous portraits. Art historians term this contrast pictorialism. In sculpture, human flesh tends to be rendered with a highly polished, ultra-white sugar cube-like consistency accomplished through widespread use of Cycladic island marbles. The eyes of the portraits have drilled pupils and heavy eyelids that remind one of the sleepy look of actor Sylvester Stallone. It is a trend that will continue well after the mid-second century in Imperial portraiture.

Fig. X-27 View of the Pantheon today showing the poorly effected join of the front pediment to the middle block of the building. Photo Credit: Noelle Soren. University of Arizona Photo Archive.

THE PANTHEON

In architecture, Hadrian is best remembered for a construction that typifies his approach to building: the Pantheon or temple to all the gods constructed in the Campus Martius in Rome (Fig. X-26). There had already been a temple to the gods on this spot in the Augustan Period, erected by Agrippa, whose name appears on the architrave of the present building, showing the affection Hadrian had for this venerated Roman and for the Augustan Period in general, but the surviving structure is completely Hadrianic and not Augustan in date. The visitor today comes upon it at the level of its top step (Fig. X-27), because the ground level has risen about 15 feet over the centuries. This ruins the effect of standing at the base of the now-hidden temple steps and looking up at the commanding edifice. Also, the Pantheon once stood within an extensive colonnaded piazza that would have helped to mask the rear area of the temple and heighten the visitor's surprise upon entering it.

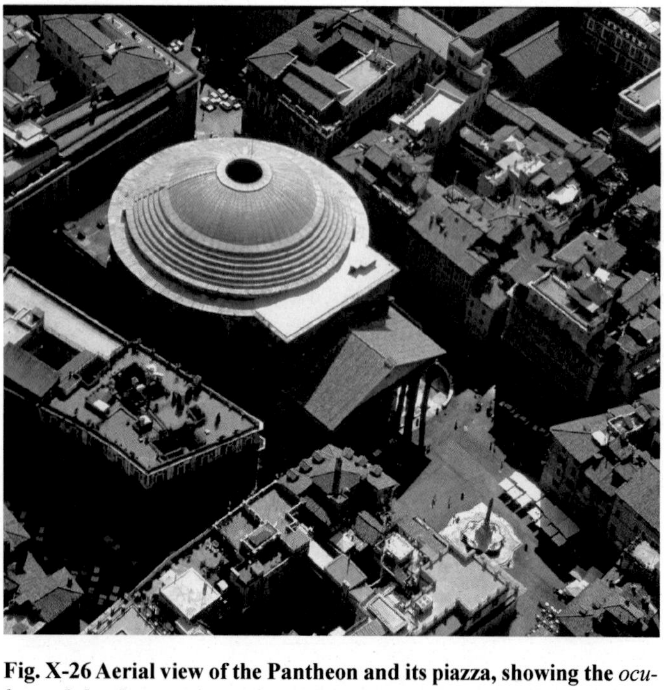

Fig. X-26 Aerial view of the Pantheon and its piazza, showing the *oculus* and the three main sections of the structure. Photo Credit: Alinari / Art Resource, N.Y.

The Pantheon is no ordinary Greco-Roman temple, for the emperor Hadrian was an architect with a definite sense of style. He liked Greek architectural forms, such as columns and architraves, but preferred them to be fitted with careful and precisely carved moldings. Color contrast was important in his buildings also; for example, white marble forms were contrasted with vari-colored Egyptian granite. Geometric precision was of such interest to this emperor that he enjoyed playing with circles and squares and alternating curvilinear and rectilinear forms in his structures. Hadrian was not just a lover of Classical Greek architecture but enjoyed using his buildings to surprise and astonish the viewer in a Baroque manner that recalled Sulla, Nero and Domitian. Thus the Pantheon combines the Greek temple form and traditional classicism with Roman Baroque dynamism to produce architecture that is innovative, elegant and dramatic and is intended to be experienced dramatically by the visitor. Sometimes, his fusion of daring vaulted forms and traditional Greek post-and-lintel architecture led to the construction of imaginative structures that were often completely unstable, particularly as he experimented with them in his villa at Tivoli! Fortunately, the Pantheon works both as an aesthetic composition and a functional building.

Fig. X-28a Reconstruction of the interior of the Pantheon in the Hadrianic Period by Bernard M. Frischer and Rome Reborn.

From the front the Pantheon appeared at first glance to be a typical Greco-Roman temple. The façade was gabled and there were Corinthian columns and an architrave. One would expect to encounter a cult statue in its place inside at the rear of the *cella,* but such was not the case. Instead one entered into a colossal rotunda, a symphony of curvilinear and spherical form, which contrasted with the rectilinear Greek entrance (Fig. X-26). On the floor, patterns of *opus sectile* or decorative cut stone slabs show square and curvilinear forms arranged in decorative sequences and pick up the effect highlighted in the architecture. The colossal interior featured a ceiling of gilded coffers, which seemed to float above the structure (Figs. X-27, 28). There were a series of *exedrae* or niches inside, each with images of the gods and which could be glimpsed between delicate columns. Although the little columns appear to be supporting the upper interior walls, that task is actually accomplished by massive piers.

The rotunda is linked to the façade of the temple by a third part, a middle block, which allows for the transition from the circular rotunda to the rectilinear façade. The enormously thick walls allow for hidden staircases, corridors, and specially constructed brick relieving arches to occupy the spaces and provide access for repairs. Relieving arches took the weight and thrust of the building as it settled and channeled them away from open spaces that might crack under pressure from above. The architects knew that openings within the structure could develop fissures soon after the building was made or over time, so they took great pains to protect against potential trouble spots. There were also rooms used as drying chambers that were key-shaped in plan. These provided space for expansion and contraction within the building as the concrete was drying and they were designed to prevent cracking.

At the top of the structure is an *oculus* or central opening that was built up to by a series of concentric steps on the roof. These steps were originally placed not only to provide a heavy support from which to suspend the dome but also to provide a surface that could be sheathed in bronze to provide additional support. The dome was built of concrete that got thinner as it soared away from its supporting walls. This concrete was prepared with a light stone aggregate as it approached the *oculus* so that it would be sturdy, yet relatively light and would stand for a long period of time. That these many hidden architectural refinements of the Pantheon were both practical and well-reasoned is exemplified by the fact that the building has survived for almost 2,000 years despite having little structural restoration. In fact many of its safeguards such as the bronze sheathing of the step rings of the dome and the ceiling beams of the entrance have been stripped off by the popes over the centuries, and in the 17th century massive towers were added to the façade by the Baroque architect Gianlorenzo Bernini. These towers caused such a furor among the local populace that they became known as the "Asses' Ears" and were eventually removed.

The Pantheon has been praised by artists and architects for generations. Rome's director of antiquities in the early 16th century was the painter Raphael, who admired it so much he was buried in it. What Renaissance designers appreciated was the precise symmetry and proportion of the building, the sense of wonder its interior creates, the sheer size, and the curious recession of the gilded coffers that create an ambiguous sense of just how high the building is. The interior is a complete world created by an architect, possibly Hadrian himself, in order to send a message of Rome the world-maker at the time when the Empire had reached its zenith. The sun itself is captured and brought in to pan around the *exedrae* or recesses in the bottom story illuminating the divinities of Rome.

Fig. X- 28b View of the interior of the Pantheon today. Photo Credit: Noelle Soren. University of Arizona Photo Archive.

Behind the Pantheon, the building is buttressed by the massive Basilica of Agrippa. A medieval street shaved off most of the Basilica, but its two-story side wall, which provides essential support to the Pantheon, still stands, showing that these two completely different buildings were joined together. They were ingeniously designed to support each other and continue to do to so to this day despite the removal of most of the Basilica.

The Pantheon, however inspiring and wondrous, was not a complete success architecturally. Something appears to have gone wrong with the shipping of the columns from Egypt used in the façade. The columns appear to have arrived shorter than had been anticipated and the construction of the rest of the building had already gone too far to permit a change in the order. That is the most popular current theory to explain why the façade of the building fails to properly link and line up with the middle block of the building in the gable area (Fig. X-27). Tourists today seldom notice how the gabled area of the middle block rises awkwardly above the back of the front gabled area, but this construction flaw shows that even expensive Imperial projects sometimes required compromise and adjustment in order to reach completion in a world where instant communication did not exist.

Fig. X-29 Model of Hadrian's Villa (Villa Adriana) in Tivoli, in the early second century CE. View from the west showing the so-called *Stoa Poikile* in the foreground. Location: Museo della Civiltà Romana, Rome, Italy. Photo Credit: Vanni / Art Resource, N.Y.

HADRIAN'S VILLA AT TIVOLI

The problems with the construction of the Pantheon did not stop Hadrian from continuing to pursue his interest in architectural experimentation, but Rome was a crowded environment, and the architect-emperor needed a broader landscape in which to practice. He found it in the plain below Tivoli, where a huge villa complex was constructed, no doubt to his specifications. Hadrian's Villa at Tivoli remains one of the greatest expanses of Imperial architectural experiment built over a short period of time (Fig. X-29).

Names, which are not always accurate, have been assigned to the various sections of the villa. It seems that the emperor, who loved travel, was attempting to present his interpretations of the extraordinary places he had been by building architectural tributes to them. They were not intended to be precise reconstructions of any particular building in any area but rather impressions or sensations of these places or attempts to explore new and innovative architectural concepts. In short, it was an expensive hobby that few but the wealthiest could indulge.

The so-called *Stoa Poikile* may not have been an attempt to emulate the famous Painted Stoa excavated in recent decades in the agora or market place of Athens, but it was a vast world unto itself where the emperor and friends could dine in a magnificent tri-lobed hall, which allowed light, air and water to be present on three sides of banqueters. It also provided a chance to walk out into a great porticoed space opening onto an enormous *piscina*, possibly intended as a giant swimming pool or fish pond. The hall features sugar cube-like polished columns with ultra-precise, evenly spaced shallow decorative ornament in the Hadrianic tradition.

Among the many innovative sectors of the villa is the so-called Maritime Theatre (Fig. X-30). It is an intimate private retreat which, characteristically, is a geometric architectural exercise, being designed to fit into a circle surrounded by a moat, complete with drawbridge. If the emperor wanted to get away from his duties, perhaps with Antinous, for a period of recreation, he had only to step across the drawbridge into this mini-villa, which featured a private bath, sleeping quarters, sitting rooms, and a quadrifoil central court complete with curvilinear linked architraves decorated with cupids.

Another section, the so-called *Piazza d'Oro* or Golden Piazza gave full reign to Hadrian's predilection for gourd-like vaulted spaces. Huge vaults that resembled sections or segments of a gourd spanned the entry vestibule. Throughout the Roman Empire this type of construction is found only in the Hadrianic Period. Trajan's architect Apollodorus of Damascus is reported to have become so frustrated with Hadrian's meddling in one of his Imperial projects that he spoke sternly to the emperor: "Go and draw your gourds!" It is the last we ever hear of Apollodorus.

Fig. X-30 Island Villa, Hadrian's Villa (Villa Adriana). Emperor Hadrian designed and had his villa built in 118-34 CE. This building, probably a private residence of the emperor, is also known as the Maritime Theatre. Location: Hadrian's Villa, Tivoli, Italy. Photo Credit: Vanni / Art Resource, N.Y.

Fig. X-31 View of the Canopus Area. Photo Credit: Noelle Soren. University of Arizona School of Anthropology Photo Archive.

Among the large and small baths, areas of contemplation, libraries and still undetermined spaces is the most famous area, the so-called Canopus (Fig. X-31). Apparently this was intended to evoke an area of ancient Alexandria, complete with a Temple to Serapis, the Hellenistic deity devised by the ruling Ptolemies to become a main divinity of Egypt. In Hadrian's version, the arched pediment of the temple, which was typical of Egyptian temples of Alexandria and Rome in the Imperial Period, has been transformed. The entry to the temple has become a series of niches, one featuring a waterfall supplied by a specially brought in aqueduct channel that is hidden on the top of the temple. Hadrian used the higher land behind the temple to mask massive water conduits and to shower water down in front of unsuspecting visitors. The interior of the temple is itself a series of pools and a water show rather than a traditional *cella*. The interior of the façade is topped with a half-domed gourd vault.

In front of the temple, pools stretch out and are lined with caryatid figures. These had nothing to do with Alexandria and were inspired from the later fifth century BCE *Erectheum*, the most sacred temple on the Athenian Acropolis. The same figures had inspired Augustus for his Forum a century earlier (see Chapter VII; Fig. VII-13). This borrowing of styles and cultures delighted Hadrian and was typical of his eclectic taste, but whatever he borrowed he organized into carefully planned symmetrical spaces. Even the crocodiles found here show great attention to detail; they were carved in mottled blue-grey *bardiglio* marble from Carrara to make them appear scaly and to startle the visitor. They were placed on a riser in the pool water and were actually fountains with lead spouts in their mouths. The surrounding colonnade of the Canopus area features non-traditional alternating straight and arched lintels, one of the rare times this particular feature, so popular in Pompeian painting beginning in the middle first century BCE, has been found in an actual mid-Imperial construction. Throughout the villa elegant quarters feature geometric mosaics and *opus sectile*, all made with precision, delicacy and a fondness for intricate interconnecting designs (Fig. X-32). The mosaics have designs that are less powerful and weighty than those at Timgad in the Trajanic Period and are typically rendered in black-and-white rather than in the vivid North African colors.

The visitor is overwhelmed by the size of the villa and its unity of design and purpose. New parts of it such as a whole area devoted to Antinous are still being discovered and excavated. It became a vast study source for later architects such as Francesco Borromini, who is said to have been inspired for his curvilinear Baroque church designs, such as San Carlo alle Quattro Fontane in Rome. Borromini observed Hadrian's astonishing dining pavilion at the back of the *Piazza d'Oro* and may have been inspired by its undulating central courtyard.

Hadrian may have had one problem however. He enjoyed using Greek post-and-lintel systems, columns and architraves, so much that he sometimes could not resist placing gourd or segment-vaulted domes on top of them. This resulted in structures that were not stable, as the ruins of the domed room of the *Piazza d'Oro* show, but one can imagine that Hadrian must have enjoyed designing and erecting these fantastic complexes.

Fig. X-32 Hospitalia (Guest Quarters), Hadrian's Villa (Villa Adriana). Location: Hadrian's Villa, Tivoli, Italy. Photo Credit: Vanni / Art Resource, N.Y.

Fig. X- 33 Underground gourd-vaulted basement room at Bulla Regia in Tunisia. Photo Credit: Noelle Soren. University of Arizona School of Anthropology Photo Archive.

Fig. X-34 Reconstruction of the Mausoleum of Hadrian and the Pons Aelius (Aelian Bridge over the Tiber River). From the Museo della Civiltà Romana. Photo Credit: AKG Images/Bildarchiv Monheim.

Hadrian's influence in architecture was not limited to Italy. In Bulla Regia, Tunisia, a Hadrianic bath complex has revealed a little published underground room (Fig. X-33). It has a series of corridors and a central space, which seems to contain an *oculus*. Was it an underground dining room in the manner of the *Domus Aurea*'s octagonal room? That is one hypothesis, although it has also been proposed that it was a club room or a room for a secret society or religious organization. In any case, the entire ceiling has been transformed into a gourd-vaulted delight that still dazzles the visitor.

HADRIAN'S MAUSOLEUM

One of the most readily recognized landmarks of Rome, located on the right bank of the Tiber, is the Castel Sant'Angelo, incorporating Hadrian's Mausoleum (Fig. X-34). Hadrian commissioned this as the burial place for himself and Sabina, but it was finished only shortly after Hadrian's death by his successor, Antoninus Pius, who was also buried here along with other members of the dynasty. Like many large structures, Hadrian's Mausoleum was incorporated into the city's defenses, sometime between the mid-third and the early-fifth century. Afterwards, it played an important role in the fighting between the Byzantines and Goths in the sixth century, and then became a fortress refuge for the popes, with significant rebuilding during the 15th and 16th centuries.

Its subsequent history means that it is difficult to reconstruct the design of Hadrian's Mausoleum. Nevertheless, it is clear that it belongs to a class of funerary monuments with various antecedents at Rome: a cylinder set on a square base. It obviously rivals the Mausoleum of Augustus, another such monument, nearly opposite which it stands. A bridge built by Hadrian connects his mausoleum to the Campus Martius, containing Augustus' Mausoleum. As in the case of the Mausoleum of Augustus, there is much scholarly debate about the appearance of the upper part; the existing upper story is medieval and modern. Did it have another smaller cylinder? Was it finished in an earthen mound? It is certain from Renaissance architectural drawings and from fragments that Hadrian's Mausoleum was sheathed in white marble from Luni (in the Carrara area of eastern Liguria and northern Tuscany) with rich sculptural decoration. The surviving core of the Mausoleum contains a helicoidal or corkscrew-like ramp leading to a corridor giving on to the funerary chamber in the center of the cylinder.

HADRIAN'S WALL

Hadrian built a spectacular wall across England from the Tyne River to the Solway Firth and the series of camps and forts he developed to defend and regulate the flow of peoples in this troubled area (Fig. X- 35). This remote, often freezing cold area was the site of the garrison of Rome's northwest frontier, where soldiers might spend as much as 25 years, the full period of their military service. Already in the Flavian Period there had been trouble along this border, which caused Agricola's army, including the 9th Legion, to head into what is now Scotland to celebrate a great victory. However, unrest continued in the north of England and Scotland, and the scattered forts that dotted the Tyne-Solway area were considered too dangerous, with the result that Hadrian's

Fig. X-35 Hadrian's Wall in England. Photo Credit: Noelle Soren. University of Arizona School of Anthropology Photo Archive.

enormous wall was quickly erected across almost 100 miles of territory. It was constructed by Aulus Platorius Nepos, the *legatus* of Britain between 122 and 126 CE, over the shortest width of land possible to defend. The wall was also located near legionary fortresses such as York and Chester.

The wall is remembered as one of the most significant Roman engineering and architectural accomplishments, but often it is forgotten how much trial and error goes into an undertaking of this scale. Hadrian's Wall was, like so many Hadrianic and Roman projects, designed one way and actually built in another. The original plan was apparently to make the wall 10-Roman-feet wide and about 15-feet high with a walkway on the inside. Soon after the work had begun, but not before 10-foot foundations had been built for some distance to the west beyond the stretch of broad wall, the width for the rest of the wall was narrowed to 8 feet and sometimes 6 feet. These parts of the wall were constructed of rubble with facings of roughly dressed stone, mostly locally quarried sandstone. Some sections toward the east, however, were constructed in turf and rebuilt in sandstone later during Hadrian's reign. The reason for narrowing the width and indeed for choosing such a broad original width remains unclear and is debated by archaeologists, as is the reason for building sections in turf and replacing them in sandstone. The unusual width of the broad wall may have been intended to create a military monument for Hadrian—but then why not continue? Sandstone was available near the turf stretches, as the subsequent rebuilding shows—so why not use it from the start? Hadrian's Wall was planned to have milecastles 1620 yards apart. Between the milecastles were turrets in the wall. Along much of the wall, a ditch shaped like a V was dug to the north. In a modification of plans during construction, it was decided to replace the forts in the area a few miles to the south of the wall with forts on the wall itself.

The *vallum,* located to the south of the wall, was added after the decision was taken to move the forts to the wall, as the building sequence shows. It was a flat-bottomed ditch about 10-feet deep and 20-feet wide with earth piled up above it in two mounds to the south and north of the ditch. Apparently, this feature was designed to provide protection for the wall from the south.

What was the purpose of Hadrian's Wall? It certainly was not the equivalent of a city wall, with defenders on it combating attackers below. There is no evidence for a fighting platform on the wall, nor was there enough manpower to use it in that way. Hadrian's Wall was also not a border such as modern states have. Regular opening in the forts and milecastles allowed soldiers to leave easily for operations toward the north. There were even forts north of the wall under Hadrian, and his successor built another wall between the Firths of Clyde and Forth in modern Scotland. It seems clear that the Hadrian's Wall was intended to form a barrier across a gap in which natural barriers were lacking. There is no doubt that it provided effective control of movement between north and south, which may have been designed as much to isolate the restive population to the south of the wall as to keep out the people to the north.

Fig. X-36 Officers in the Roman army of the later first century CE: ***centurion*** **(Latin:** ***centurio*****) (foreground), standard bearer (*****signifer*****) with standard (*****signum*****) (left), Horn and trumpet players (*****cornicen & tubicen*****) (middle), commanding officer (*****legatus*****) standing to right, and the emperor Vespasian sitting on a folding Roman campstool. Watercolor by Peter Connolly. ©akg-images / Peter Connolly / The Image Works.**

THE ROMAN LEGIONS

Visiting this English countryside today, it is easy to forget that men were stationed here and the area teemed with the activity of patrols and groups of various tribes passing back and forth on business. The wall was constructed by Roman Legions, which at this time consisted of 10 *cohortes*, each with 6 *centuriae.* This totaled about 5,000 men, who formed the infantry. The men were not allowed to marry although some did create common-law families. Legionaries had to be Roman citizens and served for 25 years. In Hadrian's time the legions known to be present in Britannia were the *II Augusta* (with headquarters at Caerleon-on-Usk), the *XX Valeria Victrix* (with headquarters at Chester) and the *VI Victrix* and *IX Victrix* (both with headquarters at York).

A *legatus* commanded the legion, assisted by a senior military tribune, a young man of Senatorial rank at the beginning of his career. The third-in-command was the *praefectus castrorum*, in charge of the day-to-day running of the camp. Five military tribunes of equestrian rank with previous administrative experience completed the staff. Each *centuria* was under the command of a *centurio* (Fig. X-36). The auxiliaries, who were non-citizens recruited throughout the empire and beyond, supplied non-infantry units, especially cavalry but also archers, for example. Often auxiliaries from very distant lands were called upon to serve far from their homes. This helped to ensure that they would not foment revolt with the natives, to whom they could not speak. The forts on Hadrian's Wall were manned by auxiliaries.

Fig. X-37 Housesteads (England), Roman fort along Hadrian's Wall (started 122 CE). Reconstruction of the *castrum* and village outside the walls at Housesteads c. Third century CE, with the camp headquarters (*principia*), the commander's house (*praetorium*), hospital (*valetudinarium*) in the central area. Watercolor by Peter Connolly. ©AKG-images / Peter Connolly / The Image Works.

THE CASTRUM

By Hadrian's time, the *castrum* or military fort had a relatively standardized form with essential buildings and spaces (Figs. IV-19; X-37). One good place to investigate this is Housesteads, located almost due west from modern Newcastle upon Tyne, the most complete example of a British fort yet excavated. Seen today, the layout is relatively simple. A main street, the Via Principalis links two of the four gates of the walled camp. The central part of the space is devoted to the principal buildings: the spacious house of the fort commander (*praetorium*), the headquarters of the staff (*principia*), a hospital (*valetudinarium*), a granary (*horreum*), ample latrines (*latrinum*), large barracks area (*castra*) and a section of Hadrian's Wall that runs alongside the camp.

The *praetorium* was a lodging, a series of rooms around a courtyard, the largest single building on site. The courtyard provided shelter from the notorious howling winds of Housesteads. The camp commander enjoyed the privilege of two separate hypocaust systems. These were probably a heated dining room and private bathing facilities for his family. A latrine was found at the northwest corner of the house and a kitchen to the northeast. The structure was frequently remodeled, probably at the whim of the various officers and their wives who stayed there over 300 years. The adjacent *principium* or headquarters functioned as a protected forum complex for the officers and principal staff, serving both military and religious functions. There was a large courtyard, at the back of which was a large hall or basilica, which calls to mind the arrangement of the Forum of Trajan in Rome. Here trials could be held, meetings could go on even on rainy or bitter cold days, and addresses could be given. A central room on the north served as a small shrine or *aedes*, which housed the military standards of the regiment. It was considered the greatest disgrace if these were surrendered or captured, and they were placed in a location near to where images of protective divinities might be found. This building also contained statues of the emperor and his family, and there would be altars to Jupiter and the female personification of Discipline.

In the heart of the camp was the granary or *horreum*, which was a long rectangular building with a wooden floor raised up on supports to provide a dry facility away from rodents or other vermin (Fig. X-38). Grain was stored in sacks and stockpiled for use. A row of piers divided the structure in two lengthwise. Equally critical to any camp was the hospital or *valetudinarium*, which was constructed in typical Roman fashion, with a series of rooms for offices and patients placed around a central colonnaded courtyard. A *medicus*, usually of *centurion* rank, would be in residence to look after the troops along with his staff of bandagers and orderlies. There would likely be a shrine to Roman divinities of healing and health here: Asculapius and Salus. Anesthetics were in short supply and included poppies, henbane and mandrake, but surgery was something dreaded by all and accompanied frequently by cries of agony.

The housing facilities or barracks for the single men were very cramped. They lived in buildings that were subdivided into 10 units called *contubernia*. A *contubernium* was in fact the name given to each eight-man division of a century within the Roman army. Larger apartments in these units were no doubt occupied by the *centurion*, whose task it was to look after the men. The front room of the barracks was the *arma,* where equipment was stored for each soldier. When all the equipment was hung up, there was barely any room to turn around. Soldiers seeking relaxation needed to confine themselves to their beds or go outdoors. The

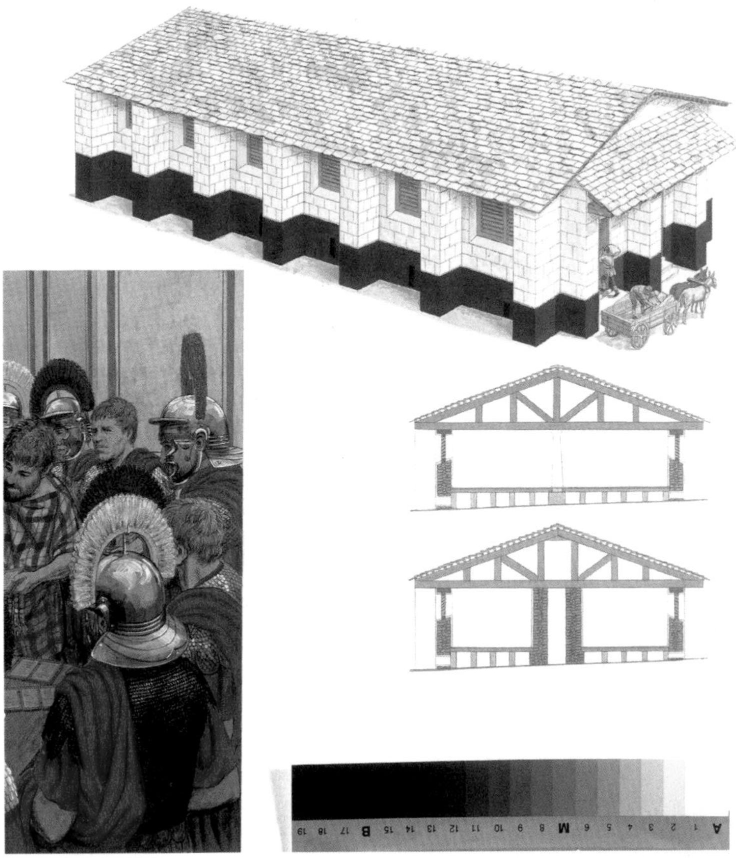

Fig. X-38 Reconstruction of the granary at Housesteads fort in England in which grain, vegetables and meat were stored. Watercolor by Peter Connolly. ©AKG-images / Peter Connolly / The Image Works.

papilio was the sleeping room with an arrangement of bunk beds in a confined space.

Life on the frontier was hard. The average soldier spent a full day on patrol or cleaning out facilities, and there was little to do in the evenings other than devising one's own entertainment. Diversions could be found through religious worship, particularly of divinities such as Mithras, who proved popular with Roman troops. Sports activities were high in priority and there were inter-service competitions in wrestling, horse racing, tugs of war and the like, but there is no evidence of the use of amphitheatres anywhere along Hadrian's Wall. It may be that the popular animal hunts and lavish set design could not be offered here because of the remoteness of the region and simple fighting could be staged, *gladiator*-style, without need of a massive building. Hunting was always popular, particularly for wild boar. Games were popular with the troops including, particularly, variations of checkers and craps shooting. For the limited time when soldiers had furloughs prostitutes were readily available in neighboring towns, and drinking could be done in local *tabernae*. Given the risk of injury and illness in such an environment, fortune tellers also had a lively trade, One attraction for auxiliaries was the eligibility for Roman citizenship after serving 25 years.

OSTIA AND THE GRAIN TRADE

The principal supply harbor for Rome was Ostia (Fig. X-39). Although many varied products came into this port and were stored and distributed for Rome and its environs, the most important commodity that was imported, primarily from Africa, was wheat. Much of the architecture of the town was created because of the need to deal with the wheat trade and is therefore largely functional in nature.

For antiquity, wheat was not merely a trade item. Its position was similar to crude oil today. In fact, in both cases it is the most significant source of energy. In the ancient world, the main source of energy was muscle power from animals and people. Therefore, obtaining the principal human food source was a major concern.

Wheat owed its position to various factors. First, the geology and the climate of the Mediterranean do not permit large-scale cattle-raising, which is the foundation of the meat-based societies typical of Northern Europe. Thus, a cereal had to be the basic food source. Second, wheat is the only one of the cereals known to the Romans that could be made into bread. For the study of the Roman economy, wheat holds particular importance, because we know that the state intervened in its distribution and trade. Unfortunately, grain does not lend itself easily to archaeological study, because both it and its containers are perishable. Nevertheless, it must be taken into account.

Wheat has certain properties that make it difficult to store. It is not only heavy and bulky but also mobile—it behaves almost like a liquid, with considerable lateral thrust. It is also alive and must be kept in special conditions. It supports humidity of 10-15% before beginning to mold. And it needs a temperature of less than 15.5° C in order not to be attacked by insects. These factors had to be kept in mind because wheat had to be stored; it had to be kept for years in case of poor harvests or of the need to export it to less fortunate areas.

It has been argued that the ancient world lived under the constant threat of a food crisis. The reasons are to be found in the variability of the weather on the one hand (particularly in Late Antiquity) and in human factors (such as the instability of governments and the impact of wars) on the other. Famine was, on the contrary, unusual. Bad harvests in succeeding years were much less frequent than those in single years, at least up until the fifth and sixth centuries. Often the sources associate famine with bad harvests and war or epidemics. Therefore, ancient communities were chronically susceptible to food crises and were always concerned about the food supply. Nonetheless, these societies were able normally to find a solution to disruptions in the food supply before the problem became a famine. To do so, most ancient communities relied on the importation of additional supplies and on the distribution of these supplies for the benefit of weaker consumers (often at the expense of the rich, who could thereby dampen calls for overall reform and further their individual political careers).

Before the late Republican Period, Rome acted much like any other ancient state, developing *ad hoc* solutions as problems arose in the grain supply. Although the sources are sketchy for the earlier part of Roman history, it seems clear that there were repeated food crises during the fifth century BCE, a time when the Roman state was unable to use resources gained by conquest to alleviate the needs of the poor. Climate factors may have also played a significant role.

In the late Republican and Imperial Periods, Rome created a structure that was unique in the ancient world to guarantee the grain supply to the capital. The origins of the structure go back to

Fig. X- 39 Reconstructed full overview of the Roman port town of Ostia. Reconstruction by Angelo Coccettini (computer architectural reconstruction specialist) and Marzia Vinci (consulting archaeologist).

the late third and the first half of the second century BCE, when Rome conquered three outstanding wheat-producing provinces or "breadbaskets"—Sicily, Sardinia and Africa—and instituted taxation in grain. In 123 BCE the socially conscious tribune Gaius Gracchus established the first regular distribution of grain to citizens. The details of the distributions between that date and the time of Augustus are uncertain and debated, but it is clear that they were low-cost rather than free (as they became later) and that they were troubled by the hostility of some aristocrats towards them and by the disorder of the civil wars. The system assumed its definitive form under Augustus. In 22 BCE he was charged with the *cura annonae*, that is with the care of the entire grain supply for Rome. A considerable innovation was the addition of Egypt to the grain-producing provinces serving Rome. From Augustus onward, guaranteeing the grain supply was an essential function that the emperors always held.

At an unknown date Augustus created the prefecture of the *annona* to carry out the task. The *cura annonae* had two duties: assuring the grain necessary for the free distributions (which, however, were given only to a part of the population of Rome and were not intended to meet the recipients' entire family needs) and guaranteeing the presence on the market of enough grain for sale to cover the demand of the remaining population.

The head, the *praefectus annonae*, was one of the four prefects at the top of the equestrian career, and in the first half of the first century he was the most prestigious of the four. Later, to judge by promotions, he seems to have been tied in third place with the prefect of the *vigiles* (the fire-fighting and policing service) below the prefect of Egypt, who was in turn below the praetorian prefect. He was chosen for his qualities as a financial administrator rather than for technical competence. In fact, there is no known case of a prefect promoted from the lower ranks of the prefecture. His job was to oversee the grain supply in the entire Mediterranean from the capital.

The prefect had subordinates both at Rome and Ostia as well as in the provinces. In the upper ranks they consisted of equestrians and freedmen, some nominated by him and some by the emperor. The lower ranks were filled by Imperial slaves and soldiers, as far as we can tell from epigraphic evidence at Rome and Ostia. It was not a large establishment. Evidently the prefect had to rely also on local functionaries from provincial governors on down to lesser officials.

Grain merchants and shippers were the most important private individuals involved in the grain supply. Apparently these were originally completely autonomous. Between the reigns of Claudius and Trajan, however, the state took steps to encourage the transportation of grain to Rome. These did not imply the existence or creation of corporations, but the shippers' and merchants' desire to see their rights respected seems to have led them to create associations, which were useful to the prefects in drawing up lists of those who held rights. Under Trajan, it became normal to reason in terms of corporations of shippers and merchants. By the beginning of the fourth century, these corporations were hereditary and under state control.

Other private individuals who worked for the *annona* were the *mensores*, whose task was to check and measure the wheat. This took place at each stage of its production, from the harvest in the provinces through the various stages of its transportation and storage until distribution. There were therefore numerous *mensores*, grouped together in professional associations. The quality of the grain was checked on samples that were sent with the shipments. The measurements were made in a cylindrical container called the *modius* containing 8.75 liters into which the grain was poured and leveled off with a stick called the *rutellum*. The continual measuring of the grain was so characteristic that the two utensils became symbolic of grain.

At a lower social level among the private but free individuals involved in the grain trade were the *saccarii* or sack-carriers, whose importance is obvious, although they are not well attested in the sources or epigraphy. The construction of the granaries with steps makes it certain that the grain was carried in and out rather than brought by carts, for example. This group does not appear to have enjoyed any privileges or organizations to encourage their activity.

One of the main problems in evaluating the grain trade archaeologically is that neither the merchandise nor its containers (sacks) survive in the archaeological record. This may mean that grain tends to be taken less into consideration than other foodstuffs, such as wine and olive oil, for which we have the amphorae or vessels in which they were transported. Therefore, we have to rely on indirect evidence for grain. At the macroscopic level one can cite the entire port system of Rome and Ostia, which we know from the sources was intended chiefly to receive grain. Then there are single buildings that can be connected functionally to the grain trade. Finally, there are places that show connections with the grain trade through inscriptions or figural decorations.

Ostia does not possess a natural harbor, and the increasing importance of the grain traffic made this an unsatisfactory situation. Throughout the Republic and into the first century CE, all ships except the smallest had to stand off the mouth of the river to unload their cargoes into boats that carried them into the Tiber, where they were unloaded onto the banks of the river and ultimately delivered to Rome. A row of inscribed stones dating to the late second century BCE recalls that the river banks were public property not to be encroached upon. The first radical attempt to improve the situation came under Claudius, when a large artificial harbor was built just north of the mouth of the Tiber. It consisted of a large area surrounded by breakwaters projecting from the coast. It proved to have defects, particularly in not being perfectly protected from winds, and there were severe storms that destroyed shipping in the artificial harbor.

With this in mind Trajan added another segment to the system. His artificial harbor was cut into the land behind the earlier harbor and so was landlocked and better protected. He also had a second mouth of the Tiber, the *Fossa Traiana*, cut to connect the port complex to the Tiber. Thus, from the early second century there were an outer port, an inner one surrounded by warehouses and a direct connection to the river.

This was, however, only part of a much larger whole. A joint project of the Deutsches Archäologisches Institut and the American Academy in Rome was able to prove that there was a small harbor facility just inside the mouth of the river, dating to the first century CE (probably before Domitian) but extensively rebuilt in the mid-second, including a dry dock and a temple probably dedicated to Castor and Pollux, the protectors of sailors. Ostia and Portus were themselves only the center-point of an extensive system of secondary ports reaching at least from Anzio (Antium) to the south and Civitavecchia (Centumcellae) to the north (each about 40 km away). In a sense the southern end can be considered to include Pozzuoli, which continued to be the major destination for the eastern trade, including the all-important grain fleet from Egypt. These ports all fed Ostia and Portus—so that it is not a mistake to talk about Rome's *façade maritime*.

THE FUNCTIONAL ARCHITECTURE OF THE GRAIN TRADE

Granaries are the prime example of single buildings functionally connected with the grain trade (Fig. X-38). They must be sturdy buildings in order to withstand the lateral thrust of the grain and also be able to hold large volumes of it. These characteristics help to distinguish granaries from other general warehouses (or *horrea*). It is certain that a warehouse was intended for grain when it has floors raised on *suspensurae* (small pillars) to permit the ventilation necessary for the storage of grain. Their absence is not, however, necessarily an argument against a building's use as a granary, since the raised structure could have been made of wood and not survived. From the ancient names of many *horrea* at Rome, it is possible to deduce that they were originally built by private individuals belonging to members of the great families, probably as investments to rent out. They pass only later into the hands of the emperors, who add others commissioned directly as public property. At Ostia, on the contrary, it seems that publicly erected *horrea* were the norm.

Ostia gives us the best picture of warehouses in general and granaries in particular (Fig. X-39). Among the oldest surviving warehouses are the Horrea of Hortensius, dated to the first half of the first century CE. The structure is dominated by a large porticoed courtyard around which there are rooms. There is no trace of raised floors. Nevertheless, it has been suggested that this warehouse was publicly owned and intended for grain because of its size and importance, as well as for its easy access from the Tiber.

The largest warehouse among the many at Ostia, the Great Horrea, is located near the center of the city on the Tiber (Figs. X-40, 41). It was first built toward the middle of the first century CE and then renovated toward the middle of the second century and again during the reign of Commodus. It is undoubtedly to be

Fig. X-40 View of the Great Horrea of Ostia by Angelo Coccettini and Marzia Vinci.

Fig. X-41 Reconstruction of the façade of the *Horrea Epagathiana et Epaphroditiana* by Angelo Coccettini and Marzia Vinci.

considered a granary because of its raised floors and the strong walls. Its position, size and massive nature suggest that it must have been a public property. The pressure on space is shown by the use of the courtyard to hold an additional block of rooms.

Ostia possesses a further complex directly connected with the grain trade—the headquarters of the Association of Measurers in Via della Foce. A mosaic, dated to the Severan Period, was found in the meeting room there (Fig. X-42). It shows the *mensores* at work. A *saccarius* approaches the *mensor*, who holds a *rutellum* (to the left of a *modius*). A bearer, who has already emptied his sack, looks on from behind the *modius*. A probable functionary of the *annona* looks on from the right, the only personage not barefoot. A small man at the center is probably keeping count. The rest of the block is taken up by the so-called Horrea of the Mensores. The alternation of normal long and narrow rooms with others that are wide, open, and spacious suggests that this was a place where the *mensores* carried out their checks rather than an actual warehouse.

Fig. X-42 Mosaic of the *Mensores* (grain measurers) from the Via della Foce at Ostia. University of Arizona School of Anthropology Collection.

The Barracks of the Vigils (Figs. X- 43 through 47) is an outgrowth of the grain trade at Ostia. We know from the written sources that the stationing of a cohort of vigils or watchmen at

Fig. X-43 Reconstructed theatre and corporation plaza along the *decumanus*. The reconstruction also shows the Baths of Neptune below the Piazza of the Corporations and, to the right of the Baths, the Barracks of the Vigils. Reconstructions by Angelo Coccettini and Marzia Vinci).

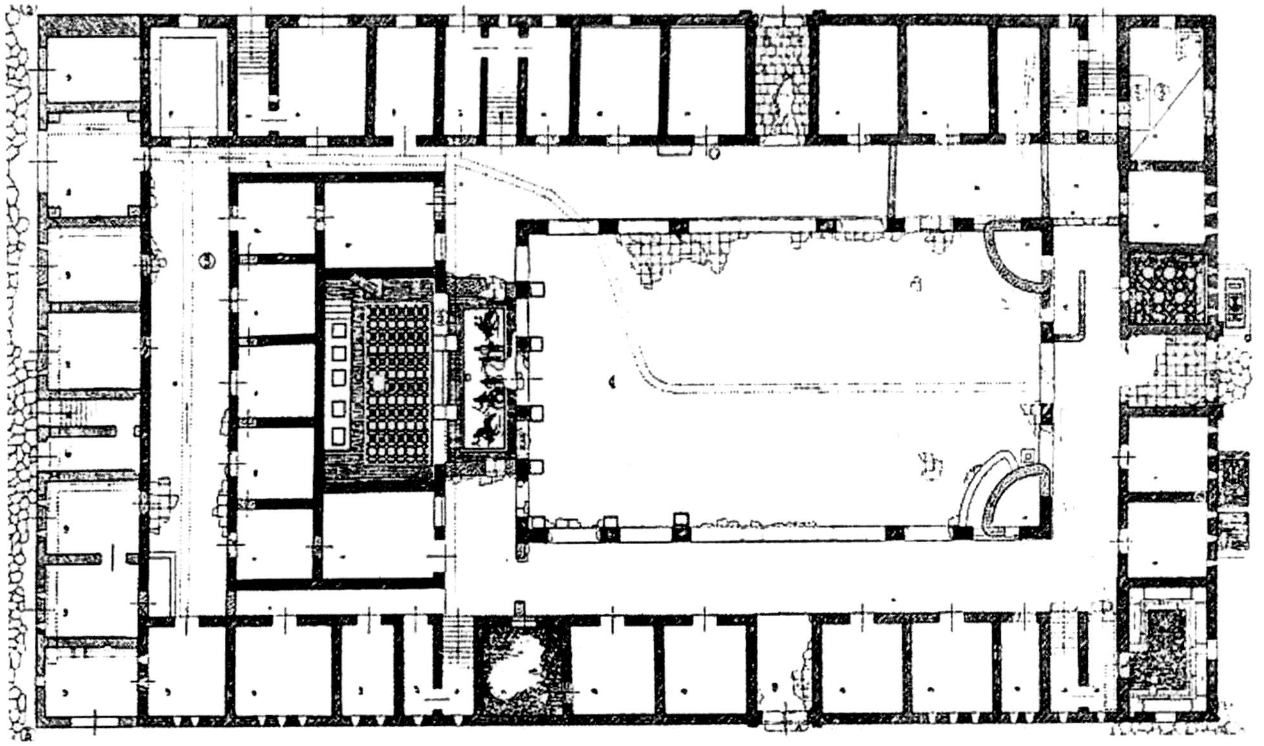

Fig. X-44 Plan of the Barracks of the Vigils. University of Arizona School of Anthropology Photo Collection.

Fig. X-45 (above) and X-46 (below) Reconstruction of the Barracks of the Vigils at Ostia. Reconstruction by Angelo Coccettini and Marzia Vinci.

Ostia was motivated by the fear of fire in the granaries and more generally in the establishments of the *annona* and port. Augustus and later Claudius had sent military units to Ostia with firefighting functions, but it was only from the time of Domitian that the cohort was stationed there permanently. The barracks to be seen today, built on top of the Domitianic structure, dates to the time of Hadrian. It is a functional building structured around an interior courtyard, with latrines, a sanctuary and the space necessary for exercises.

The Piazzale delle Corporazioni at Ostia is the most outstanding example of a monument connected to the grain trade because of its inscriptions and figural decorations (Fig. X- 43, 47, 48, 49). It is one of the most imposing monuments in the city, a large square located directly behind the theatre with porticos on the three sides away from the theatre. Such squares are a common feature of theatre complexes, serving as a place where the spectators could walk in the intervals between programs. Originally the complex, dated in its first phase to the Augustan Period (like the theatre itself), was nothing more than this. In its second-century phase, however, one aisle of each portico was divided into rooms giving on to the remaining part of the portico. The mosaic floor of the porticos is decorated with motifs that invite the passerby to stop and turn 90° toward the rooms off the portico. Most of the motifs are schematic representations of the activities of the owners of the rooms, who are often also named in the mosaic alongside the representation. Frequently the owners are identified by labels as shippers from some place in the provinces. Naturally the shippers' motifs often involve maritime subjects (ships, dolphins, the lighthouse at the harbor of Portus), but together with them or indeed in place of them there are indications of the goods traded, mostly grain, although there are others, such as an elephant alluding to the exotic animals supplied for the games at Rome. Thus, we find ears of wheat or the *modius* and the *rutellum*. Current thinking holds that the spaces may have served for corporate hospitality—the rooms are certainly too small to have functioned as the offices of the corporations as the older literature on Ostia suggests. These rooms with their decorations

Fig. X-47 Panorama of Roman Ostia including the *decumanus*, theatr and the Piazza of the Corporations. Reconstruction by Angelo Coccetti and Marzia Vinci.

Fig. X-48 (above) Detail of the Reconstruction of the Piazza of the Corporations showing also the central temple, often proposed as dedicated to Ceres. Reconstruction by Angelo Coccettini and Marzia Vinci.

Fig. X-49 (left) View of the floor mosaics in the Piazzale delle Corporazioni, at Ostia. Location: Piazzale delle Corporazioni, Ostia, Italy. Photo Credit: Alinari / Art Resource, N.Y.

and inscriptions show the importance of shippers and particularly of the grain trade at Ostia.

What happened to the grain after it was processed through Ostia? Rome was, of course, the destination of grain imported by the state and private individuals, which was taken up to Rome as needed. There were various ways to transport it. There was some road traffic, with an association of teamsters, the *cisiarii*, who have left a building at Ostia with a bath decorated with mosaics showing them in action. The most important way of moving grain was with *naves codicariae*, proper small ships with a hold and a mast. The mast, besides holding sails, could be used for hauling the boats upriver with ropes pulled by men or animals. At Rome itself there were extensive port facilities on the Tiber River. Significantly, those in the south of the city were rebuilt extensively under Trajan to allow docking at all times, normally at an intermediate level but also at a low one and a high one for exceptional conditions. Rome's granaries are little known, however. The main source of information about warehouses at Rome is the *Forma Urbis*

Fig. X-50 Fragment of the *Forma Urbis Marmoria*, in which were delimited streets, porticos, taverns and possibly even granaries of ancient Rome. Location: Museo della Civiltà Romana, Rome Photo Credit: Gianni Dagli Orti / The Art Archive at Art Resource, N.Y.

Marmorea, the marble plan of the Severan Period (late second to early third century CE) that was found in a fragmentary state in the *Templum Pacis*. It shows mostly buildings with courtyards such as are known at Ostia. From the plan it is impossible, of course, to determine which were used for grain (Fig. X-50).

It is impossible to realize the importance of the grain trade without the knowledge of the ancient written sources. Archaeology can, however, illustrate and supplement the picture drawn from the sources. This is especially the case at Ostia, a city dedicated largely to this trade which became a bustling worker community in the glory days of the second century.

CRITICAL THINKING EXERCISES

• 1 After the death of Domitian by assassination, how did the Romans proceed to name a new emperor?
• 2 What do Trajan's monuments say about how he wished to be remembered?
• 3 How are the vanquished portrayed in the Forum of Trajan and on the Column of Trajan and why?
• 4 What provisions did Trajan make with the food supply of Rome and Italy?
• 5 How did Romans use spa resorts or retreats for healing functions? What medicinal and religious elements did they combine?
• 6 How was the Roman army organized? What were the elements articulating a *castrum*?
• 7 How did Hadrianic sculpture differ sharply from preceding styles and vogues?
• 8 What role did Antinous play in Hadrian's life and in religious history?
• 9 What is the principal message being conveyed by Apollodorus of Damascus in the Forum of Trajan and on the Column of Trajan?
•10 How was the Roman army organized?
•11 What are the characteristics of Hadrian's architectural vision?
•12 Why is it often said that the Pantheon is a typical example of the Romans' use of architectural space?
•13 Describe life in the army along Hadrian's Wall in England.
•14 Assess the importance of the grain trade for the Roman Empire and discuss the evidence for its importance at Ostia.

THE ROMAN FORUM IN THE HIGH EMPIRE

Fig. X-51 Reconstruction of the Roman Forum in the High Imperial Period looking through the Arch of Septimius Severus towards the Basilica Paulli, the Lapis Niger, and the Temple of the Deified Julius Caesar and its rostrum. Courtesy of Bernard M. Frischer and Rome Reborn.

In our filmed interview, the archaeologist and authority on the Forum, Nicola Terrenato, Professor of Classical Archaeology at the University of Michigan, has offered his vision of what the Roman Forum felt like to experience in the High Imperial Period (Fig. X-51):

> We know the Imperial Forum of Rome so much better than we know the Republican Forum. A lot of the buildings more or less preserve a phase of the early Empire. In the high Empire we would see a dazzling white scenario of course but with a lot of color painted on the sculpture. We would see massive Corinthian temples surrounding the Forum. We would see this white dazzling travertine floor of the Forum with a large inscription across it commemorating the builder of the floor. We would see of course massive basilicas along the long sides and a bustle of people going in and out of them, and trials and money changers and hawkers of every kind. We would see smaller temples like the Temple of Vesta, elegant structures. We would see some of the earliest triumphal arches with inscriptions, with carvings commemorating the great victories and the great triumphs of the emperors. At that point really the Forum became one of the marvels of the world and it would stay that way for centuries. Even after Rome has lost the status as Imperial capital, people will still travel to see the Roman Forum and Imperial Fora to view them as wonders of the world.

Chapter XI
The Antonine Emperors and the Severans

Hadrian planned for his own successor's accession to be a graceful one. Antoninus Pius is not a well-known emperor, although he ruled from 138 to 161 CE, a considerable time (Fig. XI-1). His distinguished family was from Nemausus, now Nimes, in the south of Gaul, although he was born near Rome and raised there. Thus, he was now the third emperor in a row with a provincial background. He was not a megalomaniac builder, had no particular obsessive behavioral traits and loved his wife. Neither his architecture nor his sculpture were particularly distinctive or innovative. As is so often the case in history, those who do their job with distinction and without scandal are considered too dull to be remembered; that may be said of this emperor as well.

Fig. XI- 1 Portrait of Antoninus Pius (ruler 138-161 CE). Roman Emperor, c. 150 CE. Marble. Photo: Elke Estel / Hans-Peter Klut. Location: Skulpturensammlung, Staatliche Kunstsammlungen, Dresden, Germany. Photo Credit: Art Resource, N.Y.

Antoninus' reign was the most peaceful of any emperor's. He undertook no military campaign himself, and there was no serious fighting during his time. His most notable endeavor was the establishment of a wall to the north of Hadrian's Wall but within territory which the Romans always considered their sphere of activity. The Antonine Wall, a simpler structure of turf and stone, crossed the narrowest point in Britain, between the Firths of Clyde and Forth. Although it was not long-lived, being occupied for only some 20 years under Antoninus Pius and again for a few years under Septimius Severus and otherwise abandoned in favor of Hadrian's Wall, its shorter line possessed some military logic. The line of fortification in Germany between the Rhine and the Danube was also adjusted to a slightly advanced, shorter route.

Antoninus' reign marks the beginning of the rule of the Antonine *gens* that was almost as long-lasting as the Julio-Claudian dynasty, continuing in power until nearly the end of the second century. So revered were the good Antonine rulers that the next dynasty to rule, the Severans, claimed connections to them that were probably not true.

SCULPTURE

The sculpted portraiture of this period shows a pronounced dematerialization of plastic form as if non-Classical, popular art with its simplified forms and weakened structural sophistication was now forcing its way through into official Imperial art. The heavy eyelids that had typified Roman sculpture since the time of Hadrian continued but the face started to become less a realistic portrait and more a bilaterally symmetrical mask (Fig. XI-1). The highly polished, sugar cube-like look of Hadrianic sculpture persisted, although in a more muted form. These new trends intensified under the next emperor Marcus Aurelius whose co-reign with the much less apt Lucius Verus was anything but happy. Both highly Classical and simplified popular art trends continued into this period in official and local artistic works.

SARCOPHAGI

During the second century a new tradition grew throughout the Empire: burying the dead intact in sarcophagi. The tradition of inhumation in a sarcophagus was widely practiced by ancient Egyptians, Greeks and Etruscans, but for the Romans, with the exception of some notable families such as the Scipios, cremation and the placing of bodies in urns was the norm. Now all manner of sarcophagi were being made in various parts of the Roman world, decorated with scenes intended to commemorate the life of the deceased. Scholars still

Fig. XI- 2 Sarcophagus of the 9 Muses. Roman, c. 150 CE. Marble, 61.5 x 205 x 68 cm. Photo: Hervé Lewandowski. Location: Louvre Museum, Paris, France. Photo Credit: Réunion des Musées Nationaux / Art Resource, N.Y.

debate why this vogue that seems to have begun under Trajan grew so rapidly under Hadrian, but no satisfactory answers have yet been offered. One suggestion is that during the time of highest prosperity in the Roman Empire, wealthy people commissioned sarcophagi as a way to memorialize themselves with magnificent carvings that could be appreciated long after their death. Thus the sarcophagus became a gaudy status symbol.

Not surprisingly the subject matter of the sarcophagus varied. There could be a portrait, sometimes quite realistic, of the deceased accompanied by scenes showing the four seasons or cupids as symbols of divine love. Battle sarcophagi were extremely popular for those with a distinguished military career. The rich with intellectual pretensions might place themselves in the company of Muses in order to appear sophisticated, refined and cultured or they might be followers of Apollo Musagetes or other religious or philosophical sects that would approve of such imagery. Muses were also thought of as intermediaries, figures who might help the deceased traverse the mysterious realm of the afterlife in order to dwell on a higher plain (Fig. XI-2). Wealthy citizens might have their sarcophagus custom-designed while the middle class might visit a workshop specializing in such sculptures. They could select a prefabricated one featuring appropriate images and themes, and then have the reclining figure on the lid carved into a portrait of the deceased. Sarcophagi were, in fact, frequently exported semi-finished from the marble quarries. The quality of the sarcophagus varied enormously, depending on how much one wanted to pay for one, just as the quality of casket varies in a modern funeral home.

The trend was both widespread and diverse. In Rome sarcophagi had decoration on three sides and often featured a reclining image of the deceased on top that recalled Etruscan predecessors (Fig. XI- 3). These are known as *gisant* or reclining figure style. Sometimes the top might be flat with barbarian heads at the corners (Fig. XI-4). Examples from Greece and Asia Minor were often four-sided and fashioned in the manner of little temples or a big couch showing regional influence from the sarcophagi of the Hellenistic Period in that region.

Fig. XI- 3 Battle of the Greeks and Amazons on a Roman sarcophagus, c. 180 CE. Marble, 230 x 81 cm. The lid shows a reclining couple (*gisant* type). Photo: René-Gabriel Ojéda. Location: Louvre Museum, Paris, France. Photo Credit: Réunion des Musées Nationaux / Art Resource, N.Y.

Fig. XI- 4 Battle between Romans and Gauls, Vigna Ammendola Sarcophagus. Probably c. 150 CE. Location: Musei Capitolini, Rome, Italy. Photo Credit: Alinari / Art Resource, N.Y.

THE VIGNA AMMENDOLA SARCOPHAGUS

Although designs and themes were constantly repeated, some sarcophagi were masterpieces and sculptural *tours de force*. One example probably made in the time of Antoninus Pius is the Vigna Ammendola Sarcophagus, found in a vineyard of the Ammendola family along the Appian Way in 1829 and now located in the Capitoline Museums in Rome, a fine example of the battle sarcophagus so much in vogue during this period (Fig. XI-4).

It is a pastiche of stock scenes of battle, all thrown together in an intricate tapestry of interwoven arms, legs, anguished faces, horses, shields and battle trophies, a clutter in the tradition of the much earlier Alexander Mosaic (see Chapter VI; Fig. VI-18). Roman sculptors enjoyed showing off their technical virtuosity in creating these works, which were no doubt sketched preliminarily. The sculptor used battle images familiar to Romans from paintings, coins and public monuments. His unique contribution is not in the creating of new poses but rather in the complex integration of these traditional ideas and stock images into a coherent interlocking scene. Thus we can recognize in earlier sculptural works the naked soldier with sword viewed from the rear and the Dying Gaul in the lower center, who was "borrowed" from a dedicatory monument erected on the Pergamene acropolis in the Hellenistic Period by the Attalid Kings of Pergamum. The bound captive by a trophy was a staple of Roman coinage and victory monuments. All this borrowing of earlier forms shows that the Romans were familiar with Greek masterpieces and copied and admired them. Placing them in their own design was not considered plagiarism but rather an *homage* or invocation of the fine works of earlier times and showed refinement on the craftsman's part as well as erudition on behalf of the patron.

The surface of the battle sarcophagus was normally organized into set pieces with captured barbarians sitting at the ends beneath a trophy hung with captured enemy spoils and looking back into the frame. The center piece is often a powerful scene, grouping the figures into a geometric pattern. In this case the sculptor created a group formed by the soldier on horseback hiding his face, a horseman coming up in the upper right, a powerful naked warrior seen from behind, a fallen horse and a noble half-naked barbarian stabbing himself. Between the ends and the center another grouping is placed on either side. At the left is a Roman soldier in full armor looking backwards and holding what may be a lance while beneath him a naked barbarian falls dramatically from his horse. This is flanked on the right by an advancing Roman foot soldier about to slash a fallen naked barbarian while an armed Roman soldier appears above. These are the set pieces around which other figures are grouped and interrelated. The military theme is also reflected on the lid, carved with images of defeated and disconsolate barbarians. The ends of the lid feature severed barbarian heads, a sign of Roman triumph already familiar from the Column of Trajan (see Chapter X) and which would be reused on the Column of Marcus Aurelius.

In this sarcophagus the typical Antonine–style of around 150 CE is clear. The figures still reveal a measure of plastic form and are not yet stumpy or doll-like, showing that Classical influence could still be brought to bear in the rendering of the figures and their proportions. The relief is deeply cut, creating vast pockets of shade that flicker amid the highlights, giving an almost three-dimensional effect. The figures are muscular and given to dramatic poses, showing the influence of the Pergamene Baroque–style, suggesting that the subject matter is the Greeks against the Gauls, a popular theme in Hellenistic Pergamene sculpture and now-lost paintings. The attention to detail of the brave Gallic warriors with their wild hair and metal neck ring known as a torc further suggests that there was a specific Pergamene prototype for the basic scene that was borrowed and then embellished by the Roman sculptor. Romans so delighted in the wild interweaving of forms that some subsequent sarcophagus sculptors took it to radical extremes, even increasing the verticality of the stone casket so they could fit in more elaborate tapestries of intertwined bodies.

The particular painting that may have influenced this sarcophagus was done in Pergamum in western Anatolia around 165 BCE. There the King Eumenes II of the Attalid Dynasty won a major victory over the Gauls but was too sickly to fight himself. His triumphal painting had the head of the conquering general not quite visible, exactly in the manner shown here. Of course sarcophagi such as this could have a wide circulation because they might be prefabricated with a conquering generic general and simply purchased by a client wanting a battle scene in honor of his own military career. That his victory was being compared to the conquest of the Gauls would have been a perfectly acceptable reference for a Roman military man because the Romans had had their own problems repelling the Gauls in the early and middle Republic.

THE HOUSE OF THE CASCADE IN UTICA, TUNISIA

The degree to which Roman domestic architecture had evolved by the Antonine Period is shown by a remarkable upper class house found at Utica on the northern coast of Tunisia (Figs. XI-5 through 9). Utica, located near ancient Carthage, had been a thriving Punic community before the Romans defeated the Carthaginians for the last time in 146 BCE and took over their lands. In the time of Augustus, the area was surveyed and laid out in a grid of *insulae* or city blocks each with 12 houses, and each of equal size. This layout was suitable for a new Roman colony and could be an effective way to settle veterans, poor people or just to remove overpopulation from major cities such as Rome.

However, in Roman communities where *insulae* are found, invariably somebody gradually acquires more wealth than his neighbor and begins to expand by buying up several of his neighbors' lots. Such was the case with the so-called House of the Cascade, which sprawled over five lots in the later first century CE, then was remodeled extensively in the time of Antoninus Pius. The elegant house is so well preserved that one can imagine what attending a dinner party there must have been like.

At the entry there was a lovely fountain that greeted the guests, who then proceeded up one of two ramped corridors that were probably lined with portraits of the *dominus* and his family. Finally the central part of the house or peristyle was reached with corridors on four sides around a beautiful porticoed garden complete with sundial. To the left was a series of five guest rooms, simple chambers floored with elegant mosaics of the later first century CE and separated from each other by thin curtains. The mini-rooms were suitable sleeping quarters for guests staying the night. The thin and removable curtain walls between the rooms could likely be pushed aside or removed to put rooms together and provide either more space for a family or an optional more intimate setting for guests in separate rooms.

House of the Cascade, Utica, Tunisia c. 150 CE.

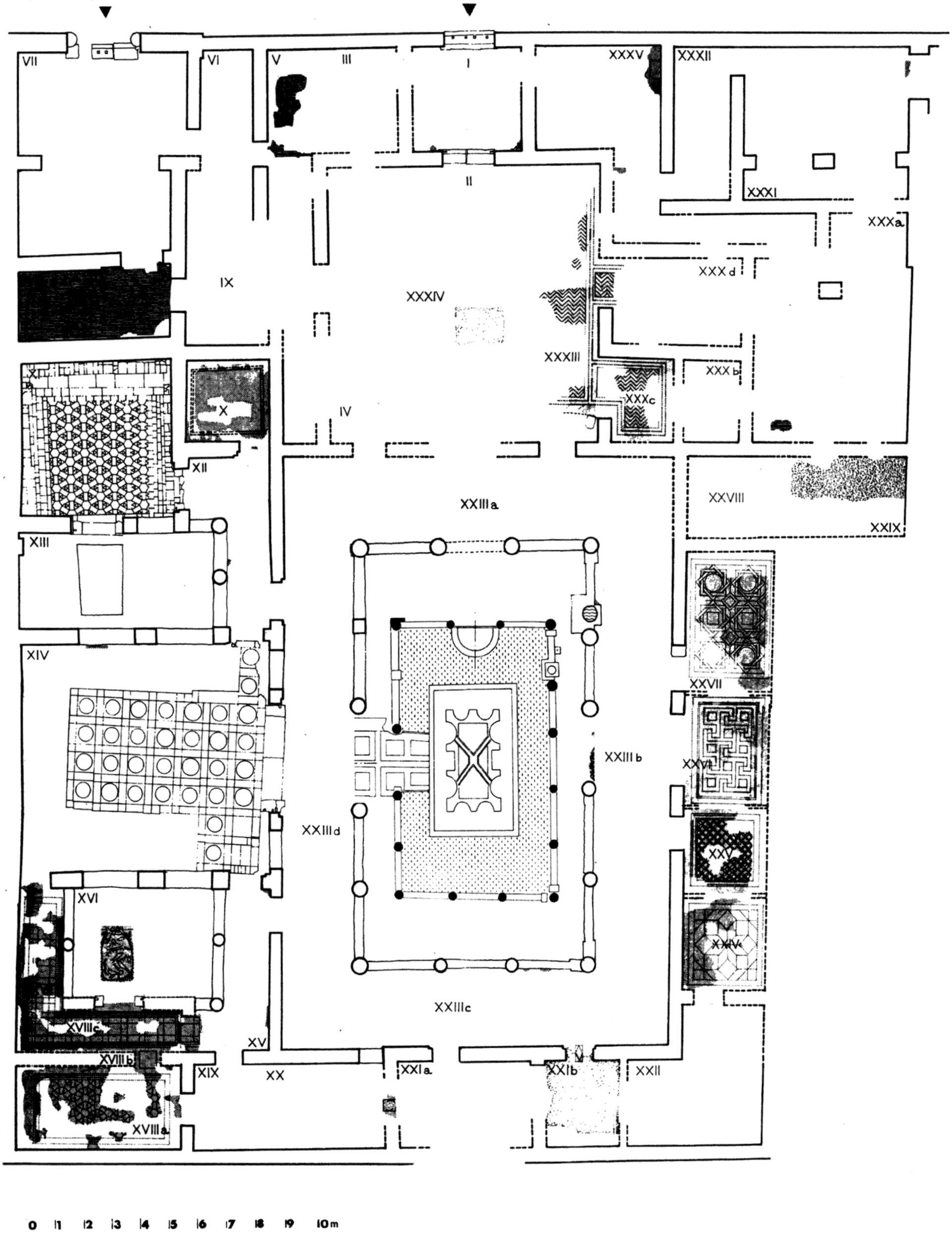

Fig. XI- 5 Plan of the House of the Cascade (Maison de la Cascade), Utica, Tunisia, constructed in the later first c. CE and remodeled in the Antonine Period. Courtesy of David Soren.

Fig. XI- 6 View over the central court and fountain of the House of the Cascade. Photo Credit: Noelle Soren. University of Arizona School of Anthropology Archive.

Across from these was a large *triclinium* or central dining room with spaces for couches to be placed around three sides near the back. It was paved in luxurious *opus sectile* or cut stone geometric pieces of flooring (Fig. XI-9). The banqueters could recline on the couches while servants wheeled in food on little carts and served it already cut up as finger food (by an attendant known as a *scissor*) on small tables. The food for the elaborate *cena* would include multiple courses prepared in a nearby kitchen area across the courtyard. Flute players might be brought in to accompany the meal. The banqueters would have light, air and water surrounding them on three sides thanks to the arrangement of the rooms in the main dining area. For example, after dinner, guests could proceed to the courtyard to the north to view a mosaic of various Mediterranean fish being caught in a big net by fishermen in a boat. A fountain at the top of the ramped mosaic allowed water to cascade down over the fish. Some of the fish had highlights of their bodies picked out with glass *tesserae* to make them appear to shimmer and swim as the water cascaded down over them (Figs. XI-7, 8).

The *triclinium* opened in front onto a central *viridarium* or garden with a large fountain full of alternating rectilinear and curvilinear niches, a Baroque touch. At the top of the fountain lead pipes had been strung in a figure-eight pattern and no doubt perforated to allow for a dancing water show. Water was brought into the villa by an aqueduct and funneled from there to lead pipes. The aqueduct had been introduced into Utica in the Hadrianic Period (c. 130 CE), allowing wealthy home owners to respond accordingly, being able for the first time to introduce elaborate fountains into their homes relatively inexpensively. This extensive lead piping caused earlier mosaics to be torn up not only to install the pipes but also to put in drains to evacuate the ever flowing water. Thus the local mosaic industry also saw a boom in the second century CE because of the extensive house remodeling required to modernize and keep up with the latest trends in interior design locally and in Rome.

Fig. XI- 7 View of the fish cascade of the House of the Cascade (Maison de la Cascade) also known as the House of the Waterfall, Utica, Tunisia. Mosaic-decorated fountain. Photo Credit: Gianni Dagli Orti / The Art Archive at Art Resource, N.Y.

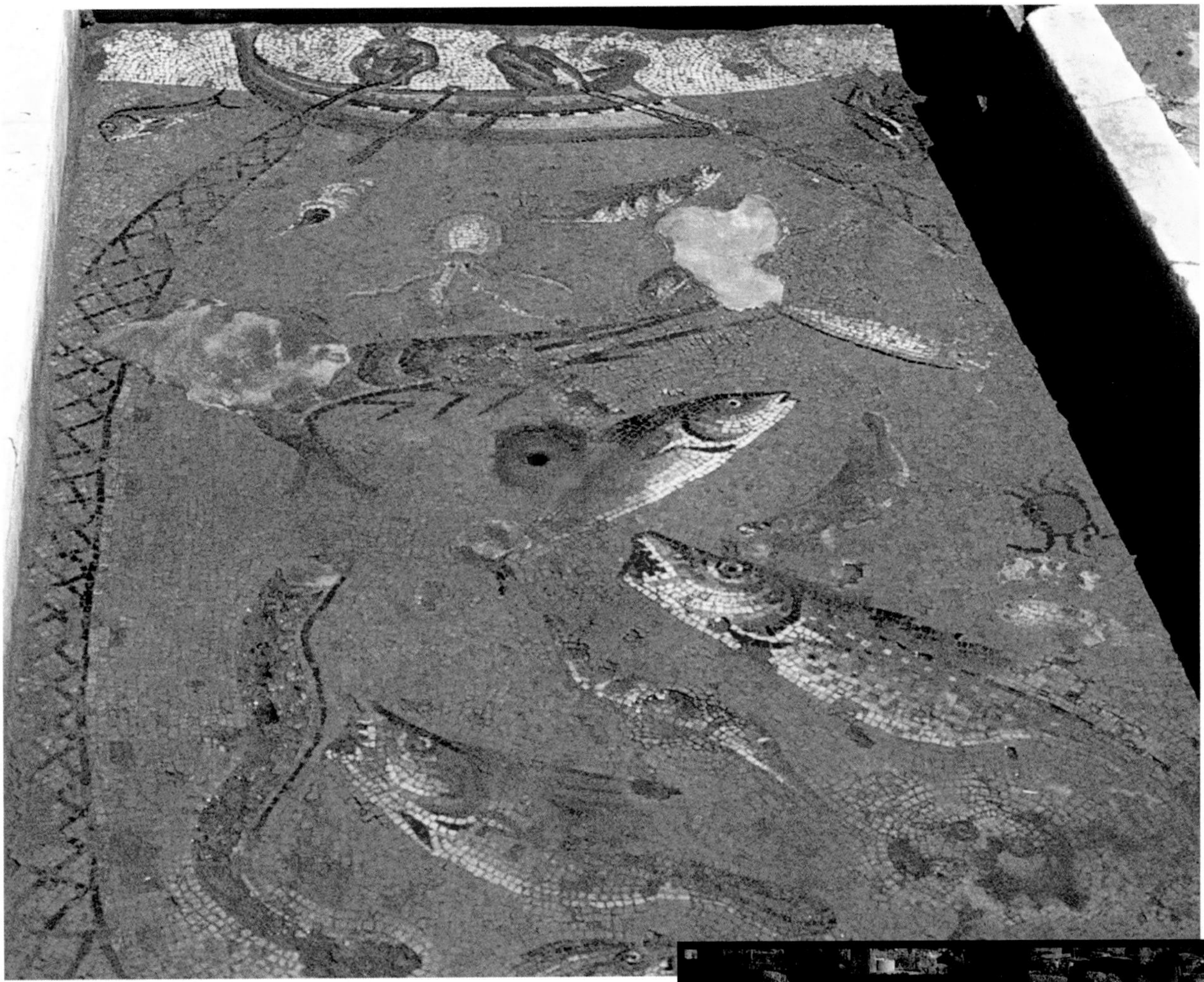

Fig. XI-8 Detail of the fish mosaic of the House of the Cascade, Utica, Tunisia. Photo Credit: Noelle Soren. University of Arizona School of Anthropology Archive.

Fig. XI- 9a (above) and 9b (right) Detail of the main *triclinium* or dining area of the House of the Cascade, Utica, Tunisia, paved in *opus sectile* in the Antonine Period. Photo Credit: Noelle Soren. University of Arizona School of Anthropology Archive.

Fig. XI- 10 Detail from the interior of the Tomb of the Pancratii in Rome. Stucco panel depicting Priam in front of Achilles, located in the sepulchral room of the tomb. Location: Via Latina, Rome, Italy. Photo Credit: Alinari / Art Resource, N.Y.

THE TOMB OF THE PANCRATII

Wall painting also followed its own vogues in the second century CE. Much of it was pedestrian and lacked the dignity and careful execution of the earlier Pompeian product, especially the early years of the Third Style. Occasionally beautiful walls were produced as in the Tomb of the Pancratii, owned by a burial *collegium* and situated along the Via Latina on the outskirts of Rome (Fig. XI-10). Discovered in 1857, it has been off-limits to tourists and remained well-preserved. The privileged few who do get to see the two-story high structure can delight in its geometric paneling typical of its age, its magnificent stucco work and its careful execution. Dated to no earlier than the year 159 CE by its brick stamps, the art work mixes painting and stucco and offers a pleasing image of flat, geometric wall designs with rectangular panels, often featuring figures and figural scenes. In the center of the ceiling Jupiter appears with his eagle, a sign of *apotheosis* or transport of the soul to an afterlife among the gods. There are scenes from the works of Homer, sacral-idyllic landscapes, centaurs fighting with lions, and still lives. It is hard to interpret what each image means; many seem to be simply decorative or the result of the desire to surround the dead with images of the heroic individuals who had passed on before them (and whom they may hope to join). Much of the art is just pleasant images such as flowers that would be delightful to contemplate in the afterlife. The overall effect is that of a Rococo interior of the 18th century in France or Austria: delicate and precise ornament, attractive floating and flying figures such as *putti* or cupids, shell decorations, and thin architraves that push out and pull in. The workmanship is of extremely high quality.

MITHRAS

During the second century CE, oriental religions became enormously popular, particularly the cult of Mithras, an eastern divinity of disputed origins, who became especially popular with soldiers and officials, probably because of its emphasis on hierarchy and duty. *Mithraea* survive around the Roman world (even as far away as Londinium or Roman London). They are readily recognized because they have banqueting couches on either side with a sacred niche at the end and imitate the appearance of caves because Mithras was supposedly born from rocks (Fig. XI-11). In the sacred niche Mithras, wearing a Phrygian or Anatolian cap and sometimes holding a disc (the symbol of the world) in his

Fig. XI-11a *Mithraeum* beneath the Church of San Clemente. This underground sanctuary is one of 45 shrines, dedicated to the worship of Mithras, which have been found in Rome. Third c. CE. Location: San Clemente, Rome, Italy. Photo Credit: Werner Forman / Art Resource, N.Y.

Fig. XI-11b Artist's reconstruction of the *Mithraeum* of the Seven Spheres at Ostia, c. 170 CE by Angelo Concettini (computer architectural reconstruction specialist) and Marzia Vinci (consulting archaeologist).

Fig. XI- 12 Mithras *Tauroctonos* (Mithras the Bull Slayer). Marble. Imperial Roman. Second century CE. Location: Sala degli Animali, Museo Pio Clementino, Vatican Museums, Vatican State. Photo Credit:.Vanni / Art Resource, N.Y.

right hand, was depicted heroically slaying the bull (Fig. XI- 12). Men—only males could participate in the cult—entered his realm to be purified, became initiates and learned ethical and spiritual life codes. There were seven grades of initiation to the cult that were attained through devotion and mystical religious practices. Ceremonies involved the sacrifice of bulls, symbolic of the fertility that Mithras brought to the Earth, and ritual meals. There were many parallels with Christian liturgy, including the need for purification and the baptismal *dolium* or jar with holy water at the entry. It is much contested whether these practices were adapted rather than innovated by the Christian groups as their own numbers grew rapidly. For a time during the second and third centuries CE, Mithraism appeared to be the most popular and fastest growing cult of the day, especially among the Roman soldiery, but it was gradually eclipsed by Christianity. It was also particularly popular in Rome and Ostia, where cult centers might appear within apartment complexes and even public bathing facilities.

HOUSING IN THE second CENTURY

Because of centuries of overbuilding, very little survives to view today in Rome of ancient domestic architecture in the densely packed metropolis. However, a visit to Ostia provides a unique opportunity to study Roman quarters in detail (for more on the commercial life of Ostia see Chapter X). The *insulae* feature commercial establishments with ready-to-eat food in the manner of a modern snack bar (*thermopolia*) and neighborhood baths (*balneae*), but unlike Pompeii or Herculaneum, the housing is packed close together because real estate was expensive. Apartment houses are the rule rather than the more sprawling Pompeian house type (Fig. XI- 13). The four and five story structures arose some 50 feet in the air and featured balconies, central courtyards and sometimes little shrines. Some reports suggest that structures as high as 70 feet were built and reached seven stories.

One of the most famous of the apartment complexes is the House of Diana located east of the Forum. The name comes from a small terracotta relief sculpture in the central courtyard of the building showing the huntress goddess. This house is unusual in that it has some communal features, such as a porter's lodge, which have led to the suggestion that it served as a hotel or that rooms were perhaps rented to travelers. Near the courtyard are two rooms which were

Fig. XI- 13 Apartment house at Ostia (House of Diana), on the Via di Diana. Photo Credit: Noelle Soren. University of Arizona School of Anthropology Archive.

transformed into a small *mithraeum* that once held statues of the cult divinities. The ground floor had shops along the street on two sides. A balcony overlooks the street from the first floor; balconies were essential in high-rise apartment dwellings to enable firemen to battle blazes and for ropes to be lowered down to facilitate escape. After the great fire of 64 CE in Rome, firefighting balconies became mandated by law. A pleasant piazza or mini-park occupied the area across the street, flanked by a little marble altar dedicated to the *Lares* or protective divinities of the quarter. A snack bar was close at hand to serve the occupants. The feeling is one of pleasant and vibrant neighborhood life.

Elsewhere at Ostia, apartments were available in more up-scale or simplified versions. Whether elaborate or basic, apartments served Ostia's middle classes, since people lower down the social scale lived behind their workshops and in other less formal spaces. There were bigger, more richly decorated apartments, which might be located amidst gardens and in complexes with more amenities. There were also ones that offered only the basics. Nevertheless, the plan was often similar—two large rooms at either end joined by a corridor with the entrance on one side and smaller rooms on the other. When the apartment houses of Ostia were discovered in the first half of the 20th century, they created a sensation, both because they were so different from the single-story, single-family houses arranged around an *atrium* and a peristyle described by Latin authors and known at Pompeii and because the houses they were discovering were not unlike the ones in which they lived themselves.

LATE ROMAN PAINTING AT OSTIA

Ostia is also an important place to observe Roman wall painting after the fall of Pompeii. Although most of the houses are not in the same fine condition as those buried under ash or lava in Pompeii, Herculaneum or Stabiae, enough survives to give an indication of the styles and trends of the later Empire. With the new harbor built under Trajan between 100 and 106, the town boomed and intensive building continued until well into the third century. Generally, the quality of the wall decoration is disappointing when compared to the earlier Pompeian styles; the poor degree of preservation does not help this overall impression.

The House of Ganymede in Ostia, decorated around 180 CE, has all the flashy character of later second-century CE Roman architecture (Fig. XI-14). Its painted decoration is dynamic but illogical, full of flat surfaces and partially glimpsed vistas that have colonnades that do not make architectonic sense and seem to be carelessly added rather than a logical part of any architectural scheme on the wall. The color scheme is always lively, emphasizing yellow and red and there is an emphasis on geometric panels. Figures float within panels but seem poorly or quickly executed and not well centered. There is a tendency towards reedy and linear architectural forms such as columns or moldings that recall the Third Style at Pompeii but are rendered here in slapdash fashion. Occasionally landscape scenes are attempted but they are sketchy and often tiny. Overall, there is the feeling of second-rate Rococo here, decorative elements that exist with great delicacy but are divorced, perhaps deliberately or indifferently, from all logic. Figures are not centered and the wall does not appear to

Fig. XI- 14a (above) and 14b (below) Painting in the House of Ganymede in Ostia. University of Arizona School of Anthropology Photo Archive.

show any concern about being carefully arranged, pre-planned or symmetrical. Prospects or vistas lead nowhere. The artist has borrowed from earlier styles for decorative effect but seems to have nothing to say or to care about saying it. The work suggests artisans are covering the surface with no interest in producing high art or in developing elaborate pre-painting layouts.

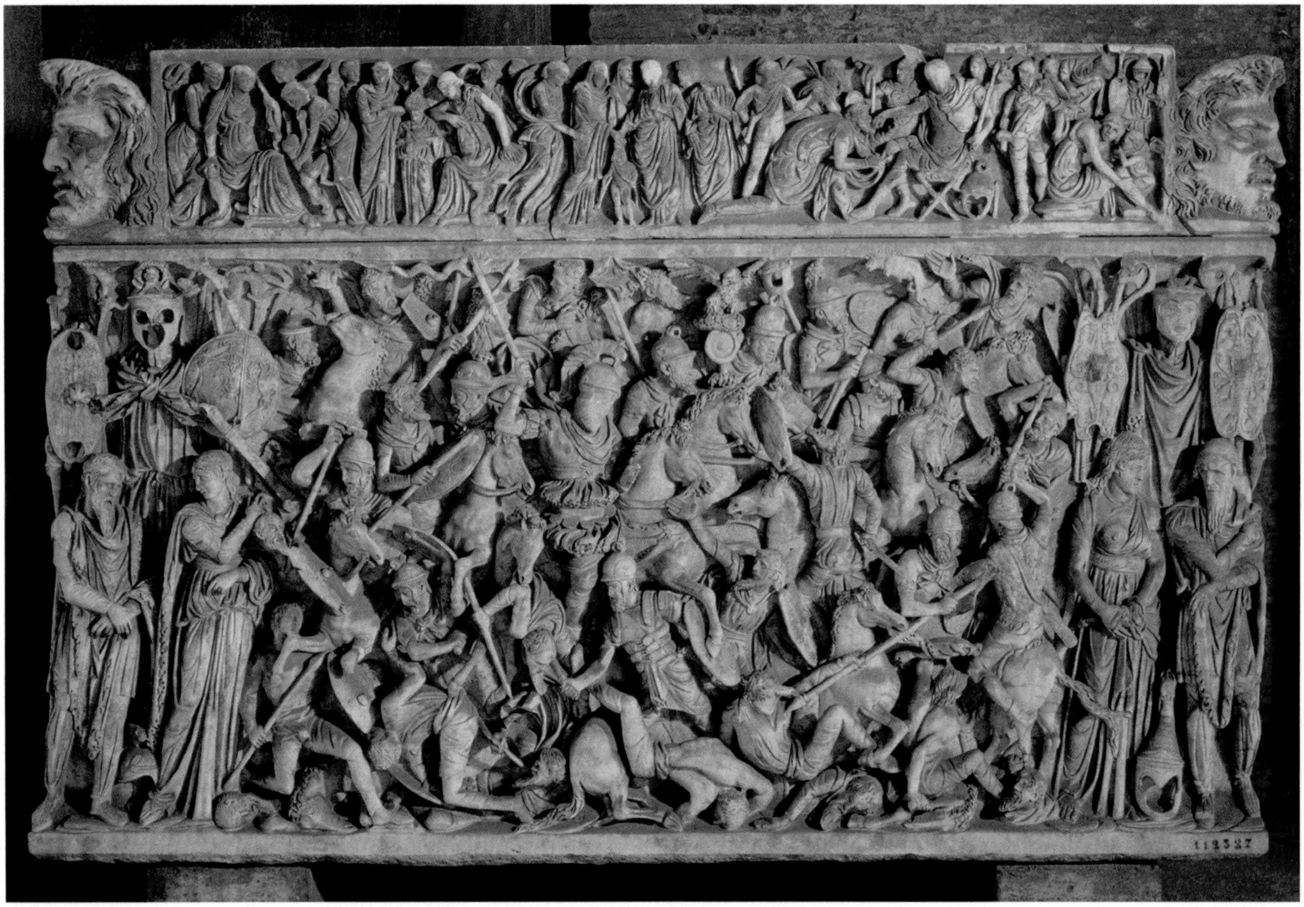

Fig. XI- 15 Battle between Romans and Barbarians. The Portonaccio Sarcophagus, from Portonaccio, Via Tiburtina (near Rome). Antonine dynasty, c. 180-190 CE. Location: Museo Nazionale Romano (Palazzo Massimo alle Terme), Rome. Photo Credit: Scala / Art Resource, N.Y.

THE VIA TIBURTINA SARCOPHAGUS

The 150s were a time when many Romans enjoyed the good life. However, although North Africa remained prosperous and imports continued to stream into Rome, times were already changing in the great metropolis. The 160s became an age of war, a theme reflected on the battle sarcophagi of this period that reveal more of the hell of the battle than the pride in the Roman army shown on the Column of Trajan. It was an age where wars on the Rhine, in Northern Italy and in Parthia (Iran) touched nearly every Roman family in some way. The expressions of agony on the faces of sculpted figures of the later second century reflect contemporary feelings in Rome and were at odds with the general tendency in portraiture to dematerialize human form and create iconic masks. This can be seen on the Via Tiburtina Sarcophagus now in Rome's Terme Museum (Fig. XI-15). Dating to around 190 CE at the end of the Antonine Period, it displays a living tapestry so interwoven with figures and so tumultuously overblown that one can scarcely make out the details without repeated viewings. This is no allegorical event but a real-life battle between Romans and Germans. Again book-ended by captives, this time standing beneath a captured trophy, the triumphing general now fully occupies the central position.

The emphasis now is on chaos, violence and emotion with figures sprawling into every nook and cranny as the emperor cuts his way through the enemy lines while on horseback. The Roman armor contrasts with the half-naked foe. If the original paint had survived the scene would have been even more chaotic and brilliantly flashing. The figures are beginning to lose their Classical plasticity and become increasingly stumpy and ill-proportioned. The captives at the ends are strangely elongated to match the increased verticality of the sarcophagus. The sculptor has gone as far as he can here with undercutting, planned overlapping, Baroque poses, dramatic emotion and multi-level staging. Even the Roman soldiers show the stress, although not as much as the sad, anguished barbarians.

It was indeed a stressful time. After Antoninus Pius, Rome entered into an age of constant warfare and insecurity. Marcus Aurelius (161-180 CE; Fig. XI-16) brought a measure of steady leadership to the period, but the economic crisis, plague and constant warfare drained manpower reserves and sapped the physical health of the Empire. Barbarians almost at the gates of Rome led many to believe that life had become depressing and full of suffering and despair for the future. The grisly world of the Via Tiburtina Sarcophagus revealed a universal hell of war for one and all.

Fig. XI- 16 Equestrian statue of Marcus Aurelius. Gilded bronze, c. 175 CE. Marcus Aurelius Exedra, Palazzo dei Conservatori, Musei Capitolini. Rome, Italy. Photo Credit: Vanni / Art Resource, N.Y.

THE EQUESTRIAN STATUE OF MARCUS AURELIUS

Piazza of the Capitoline Museum showing the Marucs Aurelius equestrian statue replica.

Visitors to the Capitoline Museums can see the bronze equestrian statue of Marcus Aurelius, a rare example of a surviving Antique bronze life-sized equestrian sculpture (Fig. XI-16). Restored in the 1980s, the original stands inside while a replica now greets visitors to the Piazza del Campidoglio at the top of the Capitoline Hill. The remarkable statue survived antiquity because it was believed to be a portrait of the emperor Constantine and had stood in the Piazza of the Lateran in Rome from at least the eighth century CE until 1538 when it was transferred to the Capitoline. Many other similar equestrian statues or *equi magni* of this type existed in Rome but this is the only one preserved. Dating probably to around 175-180 CE, the time of Marcus's victories over the Germanic tribes, the piece has inspired considerable discussion because the emperor is not in military armor, yet seems to be addressing or commanding his subjects in a powerful manner.

The emperor wears a cloak over his tunic. The folds of the drapery are intricately modeled and the horse's legs and head are particularly well modeled. The attention to the detail of the horse's trappings and even the wrinkles in the animal's neck reflect the high quality of the workmanship. There appears to be a fringed coverlet instead of a saddle beneath the emperor and no stirrups are visible (stirrups were introduced to Europe only in the Middle Ages; the Romans may have occasionally employed simple saddles from the late Republican Period on). The statue was also coated with gold leaf, traces of which survive.

Despite the plasticity of the clothing and horse, the head of Marcus is more a mask than a portrait. The heavy eyelids are characteristic of the period and the contrast between the smooth, bilaterally symmetrical face and the hair and beard curls full of restless texture and deep pockets of shadow reflects the trend to pictorialism that had begun with Hadrian. The growing emphasis on showing the most important subject matter in an overlarge manner, a tendency that was common in popular art and not present in Classical art, may explain why the head appears larger than normal and why the entire figure of Marcus appears so ample with respect to the horse.

The eyes also appear unusually large and opened very wide, another characteristic of the time. The drilling of the pupils, a technique employed primarily from the time of Hadrian on, adds a dimension of intensity and power to the expression, a majesty that is heightened by viewing the sculpture from below. Unlike the Column of Marcus Aurelius and some of the intense battle sarcophagi of the period already discussed, this statue combines extraordinary realistic detail (all the more difficult to obtain in the bronze-working process on this scale) with an other-worldly quality emphasized by the lack of correct proportions, the mask-like facial features, the pictorialism, and the drilling of the eyes. This Marcus, like the historical one, seems to be engaged in introspection, looking beyond this world and towards the next.

BARBARIAN INCURSIONS

In the middle of the second century CE, with the Empire at its most sprawling, barbarian unrest grew in the east, west and north. A shocking defeat at Elegeia during a military campaign in Armenia aroused the emperors Lucius Verus and Marcus Aurelius to the gravity of the situation. Lucius Verus, a mediocre troop commander, took charge of the troops in 162 and engaged in the *Bellum Armeniacum et Parthicum*, a huge war which took place in the areas of Syria, Media, Cappadocia and Armenia, with Lucius finally earning a triumph in 166. The war was enormously expensive in funds and manpower and forced the depletion of the legions on the Danubian frontier. Lucius Verus' soldiers brought diseases back to Rome, perhaps smallpox or measles, that caused a pandemic called the Antonine Plague (we are still not quite sure what they were, although they are usually described in texts as "the plague") that decimated the Roman troops and took his life.

The barbarian incursions that followed from the northern frontier regions were precursors of the invasions and migrations that eventually contributed to the downfall of Rome several centuries later. Two allied Germanic tribes known as the Marcomanni and the Quadi even marched on Italy itself. Marcus wrote about the hard times he was facing in his *Meditations*, yearning for a better world and desiring to reflect upon one's place not in this world so much as in the cosmos. In this age of constant fighting and major threats to Rome itself, alternative religions became increasingly popular, offering hope of a better life in the next world. The traditional philosophy of stoicism, once embraced by most Romans including Marcus Aurelius, now was becoming replaced by religions offering salvation, escape, and celestial reward. Among them was Christianity which had previously had less impact in Rome.

In these religions there was often the notion that the body was a prison from which one could be liberated spiritually in this life and actually in the next. Physical form was thus insignificant and a body of art grew up that de-emphasized the Classical tradition and showed figures with large eyes, hands and feet and all but dematerialized bodies. Non-traditional imagery even began to

Fig. XI-17 Decapitation of German Nobles. From the Column of Marcus Aurelius, Piazza Colonna, Rome. Completed 193 CE. Photo Credit: Alinari / Art Resource, N.Y.

show up on traditional monuments such as the commemorative Column of Marcus Aurelius. Among the images carved on it was a mysterious rain god who allegedly produced a torrent of water to save the Romans from certain defeat in battle versus the Marcomanni and Quadi. In an age of disease, despair, and constant war, deliverance and hoped-for miracles were more than welcome.

On the Column of Marcus Aurelius, panels vividly portray brutal events such as the decapitation of the captives (Fig. XI-17). The Roman cavalry implacably surveys the area at the top of the panel while captives await execution with terror in their faces, and disembodied heads roll on the ground. The executors may also be Germans from a tribal group loyal to Rome. The simplified artistic form, featuring tiering of figures, stylized bodies, overlarge heads and hands, and simplified drapery modeling, adds to the raw power of the scene. The figures on the right of the scene link to the next panel and are shown begging for Imperial mercy.

SAN CLEMENTE

San Clemente is a church located near the Colosseum in Rome. It is extraordinary because it allows one to go back in time level by level by descending staircases that lead to successive earlier structures excavated and preserved beneath the present one. The modern church is built directly over a fourth-century Christian basilica that lies over a large complex of earlier structures that were part of a city block of Imperial Rome (Fig. XI-18). Why was this place sacred to Christians? A long-established tradition holds that Pope St. Clement I (88-97 CE), to whom both the lower and the upper basilica are dedicated, lived here. In the mid-19th century it was attempted to make a connection between Clement I and Titus Flavius Clemens, grandson of the emperor Vespasian's brother and once consul of Rome. Titus Flavius Clemens was put to death in 96 CE for his religious convictions but it is not clear if he was a Jewish sympathizer, a pro-Christian activist, or an atheist. His wife Flavia Domitilla, who was Vespasian's granddaughter and the niece of Titus and Domitian, was banished to rocky Pandateria, a desolate island with little food off the coast of Cumae in southern Italy. More recent scholars believe, however, that Clement I and Titus Flavius Clemens cannot be the same man, since Christian sources indicate that the pope had servile origins and died only in 97 CE, after Domitian's assassination. It has also been suggested that the house under the first church was actually Titus Flavius Clemens' but mistakenly considered Clement I's in the fourth century.

The location was adjacent to a *Mithraeum* and the Mithras cult was installed here about the time of Caracalla. Like all other pagan cults, Mithraism was outlawed in 395 CE by the emperor Theodosius, and the basilica apparently expanded at that time over it. Thus, the Basilica of San Clemente effectively replaced the worship of Mithras with a Christian center.

In the Norman invasion of Rome by Robert Guiscard in 1084 CE, San Clemente was burned to the ground. The church was then rebuilt and subsequently underwent substantial restoration. It was given a new facade in the 18th century. It has, since 1677, been the place of refuge for Irish Catholic Dominicans from persecution in Ireland. Today one can visit San Clemente and hear English spoken throughout as members of the order study religious works, give tours, sell souvenirs, and engage in restoration projects. The fathers began the excavation of the lower church and of the house beneath that in 1857. They found frescoes depicting stories of Clemens I, which are important testimonies of medieval Italian art and in a caption contain one of the earliest uses of Italian. The lower church is also the resting place of St. Cyril, for whom the Cyrillic alphabet is named, because he brought Clement I's relics back to Rome from the pope's place of exile in the Crimea and then died at Rome.

Fig. XI- 18 San Clemente, view down the nave towards the altar. Location: San Clemente, Rome, Italy. Photo Credit: Alinari / Art Resource, N.Y.

Fig. XI- 19 Bust of Commodus as Hercules. (Emperor from 180-192 CE). Location: Musei Capitolini, Rome, Italy Photo Credit: Scala / Art Resource, N.Y. sourced from http://en.museicapitolini.org/collezioni/percorsi_per_sale/museo_del_palazzo_dei_conservatori/sale_degli_horti_lamiani/busto_di_commodo_come_ercole)

Fig. XI- 20 Septimius Severus, Roman Emperor (193-211 CE). Marble bust. Photo: Alfredo Dagli Orti. Location: Musei Capitolini, Rome, Italy. Photo Credit: Art Resource, N.Y.

THE MURDER OF COMMODUS

The Antonine rulers lasted in Rome through Antoninus Pius, Marcus Aurelius (Figs. XI-1, 16) and the violent, inept Commodus (Fig. XI-19). After the murder of the last Antonine in 192 CE in a palace coup, the Empire fell into a chaos so profound that the praetorian guard actually put their support up for auction and the Empire was purchased by a rich Senator named Didius Julianus. Immediately rival claimants for the throne appeared, recalling the unrest of the year 69. When the battles ended only one man was left, the governor of Pannonia (a province comprising Austria and western Hungary and the northwestern part of the former Yugoslavia): Septimius Severus (Fig. XI-20). However, Severus ushered in a dynasty in Rome that was anything but typically Roman. Hailing from the town of Lepcis Magna in what is now Libya, the new emperor never fully mastered Latin and always spoke with an accent. His wife Julia Domna was a devotee of Syrian mysticism and a member of a royal family and mystical cult from Emesa. She and Septimius had two sons, Geta and Caracalla, but the latter was an aggressive and ruthless heir, who murdered his brother in 211 shortly after Septimius Severus died when they became co-emperors.

ARCH OF SEPTIMIUS SEVERUS IN THE ROMAN FORUM

The Severan dynasty is best known for a series of triumphal arches that were built around the Roman Empire. The most widely known of these is the Arch of Septimius Severus in the Roman Forum (Figs. XI-21, 22). It was the first major Imperial commission carried out in the Forum in decades. It commemorates Septimius' victory against the Parthians, Rome's traditional rival empire. The inscription indicates that the arch was dedicated in 203 CE by Septimius Severus and his two sons Geta and Caracalla. Clearly, with the placing of this arch, Severus had in mind both the raising to the ranks of Augustus and Caesar the two sons, establishing a dynasty in the manner of Augustus and Antoninus Pius. The reference to Geta was removed when Caracalla took sole power after Septimius' death and had Geta murdered.

Although it is arguably the best preserved monument in the Forum, its ungainly sculpture and weathered condition make it a monument all but ignored by modern tourists. It was placed adjacent to the *rostra*, which were flanked on their opposite side by the much smaller Arch of Tiberius, now no longer there. Visible as one descended the Capitoline Hill to the northwest side of the Forum or as one descended the *Clivus Argentarius*, a winding road that led by the Forum of Julius Caesar to the northwest, the Arch of Septimius Severus simply could not be avoided in antiquity as well as now. It partially obscured the Temple of Concord, offset the balance of the *Curia* piazza and gave a hemmed in effect to the

Fig. XI- 21 View from the Capitoline Hill of the Arch of Septimius Severus in the Roman Forum with the Column of Phocas, Temple of Castor and Pollux and *Basilica Iulia* in the background. Photo by Dan Duncan.

XI- 22 Arch of Septimius Severus in the Roman Forum, detail. Septimius Severus (upper right) and Roman army besiege a walled city, perhaps Seleucia on the Tigris River in Mesopotamia, as the defenders flee or surrender. Photo by Dan Duncan.

center of the Forum, but it accomplished its objective: to put the accomplishments of the emperor in the face of everyone.

Severus's accomplishments were extraordinary. He brought the Empire back from anarchy to relative stability, at least for a time, and conducted successful campaigns at the extremes of the eastern empire against the Osroeni and Parthians. Osroene was a kingdom in northwestern Mesopotamia on the Euphrates which had been nominally conquered by the Romans in the 160s but now supported Parthia, long-time threat to Rome and particularly unfriendly to Severus. Parthia had its core area in what is now Iran and Iraq but spread out to become a danger to Roman provinces and interests in the East intermittently from the time of Augustus. The first Roman Emperor Augustus had built his arch in the Forum to commemorate the return of the standards captured by Parthia (see Chapter VII) and now this emperor with Punic roots, Septimius Severus, could claim his link to Augustus with the diagonal placement of his arch across the Forum.

The Arch of Septimius Severus stands at the bottom of the Capitoline above the *Comitium*. It presents three passageways (a larger central one and two smaller lateral ones framed by columns) surmounted by an attic. It is richly ornamented with architectural decoration, relief sculpture and a monumental inscription on the two main sides. Originally there was a triumphal *quadriga* in gilded bronze above the attic. The structure consists mostly of travertine and marble (Pentelic for much of the exposed masonry, Proconnesian for the columns and possibly Luna for the major elements of the relief).

The sculptural decoration on the façades of the arch appears on the pedestals supporting the columns, the keystones of the arches, the spandrels of the arches and especially the two panels over each lateral passageway. The figures outside the panels are fairly standard: Roman soldiers, barbarian captives, river gods, personifications of victories and seasons. Parthians in their distinctive costumes are shown captured on the pedestals and the triumphal procession with the Parthian booty is shown running around the arch above the level of the side arches. In the spandrels—the spaces left over above the central arch, below the architrave and next to the columns—victories rendered in a stiff Classical manner carry Parthian trophies just to underscore the message of conquest.

The panels probably narrate the events of the campaigns against the Parthians, although the details are still disputed. The weathered look of these sculptures has made it difficult to determine exactly what scenes are being shown in the panels above the side arches; they appear to show the great Parthian campaigns of the emperor. One of the panel groups on the north area of the arch facing the Capitoline Hill shows what may be the capture of Babylon or Seleucia on the Tigris, done in a narrative sequence beginning at the bottom.

First, Parthian defenders make a last-ditch stand inside the city walled with clearly indicated ashlar blocks. The tilt-down perspective allows us to look inside and glimpse multistoried buildings dwarfed by the defenders who are made extraordinarily large. Some of the city defenders have already given up and flee on horseback, their capes blowing out behind them, to the upper right and upper left of the city. At the middle left, what may be water flows into a double box that might indicate the city water supply held in giant rectangular cisterns. Perhaps these cisterns were cut off, leaving the city without water and triggering the surrender about to occur. More city dwellers flee to the lower left, this time on foot while at the bottom a roughly textured area might indicate the rocky terrain. At the lower right a badly preserved group of Roman soldiers wearing chain mail armor huddle in a fort and prepare to assault the city. In the scene above, the city and its cisterns appear again with the defenders primarily standing in front of it, surrounded on all sides by the Romans. The emperor may have appeared at the upper right, but the figure has now lost its head. His troops surround him carrying legionary standards and flags. The victory is complete.

Relief panels depicting historical episodes are, of course, nothing unusual in Roman art. The intention of the Severan panels is new, however—laying out a continuous narrative on a triumphal arch. The columns of Trajan and Marcus Aurelius had done this with unbroken spirals (see Chapter X), but the Severan sculptors had to adapt the model to a flat surface and place it in registers with simplified and reduced connecting elements. Technically the panels are innovative in their extensive use of the drill, which can penetrate more deeply than the chisel and create effects of shadow. There are differing opinions among scholars whether the panels were designed by a single artist or by two (one probably older and working in the Antonine tradition of individualized figures and the other a forerunner of the Late Antique tradition of anonymous masses of figures). Some scholars also feel that much was owed in the composition of the panels to triumphal military painting. Little doubt exists, however, that the figures outside the panels draw on earlier models.

Overall, the artistic design of the Arch of Septimius Severus is a mixture of styles. Unable to decide between traditional Classical imagery and the popular simplified look of the day, the designer uses both. The Classical style is reserved for the spandrels and column podia. The popular art style, in the tradition of the Columns of Trajan and Marcus Aurelius, has progressed further here. Figures are not only ill-proportioned but stumpy and flat and their drapery features simplified slash modeling rather than catenaries or smooth chains of indicated folds. The overall composition, even taking into consideration all the weathering and defacing of the images, lacks clarity, readability and a sense of artistic composition. However, scholarly defenders claim that the reliefs of the Arch of Septimius Severus represent a Late Antique resurgence of narrative folk art.

THE "ARCH" OF THE ARGENTARII IN ROME

It is useful to compare the Arch of Septimius Severus with the so-called Arch of the Argentarii or Money-Changers in Rome. This monument—actually not an arch at all but a gate with a lintel and jambs—stood at the end of the *Vicus Iugarius* (the street leading from the Forum) by the entry to the *Forum Boarium* by the Tiber River (Fig. XI-23). Its inscription indicates that it was erected privately by the money-changers of Rome (*argentarii*) in 203/4 in honor of the Imperial family. Besides Septimius Severus, his wife and Caracalla, it showed Caracalla's wife, his father-in-law and Geta, all of whom eventually fell into disgrace, causing the monument to be altered three times. The relief sculptures highlight military and sacrificial scenes, the former dependent on earlier models but the latter of Severan creation.

The monument shows particularly well the Severan traits that foreshadow Late Antique art. The architectural decoration is seen as a means of filling space. There is a tendency towards frontality and two-dimensionality in the relief, particularly in the sacrificial scenes, emphasizing the figures' role instead of their individual personality or shape. These traits perhaps came to the fore here because a private monument was less constrained by tradition than an official one. Without earlier models for some of the scenes, the sculptor relied more on native folk art styles.

THE BATHS OF CARACALLA

Rome's most famous public works project, the Baths of Caracalla (Figs. XI- 24 through 26), was in fact built by Caracalla. Situated in a relatively poor district in the southern part of Rome, it was intended as the ultimate neighborhood bath, a chance for the lowest levels of Roman society to surround themselves with luxurious mosaics, painting and statuary. As we have seen, the concept of the giant Roman bath complex evolved slowly from Greek predecessors. Now it had become colossal.

The Baths of Caracalla was not only a bathing establishment but also a giant entertainment center. There were several stories of offices and shops, and people providing services of all kinds from

XI- 23a (left) and 23b (above) Arch of the Argentarii in Rome, including detail of the Severan family sacrificing. Photo Credit: Noelle Soren. University of Arizona School of Anthropology Archive.

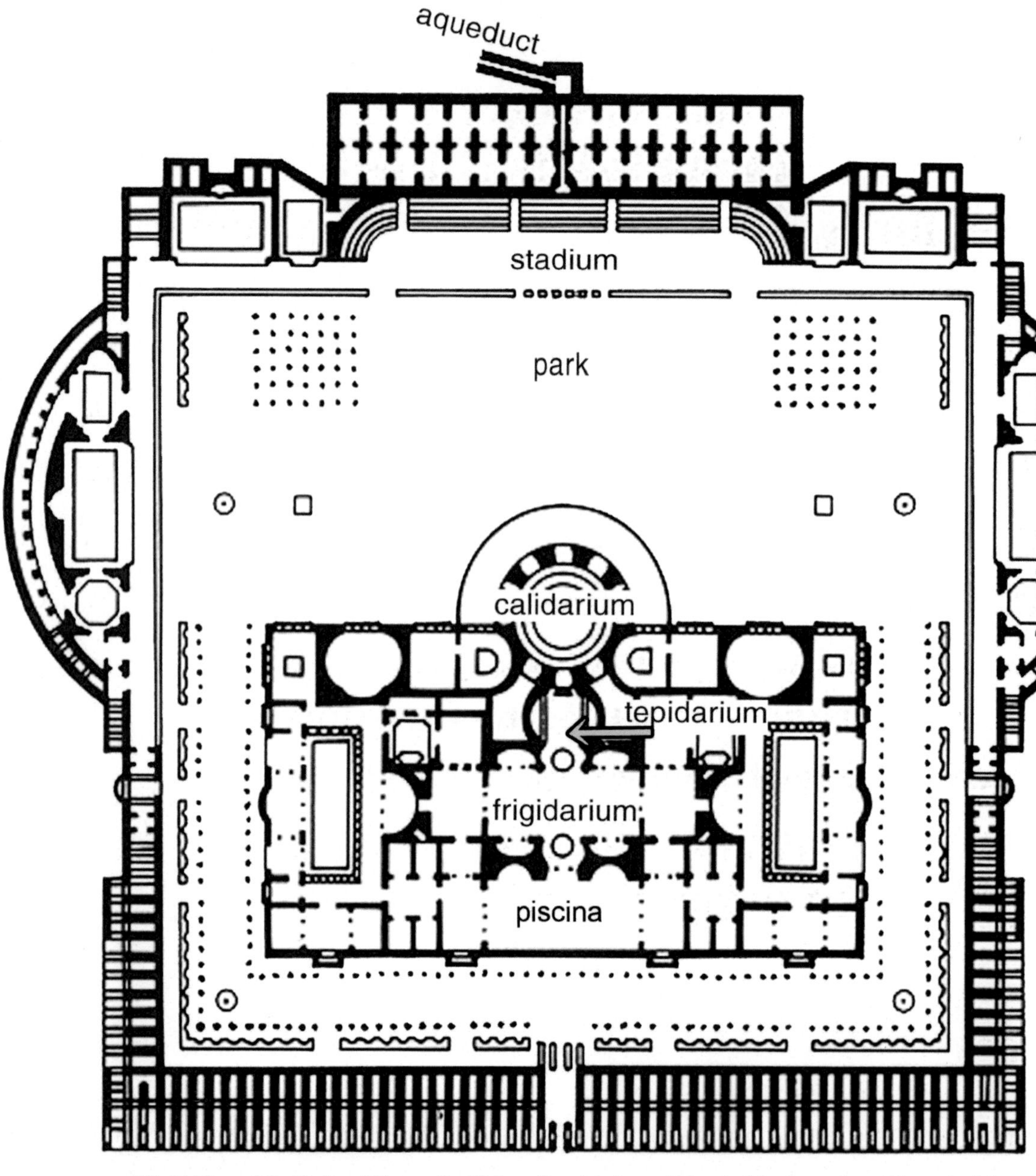

XI- 24 Plan of the Baths of Caracalla. University of Arizona School of Anthropology Photo Archive.

assistance in reading documents to visits with prostitutes. Unlike a modern shopping mall, however, the main social attraction and focus was the bathing. Raised up on an artificial platform that spanned some 25 acres, the Baths of Caracalla took four to six years to construct and remained in use for more than 300 years, accommodating up to 10,000 people at once

Once inside the massive enclosure, bathers found many different rooms and could follow their own route through them. There were several places to disrobe (*apodyteria*) fitted out with waiting benches and lockers where clothing could be checked. One could proceed directly to the *frigidarium*. It was more than just an unheated room with a pool. By the third century, it had become the showcase room of the baths, a vast triple-groin vaulted hall that towered high above the humbled bather. There were sculptures of muscular athletes to inspire you to get into shape. Even if you did not wish to bathe extensively, the *frigidarium* could be a place to meet friends and enjoy conversation in elegant surroundings.

From the *frigidarium* the bather passed to the *tepidarium* which was a room with a hypocaust floor, but the furnace was far away and the heat secondary. It provided a transition from the cold plunge of the *frigidarium* and led into the very hot rooms of the baths. The principal hot room or *caldarium* was pushed out from the giant rectangular block of the bath. This allowed for tubs to be placed by picture windows with views onto the esplanade beyond (see Chapter IX for further discussion of Roman baths).

Of course the furnaces would have to be well primed to generate enough heat to extend to the various hot rooms of the bath complex. Temperatures of up to 80 degrees centigrade were possible and in some ultra-hot hypocaust rooms reminders in mosaics were placed to warn bathers they might burn their feet. The little entry mosaics showed pictures of shoes, perhaps wooden clogs, actual examples of which were no doubt readily available there. Rooms reached levels up to 55 degrees centigrade (131 Fahrenheit) in *caldaria* and one account tells of slaves revolting against their master and

XI- 25 Reconstruction of the Baths of Caracalla showing the *piscina* or swimming pool and the view into the *frigidarium*. AKG-Images 5IT-R1-O2-1880-1-B. Woodcut reconstruction by Viollet le Duc, c. 1880, later hand colored.

holding him down so he was scorched by the hot floor. It is estimated that the hypocausts may have been kept around 50 to 70 degrees normally, the floor 35 (95 Fahrenheit) and the atmosphere under 30 (86 F) in order to avoid elderly people getting overcome. That the temperatures in the hypocaust space were hot is attested by the Roman baths of Glanum in southern France where the sandstone *suspensurae* were dissolved by the heat.

Having gone through the basic circuit of the Baths of Caracalla, the bather had still more options, because it was not necessary to return the same way one entered. There was usually a side track with various rooms for private rubdowns as well as a *laconicum* or Spartan hot bath where the temperatures could be more elevated than in the *caldarium*. Side tracks led back to the dressing room or out to the exercise ground for a game of rugby or volleyball. In front of the *palaestra* a colossal *piscina* or pool invited the bather for *natatio* or swimming. There were also bowling rooms for a game of ninepins, halls of philosophy, and even places for religious worship within the bath complex. The cult of

XI- 26 Aerial view of the Baths of Caracalla, Rome, Italy. Photo Credit: Alinari / Art Resource, N.Y.

GLADIATOR: THE MOVIE

The most successful film about ancient Rome made in modern times is Ridley Scott's acclaimed *Gladiator*. It is set in 180 CE at a time when the Roman Emperor Marcus Aurelius (portrayed by Richard Harris) is elderly and the Roman Empire is exhausted from decades of war both in the Roman East and along the Danube River. There is much discussion about who will be the next emperor. Rome's greatest general is known as Maximus (Russell Crowe), a one-man wrecking crew operating in Germania in a world of cavalry, catapults and constant battles. Following an old Roman tradition dating back to the dictator Cincinnatus, Maximus seeks only to do his duty, then return to his wife and child and plow his fields in Italy, but Marcus Aurelius wants Maximus to be the next emperor of Rome "to give Rome its true self" and the emperor rejects his own scheming and immoral son Commodus (Joaquin Phoenix) who is intriguing with his sister Lucilla (Connie Nielsen) to obtain power. In the movie, Commodus murders Marcus but Maximus refuses to accept the new emperor, touching off reprisals against the soldier's family and years of slavery and fighting in the arena.

Gladiator poses some problems for the student of ancient Rome. The premise of the film, that a Roman citizen could be held in slavery although everyone recognized him as the well-known general, goes against Roman law. Nor do the specifically archaeological elements hold up. The Colosseum is shown with its *velarium* or awning but no pulleys or ropes to hold it up, and all the buildings in Rome are made white whereas in reality they were sumptuously decorated in color. In one sequence, the camera lovingly presents an aerial tour of the Roman Forum (again, all white) but includes the *Basilica Nova*, also known as the Basilica of Constantine, which was not built until more than 100 years later at the eastern end of the Forum near the Colosseum. At other times, the buildings of the Forum and the area of the Colosseum bear no resemblance whatever to what had been previously shown. This is because the aerial pan of the Forum and Colosseum area was modeled on the famous (and all-white) model of Rome begun in 1935 by the architect Italo Gismondi which is now in the EUR district of Rome, erected by Benito Mussolini during the Fascist era to give an idea of the look of Rome in the time of the emperor Constantine, but the set design used for the close-ups disregarded the model and highlights fantasy architecture instead. In the arena the film highlights a re-enactment of the great Carthaginian general Hannibal's defeat at Zarma in 202 BCE but in fact the site was known as Zama with no r.

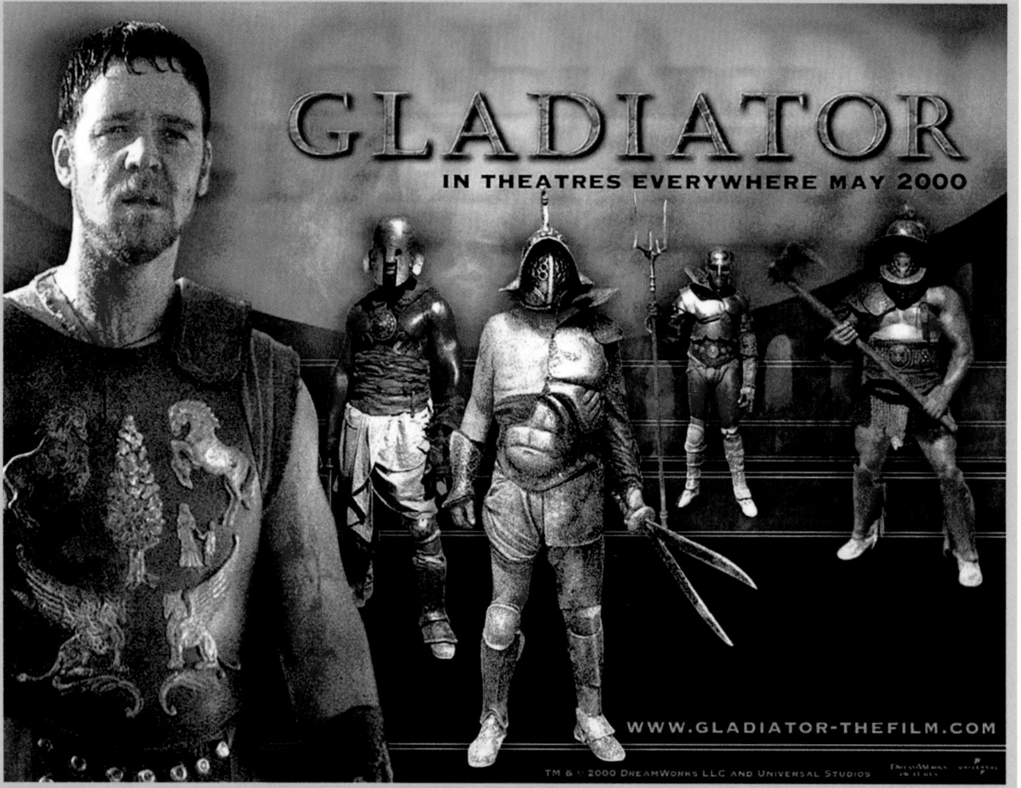

Pre-release advertising for *Gladiator*. Photo credit: Universal Pictures, DreamWorks SKG, US. Released to U.S. theaters May 1, 2000.

In one sequence representing the Forum area an enormous building appears at the right that has strange bulging columns and seems modeled on the Doges Palace in Venice of the early Renaissance. In another scene the Arch of Septimius Severus at the western end of the Roman forum is moved in front of the Colosseum. The Forum itself is made much too wide and seems intended to emulate a huge Nazi rally field such as that used by Hitler at Nuremberg in 1934, designed by Albert Speer, and seen in the film *Triumph of the Will* (*Triumph des Willens*) by Leni Riefenstahl. Perhaps *Gladiator*'s director had in mind to equate the Romans with Nazi Germany. Whatever the reason, the set design for *Gladiator* is among the strangest visions of Rome ever put on film and has sparked ample discussion among ancient architectural historians and archaeologists.

Mithras, much in vogue in the third century in Rome and Ostia as we have seen, had an underground temple right in the heart of the enclosure of the Baths of Caracalla.

Some bathers preferred to take a quick plunge in the *caldarium* first, then get scraped down in a private room (*destrictarium*), and then go to a small sweat bath to have all salts removed from the body. Then the bather might go back to the hot bath followed by a good bracing plunge in a cold pool, and a massage with perfumed oil taken from the *eliothesium* or repository for oils and unguents. But each bather had different preferences. Older or sickly bathers avoided shocks to the system and some athletes didn't like the hot baths at all.

However the bather wanted to experience them, the Baths of Caracalla provided a world of entertainment and helped to keep quiet the restless Roman urban poor. Wealthier Romans rarely came here; it was too far away from center city, where they preferred the Baths of Nero in the Campus Martius or those of Trajan on the Esquiline or if they were really wealthy, they had their own baths in their homes or belonged to private clubs.

The Baths of Caracalla also became an inspiration to the American architect Charles Follin McKim of the prominent New York firm of McKim, Meade and White in the early 20th century. McKim decided the baths were the perfect model for the original Pennsylvania Railroad Station in Manhattan (since demolished). The *frigidarium* was transformed into a colossal waiting room and ticket purchase area while the *apodyteria* became restaurants and the *tepidarium* the access area to the tracks. The *caldarium* was missing, replaced by the train tracks and trains.

CRITICAL THINKING EXERCISES

• 1 Why did sarcophagi become enormously popular in the second century CE? What are some of the themes they commonly depict and the reasons for them?
• 2 Discuss some of the characteristics found in the Roman painting of the high Empire and how they differ from earlier Pompeian painting.
• 3 In the second century CE traditional Roman religion was challenged by other religious movements. Discuss the rise in popularity of Mithraism, Christianity and other cults.
• 4 How did the housing at Ostia differ from that of Pompeii?
• 5 What were some of the crises that plagued Rome in the second half of the second century CE?
• 6 How were the campaigns on the frontiers reflected in official art?
• 7 Describe the experience of a bather going through one of the gigantic baths.
• 8 How accurately did the movie *Gladiator* depict life in ancient Rome?
• 9 How did Roman portrait sculpture change from the time of Hadrian on?

Chapter XII
The Third Century CE—Years of Crisis

Fig. XII-1 Caracalla. 198-217 CE. AR *Antoninianus* (diameter: 22mm, 5.10 g). Rome mint. Struck in 215 CE. The obverse shows the emperor radiate, draped, and cuirassed with bust right. The reverse has Sol standing right, head left, holding a globe and raising his hand. Courtesy of Classical Numismatic Group, Inc.

THE LATER SEVERANS

During the reign of Septimius Severus' son, Caracalla (Fig. XII-1), the Roman Empire was in the grip of a ruthless tyrant who killed any potential rival, including his own brother Geta, while at the same time tried to fend off a mounting threat by the Parthians. Caracalla was murdered in a palace mutiny led by the praetorian prefect Macrinus, a Mauretanian (Moroccan) of lower class family. Palace intrigues continued as Caracalla's aunt Julia Maesa conspired to have Macrinus killed (Fig. XII-2). She herself was Syrian royalty and was able to provoke a mutiny in her native area, which led to the death of the emperor. The reason behind Julia Maesa's plot was not to save Rome but rather to install her grandson Bassianus on the throne.

Varius Avitus Bassianus became emperor in 218 CE. The art that developed during his time exemplified the Roman mixture of traditional Classical imagery and provincial artistic forms that became increasingly important in the third century. His coins followed the Antonine Classical Roman tradition, and he even changed his name to Marcus Aurelius Antoninus, evoking memories of the Antonine emperors with whom the Severans claimed to have blood ties. However, Bassianus was also a Syrian priest in the sacred city of Emesa and a devotee of the sun god *Sol Invictus Elagabal*, and he became known as Elagabalus to the Roman people (Fig. XII-3). Turning from traditional Roman religion in this time of chaos and ephemeral emperors, he was able to introduce into Rome the worship of a baetyl or large fetish stone that became the aniconic symbol of his Syrian faith. Although widespread in Syria, this religion was alien to Rome and marked a shocking departure from the worship of the state gods. Earlier members of the Severan family had embraced it but had the wisdom not to trumpet their beliefs in Rome. Now the

Fig. XII-2 Julia Maesa, Augusta, 218-224/5 CE. AR *Antoninianus* (diameter: 23mm, 4.65 g). Rome mint. Struck under Elagabalus, 218-220 CE. The obverse shows her, draped bust right, wearing the stephane (small crown), and set on a crescent. The reverse has *Pietas* standing facing, head left, extending hand and holding an *acerrum* or incense box; there is a lighted and garlanded altar to lower left. Courtesy of Classical Numismatic Group, Inc.

emperor sought to build an enormous temple on the Palatine Hill right by the Colosseum, putting the cult of Jupiter in lower position. The religion was too extreme and Elagabalus too unhinged to last as he strutted about wearing purple and gold embroidered silk and jewelry. He was eventually murdered along with his mother in the Castra Praetoria or camp of the Praetorian Guards in Rome in 222 CE.

Elagabalus was succeeded by his cousin, Alexander Severus, another grandson of Julia Maesa. Alexander Severus reigned fairly successfully until 235 CE, when he was assassinated by his troops on the German frontier, enraged that he attempted to buy off rather than fight the Germanic tribes. Alexander Severus was the last emperor of the Severan dynasty. His demise marked the beginning of the greatest crisis in Roman history since the civil wars of the late Republic.

Fig. XII-3 Bronze coin (*assarion*) from province of Moesia, minted in Marcianopolis. Shows the Roman Emperor Elagabalus. 218-222 CE on an. Æ (17mm in diameter, 2.72 g). The emperor is laureate, head right. The reverse features a bunch of grapes with stem. Courtesy of Classical Numismatic Group, Inc.

THE CRISIS OF THE THIRD CENTURY

With the exception of Macrinus, the emperors from Augustus to Alexander Severus had always been Senators or came from families of Senatorial rank, even if they had provincial roots. The city of Rome was always the center of power, and claimants to the throne who weren't already there took care to secure their base there. The exception is once again Macrinus, who remained in the East during his brief rule, and arguably lost his position because of that.

All that changed in 235 CE. The army chose as emperor Maximinus Thrax, who had been born to a peasant family probably in Moesia (a Balkan province) and had risen through the ranks from a common soldier. Thus, he was in no way an aristocrat, had not had a political career, and had no connection to the city of Rome. Unlike Macrinus, he was just the first of a series of mostly short-reigned emperors of similar background that lasted until the late third century, when the greatest of them, Diocletian, re-established the Roman state on a new basis. Many of them came from the Illyrian provinces (roughly the area of the former Yugoslavia). This region was of strategic importance because it stood as a hub for communication between the western and eastern parts of the Empire and because the barbarian threat to which they had to respond was most intense in this area. For these reasons, the emperors tended to establish themselves in or near this region. Many spent time at Sirmium (Sremska Mitrovica west of modern Belgrade) on the Sava River just behind the Danube frontier.

This series of emperors is merely the institutional face of a more widespread crisis. This period saw the collapse of the monetary system based on the silver *denarius*, which had served Rome since the time of the Republic. Beginning under the Severans, the emperors reduced the coinage's silver content to nearly nil in successive stages, particularly in order to pay for their major expense—a larger army and repeated distributions of money to the soldiers to mark the Imperial accessions. This affected even a new silver coin, nominally a double *denarius*, introduced under Caracalla and known as the *antoninianus* (from the emperor's family name), which saw its silver content debased to practically nothing over the following decades (Fig. XII-1). The debasement of the coinage, of course, led to wild inflation and often the resort to payments in kind. The larger army was needed in order to face the pressure from peoples outside the Empire, who were probably both attracted by the higher standard of living within the Empire and also pushed by pressure from behind them. Furthermore, there was repeated civil strife between rival claimants to power. As a result, many cities began to feel the need to build new walls, including Rome, or to revamp old ones after centuries during which they were not considered necessary.

As Rome's difficult third century continued, one Roman Emperor—Publius Licinius Egnatius Gallienus—managed to last for 15 years (from 253-260 as co-emperor with his father Valerian, and alone from 260-268), although his reign was marked by constant fighting and instability. Gallienus became the troop commander on the Rhine front. His father fought the Persians unsuccessfully and was eventually captured by them, a great disgrace for the Roman Empire, especially as he was supposedly subjected to humiliations such as being used as a footstool by the Persian emperor in mounting his horse (Fig. XII-4).

Between 280 and 285 CE no fewer than five claimants to be emperor were murdered. Probus, another soldier emperor from Sirmium, killed Bonosus, a British usurper and one of Probus' generals, in 280. In the same year another of his generals, Saturninus, revolted in Alexandria but was killed by his own troops. Then Probus himself was murdered at Sirmium in 282 by his own men. He was succeeded by his praetorian prefect named Carus, the patron of Diocletian. Carus was allegedly the only emperor to die after being struck by lightning in 283, while he was on campaign in the East. Carus was succeeded by his son Numerian in the East and by his elder son Carinus in the West, perhaps a sign that Carus' death was natural. Numerian was murdered in 284 by the new praetorian prefect. Carinus was murdered by his own soldiers in 285 while fighting against Diocletian. It seemed that no one could restore stability to an Empire fragmented from Britain to Persia, but into this seeming abyss stepped Diocletian who had already been declared emperor to replace Numerian before Carinus was killed.

NEO-VERISM

The third century was an international age that blended Classical art with simplified popular and regional art. The need to escape the difficulties of everyday existence and near constant warfare led many to follow alternative philosophies and religions, such as Christianity in various forms, Neo-Platonism, Egyptian

Fig. XII-4 Publius Licinius Egnatius Gallienus who ruled jointly with his father Valerian 253-60 CE and then as sole Roman Emperor to 268. Marble head. Museo della Civiltà Romana, Rome. Photo credit: Art Resources, Inc.

cults such as the worship of Isis, Mithraism and the cult of Sol Invictus, the unconquered Sun. This breakdown and reassembling of traditional beliefs created a hybrid art drawing on the Greco-Roman tradition but infusing it with an emphasis on eyes, gestures and frontality to the detriment of plasticity of the human form.

Another factor also conditioned Roman art of the third century. The Romans followed trends and vogues in style that achieved a certain distinctive look for each period. In the first half of the third century, portraits tended to look more realistic or veristic, attempting to revive the look of the Republican Period or revered military emperors such as Vespasian (Fig. IX-1). At the same time portraits developed a quality that was diametrically opposed to verism: an other-worldly dematerialized look created by the use of huge deep-drilled wide-open eyes and an increasing reliance on simplified geometric forms. The tendency towards dematerialization of sculptural form had been growing stronger in Rome since the mid-second century CE. A kind of *Kubismus* or reversion to geometric forms common in popular art (see Chapter V) was turning the face into a prefabricated mask. From 150 to 200 CE this *Kubismus* gained ground, but in 200 CE changes occurred to integrate the veristic and the geometric images into a new style.

This new synthesis of *Kubismus* with veristic facial detailing is known as neo-verism. It is apparent in the Imperial portrait art made from 200 to 260 CE., an example of which is the emperor Maximinus Thrax now in the Capitoline Museum (Fig. XII-5). His portrait is veristic and yet the psychedelic eyes give an other-worldly quality to the face, which is reinforced by the simplified forms and the ropy brows. The short beard or five o'clock shadow is another indication that the portrait is neo-veristic, for such beards were in vogue from the time of Caracalla to about 260 CE.

Fig. XII-5 Maximinus Thrax. Marble bust of the emperor, c. 235-238 CE. Neo-veristic Style. Hall of the Emperors, Palazzo Nuovo, Musei Capitolini. Rome, Italy. Photo Credit: Vanni / Art Resource, N.Y.

Fig. XII-6 Portrait, possibly of Roman Emperor Trajan Decius from the Bardo Museum, Tunis, Tunisia. The man has poppies which may associate him with Ceres, a hunting dog associated with Silvanus and the clothing of Hercules. Photo Credit: Noelle Soren. University of Arizona School of Anthropology Archive.

The collision of verism and dematerialized forms reached a crescendo in the bizarre portrait of what may be the Roman Emperor Trajan Decius (249-251CE) (Fig. XII-6), who came from Pannonia. Found at Bordj-el-Amri in modern Tunisia, it is now in the Bardo Museum in Tunis. The face is instantly recognizable as a particular middle-aged person, but that is where the similarity to an actual man ends. The statue was intended to be experienced frontally and so has no sides, being just a few inches thick and featuring a plain back that would have been set against a wall or into a niche. Although the head is modeled in tremendous detail, the body and clothing are summarily done.

It is an important figure, whoever it is, and seems to be equated to several divinities rather than just one. A crudely rendered hunting dog is shown at the feet, perhaps indicative of the god Silvanus, but the lion skin around the head indicates a portrait of Hercules, and the figure is holding poppies, symbolic of the goddess Ceres. Could a Roman Emperor be divinized into a *female* deity? That would explain the apparent indications of breasts, which when combined with the veristic face and beard is a strange sight indeed. It may be that the symbols of the divinities are more important than the sex. The philosopher Plotinus in the mid- and later-third century preached that the body was a prison, a shell from which one could ultimately escape to a higher plane of existence known as the cosmic mind, which led to a *logos* or pure wisdom and inspiration. If indeed a sculptor had this sensibility, then the body could be transformed into a billboard of divine quotations to honor the emperor, regardless of the sex of the god or goddess.

THE PORTRAITURE OF GALLIENUS

By the mid-third century portraiture was turning away from the neo-veristic and veering towards a more dematerialized look while still not forgetting the great figures of the past. The emperor Gallienus, for example, attempted to effect in his portraiture a return to the glory days of Rome, sometimes presenting himself as a new Augustus or a Hadrian (Fig. XII-4). He added a distinctive style of beard and eyes that were opened even wider than was done in previous portraits, thus again fusing the traditional Classical Idealism with the stylized dematerialized look. After Gallienus, though, Imperial portraiture became increasingly stylized and simplified during the second half of the third century. The pictorialism that had begun with Hadrian had produced a bilaterally symmetrical mask. The surface of the face was again smooth and lacked the ultra-realistic details of Neo-Verism. In fact it is no longer possible to recognize a particular individual at all; instead, an iconic superman with overlarge, deep-drilled eyes and simplified, stylized hair became the vogue now. The emperor was becoming a divinity, his body or material form being of decreasing interest. Emphasis fell on his widely opened eyes which looked away from the horrors of this world towards a higher reality.

THE CATACOMBS

Near the end of the second century CE the Christian community in Rome began to use underground networks of galleries and tombs to bury their dead. Forty to 50 or more catacombs of varying sizes have been found at the outskirts of Rome, mostly Christian but also pagan, Jewish and mixed.

Fig. XII-7 Catacomb burial niches (*loculi*). Early Christian. Location: Catacomb of San Callisto (Saint Callixtus), Rome, Italy. Photo Credit: Erich Lessing / Art Resource, N.Y.

The catacombs have always been a special branch of Roman archaeology since excavations began in the late 16th century. The father of catacomb research was Antonio Bosio (1575 or 1576-1629), who wrote a book on his findings called *Roma Sotteranea* (*Subterranean Rome*), which remained the definitive reference work on Christian catacombs until the 19th century. It is considered a pioneering work in archaeology because of Bosio's topographical research and the building block for future researchers such as Giovanni Battista de Rossi (1822-1894. His three-volume *La Roma Sotterranea Cristiana* (*Subterranean Christian Rome*) remains essential reading for catacomb scholars.

The term catacomb comes from two Greek words *kata kumbas* meaning near the hollows and probably refers to the area near the Via Appia where tufo stone had been quarried adjacent to the Catacomb of Saint Sebastian. Christians would have referred to each complex as a *coemeterium*, derived from the Greek *koimeterion* or sleeping place and giving us our word cemetery. The ancient Romans normally used the term *sepulcrum* for graves, but Christians preferred sleeping place with its implications of resurrection at the return of Christ. By the sixth century Christians began to bury bodies near churches but continued to venerate and visit catacomb sites, where they might encounter the remains of many church leaders and martyrs. Because the countryside had become less safe and the city had shrunk, many relics of saints were transferred from the catacombs into churches within the city walls, beginning in the middle of the seventh century. After the ninth century visits to the catacombs tapered off and eventually stopped.

It is not likely that the catacombs were secret places used by Christians to meet in order to avoid persecution. This has often been speculated, but the catacombs were normally placed near major public thoroughfares, and everyone in the area, whether Christian or pagan, knew where they were.

The work of digging these enormous passages and tombs was done by *fossores* or professional diggers using pickaxes. They constituted a guild and worked under the auspices of the clergy. Their only light was provided by simple clay lamps fueled with olive oil and flax wicks. The soft volcanic stone was easily worked and their pick marks can be viewed today. Periodically, *lucernaria* or light and air shafts leading to the surface were cut. The *fossores* learned to take advantage of softer areas of stone and to avoid the firmer lithoid tufo of the area in making their corridor tunnels along which the tombs were cut.

Depending on the social and ecclesiastical position of the deceased, the burials varied. Most common were the *loculi*, rectangular niches cut in rows along the walls of a gallery (Fig. XII-7). The body was placed inside and the burial space sealed with a stone slab or tile on which an inscription could be carved. There were also larger family tombs

Fig. XII-8 Hercules bringing Alcestis back from Hades to her husband Admetus. Lunette in *arcosolium* of *Cubiculum* N, Early Christian fresco, c. 320-50 CE. Location: Ipogeo (Hypogeum) of the Via Latina, Rome. Photo Credit: Scala / Art Resource, N.Y.

known as *hypogea* or *cubicula* designed for multiple burials. Often these contain *arcosolia* which are arched niches often painted (Fig. XII-8). Sometimes these *arcosolia* are large enough to hold a sarcophagus or simpler coffins (*solia*), an indicator of some wealth on the part of the family interred there.

THE CATACOMB OF SAINT CALLIXTUS

One of the most famous is the Catacomb of Saint Callixtus, located along the Via Appia south of the city and including at least 20 km of galleries (Fig. XII-7). It was a large complex, consisting of originally independent parts brought together at the end of the second century or beginning of the third. It drew its name from a man called Callixtus, appointed administrator of the catacombs by Pope Zephyrinus, Bishop of Rome from 199 to 217. Apparently it was an important position, because Callixtus became the next Pope. It was the burial place for 16 popes, as well as other high ecclesiastical dignitaries, although curiously not of St. Callixtus.

At the Catacomb of Saint Callixtus is the famous Crypt of the Popes, where an inscription placed by Pope Damasus (who served from 366 to 384) commemorates the burial of five early Bishops of Rome (Fig. XII-9). Other Christians sought to be buried as near to these august religious leaders as possible, causing a huge number of burials to surround the crypt.

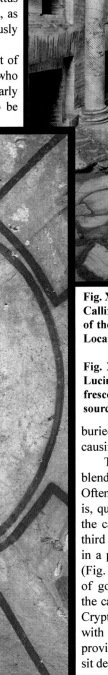

Fig. XII-9 (above) Crypt of the Popes in the Catacomb of Saint Callixtus. Early Christian tombs. Third c. CE and after. Some of the early popes of the Christian Church were buried here. Location: Rome, Italy. Photo Credit: Scala / Art Resource, N.Y.

Fig. XII-10 (left) Jesus as the Good Shepherd from crypt of Lucina in the Catacomb of Saint Callixtus . Early Christian fresco, early third CE. Rome. Photo Credit: Scala / Art Resource, N.Y.

The paintings in the Saint Callixtus catacomb often blend overtly Christian images with Classical motives. Often the figures are done in *compendium* technique, that is, quick strokes that outline the essential details. This is the case in the Crypt of Lucina where there is an early third century painting of Jesus as The Good Shepherd in a pose known since the sixth century BCE in Greece (Fig. XII-10). He is flanked by a cock and dog, symbols of good fortune and fidelity. Another popular scene in the catacombs was the Eucharistic banquet, shown in the Crypt of the Sacraments (Fig. XII-11). There are baskets with bread celebrating Jesus' miracle of the loaves, providing bread for the famished in the desert. Banqueters sit depicted in the Roman fashion, all sitting on one side of a semicircular table.

Fig. XII-11 Crypt of the Sacraments from the Catacomb of Saint Callixtus. Eucharistic banquet. Early Christian fresco, early third century CE. Rome. Photo Credit: Scala / Art Resource, N.Y.

THE CATACOMB OF VIBIA

Not all the catacombs were Christian however. Just opposite the Catacomb of Saint Callixtus along the Via Appia is the small Catacomb or Hypogeum of Vibia, of which portions date to the beginning of the fourth century CE (Fig. XII-12). Vibia was the wife of Vincentius, who was a priest in the cult of Sabazius, which had come to Rome from Thrace and Anatolia and become syncretized or blended with the worship of the Roman divinities Bacchus and Jupiter. Paintings in the tomb show a religious belief that seems a curious hybrid of Christian and pagan ideas. The scenes and figures are fortunately labeled for our convenience. First, Pluto takes Vibia into the Underworld, where Mercury stands ready to lead her descent. Vibia faces Pluto (here known as Dispater) and possibly Persephone (Aeracura) at a tribunal of divinities and the three fates, where she is judged faithful and good. She is then led by a good male angel (Angelus Bonus) through a gate in order to participate in a banquet in the afterlife, much in the spirit of such scenes common to the Etruscan tombs of Tarquinia. The scene here takes place at another semicircular

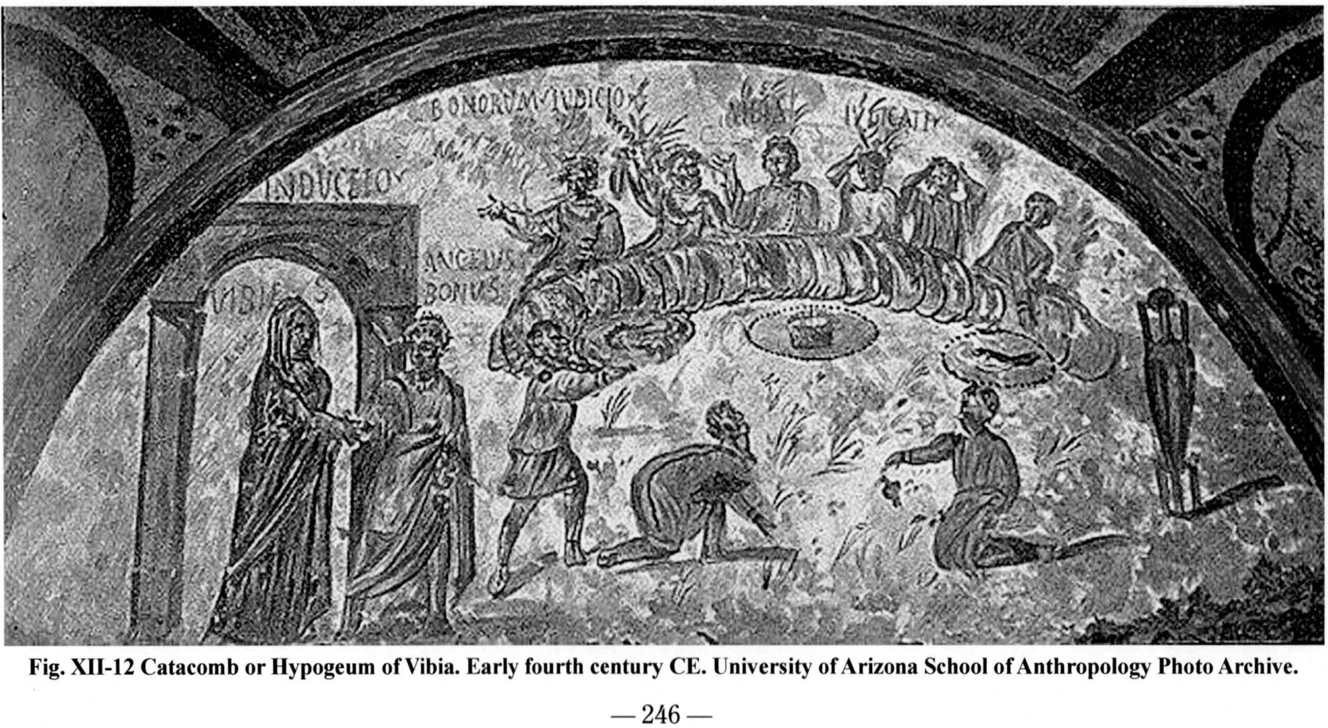

Fig. XII-12 Catacomb or Hypogeum of Vibia. Early fourth century CE. University of Arizona School of Anthropology Photo Archive.

table, this time located in a garden. The banqueters consume fish, bread and wine. An inscription on the tomb records that it belongs to Vincentius, husband of Vibia, and that what we are viewing is the gate of repose. The inscription concludes with some words for the viewer to ponder:

> Many have gone before me. I await all. Eat, drink, play and come to me. While you live, do good and this you'll carry with you. Vincentius, priest of Sabazius. It is he who served the holy rites of the gods with pious minds.

BAROQUE ARCHITECTURE

Despite the constant making and unmaking of emperors, important strides were made in architecture. The Roman fascination for theatricality and the Baroque, which had been manifest since at least the time of Sulla in such monuments as the Sanctuary of

THE LARGE FRIEZE OF CASA CELIMONTANA, ROME

Fig. XII-13 Painting from the Casa Celimontana under Church of Saints Giovanni and Paolo, Rome. 250 to early fourth century CE. Photo Credit: Nimatallah.© DeA Picture Library / Art Resource, N.Y.

An extraordinary wall painting was found decorating what may have been a *nymphaeum* or fountain room in a large Roman house on the Caelian Hill in Rome under the later church of Saints John and Paul (Fig. XII-13). The original frieze may have been 100 feet long, but only a small section of it survives, making identification difficult. It appears to show a nude figure of Venus, goddess of the sea from which she sprung off the coast of the island of Cyprus. She is about to drink from a cup being offered to her by a young male attendant posed with one foot on a rock in a traditional manner of the late Greek Classical Period. A royal purple garment is modestly draped across her lap, while she wears an elegant medallion about her neck and her drapery swirls behind her head in late Hellenistic fashion. But who is the mysterious figure reclining with the goddess? It might be her handsome male lover Adonis, son of a Cypriote king. Cupids surround the lovers and row boats in the sea, adding to the suggestion of a Cypriote love theme. Adonis was tragically killed while hunting by wild boar and taken away from his great divine love.

In Greek mythology, Adonis was also loved by Persephone, goddess of the underworld with whom after his death he spent a third of the year by decree of Zeus. In the summer he was permitted to live with Aphrodite. This cyclical return not only symbolized hope for lovers but also death and resurrection and the yearly cycle of vegetation. Does this image then imply that Adonis and Venus have been reunited in the afterlife among the gods? Is this the hopeful message of this giant frieze? What other gods and goddesses and themes were depicted here remains a mystery.

Even the date of this painting is still unclear, because there are so few examples of later Roman mythological friezes to which to compare it. George Hanfmann suggested a date in the Hadrianic Period, but this has not gained wide acceptance. The highly stylized rendering of the nude form, the stiffness of the poses and the fascination with epic scenes involving Venus and cupids all point to a date at least at the middle of the third century and possibly as late as the early fourth.

Fig. XII-14 a (above) & 14b (left) Theatre of Aspendos in Turkey. C. mid-second century CE. Photo credit: Noelle Soren. University of Arizona School of Anthropology Archive.

Fortuna Primagenia at Praeneste, continued into the third century (see Chapter VI and Figs. VI-20 through 24). This included the desire to surprise and astonish the visitor with unexpected vistas, to lead the visitor through a carefully controlled series of spaces, and to create innovative and trendy architectural experiments.

The Roman Baroque had become increasingly popular during the second half of the second century CE in areas such as North Africa, Syria and Anatolia. The Theatre of Aspendos in southwestern Turkey is an excellent example of the second century Roman Baroque (Figs. XII-14a and b). In this building, traditional Classical parts are fragmented, then recombined in creative ways. For example a pediment might be broken up into only its angled ends and used as a decoration. Colored stones were used to create a garish contrasting effect throughout. Each part of the building is attended to, standing out and reaching out to demand attention. Moldings were over-elaborately carved and rely on deep pockets of light and shade to create dramatic effects even though the quality of the carving tends towards the slapdash or mechanical.

LEPCIS MAGNA

Some of this particular look of the later second and first part of the third century may be ascribed to changing attitudes about architecture. Plotinus, perhaps the leading philosopher

Severan Forum Complex of Lepcis Magna, Libya

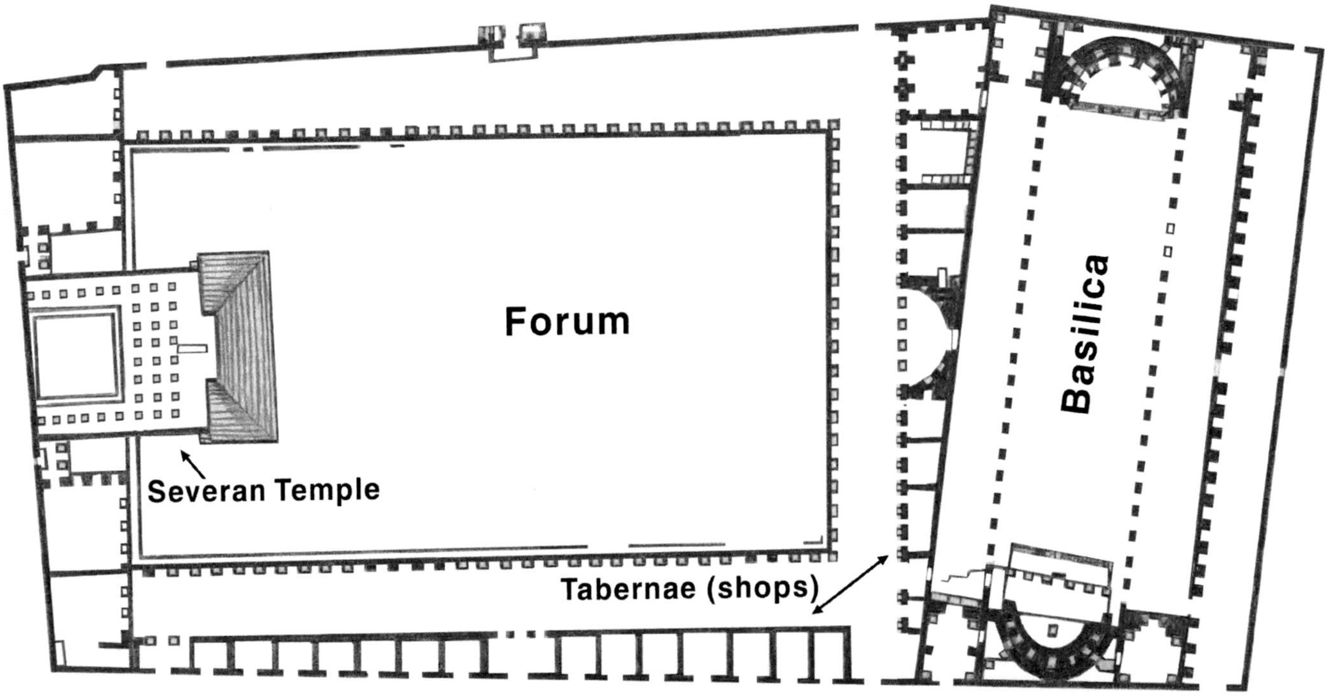

Fig. XII-15 (above) Plan of the Severan forum at Lepcis Magna by Roxanne Stall. C. 200 CE.

Fig. XII-16 (right) View of the Severan forum at Lepcis Magna featuring a medallion depicting a gorgon, placed between arches springing directly from capitals of columns bordering the forum. Location: Lepcis Magna, Libya Photo Credit: Noelle Soren. University of Arizona School of Anthropology Photo Archive.

of his age, thought each part of something was as important as the whole and worthy of contemplation on its own without regard to the overall symmetry or unity of the entire form. His ideas are the opposite of the traditional Classical views, where each part must be rigorously integrated into an overall concept and must fit in with ratios in the overall building or sculpture. A number of major third century Roman buildings are however, deliberately asymmetrical and seem unapologetic about it.

The Forum of Lepcis Magna, located in Septimius Severus' native Libya, for example, was a massive undertaking of the Severan Period. The architect placed the forum and basilica area visibly off-center with a clearly asymmetrical space (Figs. XII-15, 16). Why he didn't reduce the size of the elements to fit them more perfectly within the available space, or expand outward to form a more regular configuration of these elements is unknown. The parts employed for creating the columnar decorations of the apses of the basilica are such a bizarre fragmentation of traditional Greco-Roman entablatures that modern scholars have called into question the accuracy of the restorations, wondering just how these seemingly random bits of pediment fragments, architraves and decorative griffins were intended to interrelate and fit together (Fig. XII-17).

Fig. XII-17a (above) & 17b (left) The Severan basilica at Lepcis Magna and the controversial restoration of its apse. Photo credit: Noelle Soren. University of Arizona School of Anthropology Photo Archive.

THE TEMPLE OF BALAAT, THUBURBO MAIUS

At the provincial site of Thuburbo Maius in central Tunisia is the distinctly odd Temple of Baalat, a local divinity derived

UNCOVERING *a new* RIVAL *to* POM

How the Long-Forgotten City of Leptis Magna, Built Back in the Second Century, Is Now Being Freed From the Sands of Tripoli by Italian Archeologists

Dr. Bruno Roselli brings to America word of a marvelous Roman city which for centuries has been buried beneath African sands. It is hoped that records of a very clouded period of Roman history, disclosing trials of the early Christians, will be uncovered

Like fingers of Father Time himself the columns of temples of Leptis Magna protrude above the desert sands, calling attention to the ancient city whose glories rivaled those of even imperial Rome

Fig. XII-17 c Newspaper article on the discovery of Lepcis Magna from the *Sioux City Journal*, November 2, 1924.

Fig. XII-18 Temple of Baalat at Thuburbo Maius, showing the irregular colonnade and forecourt before the temple, altered to face several different streets arriving at differing angles. C. mid-second century CE. Tunisia. Photo credit: Noelle Soren. University of Arizona School of Anthropology Photo Archive.

from the ancient Carthaginian tradition (Fig. XII-18). The temple was placed at the intersection of three main roads of the irregularly planned community. Its surrounding colonnade could have been made rectangular or square in order to give the temple a comfortable symmetrical piazza, but instead the columns of the temple *temenos* are placed in a completely irregular fashion so that each street that leads up to the precinct can be afforded a view through the columns to the temple. This deliberate asymmetry has a purpose, allowing the land to be used either to its full capacity or in creative ways, but it is not something that an earlier Roman or a Greek would have found acceptable.

FRONTALITY

Another tendency found also in the philosophy of Plotinus as well as in art and architecture in the third century is a growing interest in frontality. As we mentioned earlier, Plotinus believed that the human body is really a shell; the divine soul of the human form, with the eyes as windows of the soul, is most important. Figures thus tend to confront us directly now and claim our attention, if not worship. This same idea holds true in architecture. In Lepcis Magna the main temple of the Severan Forum has what have come to be termed wrap-around steps, that is front steps that come out to pull you in (Fig. XII-15). They are not just front steps; rather, they push way out from the temple and even have side step access to welcome the worshipper. Around the forum above the columns are a series of arcuated or arched lintels that lead the eyes of the visitor quickly around the forum to focus sharply on the temple with its play of colored stone and its wrap-around steps. Between the arches female heads, including gorgons, stare dramatically at the visitor and provide a punctuation to the rippling arch effect around the entire asymmetrical complex (Fig. XII-16). This is not traditional Roman architecture.

In the forum at Lepcis, as well as in many other localities, including Rome, we see the popularity of the *tetrapylon* or four-sided arch emerging (Fig. XII-19). Arches were propaganda billboards from the time of Augustus, but now arched statue bases and triumphal arches alike show a fondness for the four-sided form, always there to confront the viewer directly. *Tetrapyla* remained highly popular into the fourth century.

Fig. XII-19 Model of the Arch of Septimius Severus in Leptis Magna, Libya. Built in 203 CE. The arch is built as a *tetrapylon* with four equal facades. Location: Museo della Civiltà Romana, Rome, Italy Photo Credit: Vanni / Art Resource, N.Y.

Fig. XII-20 (left) Temple of Minerva Medica, Rome. Early fourth c. CE. Location: Temple of Minerva Medica, Rome, Italy. Photo Credit: Vanni / Art Resource, N.Y.

Fig. XII-21 (below) Temple of Minerva Medica, Rome. Detail of vaulting. Early fourth c. CE. Temple of Minerva Medic. Fourth CE. Interior view. Photo Credit: Vanni / Art Resource, N.Y.

Subtle, sophisticated and innovative, the so-called temple is a gem in the history of architecture.

THE TEMPLE OF MINERVA MEDICA, ROME

There were structural innovations in the third century as well. Even though the Empire was at war constantly, and architectural commissions on a grand scale were not as plentiful as in earlier, stable times, architects and engineers continued to refine their technology to produce innovative structures. In Rome, in a neighborhood near the Termini Railroad Station, is a ruin that is little visited although visible from the railway lines. It is a remarkable structure known from a statue found nearby as the Temple of Minerva Medica (Figs. XII-20, 21). It was not a temple but probably a dining pavilion, possibly a part of the gardens of the early-fourth century emperor Valerius Licinianus Licinius (known as Licinius), if it is not slightly earlier in date.

It was a decagonal structure with nine apsed niches and an entrance. It featured a surprisingly innovative use of bricks, relieving arches to take the pressure off of critical areas, and a dome. Its upper portion was raised up in a cylinder that was pierced with windows, an innovation in domed architecture. In order to keep it stable, the dome was compartmentalized by a series of carefully constructed brick ribs that appear to be an early attempt to channel thrusts in the manner of Gothic ribbed ceilings of the 13th century. The ribs were designed to relieve any stress on the upper cylinder and dome.

Fig. XII-22 Diocletian. C. 300 CE, Roman Emperor, marble, third century CE from Nicomedia (inv. 4864). Location: Archaeological Museum Istanbul. Photo Credit: Gianni Dagli Orti / The Art Archive at Art Resource, N.Y.

DIOCLETIAN

The unrest of the third century drew to a close with a beacon of hope from an unlikely source. Gaius Aurelius Valerius Diocletianus (Fig. XII-22) came from a lower class family in Dalmatia (coastal Croatia). Nothing certain is known of his military career, except that he was commander in the war in the East at the time Numerian died. As emperor, he undertook reforms that revolutionized the Empire from within. Then Diocletian did what no Roman Emperor had been able, or indeed wanted, to do: retire.

Diocletian devised a system, called the Tetrarchy, a system of rule by four men, each assigned to a different portion of the Empire. Two were senior rulers, or Augusti and two junior rulers or Caesars who would be elevated to Augusti with the retirement or death of the senior rulers. As second Augustus, Diocletian named Maximian (Marcus Aurelius Valerius Maximianus) in 286 to oversee the western half of the Empire. In 293 the Caesars Constantius and Galerius were appointed in the West and East respectively. Diocletian ruled for years from Nicomedia in modern Turkey near the Bosphorus and retired in 305 on the Adriatic coast to a palace he had built for himself (the *nucleus* of the present city of Split, Croatia). Galerius set up headquarters in northern Greece at Thessaloniki. Rome remained the nominal capital but rarely saw an emperor and then usually only for visits.

Diocletian's power-sharing plan did not last long. Soon after his retirement, dissensions and civil wars arose. Maximian made several attempts to come out of retirement. Sons of rulers aspired to replace their fathers on the hereditary principle. Eventually Constantine, the son of Constantius, remained as the sole emperor in 324 CE.

Nevertheless, much of Diocletian's reorganization of the administration of the Empire remained, constituting what is known by Roman historians as the Dominate. In the preceding Principate, going back to Augustus, the emperor presented himself as the first among equals (*princeps*) and ruled in a kind of partnership with the Senate, preserving many of the forms of the Republican system.

Now the emperor appeared as the lord (*dominus*), detached and distant with something of a sacred character. He was at the head of a larger administrative staff and a bigger mobile army attached to him. The frontiers were strengthened and commanders were assigned to specific stretches, while provincial governors were relieved of military command. The provinces were subdivided into much smaller units, which were gathered together into dioceses. The dioceses were in turn grouped into four prefectures. Significantly, Italy, which had stood apart in the previous system as the heartland of the Roman state, was now integrated into the provincial organization like any other territory.

A new system to replace the debased silver coinage came into being under Diocletian, based on a stabilized gold coin called the *solidus* (Fig. XII-23). In a great change, silver coinage was no longer important. Bronze continued to be coined as fractional currency but with further reductions in weight throughout the fourth century. Diocletian's coinage reforms at the end of the third century would last until the end of the Roman Empire in the West and into Byzantine times in the East.

Fig. XII-23 Constantine I. emperor from 307-337 CE. AV *Solidus* (diam. 21mm, 4.48 gm). Siscia mint. Struck 335 CE. The obverse has the legend CONSTANTINVS MAX AVG, and the emperor pearl-diademed, draped, and cuirassed, bust right. The reverse legend is VICTORIA CONSTANTINI AVG, showing a Victory seated right on a shield and cuirass, inscribing VOT / XXX on the shield held by *Genius*; SIS Siscia mint mark. RIC VII 243; Depeyrot 23/2; Alföldi 601. Courtesy of Classical Numismatic Group, Inc. No. 251052.

Under Diocletian, the taxation was also reformed. Land was assessed according to its quality and produce, and the state's needs were met at least in part in kind. The heavier burden of taxation to support the new administration is thought to have led to a crisis prompting Diocletian's Edict on Prices in 301 CE. This attempted to set maximum prices for a wide range of goods. It was apparently no more successful than similar attempts in more modern times, but it does offer historians valuable insight into what was produced and where.

Another effect of the reorganization of the administration was that anyone seeking a career in the Dominate would look toward the Imperial service (or the Church once it was tolerated). A Senatorial career was no longer particularly attractive, since the Senate was not the main recruiting ground for Imperial officials as before, although it continued to exist as a prestigious body. At a lower level, a career in the service of the local city was burdensome without reward, now that it did not offer possible entry into higher social ranks. Men tended to avoid if possible the same offices that had been highly sought after in earlier centuries, and we learn of attempts to force them to serve. At the highest levels, there were immensely wealthy Senatorial families owning vast estates in many provinces, who supported palatial residences at Rome and on their lands.

Fig. XII-24 Tetrarchic sculpture from the southwest corner of Saint Marks' Basilica in Venice, Italy. Showing the augusti Diocletian and Maximian and the caesars Constantius Chlorus and Galerius. Photo credit: Scala/Art Resource, N.Y.

TETRARCHIC PORTRAITURE

Apparently, the conception of the emperor as *dominus* owes much to the example of the Persian monarchs. Its iconography privileges the presentation of the office held over the individuality of the man holding it. So it is often difficult, for example, to identify unlabeled representations of the Tetrarchs. They do not look heavenward for inspiration but shine divine inspiration from their eyes, while their faces frown with the burden of their office.

A key example is a sculpture that probably stood at the entrance to a main public square in Constantinople on top of a column (Fig. XII-24). The figures are blocky, squat, and simplified. They appear to the modern eye to be little puppets but must have been viewed differently by contemporaries with a sensitivity not governed by the Classical tradition. The figures are paired in an embrace, as if they were mirror images, with their hands on their long swords, ready to draw them from their scabbards. The message appears to be that they are all equal, united, and ready to do battle. There is considerable emphasis on the patterning of the cloaks, military cuirasses, and scabbards. Each figure wears a special cap typical of the period around 300 CE.

The faces are bilaterally symmetrical with overlarge eyes in overlarge heads. Gesture is important but not accuracy of the physical form of the body. The emphasis on unity of form suggests that concept trumps physical likeness. It has also been argued that this work represents a fall-off in technical quality. However, this kind of iconic non-Classical form is ubiquitous at this time, particularly in the East, where it will pave the way for the art of the era of Constantine the Great and, later on, for the iconic and rigidly hierarchic Byzantine art of the Middle Ages (Fig. XIV-2). Furthermore, poor-quality work is unlikely to have been done in Egyptian porphyry, an expensive stone and difficult to work, used for important commissions. The individuals depicted are believed to be the Tetrarchs themselves, Domitian and Maximian as Augusti and their appointed successors Galerius and Constantius Chlorus as Caesars.

This piece of Late Antique art may have been part of a series of works of this type, made in Egypt, where the only source of porphyry was located in the Eastern Desert at Mons Porphyrites. It was removed in 1204 during the Fourth Crusade and brought to Venice, where it was placed on one corner of the treasury of Saint Mark's Cathedral, where it remains.

DIOCLETIAN'S PALACE

Long before the breakdown of the Tetrarchic System occurred, Diocletian had built a retirement residence for himself near his birthplace in Illyria (Croatia) (Figs. XII-25 through 28). It was a combination fortress and Baroque palace full of the latest ideas in Imperial architecture, including

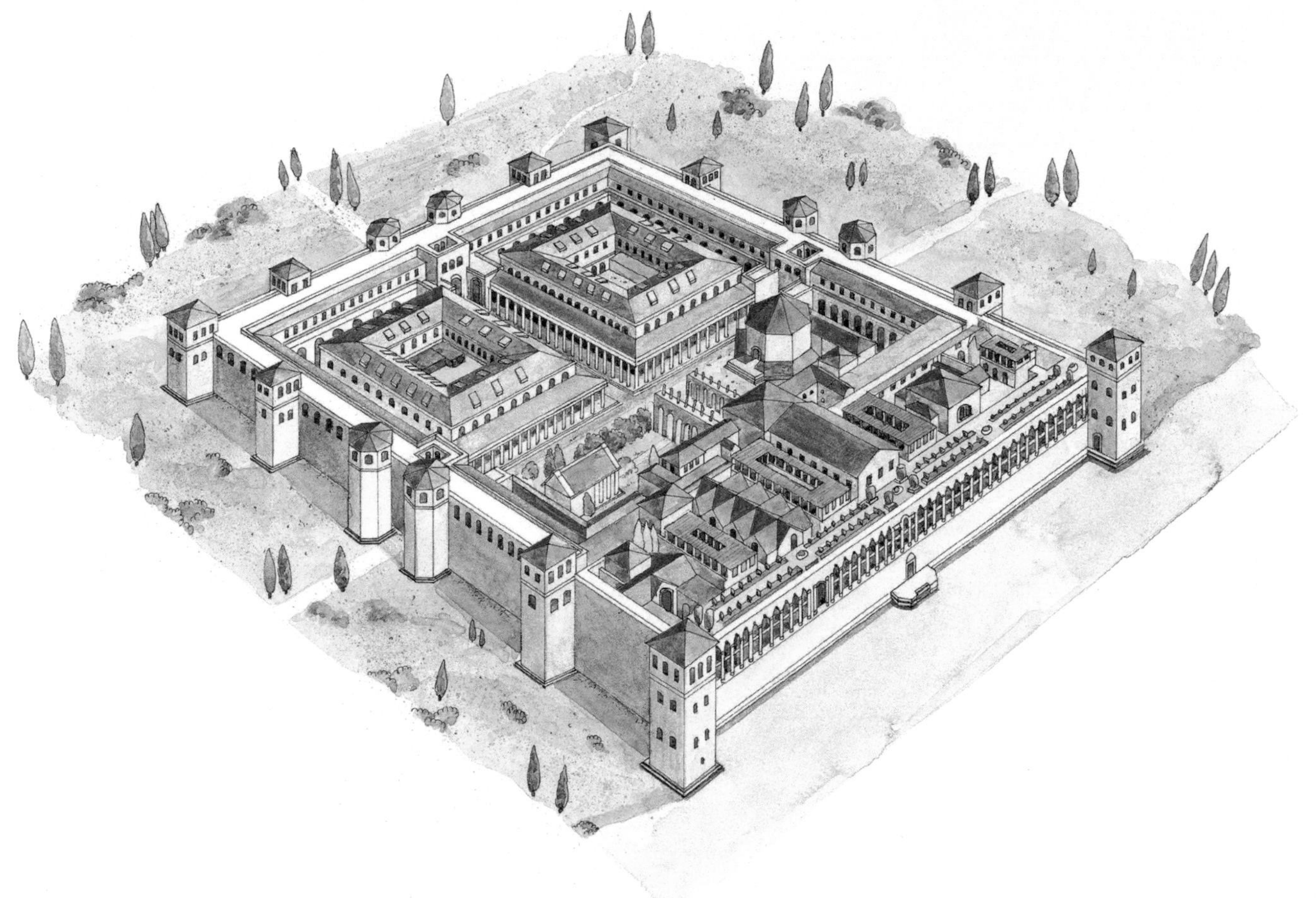

Fig. XII-25 Roman Civilization. Reconstruction of Diocletian's Split Palace. Early fourth century CE. Photo Credit: © DeA Picture Library / Art Resource, N.Y.

arched lintels springing directly from capitals. There is no indication of the name of the architect, although some architectural features and the presence of Greek letters as mason's marks suggest the involvement of people from the eastern part of the Empire.

The overall rectangular plan of the complex shows a certain symmetry. The palace is articulated by two avenues crossing at right angles with four gates opening at their ends. The big streets were lined with Corinthian porticos in the second and third century Syrian and Anatolian tradition, providing shade from the hot sun. All around the palace, small rooms can be seen, all of equal size, and no doubt intended for the palace guard. That they are so numerous and the walls of the palace so high suggest the troubled nature of the times. Diocletian's private quarters have been identified in a series of rooms in the south of the complex, all along the front overlooking the sea. They include reception rooms, as well as smaller spaces. The rest of the southwestern quadrant of the complex contains the Temple of Jupiter, the god to whom Diocletian was especially devoted. It features richly carved moldings and a vaulted roof over the interior.

Fig. XII-26 View of Diocletian's Palace at Split. Colonnade and entry to the emperor's quarters. Photo credit: Noelle Soren. University of Arizona School of Anthropology Archive.

Diocletian's mausoleum was located opposite the temple in the southeastern quadrant behind the private quarters. Its outside was an octagon surrounded by Corinthian columns and featuring a crypt within its central podium. The angled columns of the podium feature an upper *abacus* with five sides, a non-traditional form of the Corinthian capital to allow each column to adapt to the octagonal design. The columns are also not uniform: some are made of marble, some granite; some are fluted, some not. This may have been because architectural parts from earlier structures were reused in this building due to time constraints in its construction. Nonetheless, the architect was able to take a potential liability and turn it into something trendy.

The mausoleum features an extraordinary dome with an inner and outer shell. The outer dome rises to form an octagonal

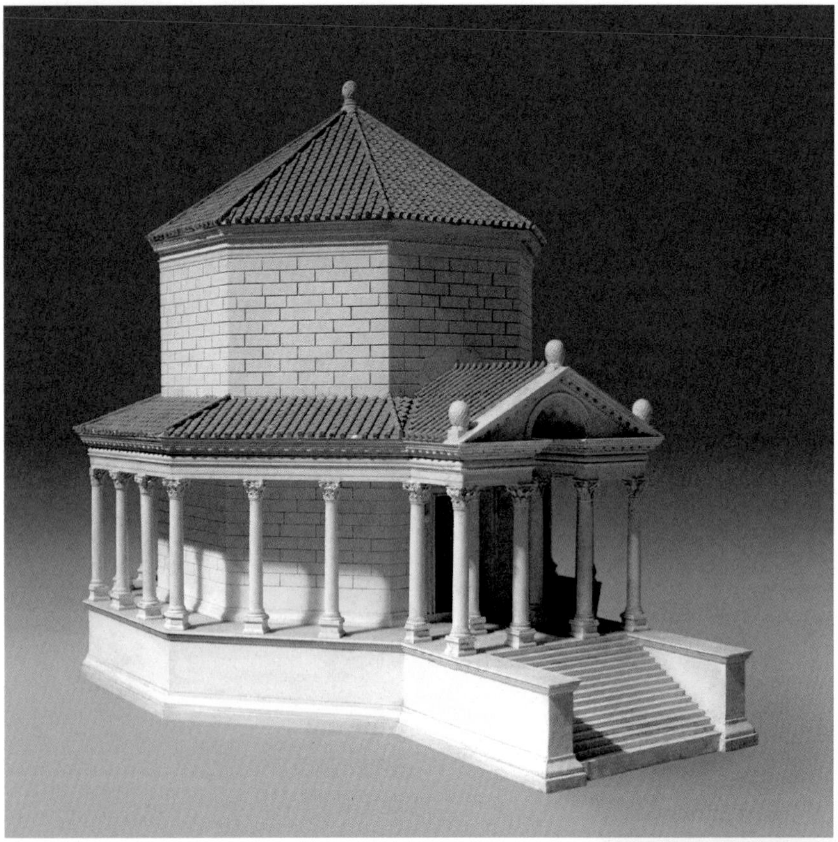

was registered as a UNESCO World Heritage site in 2007. The complex is surrounded by an irregular rectangular fortified wall with large towers, which led it to be considered a fortress for a long time, and contains various buildings (such as a palace, temples, baths and basilicas) in what appears to be a less compact plan than at Split. A funerary-sacral complex, thought to be the burial place for Galerius and his mother, is located on a hill at a short distance from the fortified complex.

PIAZZA ARMERINA

Eighteenth-century excavations in south central Sicily first brought to light a magnificent villa of the first quarter of the fourth century CE, literally covered with spectacular mosaics, forming

Fig. XII-27 (left) Model of the Mausoleum of Diocletian in Split (Spalatum), Croatia. This tetrarchic style mausoleum was begun in 293 CE. Location: Museo della Civiltà Romana, Rome, Italy. Photo Credit: Vanni / Art Resource, N.Y.

Fig. XII-28 (below) Interior of the Mausoleum of Diocletian in Split (Spalatum), Crotia. Photo credit: Noelle Soren. University of Arizona School of Anthropology Archive.

pyramid. The inner one rises over 70 feet above the ground and is constructed of a base made with 12 semicircular relieving arches. Between and above these arches are bricks arranged in a scale pattern. The idea was probably that these multiple brick mini-relieving arches would strengthen the dome. That it was not intended decoratively is suggested by the fact that most likely such an Imperial burial place would have had mosaics placed in the dome. The base and top of the dome are decorated with regular horizontal rows of bricks arranged in a circle. Just how much this curious brick experiment contributed to the stability of the building is open to debate, but one thing is certain; the dome is still standing and has never developed a crack or fissure.

Diocletian's palace offered refuge to the inhabitants of the nearby town of Salona during the barbarian invasions and formed the nucleus of the medieval and modern city of Split. It has been well-known since the 18th century and supplied inspiration to Neo-Classical architects then.

Since Roman Emperors before and after the Tetrarchic Period did not plan to retire, comparisons for Diocletian's Palace are rare. To some extent, one can look toward the palaces that emperors of the time built in the cities where they resided away from Rome, such as Thessaloniki, Sirmium or Trier, for they chose not to stay in the houses of wealthy local citizens as traveling emperors of the past had done. There is one parallel, however. Diocletian's colleague, Galerius, built a complex, called Felix Romuliana in honor of his mother, at his birthplace at Gamzigrad in Serbia for his retirement. It was identified beyond doubt by the discovery of an inscription only in the second half of the 20th century and is little known to the general public or even to many scholars from outside the region, although it the largest single expanse of such floors ever found on a Roman site (Figs. XII- 29 to 32). Excavated too quickly in the 1950s, the site was nonetheless preserved in the 1960s in a reasonable manner, with catwalks for tourists so that they could see the beautiful floors without having an easy opportunity to destroy them. Further excavations and the construction of a new roof have taken place in recent years.

Everything about the site implies opulence, beginning with a monumental triple-arched entry gateway complete with Ionic columns and gurgling fountains, leading to a massive but consciously asymmetrical courtyard. Visitors may have had to wait to gain admittance, and there was a large restroom facility just outside the entryway. An aedicule or niche for a statue showed the piety of the owner and may have housed an image of his patron divinity. In the adjacent vestibule, figures are depicted in mosaic welcoming visitors by holding laurel twigs and candles. Next at the right visitors were permitted entry into the sumptuous main peristyle or colonnaded walkway with its large pool centerpiece and column shafts imported from Aswan in southern Egypt and Euboea in Greece. Facing the visitor was the shrine of the *Lares*, the household gods.

If the visitor had traveled from afar to consult with the *dominus* of the villa, he would probably have come with an entourage, all of whom could stay in mosaic-paved guest rooms to the left of the entry to the courtyard. The formal meeting could take place in a private basilica or large official hall at the back of the structure, fitted with an apse and vaulted roof. The floors were done in elegant *opus sectile* or cut sections of fitted marble, with marble veneering on the walls. On the way to the audience hall, the visitors' attention would be drawn to an extraordinarily long ambulatory corridor paved with scenes of a great hunt, featuring the capturing of animals (including even fantastic ones) with a variety of techniques, including cages with vertical sliding doors. The animals are shown being loaded onto transport ships to be brought back to the Italian mainland or Sicily for use in the arena, zoos, or private collections.

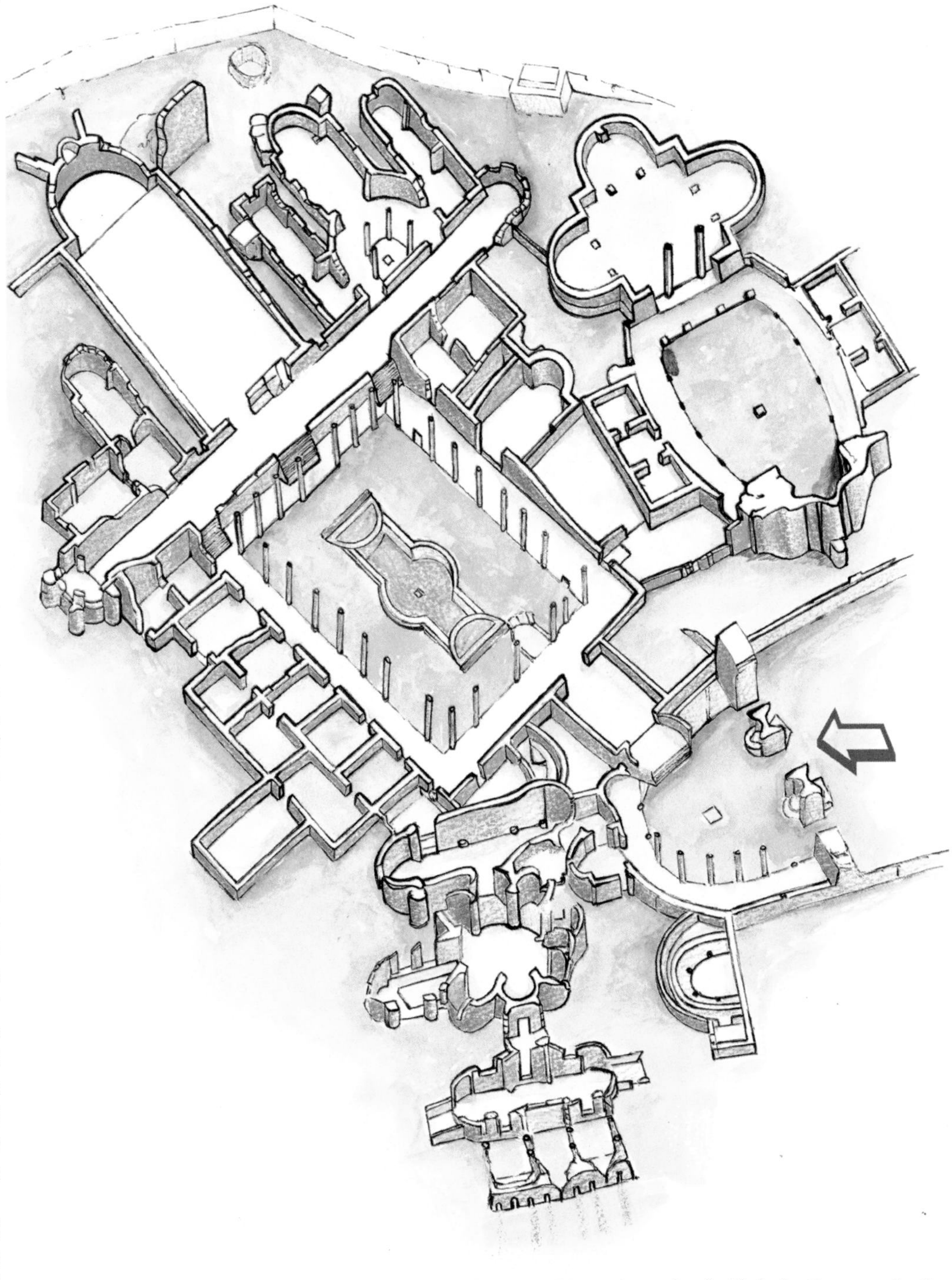

Fig. XII-29-Reconstruction of the Villa Romana del Casale at Piazza Armerina in Sicily by Roxanne Stall. First quarter of the fourth century CE. Main entry at lower right.

Bedroom suites for the family flank the large basilica and a sumptuous *cena* or dinner might be prepared for all in the tri-lobed dining room, which had several courtyards for walking about. Elaborate baths decorated with circus scenes were at the disposal of the guests as well as the family and required constant upkeep. There was a private latrine plus *frigidarium*, *tepidarium* and a number of different types of hot rooms, perhaps for steam baths, dry baths and massage, or to serve different people at the same time more privately. Despite being isolated, every attempt was made to make this villa the most up to date, even including importing mosaic artists from North Africa.

Whose villa was it? An old but now discredited hypothesis connects it with Maximian or Maxentius. It is to be noted that Piazza

Fig.XII-30 View of the Big Game Hunt area of the Villa Romana del Casale of Piazza Armerina in Sicily, showing a griffin perched above an animal trapping cage and, in the apse, a personification of Africa. Photo Credit: Vanni / Art Resource, N.Y.

Fig. XII-31 The Big Game Hunt, mosaic in the ambulatory of the Villa Romana del Casale, Piazza Armerina in Sicily. Ostriches and gazelles are carried up to the sailboat, while hunters carry other captured animals in boxes and nets. Photo Credit: Erich Lessing / Art Resource, N.Y. personification of Africa. Photo Credit: Vanni / Art Resource, N.Y.

Armerina, unlike Diocletian's Palace and Felix Romuliana, is not walled and fortified but rather a sprawling and open complex. Nor apparently does the Tetrarchic date on art-historical grounds for the mosaics necessarily hold up. Now it is thought that the villa must have been the seat of a member of the immensely wealthy Roman Senatorial aristocracy with Sicilian connections. Whoever he was, he reflected the popular taste of many men of means: a love of the circus, a great pride in hunting of big game, and a love of luxury, including fine dining and elegant bathing.

Fig. XII-32 (right) Musician with horn and palm frond and laurel crown for winner of *quadriga* (chariot) race. Mosaic from the Roman *palaestra*, Villa del Casale, first quarter of the fourth century CE, Piazza Armerina, Sicily, Italy. Photo Credit: Gianni Dagli Orti / The Art Archive at Art Resource, N.Y.

Fig. XII-33 Bikini-clad Female Athletes, Piazza Armerina, Sicily. Location: Villa Romana del Casale, Piazza Armerina, Sicily, Italy. Photo Credit: Vanni / Art Resource, N.Y.

THE FIRST BIKINI?

Aside from its major mosaics, Piazza Armerina preserves another mosaic with striking subject matter (Fig. XII-33). In the rear of two rooms, which may be for servants, is a mosaic showing young girls in bikini-like outfits, engaged in athletic contests. The halter top was known to the Greeks as a *strofion*, while brief shorts were called by the Romans a *subligaculum*. The mosaic may have been done a generation or two after the original villa was built, perhaps as part of the redecoration of the room to commemorate a prize-winning female athlete/attendant who had brought honor to the villa with her victories.

The women are shown engaging in a long jump while holding heavy weights, throwing the *discus*, running a marathon and playing ball. A victorious woman holding what appears to be a decorative wheel on a stick, almost a mini-parasol, is shown about to receive a crown of roses and a palm branch from a semi-nude young lady in a gold dress, which is slipping off her shoulder. Was the intention here athletic, erotic, or both?

The meaning is clearer in a rare group of monokinied ladies done in stucco and found in what may have been a public brothel at Dougga, central Tunisia. Here four women are shown wearing diaphanous, black-net pants made of two form-fitting pieces held together by ties from which ribbons dangle to their knees. Suggestions as to their identity have included bathers and female athletes, but the nature of their clothing suggests that they belonged to the world's oldest profession, a theory enhanced by the finding of a little cupid figure with them. Their date is unknown, but most scholars assign them to the third century.

CRITICAL THINKING EXERCISES

• 1. What were some of the accomplishments and failures of Septimius Severus and the Severans.
• 2. Septimius Severus and the Severans had many accomplishments as well as dismal failures during their reigns. Discuss several of each.
• 3. In what ways were the Severans an atypical dynasty ruling Rome?
• 4. What is meant by the term "Soldier Emperors" and why did it apply so well to the third century CE in Rome?
• 5. Compare neo-verism to the two earlier vogues in Roman sculpture for Veristic imagery.
• 6. How did Diocletian reinvigorate and transform traditional Roman thinking about government?
• 7. What was the purpose of the catacombs. Were they only used by Christians?
• 8. Roman art was often officially Classical and Greek-influenced and yet popular art became increasingly used in the later Empire. Explain the difference between these styles and give several examples.
• 9. The catacombs are usually thought of as being places of refuge used by Christians to avoid persecution. Is this true and were they only used by Christians?
•10. What are some of the characteristics of Late Antique Roman Baroque architecture? Give several examples.
•11. In some ways the art and architecture of Late Antiquity suggests a falling-off in the number of projects sponsored and the quality of workmanship and yet this is actually a time of considerable innovation. Explain.
•12.The palace of Diocletian at Split represents something of a departure in Roman Imperial architecture. Was it unique? How did it break new ground in architecture.
•13. Who lived in the massive villa at Piazza Armerina and what were some of the themes displayed on its extraordinary mosaic floors?

Chapter XIII
Rome in Late Antiquity

CONSTANTINE THE GREAT AND THE END OF THE TETRARCHY

Maximian retired with Diocletian so that Galerius and Constantius could become Augusti, with Severus and Maximinus becoming Caesars in west and east, but tensions mounted between Galerius and Constantius almost immediately as they jockeyed for control of the Empire. While Maximian had largely deferred to Diocletian and the two fellow countrymen had worked well together, Constantius and Galerius lacked trust in each other, a problem that was exacerbated by the ruthless ambition of Constantius' son Constantine. When Constantius died suddenly at York, Constantine declared himself emperor, completely ignoring Diocletian's carefully structured system of the four Tetrarchs. Forced to respond, Maximian's son Maxentius in turn declared himself emperor, the Caesar Severus led his own campaign, Galerius raised troops, Galerius' friend Licinius claimed to be Augustus of the West, and alliances were made and unmade with lightning speed as chaos set in. The system Diocletian had set up worked only if the people involved enjoyed

Fig. XIII-2 Colossal head of Emperor Constantine the Great from the *Basilica Nova*, also known as Basilica of Constantine or Maxentius c. 306-312 CE (completed in final form perhaps in the later fourth century CE). Photo credit: Noelle Soren. University of Arizona School of Anthropology Archive. Courtesy of the Musei Capitolini (Claudio Parisi Presicce, Direttore).

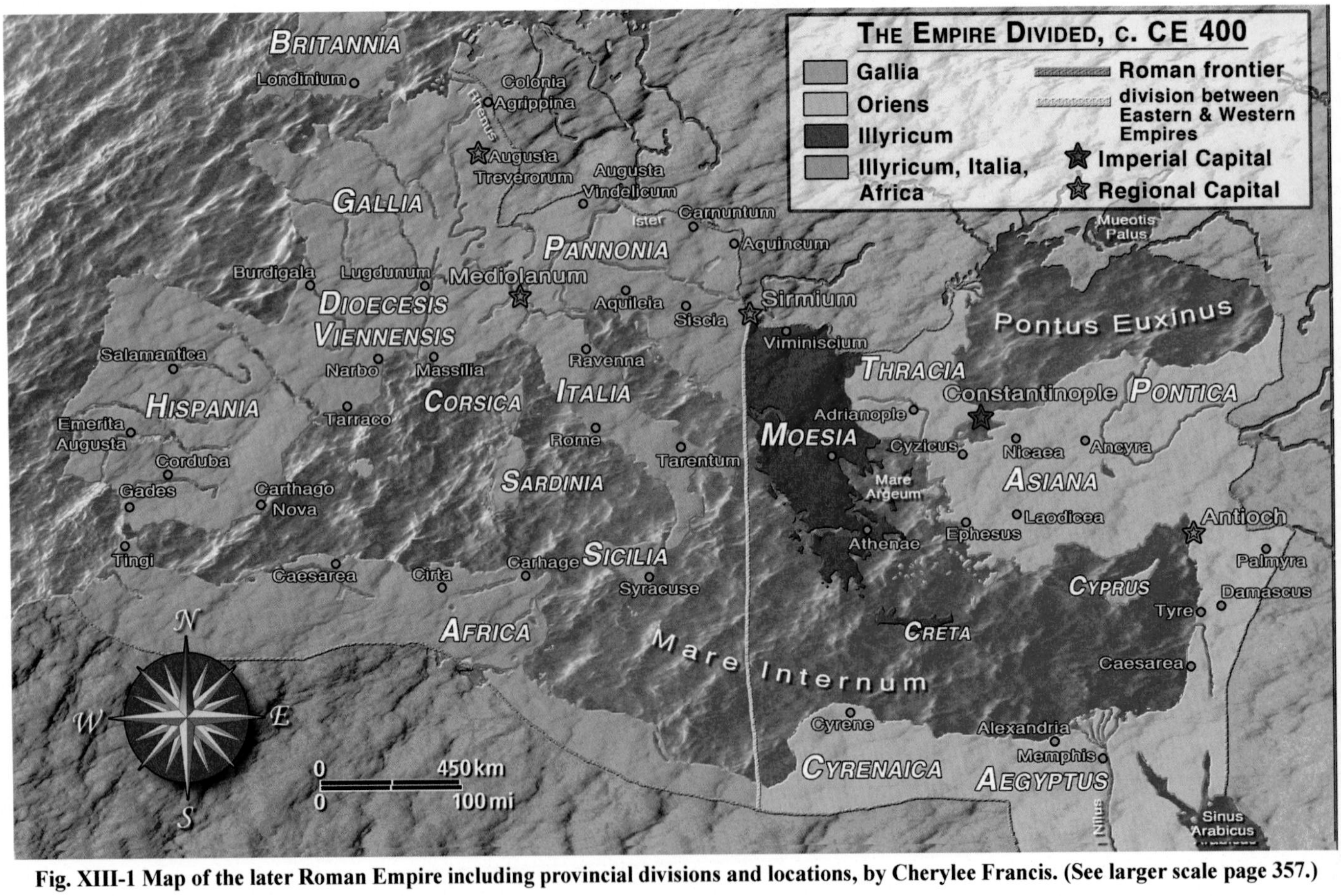

Fig. XIII-1 Map of the later Roman Empire including provincial divisions and locations, by Cherylee Francis. (See larger scale page 357.)

each other's trust. With so many people of strong will involved, the system was doomed.

The cunning and brutal Constantine played off his multiple opponents against one another and eventually cut them down one by one until he was the last man left. However, one must admit that he had no choice because if one sought to rule at this time, the only chance for success was to kill one's rivals before one was killed oneself. Consequently, Constantine attacked Maximian and killed him in Massilia (modern Marseilles) in 309. Galerius died soon after, presumably of natural causes. In 312, Constantine's major rival Maxentius, son of Maximian, was killed at a famous battle near Rome at the Milvian Bridge leaving all of northern Italy under Constantine (Figs. XIII-1, 2).

At this famous battle Constantine was said by later church historians to have become convinced that he had been saved by the god of the Christians. Newly allied with Licinius, who was wed to his half-sister, Constantine issued the Edict of Milan, bringing freedom from religious persecution to all of the subjects of the Empire. Constantine then urged Licinius, now looking after the East, to defeat Maximinus, another potential threat to Constantine's power. Despite his reported Christian conversion, Constantine did not end up a kinder, gentler ruler, for he then turned on Licinius and defeated him as well, after accusing him of intrigues, with the result that Constantine now became the sole ruler of the vast Roman Empire and gave his own family, including particularly his sons and nephews, control over the government and tremendous influence over the Christian church. Things did not always go well at home for Constantine during this period, however, as his second-wife Fausta, accused of intrigue against her stepson (or possibly with him), was suffocated in an overheated bath.

Between the Tetrarchy and the early reign of Constantine the city of Rome experienced an Indian summer. Diocletian promoted building in the city, in particular the spectacular baths that bear his name, and the much needed restoration of the *Curia* or Senate house which largely survives today. Maximian and his son Maxentius had made Rome their power base, and Maxentius was responsible for further building, such as the renovated Temple of Venus and Rome and the beginning of work on the *Basilica Nova*. Constantine spent some time in the city and promoted building there, both in the traditional civil sphere (his arch, baths, restorations) and also in the religious sphere with the first major Christian monuments.

YORK

Often the Romans needed to establish a military camp in a remote provincial location and over time the site might grow into a burgeoning town which, in many cases, still exists today. That was the case for example of Eboracum on the Ouse River in northeastern England (Fig. XIII-3). The Romans' 9th Legion established a fort there in 71 CE while they were attempting to pacify the area of Yorkshire and watching out for Caledonian tribes. Typically, it covered some 50 acres in a grid plan surrounded by a ditch or fossa backed by earthen ramparts and a timber palisade. Four gates were supplemented by guard towers and the usual internal buildings were put up: barracks, baths, a hospital, storehouses, principia for the commander to live in and a praetorium or headquarters.

It is often forgotten that families regularly accompanied soldiers living in a castrum or camp and this, as well as periods of extended peace, contributed to the rise of the camp as an actual town with many legionary retirees living in private houses and managing local businesses. In this way Eboracum became the city that is York today. As a port town, trade was essential and flourished although during its early existence an abundance of rats spread disease, and residents of Eboracum were known to live short lives and suffer from all manner of intestinal disorders, fleas and lice. As stone masonry replaced the wooden palisades of the simple fort by the early second century CE, local health appears to have improved but skirmishes continued with the northern tribes. In 208 CE the emperor Septimius Severus spent considerable time here trying to stop the barbarian influx but soon died at Eboracum in 211.

The town became an official Roman *colonia*, which was a title of the highest possible status for a community that had shown considerable growth from its origins as a camp or veteran settlement. Colonies normally featured elegant baths, sewer systems and a large forum with temples, market facilities and Imperial cult centers. Eboracum continued to have military importance in Late Antiquity as one of the centers of Western civilization. Diocletian named it the center of one of Britain's four provinces in 296, the governor of the sixth Roman legion was headquartered here as governor, and Constantine the Great was declared emperor here in 306 by the troops after the death of his father.

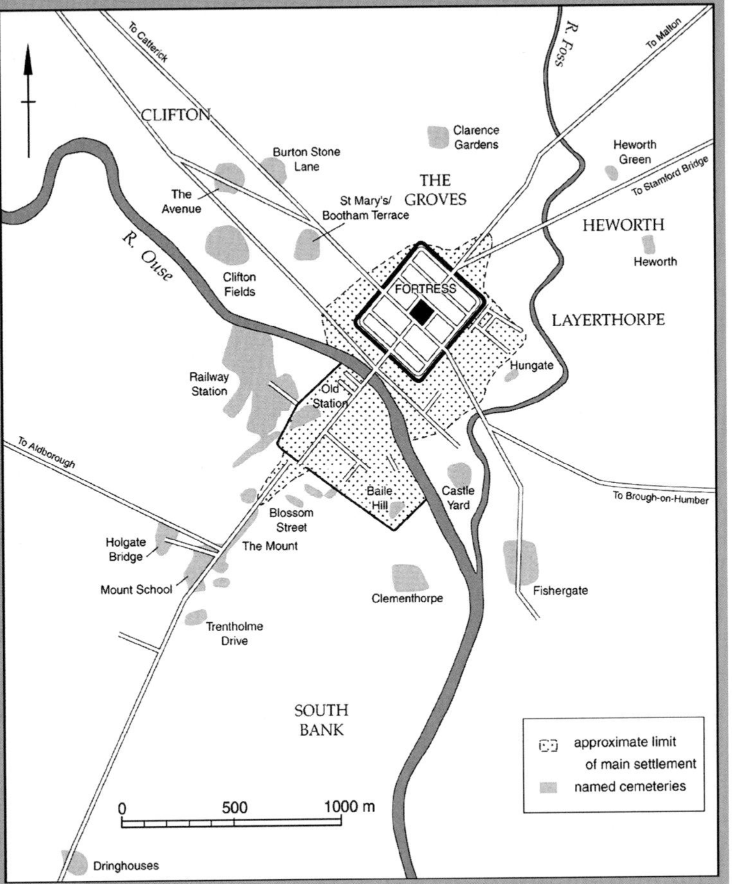

Fig. XIII-3 Plan of ancient York in England. Courtesy of the York Archaeological Trust.

THE BASILICA NOVA

The Basilica of Maxentius, sometimes now called the Basilica of Constantine but generally known as the *Basilica Nova* in the ancient sources, stands on the Velia, a saddle that joined the Palatine and the Esquiline hills until the Fascist regime cut through it to make a parade route in the 1930s from Piazza Venezia to the Colosseum (Figs. XIII-4, 5). The Basilica's northern foundations were exposed then and immediately decorated with a series of maps showing the expansion of Rome. In the 1970s the Basilica, one of the best preserved Roman ruins in the city, was used as an open air summer cinema. The location was perhaps originally suggested by a desire to recall the ancient connections of the Valerian *gens*, whose name Maxentius bore, with this part of Rome and thereby to emphasize Maxentius' association with the city, which constituted his power base in Imperial politics. Building began under Maxentius but was finished only after his defeat by Constantine.

Fig. XIII-4 Reconstruction of the *Basilica Nova*. Location: *Forum Romanum*, Rome. Courtesy of Bernard Frischer and Rome Reborn.

This Basilica is not the largest in Rome but certainly the most impressive architecturally as it was covered throughout with massive vaulting such as had been used before for *frigidaria* (central halls) of baths. The building consisted originally of a central hall or nave running approximately east-west and covered by three cross-vaults. It also had three communicating rooms on either side of the nave. The western end of the central hall finished in an apse, where the gigantic statue of Constantine now kept in the Capitoline Museums was found (Fig. XIII-2). The overall concept of the big nave and side aisles with a principal short side apse had already been developed by Domitian in the basilica of his Flavian Palace on the Palatine Hill in Rome. At a later date the entrance on the long side toward the Sacred Way was monumentalized with a porch and the room opposite it was given an apse, thus giving a greater importance to the short axis. These changes are normally attributed to Constantine, but it has been argued recently that the level of their foundations is too high for such an early date and that the alteration of the building was done in the later fourth century.

A recent interpretation put forward by Filippo Coarelli, one of Italy's foremost scholars of Roman topography, places the *Basilica Nova* in association with the *Templum Pacis* (or Temple of Peace) located in the Forum of Vespasian to the north and east. This was connected with the *praefectus urbi* (urban prefect), Rome's Chief Administrative Officer, who also administered justice for the city in Late Antiquity. It is known that the prefect began holding frequent public hearings from c. 384 CE. The apse of the Basilica offers an appropriate setting: a podium such as judges used, an element allowing the apse to be closed off from the rest of the building and a rich backdrop of niches framed by columns and pediments. Therefore, it is likely that the changes were made in the late fourth century to accommodate this function.

The colossal head of Constantine, found in the Basilica in 1486, came from a seated statue perhaps more than 30-feet high,

Fig. XIII-5 *Basilica Nova* with Statue of Constantine the Great in apse. Courtesy Bernard Frischer and Rome Reborn.

designed both to replace a colossal image of Maxentius intended to appear there and to show that Constantine had defeated Maxentius to control Rome and northern Italy (Fig. XIII-2). It had a body of various white marbles and was bare-chested with bronze drapery across the legs. It was set on a huge podium in the west apse of the Basilica. Whether or not it carried Christian imagery such as a cross-topped scepter is unknown. The head, made of Pentelic marble from Athens, does not reveal a mere mortal but rather a god-like individual with piercing overlarge eyes that appear to commune with a higher plane of reality. Typical of this age of dematerialized representation of humans are the ropy eyebrows, stylized bangs, deep eye drilling, and high cheekbones as well as the overall smooth-faced, transfixed look.

THE ARCH OF CONSTANTINE

Even more familiar than the *Basilica Nova* to tourists visiting the Forum and Colosseum is the Arch of Constantine, clearly identified by its inscription although not mentioned by any ancient authors (Figs. XIII-6, 7, 8). It stands on the Triumphal Way at a point just before the place where the procession coming from the south would turn left toward the Arch of Titus and the Forum. It is a triple arch consisting of a larger central passageway and two side ones. The passageways are framed by columns on pedestals. Above them stretches the attic or upper story, articulated by Dacian War captives standing above the columns. It is built mostly of recycled Proconnesian marble, originally quarried on an island in the Sea of Marmara in modern Turkey, but the attic consists of brick with a marble veneer. The arch owes its good preservation to its incorporation c. 1000 CE into the fortifications built by the monks of San Gregorio who were based on the Caelian Hill to the south. Then in the mid-12th century it was built into the fortress of the Frangipane family established on the slopes of the Palatine to the west.

Although intended to honor the new emperor, a large part of the decoration of the arch consists of reused sculpture. Scholars have often said that the choice reflects a desire on Constantine's part to identify himself with good predecessors, but the figures of the emperor on the recycled slabs are always reworked to be Constantine and the scenes therefore were intended to depict him. Would the average passerby have had the art historical sensibility of the modern scholar needed to recognize the styles of bygone times? The earliest pieces, placed inside the central passageway and on the short sides of the attic, come from a great Trajanic (or possibly Domitianic) frieze showing the emperor in battle and greeted by the personification of victory. The Dacian captives are clearly of Trajanic date and refer to his several major campaigns in what is now Romania.

Until recently it was assumed that the Trajanic elements were taken from Trajan's Forum, but it is now known that that Forum was not yet abandoned in the fourth century and is therefore unlikely to have been the source for these pieces, which must have come from some other monument, perhaps one not even in Rome. Eight Hadrianic roundels or rounded frames occupy a

Fig. XIII-6 Arch of Constantine, c. 315/6 CE. Photo Credit: Noelle Soren. University of Arizona School of Anthropology Archive.

prominent position in pairs over the lateral passageways on each side. They are accentuated by being placed dramatically against a red porphyry background. The use of strong color contrasts is an innovation in the Arch of Constantine. The roundels show the emperor hunting and performing sacrifices to various deities. The third set of reused decorative sculpture consists of eight-panel reliefs situated in pairs on either side of the attic above the lateral passageways. These originally showed the emperor Marcus Aurelius in war and carrying out civilian duties.

Fig. XIII-7 Arch of Constantine, detail of Hadrianic hunting relief with sacrifice to Diana. Photo Credit: University of Arizona School of Anthropology Archive.

The rest of the decoration dates to the time of Constantine. The major element is a frieze running just above the side passageways, below the Hadrianic roundels, and at the same height on the short sides of the arch. It depicts Constantine's march on Rome, the battle of the Milvian Bridge in which he defeated Maxentius, and Constantine in the city of Rome. Sculptors of the time of Constantine also executed roundels of the sun and moon gods for the short sides of the arch, river gods and victories for the spandrels of the passageways and victories and captives for the pedestals of the columns.

This Constantinian sculpture firmly rejects the Classical heritage shown in the earlier pieces in favor of non-Classical popular art that was already beginning to emerge in official art in the Severan Period, often with frontally placed figures given different sizes to reflect their importance. Art historians of the 19th and early 20th centuries generally saw this as an indication of decadence and incompetence, but scholars with a medieval background were able to argue that this reflects a different intention in art that grew out of plebeian and provincial currents less influenced by high Greek art and had long been an undercurrent in Roman art.

Inscriptions make up the other important element on the arch. The major inscription is repeated on the central space of the attic on either side. Constantine's title of Maximus (the Greatest), granted in 312 CE, means that the dedicatory inscription was placed no earlier than that year. Shorter phrases above the Hadrianic roundels recall the 10th and 20th anniversaries of Constantine's rule. Such phrases, which occur frequently in Late Antique epigraphy, are generally agreed to commemorate the former and look forward to the latter. In that case a date of 315/ 6 CE is likely for the dedication of this arch.

In light of Constantine's fame as the first Christian emperor it is important to notice that there is nothing specifically Christian about anything on the arch. The sculpture shows him doing the same things that his pagan predecessors did: making war and triumphing, carrying out pagan sacrifices, hunting, addressing the people of Rome and doing good deeds. The main inscription emphasizes his defeat of the tyrant (i.e., Maxentius). The only element that might be claimed to show Constantine's Christianity is the inscription's phrase "by divine inspiration," which is at best a veiled and debatable reference. It may be that on his arch Constantine was concerned to place himself in the Imperial tradition rather than to draw attention to his new religious beliefs or, as some scholars believe, Constantine's conversion did not occur at the Milvian Bridge despite the insistence of contemporary church historians such as Eusebius.

The date of the structure of the arch formed one of the great debates in Roman archaeology in the 1990s. The consensus had been for some time that the arch was indeed Constantinian as a structure, although it had been suggested that Constantine merely took over an existing monument. Then two research teams brought forth arguments for conflicting dates. A group from the Istituto Centrale per il Restauro (The Central Institute for Restoration) under Alessandra Melucco Vaccaro conducted excavations on the south side as part of a restoration project. They identified a foundation trench there containing second century CE material. This led them to propose an old hypothesis that Constantine reused the site of an earlier arch. Another team, from the University of Rome "La Sapienza" under Clementina Panella, which had been investigating the nearby *Meta Sudans* (Fig. IX-11), an important fountain in the center of Rome, extended its excavation area to the northern edge of the foundations. They also claimed to have found a stretch of the foundation trench with fourth-century material, thus confirming the Constantinian date. Each group was able to call on experts to bolster its hypothesis, much as a defense lawyer and a prosecuting attorney might do in a trial. A particularly telling report came

Fig. XIII-8a Arch of Constantine, detail. The emperor Constantine (now without head) addresses the people from the *rostra* while a statue of the emperor Hadrian (?) appears at the end of the platform. Photo Credit: University of Arizona School of Anthropology Archive.

from Patrizio Pensabene, also of the University of Rome, an expert on marble: he determined the types of marble used in the structure and identified them as reused pieces (*spolia*) throughout.

More recently Ross Holloway of Brown University has proposed a solution combining the evidence from the two Roman groups. He accepts the second century date for the foundations, as the fourth-century trench seems to him implausible as a foundation trench and instead appears to him to be a trench dug against the foundation. However, the lack of correspondence between the foundation and the monument above ground indicates that the foundation was not made originally for the Arch of Constantine but rather for a structure that was never built or was demolished. The systematic use of *spolia* is also incompatible with a second-century date. Holloway suggests that the arch was begun for Maxentius and then finished hurriedly for Constantine, which explains the use of brick in the attic. In this hypothesis the Constantinian frieze was carved on the moldings at mid-height because there was no other place for it and the battle scenes from the time of Marcus Aurelius were inserted into secondary cuttings on the short sides to supplement them. It remains to be seen whether Holloway's reconstruction of events gains favor, but it has the merit of taking into account all available evidence.

ROME BECOMES A MUSEUM OF ART

Although Constantine gave Rome some of its most renowned later monuments, he also sanctioned Rome's definitive relegation to the status of a symbolic capital in 330 CE by creating his new capital at Constantinople (now İstanbul) to which he moved with his court (Fig. XIII-1). From that time forward Rome was never again the seat of administration. Even when there was a Western emperor, he was never based there. Rome's symbolic status was potent—the shock of the sack of Rome by the Visigoths in 410 prompted St. Augustine to write his *City of God (De Civitate Dei)*. However, the city's history and image led Rome, like Athens, to become a museum of its own former greatness rather than to flourish as the dynamic city of earlier times.

In these different circumstances, the resources available to the city changed drastically. The Imperial administration was concerned almost exclusively with the maintenance of the necessary infrastructure. The departure of the Imperial court, however, allowed the Senatorial aristocracy to come to the fore, and this group enjoyed the revenues of vast estates located throughout the Mediterranean. Its presence is attested by the lavish Late Antique palaces in which its members lived. This aristocracy was a defender of pagan religion and maintained and restored pagan shrines until the second half of the fourth century. As Christianity gained ground and gradually won over the aristocracy, aristocrats became benefactors of Christian buildings. Finally, the Church itself passed from receiving Imperial patronage at the time of Constantine to being a wealthy entity able to act in its own right, in particular in completing its network of parishes and associated welfare installations.

EARLY CHURCHES

The emperor was directly responsible for a series of monumental churches surrounding Rome. According to some scholars Constantine wished to avoid making a play of his Christian sympathies in the center of Rome, where paganism (i.e., non-Christian religion) was still strong. Another reason for locating churches in the suburban belt was the desire to commemorate sites of martyrdom and burials of saints there. Finally, there was more space available outside the center, and Constantine could use land he owned himself.

We know little about Christian buildings before the time of Constantine. The only pre-Constantinian church building known archaeologically is far away on the Eastern frontier at Dura Europos in what is now Syria. Written sources indicate that the early Christians of Rome met in houses and other places, first as opportunities arose and then on a fixed basis. As we have seen, however, they most certainly did not hide or hold regular worship underground in the catacombs, although offering a decent burial to its members was one of the attractions of Christianity. As long as the groups were small and not particularly wealthy, they would not have made much effort to adapt the places where they met and even less effort to create a specific architectural type for their meeting places.

Thus, formal Christian architecture began under Constantine. What Christians needed for worship was very different from pagan religion. Pagan temples served most of all to house the images of the divinities, cult equipment and donations—sacrifices took place on altars, which could be outside. Christians wanted an indoor space in which to gather in groups. It is often said that the basilicas or law courts offered the model for churches, and indeed the name was eventually applied to churches. However, it is likely that churches developed more generically from halls, such as were found in many public and private buildings. This can be seen in the way that various privately endowed churches, such as S. Clemente and Ss. Giovanni e Paolo, adapted existing structures.

Of Constantine's great churches in the neighborhood of Rome, St. John Lateran (still the seat of the pope as bishop of Rome)

Fig. XIII-8b North façade, Arch of Constantine, showing (at the lower left) panel featured in Fig. XIII-8a. Photo credit: Noelle Soren. University of Arizona School of Anthropology Archive.

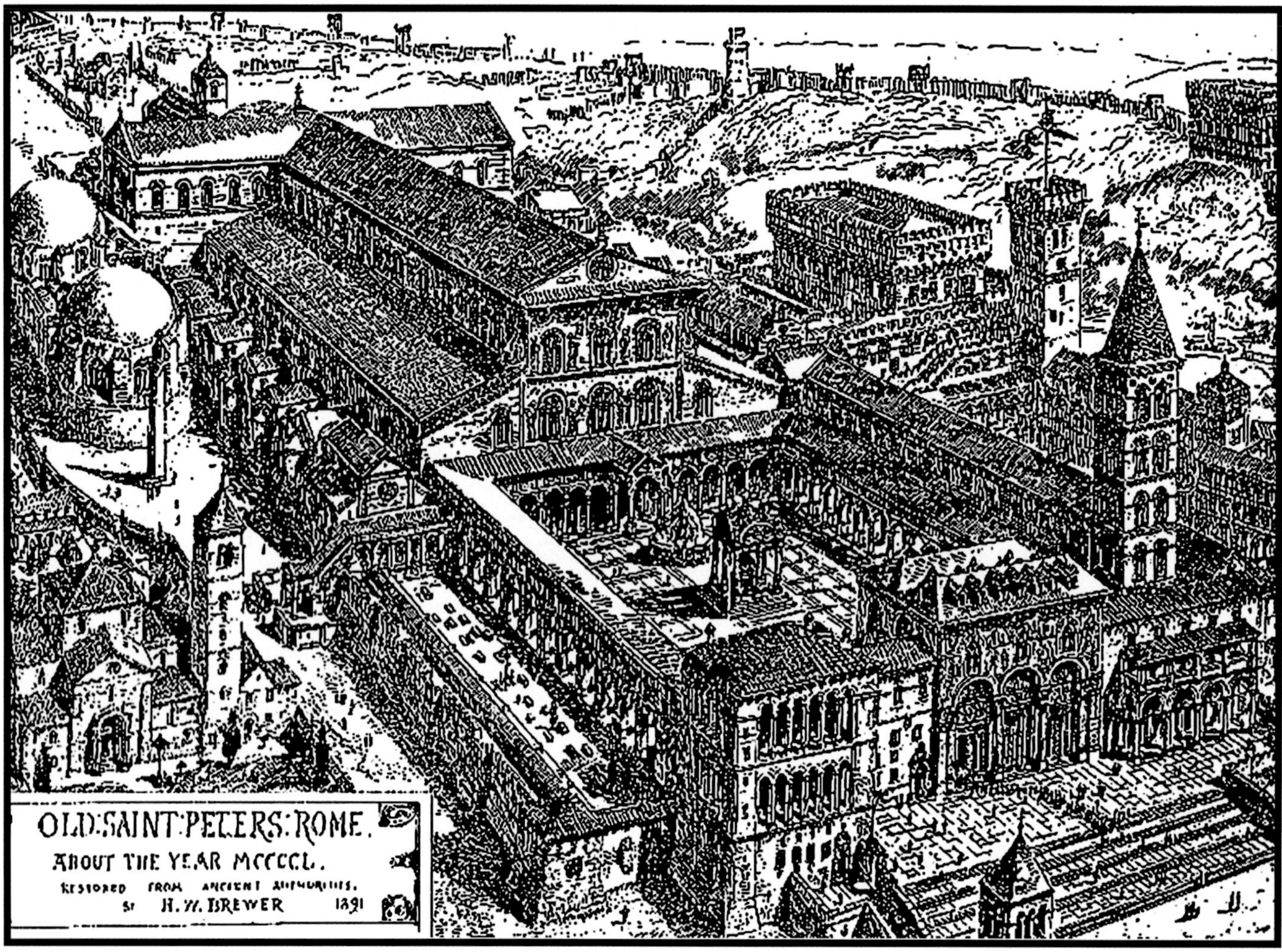

Fig. XIII-9 Reconstruction drawing of the Constantinian basilica complex of St. Peter as it looked c. 1500 CE. University of Arizona School of Anthropology Archive.

and the newly discovered bishop's church at Ostia were built in spaces cleared for the purpose, and St. Peter's in the Vatican arose over a cemetery where Peter was thought to be buried (Figs. XIII-9, 10). None was particularly conditioned by existing structures, and all benefited from Imperial benefaction. Therefore, they can give us an idea of the development of church architecture at the time of Constantine when the planners had a relatively free hand. The plans of these churches all share a nave ending in an apse and flanked by aisles. Apses had long been used as a feature to set someone off from a throng, as in law courts and Imperial and aristocratic audience chambers, and the step from that to placing the clergy in an apse for the liturgy was easy. The nave likewise was the obvious place for the congregation of the faithful. The reason for the aisles is less evident, but it can be argued that the catechumens (the unbaptized still receiving instruction), who were not allowed to participate fully in the liturgy, would have stayed there. The Ostian church shows the simplest elaboration, although it is monumental in size and was as lavishly furnished according to the written sources as the others. Besides a nave with an apse and two aisles, it had an *atrium* or large anteroom preceding the main structure. In the sixth century it was considered desirable to set the apse more apart from the nave by raising it.

The Constantinian church of St. Peter's had a nave, two aisles on either side, a transept at right angles to them and beyond it the apse in line with the nave (Figs. XIII-9, 10). The most notable feature here is the transept, which is the oldest one known. An examination of the widths of the foundation preserved beneath the Renaissance church has shown that the transept is the original part of the structure, built as a rectangular space over the presumed tomb of Saint Peter. The nave was added at a later stage of construction, as were the additional aisles, effectively turning the original structure into a transept of the completed church. The church of the Prince of the Apostles enjoyed great prestige, and the new feature was evidently also useful both practically and symbolically: therefore transepts became a standard feature of church architecture from the time of Constantine up to the modern day.

A TIME OF EARTHQUAKES

In the years following the reign of Constantine, the eastern portion of the Empire was racked with a series of major earthquakes that caused widespread suffering. Among these none was worse than the enormous earthquake and seismic sea wave of July 21, 365 CE, as recorded by the historian Ammianus Marcellinus. The quake was so bad that it caused enormous waves to crash into the harbor at Alexandria, creating enough damage to inspire the Egyptians to offer special annual prayers to keep the disaster from recurring. Boats were dislodged from their places of mooring and deposited well inland and there were many casualties as the water

Fig. XIII-10a (above) Old St. Peter's Basilica in Rome by Domenico Tasselli, 16th c. CE. Location: St. Peter's Basilica, Vatican State. Photo Credit: Scala / Art Resource, N.Y.

Fig. XIII-10b (right) Early postcard showing St. Peter's Square and the Vatican after 16th and 17th century rebuildings. Obelisk from the Circus of Caligula (originally removed by him from Heliopolis, Egypt) appears at the center.

receded from the land and then rushed back in again, killing many who had wandered out into the newly formed shoals.

To investigate such disasters, archaeologists have developed a sub-field known as seismic archaeology. This requires a

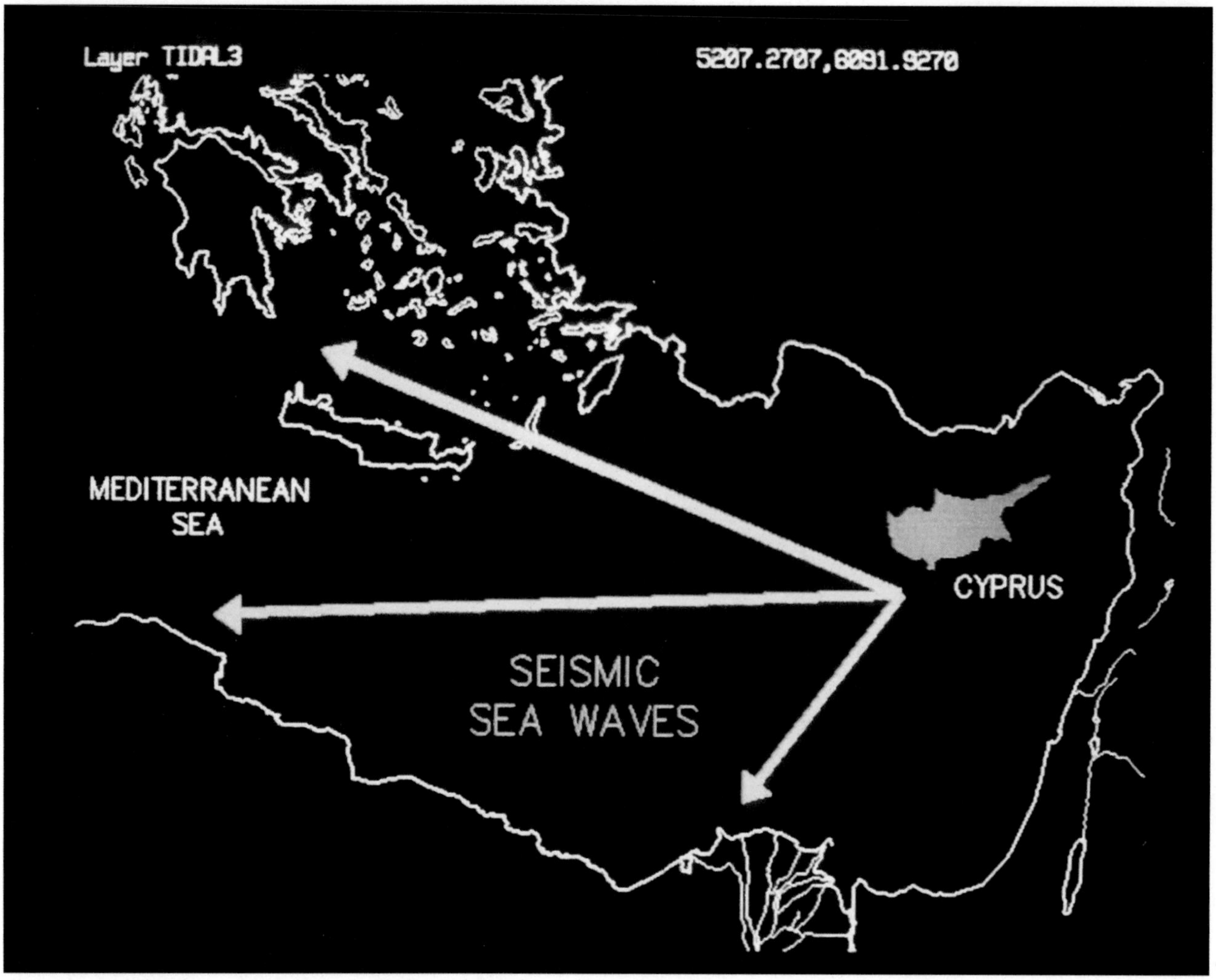

Fig. XIII-11 Map showing earthquake of 365 CE c. 25 miles southwest of the site of Kourion, Cyprus. Image developed by John C. and Peggy M. Sanders. Photo credit: Noelle Soren. University of Arizona School of Anthropology Archive.

knowledge of plate tectonics, the idea that the Earth is divided into some eight large surfaces or masses of land which come into conflict when they butt up against one another. This friction results in such phenomena as earthquakes and volcanic activity. By carefully assessing the degree of damage in a particular area one can determine the size of the earthquake, even one that occurred in antiquity. The Modified Mercalli Scale (named after Italian volcanologist Giuseppe Mercalli in 1884) gives a description from 0 to 12 of quake damage that one can observe, with numbers such as 9 and higher suggesting a major devastating event. By detecting how buildings collapse and noting the direction of falling debris, the archaeologist can begin to understand the nature of an event which may have had far-reaching consequences both on land and sea. Seismic Archaeology developed in the 1970s, after the theory of plate tectonics became accepted as fact by the majority of the scientific community. By 1978 it was being applied to earthquake-affected sites as part of the New Archaeology or Processual Archaeology movement of this era and the puzzle of the great quake of 365 CE became one of the first applications of the new approach.

The epicenter of the massive event had long been sought and was finally discovered through the excavation of a Roman town and Sanctuary of Apollo on the southwest part of the island of Cyprus in the eastern Mediterranean. The site was Kourion, known as Curium in Roman times. By observing that in the town of Paphos on the west coast of Cyprus debris from the quake tended to fall north and west, the excavator compared that tendency to the directional fall of the collapsed buildings on his own site of Kourion, where debris fell to the north and east. By consulting with geologists and geophysicists from America and Cyprus, he was able to suggest that the epicenter of the giant quake was circa 25 miles southwest of Kourion in the Mediterranean Sea (Fig. XIII-11). Further investigation revealed that this was exactly the place where the European and African plates met and where the subduction or drawing down of one plate beneath the other sometimes causes major offshore earthquakes and seismic sea waves.

The earthquake struck with great force in three enormous waves or pulses, the second of which was strong enough to throw down the Temple of Apollo in the sanctuary area. The temple blocks lay fallen in place until the temple was reconstructed using many of these blocks in 1982 (Figs. XIII-12, 13). In a house in the town of Kourion the devastating temblor had caused huge blocks to crash down. The residents had apparently been recovering from previous quakes in the area because some of the houses had already caved in and columns had been stacked in the courtyard. A once elegant façade of some probably public building lay outside the house but one of its main rooms contained a small oven and

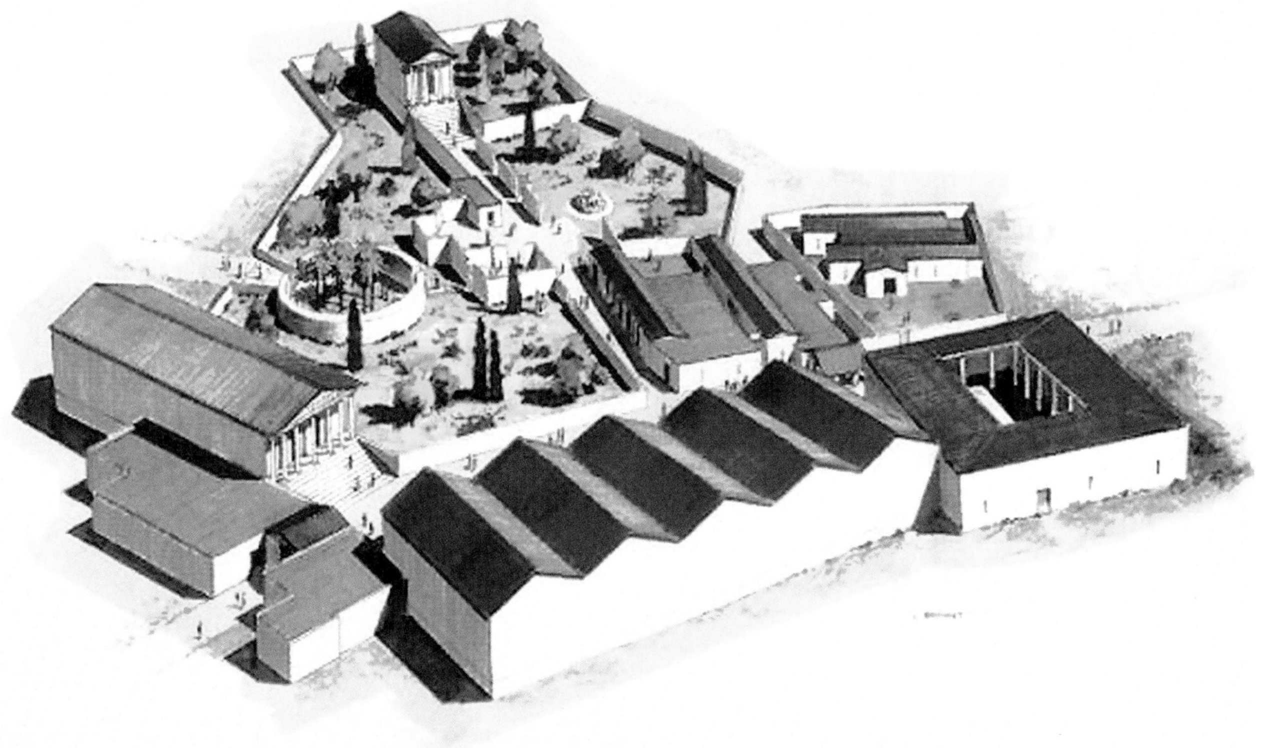

Fig. XIII-12a (above) Reconstruction of the Sanctuary of Apollo Hylates at Kourion, including the Temple of Apollo at the top, by Jim Bryant with David Soren. Courtesy David Soren. University of Arizona School of Anthropology Archive.
Fig. XIII-12b (below) Aerial view of the site. Photo credit: Harry Heywood.

probably had already sustained damage in an earlier quake or quakes.

In the house a middle-aged man had taken refuge in a doorway which collapsed against him. His head, arms and torso were found buried in the quake debris but his legs were completely missing. Since they stuck up above ground, they may have been torn off by dogs trying to survive after the disaster. In a room in the public building a young man had put his hands over his head and crouched into the fetal position, only to be buried under tons of stone (Fig. XIII-14). In a stable containing an animal-feeding trough a mule was found still tethered with an iron chain. The remains of a circa 12-year-old girl were tangled up

Fig. XIII-13 (right) Reconstructed Temple of Apollo at Kourion. Reconstruction by Stefanos Sinos based on research by Stefanos Sinos, John Rutherford, Alexandra Korn, David Soren,. Photo credit: Noelle Soren. University of Arizona School of Anthropology Archive.

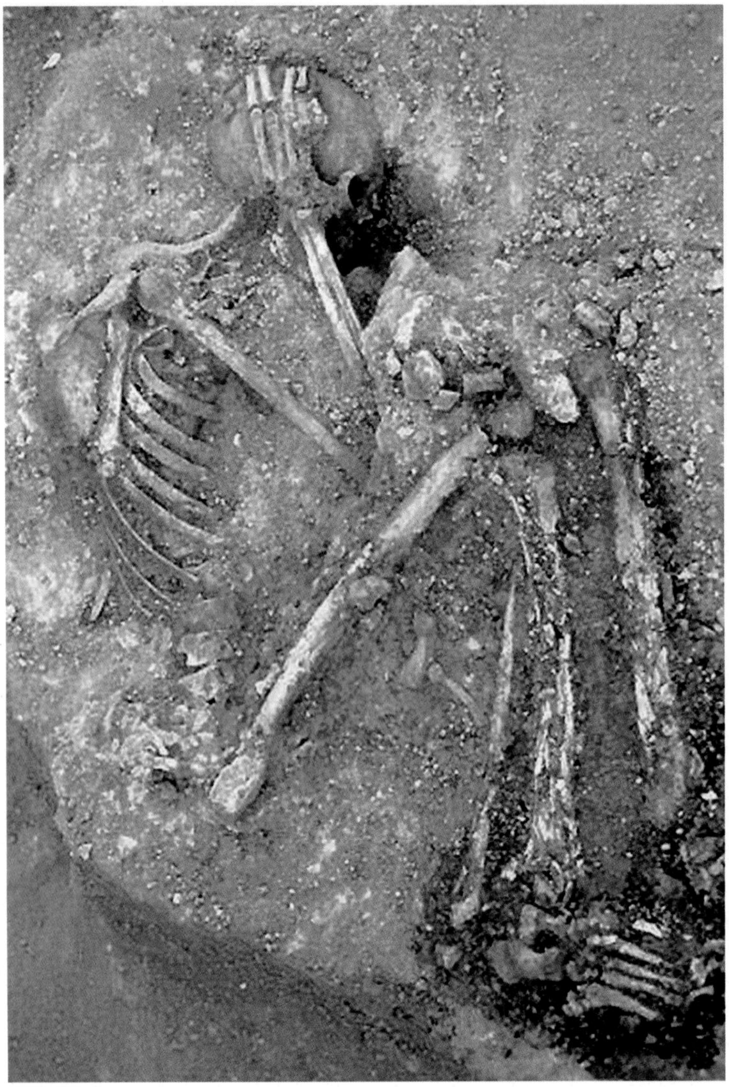

was a 1 ½-year-old infant. The original photograph, made by *National Geographic* photographer Martha Cooper, attracted worldwide attention, all the more because on the woman's finger had been a copper alloy Christian ring emblazoned with the Chi Ro, the first letters of Jesus Christ's name in Greek. Flanking the name of Jesus were the Greek letters alpha and omega, implying that the Lord was the beginning and end. However, the alpha-omega proved to be ironic here in that this was indeed the end for the ancient site of Kourion (Fig. XIII-18). After the family was trapped rodents scampered down into the crevices left by the fallen debris. They fed on the tender flesh of the child and dragged the bones a short distance from the agonal position (the position at the moment of death) of the family. Then one rodent lost its way and became trapped among the bones of the victims.

There must have been aftershocks and writers such as Libanius, a few years later in circa 380 CE, wrote of the poor unfortunate people of Cyprus. For at least 18 years there was a break in the coinage found on southwest Cyprus so that probably Kourion and Paphos were affected in a major way. No one returned to shift through the debris and recover any of the dead until 1934 and scientific investigation did not begin here until 1986.

Kourion is important because all of the finds recovered provide great help as markers to date pottery in other ancient contexts. The site also gives insight into ancient domestic architecture on the island of Cyprus and allows one to see a snapshot of a dramatic moment in Late Antiquity.

ROME IN THE LATER FOURTH AND FIFTH CENTURIES CE

The first major trauma after the removal of the Imperial court by Constantine to Constantinople in 330 came in 410 with the Visigothic sack already mentioned. The estimated

Fig. XIII-14 (above) Man in agonal position, shielding himself from falling blocks at Kourion. The excavator has posited a date of July 21, 365 CE c. 5:30 a.m. Photo credit: Noelle Soren. University of Arizona School of Anthropology Archive.

Fig. XIII-15 (bottom right) Reconstruction of the child and mule trapped in a house at Kourion in 365 CE. Artist: David Vandenberg.

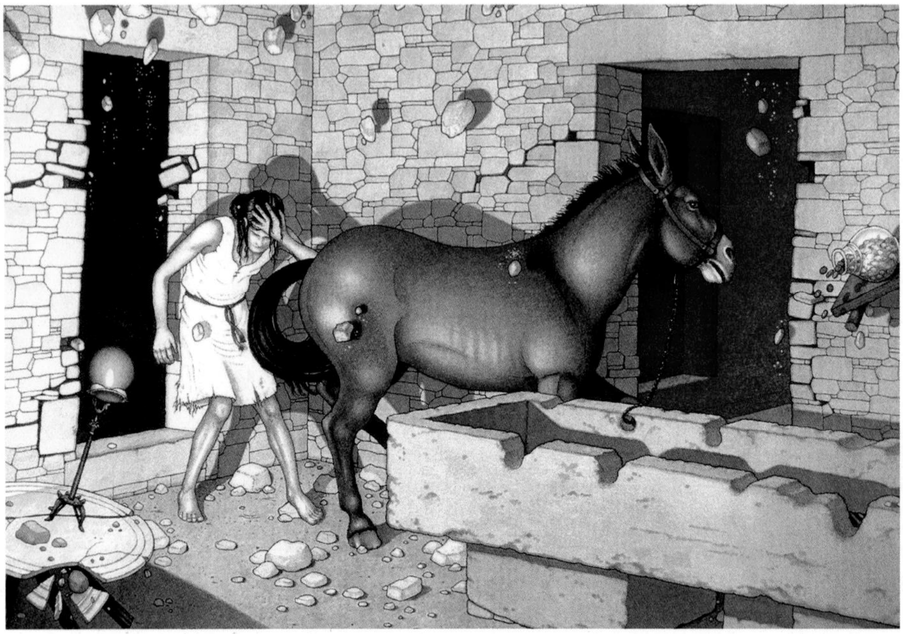

amongst those of the mule. The girl had put her hands over her head. In the same stable, a marble table top shattered, an Antique bronze lamp and lamp stand fell, and a glass jar full of coins crashed to the ground revealing coins dating to the time of the quake, or at least providing a *terminus post quem* in the reign of Valens and Valentinian I (Fig. XIII-15).

The most dramatic find was yet to come. In one room of the house a 25-year-old male and a 19-year-old woman were found clutching each other in a death grip, the man protecting the woman with his leg and arm looped around her (Figs. XIII-16, 17). It was to no avail as her neck was broken in two by a fallen block. In their arms and pressed against the mother's chin

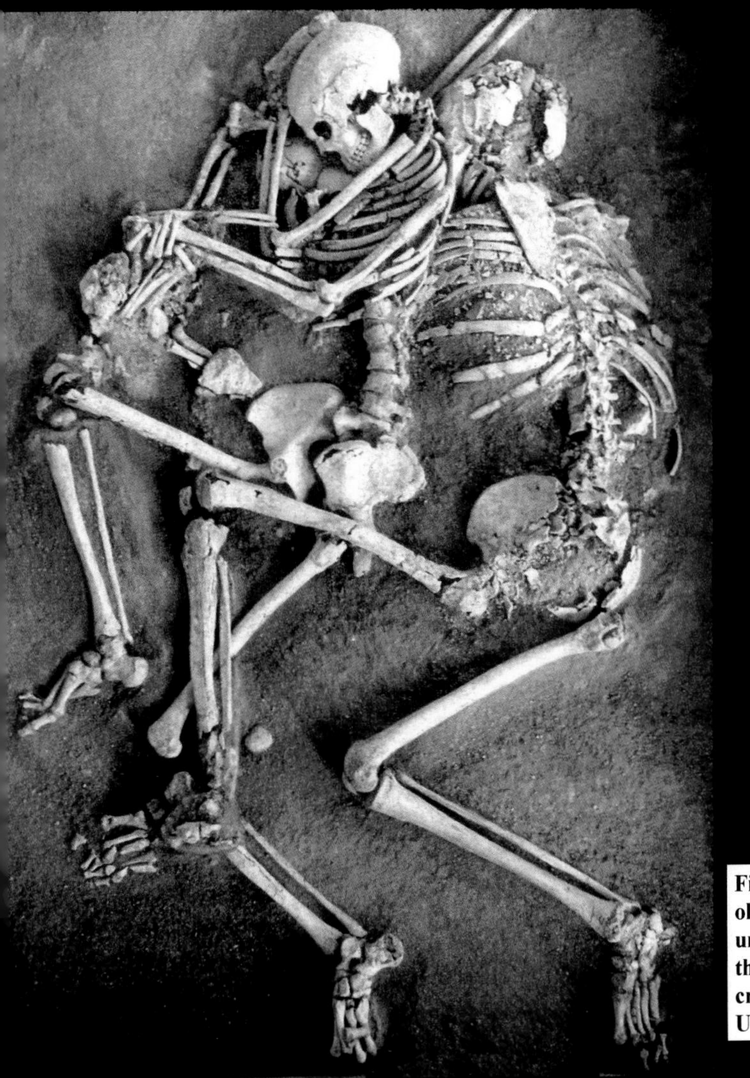

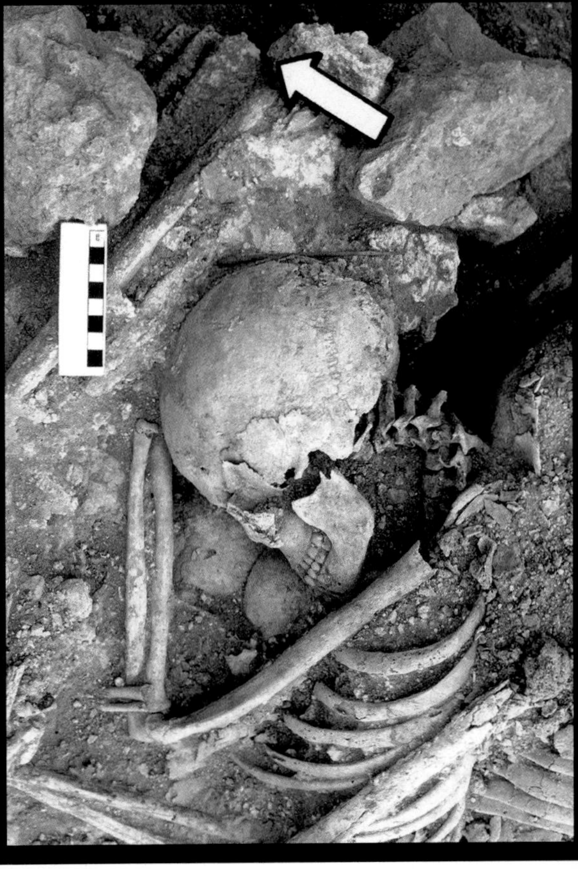

Fig. XIII-16a & 16b (upper left and right) Body of a 19 year old woman, 25 year old male and 1 ½ year old infant trapped under fallen debris at Kourion, Cyprus. Bodies prepared under the supervision of Walter Birkby, Arizona State Museum. Photo credit: Photo credit: Noelle Soren (16a), Ines Vaz Pinto (16b). University of Arizona School of Anthropology Archive.

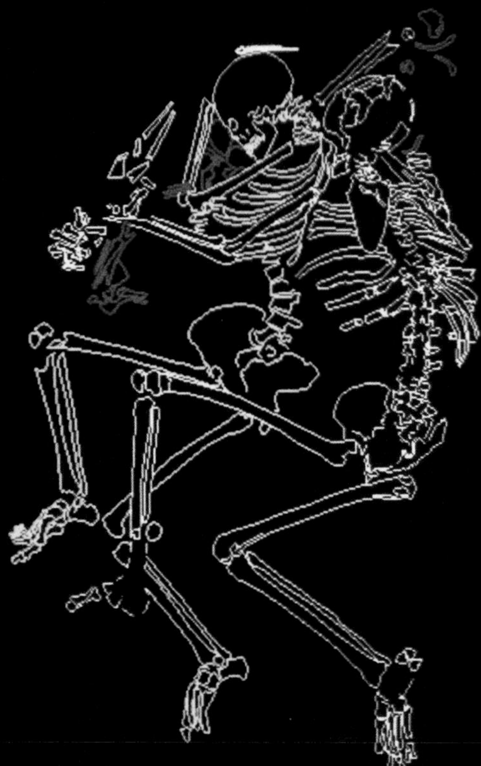

Fig. XIII-17 (left) Body of a 19-year-old woman, 25-year-old male and 1½-year-old infant trapped under fallen debris at Kourion, The infant in red has had the bones dragged by rodents. Cyprus. Digitization by John C. and Peggy M. Sanders.

Fig. XIII-18 (right) Copper alloy ring from the victims at Kourion, with symbols of Jesus Christ. Photo credit: Noelle Soren. University of Arizona School of Anthropology Archive.

THE MILDENHALL TREASURE

Imagine the thrill of discovering ancient Roman treasure in your own neighborhood. This is what Gordon Butcher did when he deep-plowed a field for sugar beets in Suffolk, England on a freezing morning in 1942 and struck a large silver platter which proved to be part of the famed Mildenhall Treasure (Fig. XIII-19). Immediately calling the man who had hired him, Sydney Ford, to help him, Butcher unearthed 34 pieces of Roman silver. Ford promptly took them home, reportedly considering them to be pewter. After keeping the horde for four years, he was found out because of local rumors and a visitor to his house who saw a spoon on his mantle.

Fig. XIII-19- The Great Dish from the Mildenhall treasure, Roman Britain, fourth century CE. The staring face in the center represents Oceanus, with dolphins in his hair and a beard formed of seaweed fronds. The inner circle, bordered by scallop shells, consists of sea-nymphs riding mythical marine creatures, a sea-horse, a triton, a sea-stag and a *ketos*, a dragon-like sea-monster. The wide outer frieze features Bacchus, holding a bunch of grapes and a *thyrsus* (a staff tipped with an ornament) and resting a foot on his panther. Location: British Museum, London, Great Britain Photo Credit: © The Trustees of the British Museum / Art Resource, N.Y.

Under the British Law of Treasure Trove, objects of gold or silver found hidden beneath the earth with the intent to cover them belong to the Crown. Objects not intended to be recovered—ones simply lost for instance or deposited in a grave—belong to the finder if no owner can be established. If the finder notifies the police promptly, he can receive compensation for the full market value of the discovery. Because the find was not reported immediately, the authorities gave Ford and Butcher each 1,000 pounds. Had Butcher reported his find to the authorities, he would likely have been given a large sum of money—the hoard was valued at £50,000 when it was finally reported—and he would have never had to touch a plow again for the rest of his life.

The non-archaeological nature of the discovery and its delayed reporting has given rise to rumors over the years. Some doubt that such a hoard could be from Britain at all. It has been suggested that it was being smuggled from the Mediterranean to the United States by American aviators stationed at the nearby airbase. Subsequent, better documented finds of a similar nature in Britain make the British provenience more plausible but have not completely eliminated doubts. More recently, evidence has come to light that some pieces may have been separated from the treasure and were never reported.

The horde uncovered by Butcher and Fox became one of the treasures of the British Museum. There are 12 dishes in the collection, plus spoons, ladles and goblets, all made of silver. The greatest dish, perhaps the most famous Roman silver dish ever found, weighs almost 18 pounds and sports a handsome head of Neptune or Oceanus in the center wearing a beard of seaweed as four dolphins appear in his hair; he is surrounded by an inner frieze of sea nymphs riding various sea creatures. The wider outer frieze shows the victory of the wine god Bacchus/Dionysus over a drunken Herakles who is propped up by satyrs, the woodland followers of Bacchus. Bacchus holds a cluster of grapes and his characteristic *thyrsus* or staff topped with grape leaves. A Silenus, eldest and most inebriated of the woodland followers of Bacchus, offers more wine to the god while a Pan and a group of satyrs and maenads dance.

Bacchic scenes were appropriate to dinner parties where wine would be served and a good time would be wished for with the help of the god. Two more plates show Bacchic scenes with reveling satyrs and maenads, the excited female followers of Dionysus. A series of flanged bowls includes one with possible imagery of Alexander the Great in the center as a young helmeted man flanked by a young woman and an older one, the latter perhaps his mother Olympias.

Despite all the pagan imagery on the serving pieces, the spoons show the Chi Ro, the first letters of the name of Christ in ancient Greek. Such a mixture of pagan and Christian motives was not uncommon in Late Antiquity. One piece has an inscription indicating it belonged to a certain Eutherius who may have been an official serving under the late pagan emperor Julian the Apostate (reigned 360-363 CE). One theory is that the service could have been given by the emperor to a wealthy Christian general serving in Britain named Lupicinus, who had been sent from Gaul by the pagan emperor Julian in 360 CE to calm the unrest in Britain.

This hoard is believed not only to have been made during the fourth century but also to have been buried late in the century. The fourth century had been prosperous for Roman Britain, but as the century drew to a close the country came under threat of sea piracy from the Saxons and of raids from Pictish and Scottish marauders. Therefore, the Mildenhall Treasure should be seen in the context of hoards of a similar composition and date throughout the Empire that were hidden as danger approached and not recovered by their owners, who died or were unable to return.

population of the city before that was 500,000 to 1,000,000 inhabitants, not far off its height in the early to mid-empire. It probably halved after 410.

THE INFANT CEMETERY NEAR LUGNANO IN TEVERINA, UMBRIA

A remarkable discovery made in 1988 has helped to fill in the picture of what happened to Rome and the countryside northwest of it during the middle-fifth century CE. At a time when Rome was being sacked and crippled by the acts of foreigners, it was also being victimized by nature. About 3 miles outside of the town of Lugnano in Teverina, along the road to Attigliano, are the ruins of one of the largest villas yet found in Umbria, the spacious Augustan structure built around 15 BCE and overlooking the Tiber River (Figs. VII-20 to 23, Fig. XIII-20).

However the elegant villa had been founded on a shifting substratum which had rendered it useless by the middle of the third century CE. Its storage magazines and kitchen and service areas which had been built against the side of the hill known as Poggio Gramignano were turned into a large infant cemetery in the fifth century CE, the only plausible adaptive reuse for this vast hilltop ruin. What was surprising, though, was the nature of the cemetery which did not evolve over a long period but which instead had buried in it at least 47 infants over a short period of time. In the several meters of fill in the reused rooms the soil was found to be loose and uncompacted, the result of a quick filling up of the rooms, perhaps over weeks or a month.

At the bottom of the fill in the rooms were single burials while higher up were found paired burials and nearer to the top came groups of up to seven infants buried

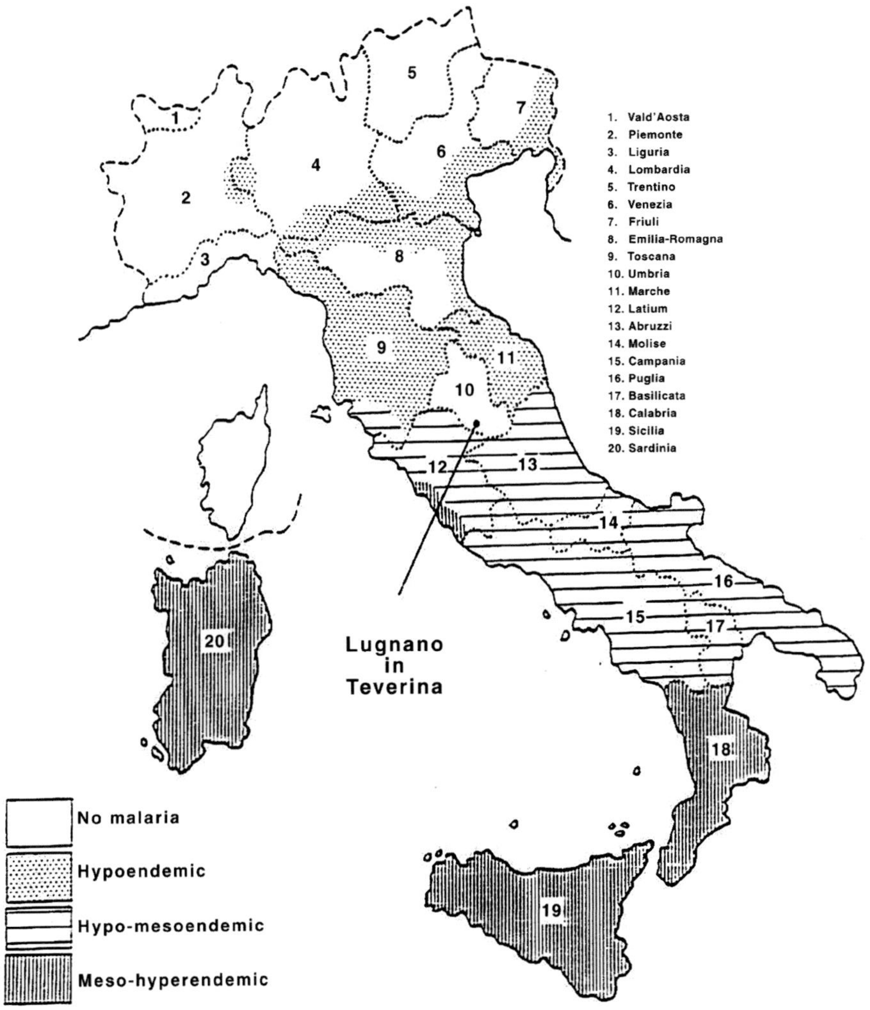

Fig. XIII-20 (top) Map showing the location of Lugnano in Teverina, Umbria in relation to areas sensitive to the development of malaria. Courtesy of Mario Coluzzi, Istituto di Parassitologia, University of Rome- La Sapienza.

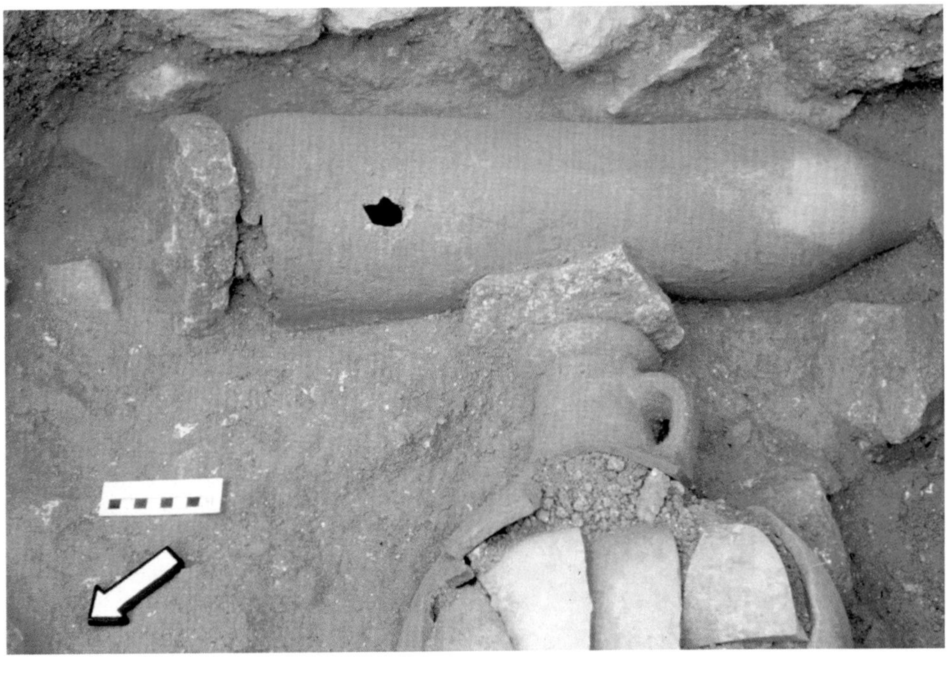

Fig. XIII-21 (right) Cluster burial of multiple infants within and outside of reused amphorae, from the infant cemetery at Poggio Gramignano, near Lugnano in Teverina, Umbria, Italy. Photo credit: Noelle Soren. University of Arizona School of Anthropology Archive.

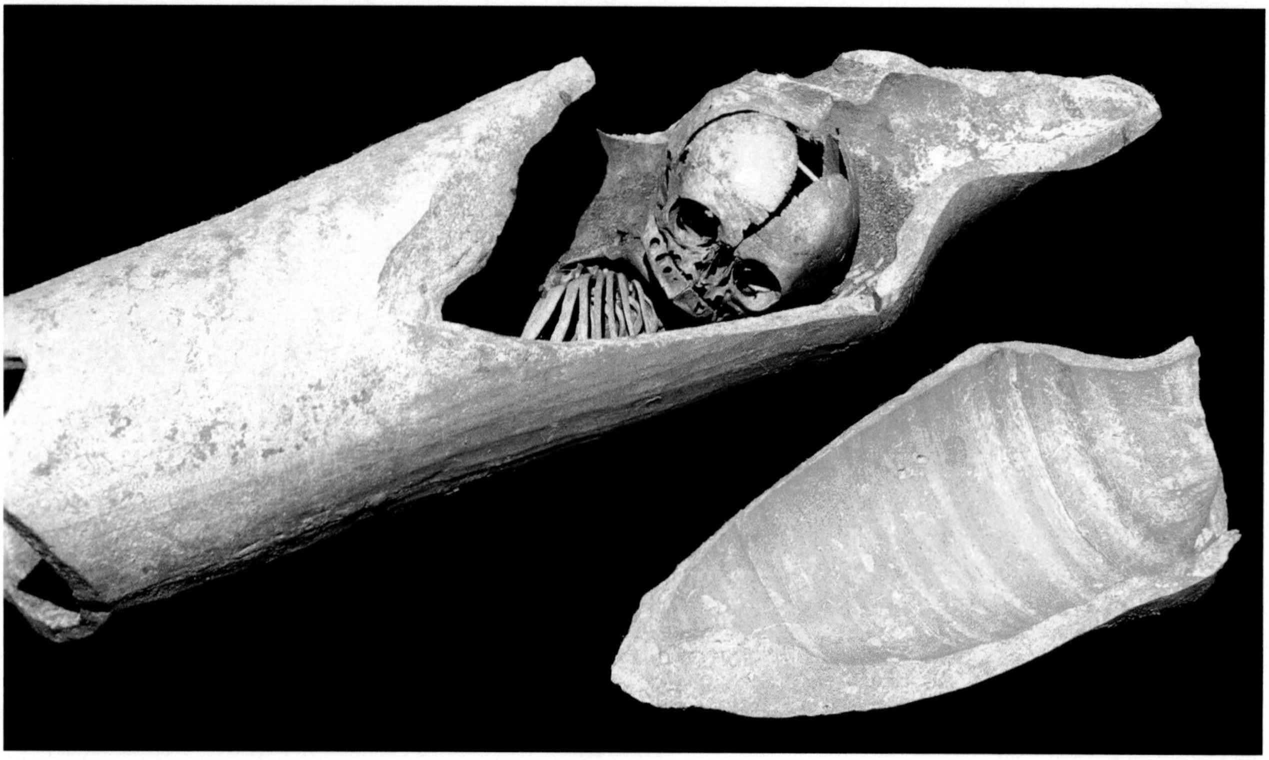

XIII-22 (above) Neonate burial at Lugnano in Teverina. Child reconstructed by Walter Birkby, Arizona State Museum Human Identification Laboratory. Photo credit: Noelle Soren. University of Arizona School of Anthropology Archive.

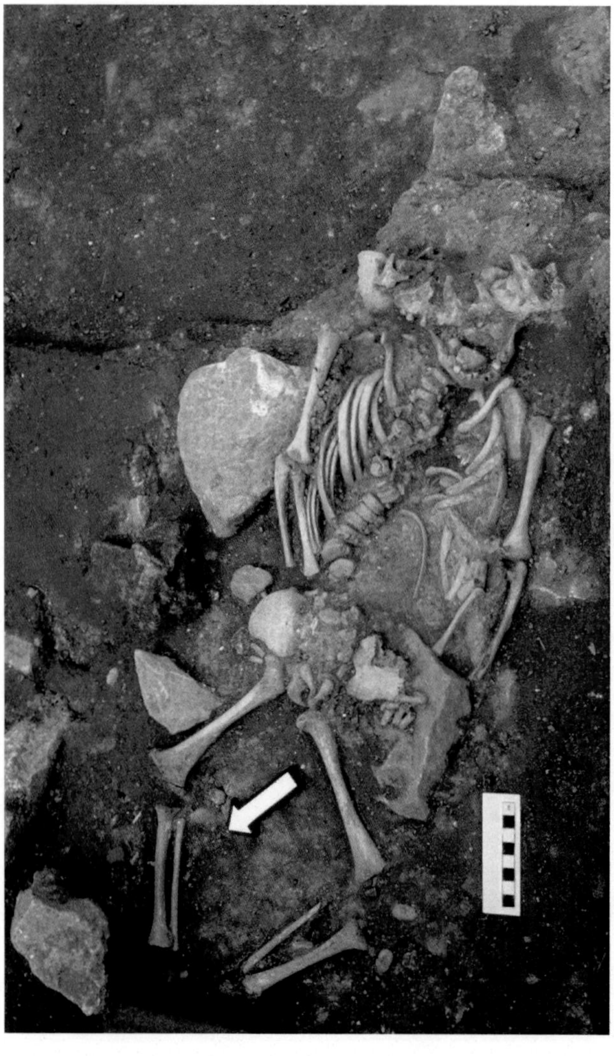

XIII-23 (left) Burial of two-to-three-year-old child at Lugnano in Teverina excavation. The infant had stones placed over the hands and a tile over the feet, apparently to prevent the child from rising after death. Photo credit: Noelle Soren. University of Arizona School of Anthropology Archive.

together at one time (Fig. XIII-21). This escalating pattern of burials intrigued the excavator who suggested that it might have resulted from an epidemic that had begun simply and then increased in deadliness over a short period of time. All of the burials were infants: aborted fetuses or neonates and a few up to five or six months of age. Just one child was 2 to 3 years old (Figs. XIII-22, 23).

No adults were found as it was typical in the fourth or fifth century to have deceased infants officially buried and yet separated from the adults. This may have been the result of a Christianized Roman Empire that required that infants be baptized and respected instead of simply discarded as Romans often did with unwanted, diseased, deformed or dead offspring. Death by drowning, exposure at crossroads or burial near their homes was common practice. No adult cemetery has yet been recovered at the Lugnano in Teverina excavation. For some reason, probably fear of contamination either physically or supernaturally, the children were isolated and buried far away from the living.

The children were arranged hierarchically. The youngest infants, including the aborted fetuses and neonates, were often all but discarded, buried along with trash swept in from the ruins of the Augustan villa, and given little in the way of formal offerings or constructed graves, although they were surrounded by puppies. Slightly older children tended to be buried in rooms away from the youngest children and were given slightly more elaborate graves, being buried within recycled roof tiles from the ruined villa or within amphorae (wine transport jars). The oldest child, 2-3 years, was found buried with sizable stones weighing down the hands and a big tile holding down the feet, as if those interring the child feared that it might rise from the dead to harm the living (Fig. XIII- 23).

Various scenarios were proposed to explain this cemetery and its victims who apparently died as the result of an epidemic. Medical and infectious disease specialists were consulted by the excavator with the result that several suggestions emerged. *Brucella* and *Listeria* are bacteria that can infect dairy products. *Toxoplasma gondii,* dangerous parasitic protozoa, could be found in uncooked red meat. All of these could cause aborted fetuses, but none would typically occur in an escalating manner, which was the case at the infant cemetery. Only one disease seemed to the excavator to fit the bill—*Plasmodium falciparum* malaria, commonly known as blackwater fever. A mosquito transmits the disease by drawing out parasite-tainted blood from one individual and depositing the parasites in another host. The parasite then invades the liver 8 to 12 days after the bite, and multiplies to hundreds of parasites that enter the blood stream, attacking red blood cells and invading them in a three- to four-day synchronized cycle. This process, which can clog capillaries and affect the kidneys and spleen, produces symptoms that initially include anorexia, headache and nausea. As the disease progresses, the individual experiences paroxysms (sudden outbursts of anguish), chills and fever, severe headache, nausea and vomiting, and severe gastric pain. The victim normally quickly develops an emaciated and gaunt appearance.

There may be tertiary symptoms, that is symptoms that occur in three-day cycles, or a daily fever. The victim is left anemic and weak, with an enlarged spleen. The disease can be fatal, especially when the blood vessels are occluded by masses of infected red blood cells. *Plasmodium falciparum* malaria can cause the intrauterine death of the fetus and may simulate *toxemia* or blood poisoning in the mother. The disease claims a few victims initially but can spread as an epidemic quickly, causing aborted fetuses. Independent studies by the Istituto di Parassitologia of the University of Rome La Sapienza directed by Mario Coluzzi indicate that this form of malaria was not common to Italy and may have been transported to this region from Africa by trade through Rome's harbor of Ostia and continued along the Tiber River to strike suddenly in epidemic form by Late Antiquity, likely in the middle of the fifth century CE as the excavation at Lugnano suggests.

Other forms of malaria such as *Plasmodium malariae* and *Plasmodium vivax* are not so severe and were known in parts of western Italy for centuries so that local populations could adapt to them, but this new strain, perhaps first reaching Italy intermittently from the second century CE on, could have been fueled by one particularly hot summer and the stagnating of Tiber River transport areas in Late Antiquity. New evidence from dendrochronological studies in the Mediterranean area indicate that this period demonstrated unusually wide ranges of climate fluctuation (known as decennial or 10-year fluctuations) so that an extraordinarily hot summer or several of them could have easily occurred.

The devastating epidemic that affected the people of the Lugnano area would have stunned the local community, and large numbers of aborted fetuses as well as unexpected and unexplained adult deaths must have caused strong local reactions. In such nominally Christian times, the local citizenry reverted to more traditional ways to combat their fear of evil: sorcery and black magic. With this idea in mind, the excavator conducted the excavations with a careful eye for even the smallest item that might have ritual significance among the burials.

Most curious was the finding of 13 puppies among the infant burials, all but one between five and six months of age. They showed evidence of being sacrificed, several revealing that the jaw of each had been ripped off in some bizarre rite and that one dog had been split in two at the midsection (Fig. XIII-24). Of course the power of puppies to dispel evil was well known not only to the Greeks and Romans but even from Hittite rituals that involved severing dogs to empower individuals or whole armies marching into battle.

Who were the divinities that these rural Late Antique Romans believed had caused the epidemic? We will likely never know exactly, but it could have been chthonic deities, *daemones* or spirits living below the Earth, rather than the traditional Roman gods such as Jupiter, Juno or Minerva. One burial featured a cooking pot containing bone scraps and was deliberately turned upside down, a

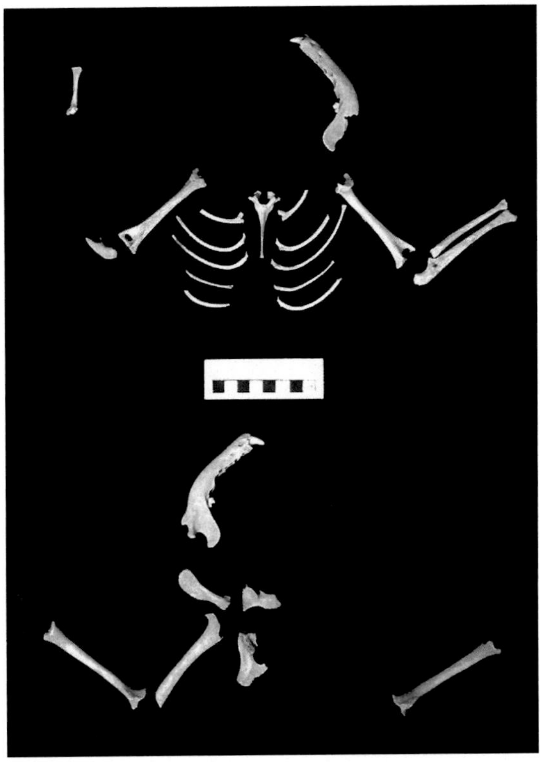

XIII-24- Five-to-six-month-old puppy found severed in two, from the excavations at the infant cemetery near Lugnano in Teverina. Photo credit: Noelle Soren. University of Arizona School of Anthropology Archive.

Fig. XIII 25a (above) & 25b (below) One of a pair of bronze cauldrons found one inside the other, from the infant cemetery near Lugnano in Teverina. Photo credit: Noelle Soren. University of Arizona School of Anthropology Archive.

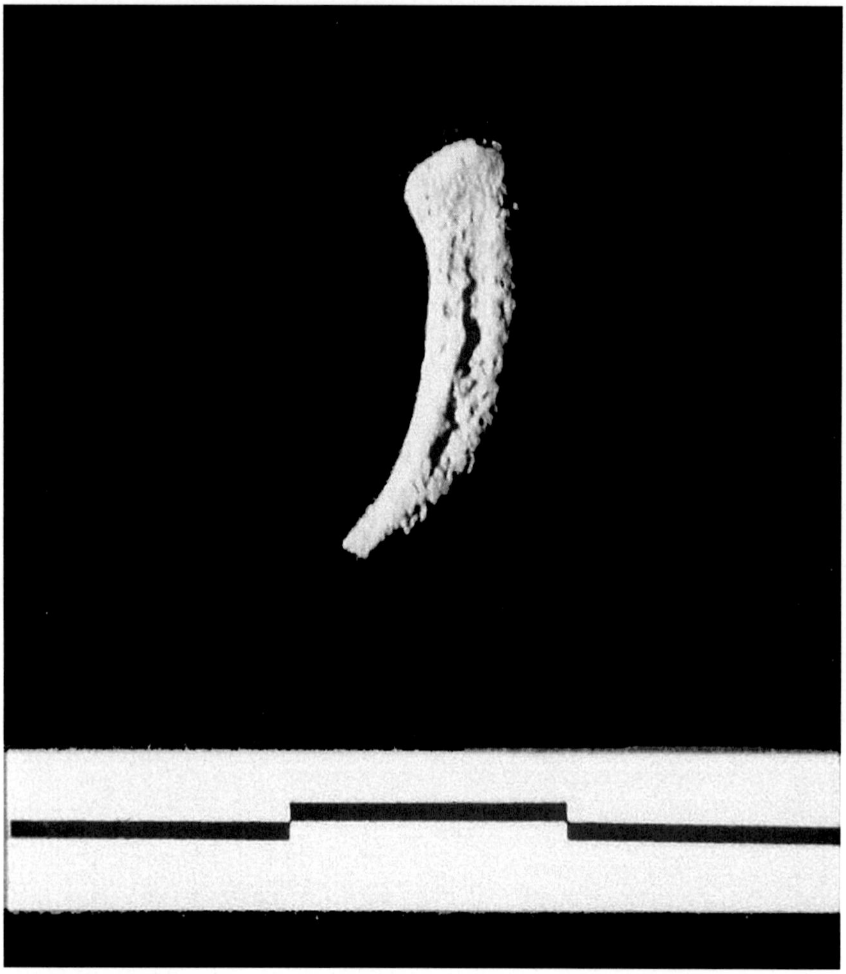

Fig. XIII 26a (above) Raven talon placed on a child burial, from the infant cemetery near Lugnano in Teverina. Photo credit: Noelle Soren. University of Arizona School of Anthropology Archive.

Fig. XIII 26b (below) *Lonicera caprifolia*, also known as goat-leaf or Italian honeysuckle. Photo credit: Videoblocks

gesture usually reserved for underworld gods. Two bronze cauldrons were also found, one stuck inside the other, and filled with ash, perhaps from offerings to ward off evil (Fig. XIII-25). These ritual practices would suit a divinity such as Hecate/Diana, mistress of darkness, whose consorts in magic rituals were puppies and dogs known as the hounds of hell. She was worshiped as one who watched over the souls of infants and aided their passage to the afterworld. Many other similar demon gods and goddesses existed whose names are unknown or unfamiliar to us. There was for example Geneta Mana, the birthing goddess, or the dog-loving Fury Tisiphone.

Symbols of witchcraft abound in the cemetery, and there may have been female and/or male witches, *sagae* or *magi*, brought into the site in antiquity to perform ritual ceremonies. One infant had a toad placed on its body, a well-known apotropaic and cure-all device that was cited by Roman writers such as Pliny the Elder for relieving the tertian or quartan fevers of a disease that seems to have been malaria. Another burial had a raven's talon, Virgil's popular talisman against evil (Fig. XIII-26a).

Apart from the objects commonly associated with black magic in the cemetery, another unusual offering was noted: a significant quantity of honeysuckle of the type known as *Lonicera caprifolia* (Fig. XIII-26b), the ancient *periclymenon.* Pliny cites it as a particularly useful cure for tertian or quartan fevers when taken for 30 days dissolved in white wine. Honeysuckle was also used as a cure for splenomegaly or enlarged spleen, a condition that can be caused by *Plasmodium*

falciparum malaria. The use of honeysuckle that blooms in the dead of summer suggests that the epidemic of Lugnano occurred in later July or August, prime time for a malaria epidemic. The presence of puppy offerings also contributes to this idea for Sirius, the dog star, rises and sets with the sun between July third and August 11th. The fevers found to occur in ancient Rome during this period—sometimes caused by simple heatstroke but sometimes due to various forms of malaria—no doubt left a person *astroboletos* (ἀστροβόλητος) or starstruck by the *dies caniculares* or dog days of summer. The summertime, the horrible season of the little dog (*atrox hora caniculae*), was frightening to the Romans who did not know what caused malaria but could recognize its effects.

The Lugnano excavation provided strong evidence that the infants of the area had been interred as a result of an escalating epidemic, posited to have been malaria, which had led to what is known to anthropologists as a revitalization movement or a desire to go back to earlier times to find possible magic practices that could relieve the community's grave problems. Black magic using assorted mystical paraphernalia was employed to try to restore normalcy. In a community without adequate modern medical care and with no mass media to reassure or provide information—no radio, television or newspapers—it is easy to see how panic would have quickly ensued and how radical, even officially unacceptable cures, might have been employed by desperate families. Furthermore, the Romans feared aborted, stillborn or short-lived infants because they believed that their souls could be used by *sagae* or *magi* to bring evil to the living.

The mothers of these infants were also likely to have been considered polluted because the Romans felt a strong need to purify themselves after a child was born. This feeling was even stronger if a child was born dead from a miscarriage, or had to be exposed. Therefore, ritual offerings had to be made. The Lugnano cemetery provides a rare and fascinating glimpse into such activities in the countryside north of Rome in Late Antiquity.

Following the excavations bone samples were taken and brought to Robert Sallares of the University of Manchester in England, an expert in DNA testing. Although the analysis of the youngest children revealed nothing and it was difficult to extract DNA from them, the older child, who was 2-3 years of age, had more substantial bones and produced positive results for *Plasmodium falciparum* malaria (Fig. XIII-23). Sallares further stated that such a find would not have been an isolated case and it was most probable that a malaria epidemic had been responsible for the strange deaths in the Lugnano cemetery. Mario Coluzzi's independent research has also shown that this deadly killer had been devastating to Late Antique Roman civilization particularly within certain susceptible zones that included the Maremma (swampy coastal area) of Tuscany and the area of the Tiber River Valley.

The Lugnano excavations also benefited from the studies of Frank Romer, who sought literary evidence that might coincide with the extraordinary archaeological results in the infant cemetery. Romer focused on Sidonius Apollinaris, an important Gallic nobleman who went south from Gaul to the city of Rome where he was going to take up his prefecture of the city in 468 CE. Heading into Italy, he crossed the Rubicon River and proceeded southwest on the Via Flaminia and soon began to feel sick and think that he was suffering from an illness that he blamed on either the Sirocco heat or the pestilential area of Etruria. He continued to the city of Rome showing symptoms of what we now know to be malaria. When he got to the city of Rome he was so thirsty he said he could drink an aqueduct dry because he did not dare stop at any of the unsafe watering holes along the way. Before entering the city he stopped at two churches to get divine help against what was almost certainly malaria and then he took up lodgings before going into the city so that he could recover from the periodic fevers besetting him.

Another piece of history that the archaeological investigations at the Lugnano infant cemetery may illuminate is the story of Attila the Hun's thwarted attack on Rome in 452 CE. It may not have been the persuasion of Pope Leo that prevented this potentially lethal enterprise but rather word of a devastating epidemic that stood in the way of the Huns. In any case an already crippled Rome had to face a bewildering and horrifying epidemic at its doorstep.

Attila, defeated the previous year in France in the Battle of the Catalaunian Plains, had intended to invade Italy at that time. However, he discovered that there was pestilence and disease of various kinds and hunger among his troops. He went back to his base across the Rhine River, and in 452 he headed to Italy, ravaging the north of Italy but also experiencing disease among his troops as he headed south. He got to the southern end of the Lago di Garda where an embassy came from Rome to warn him about what was happening in the southern areas. According to Frank Romer, there are two pieces of information that Attila received when he was at the southern end of the Lago di Garda. One of them came from the embassy from Rome which was headed by the bishop of Rome, Leo I, who gave him information about conditions in the south.

First, the famine of the previous year 451 had not fully ended and the grain production of Italy that year was not nearly normal because of the raids that Attila had already conducted in the north of the peninsula. Second, reports had come of a disease that had broken out in the south. Apparently, the information that Leo gave convinced Attila not to attack. At the same time Attila was told that the Byzantine emperor was landing troops to attack the Hunnic homeland, giving him another reason for not going further south. The story of Attila and Leo is yet another way in which archaeology and literary evidence can work together to discover the truth about conditions and events in ancient Italy.

The 450s and 460s were a critical time not only for Lugnano in Teverina and its surrounding area but also for Rome. The Vandals, an eastern Germanic tribe, who had already solidified their hold in North Africa, were affecting the grain supply from North Africa to Rome. They also had attacked Sardinia and Sicily, again probably with the Roman grain supply in mind since these were supply centers. By 455, after the threat of Attila had dissipated, Geiseric and the Vandals with their Berber allies sacked the city of Rome for two weeks and then suddenly left by the end of June. The end of June and the beginning of July marked the beginning of malaria season and malaria was well known to the Vandals and the Visigoths before them. It may be that the two-week period of ravaging Rome ended because the Vandals were afraid of the disease we now call malaria; they were likely well aware of how it was devastating this part of Italy. In any case, the Vandals had no intention of destroying the city of Rome or Roman civilization. In their new African homeland, they quickly took on a Roman lifestyle, and they incorporated their state into the power structure of the time. Their royal house even intermarried with the Imperial family at Constantinople.

Fig. XIII-27 View over Cuicul (Djemila) in Algeria. Photo Credit: Noelle Soren. University of Arizona School of Anthropology Archive.

A BEAUTIFUL CITY IN ALGERIA

Cuicul was founded by the emperor Nerva in 96-98 CE on a ridge between two wadis or seasonally active river beds (Figs. XIII- 27, 28). Its modern name, Djemila, means beautiful in Arabic and the striking vistas and lovely architecture of this ancient metropolis tell us why. In Roman times, Djemila was located in the province of Numidia on the main road to Mauretania to the west. Nerva decided to found the city to settle veterans from the third Augustan Legion as a reward for them as North Africa's pioneering pacifiers.

Fig. XIII-28 Roman theatre in Cuicul, Algeria. Photo Credit: Noelle Soren. University of Arizona School of Anthropology Archive.

With the area at peace, the town grew rapidly during the second century, featuring a colonnaded north-south main street (*cardo*) leading to a spacious porticoed forum, market, basilica, government buildings, *Capitolium* (Jupiter Temple), temples, and baths. Trade was essential to this area and a surviving inscription shows that the market was built by a wealthy Carthaginian merchant named Cosinius for 18,000 sesterces. One of the finest bath complexes in North Africa was built in the reign of Commodus (180-192), reminiscent of the elegant Baths of Trajan in central Rome. Three thousand spectators could come to the beautiful hillside theatre.

As was the case with many North African cities, Cuicul was embellished by the African-born emperor Septimius Severus with such elements as a new forum, later the site of a temple to the Severan family. Septimius Severus' son Caracalla continued this plan of building up the city by adding an arched gateway to the forum. Abundant houses dating from the second through fourth centuries CE reveal the wealth of the community. Elegant mosaics featured scenes from Greek and Roman mythology and from hunting forays, but most are of an elegant geometric quality that rivals nearby Timgad. One mosaic showing scenes from the life and rituals of Dionysus is a true masterpiece of the later second or early third century.

This paradise in a remote land could not continue forever. The third Augustan Legion ended its stay early in the fourth century and the Vandal invasions of the fifth century CE increased instability in the region, although Cuicul managed to continue to exist until at least the mid-sixth century CE at which time it received its last mention before disappearing into the sand to await the spade of the archaeologist.

Fig. XIII-29a Court of Emperor Justinian, c. 547 CE. Early Christian mosaic, 264 x 365 cm. Location: Church of San Vitale, Ravenna, Italy. Justinian appears in the center foreground. Photo Credit: Scala / Art Resource, N.Y.

ROME IN THE SIXTH CENTURY AND AFTER

By the early sixth century, after a sack by the Vandals in 455 which may not have been as devastating throughout the city as has often been suggested, as well as a siege by the Suevian king Flavius Ricimer in 472, Rome's population probably fell to a still considerable 100,000.

A decisive break in Rome came with the Greco-Gothic wars between 535 and 553 CE, which began when the emperor Justinian attempted to reassert control over Italy from Constantinople (Fig. XIII-29). Although the wars ended in a military victory for Justinian, this brought little lasting success. Nearly two decades of war up and down the peninsula created massive devastation. The interruption of the aqueducts was especially damaging—a branch of the Aqua Traiana on the Janiculum Hill, for instance, was found blocked on the premises of what is now the American Academy in Rome. Not only was the economy of Italy severely disrupted, but the Byzantines also lost control of most of the Italian peninsula within a few decades with the arrival of the Longobards. After that, the East maintained only some coastal enclaves, such as Rome and Ravenna, and for a time the route across the peninsula uniting them.

Adding to the woes of the Roman world in the sixth century CE was an event still not fully understood, which occurred in 536 and involved significant climate change. What the precise catastrophe may have been is uncertain but its effects are found throughout the world from the Americas to China. That the Roman world was also struck is documented by an eyewitness account left by the prefect of Italy for the Ostrogothic kingdom, Cassiodorus (Flavius Magnus Aurelius Cassiodorus Senator), one of the most learned men of his time. Cassiodorus was a Christian who nonetheless admired the degree of learning revealed in the reading of Greek and Latin works. Predisposed to seek empirical knowledge, he expressed considerable concern about a winter with no storms, a spring without a moderate temperature and a summer without heat. He was concerned about frozen fruits that never were able to ripen and extreme drought affecting the grain crop.

Scholars disagree on the cause of this sweeping natural disaster, with suggestions ranging from comet or asteroid impact to volcanic eruptions in the area of Krakatoa, west of Java. Whatever it was it likely fomented significant disorder and unrest, perhaps being responsible for the widespread displacement of peoples and the spread of disease through the increase or production of lifeforms that were not common to the environment previously.

Much research remains to be done with regard to the "Event of 536" and its aftermath, for it was not just a mega-event itself that caused hardship but the results of it that effected change for many years.

By the mid-sixth century Rome was inhabited by no more than a few tens of thousands of people, living in a patchwork of settlements over the area of the former metropolis. Their lack of feeling for the city as a whole entity is shown by the practice of burying the dead within the city limits, a practice that was unthinkable to the Classical mind. Finally, in 568 another Germanic people, the Longobards, took over most of northern Italy and the interior of the peninsula, leaving the greatly reduced city of Rome as an isolated outpost of the eastern Empire, along with various other places on the coasts. By this time the glorious civilization of Classical Rome survived only as a magnificent ruin.

THE END OF ROMAN ANTIQUITY

When did Roman antiquity end? The answer would have seemed obvious to generations of schoolchildren taught that the Roman Empire fell in 476 CE. Actually, it is impossible to give a simple answer. Indeed, the question is the theme of numerous recent books and conferences. Late Antiquity holds a fascination at a time when many scholars sense that our own society might be at the end of an era and transforming into something else. Scholars have proposed various dates separated by centuries.

The date of 476 marked the deposing of the last Roman Emperor in the West. He was, however, a puppet and a usurper. The matter had no relevance at all for the eastern half of the Empire, where there was no break in legal continuity. Even in the West it was a non-event to the people of the time. Those who were interested in such matters saw ultimate legitimacy residing with the sole surviving emperor in the East, while Germanic kings held actual political control much as they had for some time. The economy continued to function much as before, although by now the church had taken its place alongside the Senatorial elite as a major landholder and had assumed many of the functions of the state in guaranteeing food supplies and distribution in the major cities such as Rome.

Occasionally Diocletian's institution of the tetrarchic system in 293 is suggested as the turning point. That was indeed an important reform of the administrative system which had been inaugurated by Augustus, and it symbolizes the re-establishment of order after the turmoil of the third century. However, to consider that it marks a shift in civilization is certainly to give too much importance to political history. The time of Constantine is often considered an epochal change with dates selected such as 311 and 313 (the edicts of toleration of Christianity) or 330 (the creation of the new capital at Constantinople). A Constantinian cutoff even has official administrative backing in Greece today, where it is used by the government to mark the boundary of competence between the Classical and Byzantine archaeological services. The justification for a Constantinian date is of course religious and cultural—it marks an important milestone in the process that led to the Christian Middle Ages. There was, however, no corresponding change in the structure of the Roman world. The Empire continued to be administered much as it had been before. The economy continued to feature an aristocracy with estates and interests throughout the Empire. Material-culture specialists have shown now that there was no break in long distance trade, as evidenced in archaeological terms especially by pottery, which continued as before. Christian themes began to appear in art, craft and literature without, however, transforming them overnight.

Similar religious considerations have caused 391, the date of the emperor Theodosius I's decree closing all of the pagan sanctuaries, to be put forward. In general, the same objections can be made towards this date that were offered for a Constantinian one. In the case of the great pan-Hellenic Sanctuary at Olympia, research in recent years indicates that there was a peaceful and gradual transition to a country town in which recognizably Greco-Roman life continued until the end of the sixth century. There, the significant break came c. 600, when its Greco-Roman population abandoned the site and pagan Slavic settlers arrived.

Henri Pirenne suggested almost a century ago that antiquity ended only with the Muslim conquest of the Levant and the southern shores of the Mediterranean in the seventh century and the shift of European focus to the north under the Carolingians, leading to the break-up of the previous Mediterranean unity. His hypothesis seems justified, at least in part, by subsequent archaeological and historical research. It is generally accepted that an economic system going back to Roman Imperial times lasted into the seventh century at Rome, where pottery and amphora-borne goods were still imported from around the Mediterranean. Furthermore, documents in the papal archives also show a Mediterranean orientation which gives way only when the popes begin to look to the Carolingians rather than to the emperors at Constantinople as their main interlocutors. Recently it has been suggested that elsewhere, in particular in the East, the Muslim conquest marked less of a break in economic terms than has been thought and that the ancient way of life continued under Muslim rule for several generations after the conquest.

The answer to the question is that we should not look for any specific date that marks the end of Roman antiquity. That is especially true in dealing with archaeological evidence, which tends to bring out processes rather than events. In any case, civilizations cannot have a date of decease any more than they have a date of birth—no one could wake up one morning and say that Roman antiquity had arrived or departed. Even change that is rapid in historical terms takes place over one or even several human lifetimes. Furthermore, we can see that Roman antiquity disappeared at different times in different places and at different paces.

Change came earlier and more abruptly in outlying areas, whose Roman character depended more on the presence of the Roman army and administrative apparatus. For instance, we can say that Roman antiquity ended in southern Morocco in the late third century with the withdrawal of the troops under Diocletian and in Britain in the early fifth century, once again after the army left. In Britain there was very quickly little or nothing that recalled Rome—the incoming Saxons were pagans uninterested in the Roman way of life; the Celtic Britons maintained their Christian faith and some Latin literacy but not the urban culture that had been typical of the Romans.

The rest of the Western Roman Empire also underwent great, although somewhat less drastic changes during the fifth century. Roman political control disappeared everywhere, to be taken up mostly by Germanic warlords, who however unlike the Saxons were already or soon became Christians and were more receptive toward Roman ways. Nevertheless, socio-economic structures became much simpler. Much of the administrative apparatus

Fig. XIII-29b Italian postcard featuring famous monuments of Ravenna, including the Mausoleum of Theodoric, Ostrogoth king, c. 526 CE.

and institutions of the state disappeared. Urban life receded. Monetary circulation was greatly diminished where it survived. Long-distance trade continued mainly for luxury items. A literary education and even literacy itself became a matter for the clergy, while the aristocracy was militarized.

In Italy, the picture is more varied. The barbarian incursions in the early- and mid-fifth century created disruption. After 476, Italy was no longer under real Roman control (that is from Constantinople), although a polite fiction was maintained between the Eastern Roman Empire and Theodoric, the king of the Ostrogoths, in Italy. Rome kept its ancient character longer than many parts of the peninsula. Its population was greatly reduced from its high point in earlier centuries, but it was still supplied by maritime trade well into the sixth century. Some great families with their estates managed to survive the assumption of power by the Ostrogoths. The monuments of the city's great Imperial and Christian past were still there. More outlying parts of Italy were already taking on traits that look toward the Middle Ages, as in the contemporary West. The Greco-Gothic War between the eastern Roman Empire and the Ostrogothic Kingdom (535-554) devastated Italy. Soon afterwards, in 568, the Longobards took over most of northern Italy and the interior of the peninsula even in central and southern Italy, leaving only coastal enclaves under the control of Constantinople. Long-distance trade largely disappeared—by the late seventh century there is essentially no imported pottery in the ceramic record at Rome. Roman antiquity was well and truly past in its homeland.

In the East the ancient way of life lasted in general much longer. The eastern half of the Roman Empire did not succumb to the crisis of the fifth century, although most of the Balkan Peninsula, including Greece aside from some enclaves, was lost to the Slavs. Long-distance trade continued. Material culture, pottery in particular, shows no break until the seventh century or later. Important parts of the eastern Roman Empire, Syria and Egypt, were conquered by the Arabs in the seventh century. There, the administration continued, however, along previous lines and in the Greek language for several generations, and the material culture shows no break at the time of the conquest—life probably did not change much at first for the bulk of the population, especially since the Islamic conquerors were encouraged to live apart and mass conversion was not desired.

Much of the recent scholarship emphasizes the transformation of the Roman world rather than its fall, as earlier scholarship did. In so far as this tendency emphasizes processes, it is undoubtedly a positive development. One must not, however, lose sight of unpleasant realities. The arrival of barbarian hordes was not an enjoyable experience for most people, although slaves and other discontented sectors of the population could flock to them and others came to an accommodation with them. The unified Roman world that still existed at the beginning of the fifth century was fragmented. People could not travel easily and safely from one end of the Mediterranean to the other and beyond. No longer were needs fulfilled almost everywhere by goods produced by specialists working for distant markets. In many places, goods were produced locally or not at all—there are areas where the available pottery was technically less competent than it was before the arrival of the Romans or where production ceased altogether. The levels of competence in practically every field, from art and architecture to literacy, were lower than before. If not a fall of the Roman world, there was certainly a falling off in its transformation.

Fig. XIII-30 The Silver Amphora of Port Baratti. C. 400 CE. Photo Credit: Dan Duncan. Courtesy of Giandomenico De Tommaso and the Museo Archeologico del Territorio di Populonia (Piombino).

THE SILVER AMPHORA OF BARATTI

In 1968 near Porto Baratti in the region of Piombino, northwest Italy, a large encrusted object was hooked by an anchor from a fishing boat. The heavy vessel turned out to be a silver amphora, lacking its handles, and capable of holding 2.2 liters (74.4 ounces) of wine. Originally believed to be a Greek work of the later Classical Period, the ovoid vessel has been the special study of Giandomenico De Tommaso of the University of Florence and has been shown to have parallels with Roman silver vases found in Hungary and Moldavia which date to the later fourth or early fifth century CE (Figs. XIII-30, 31a and 31b).

Although it has been common to think of the Late Antique Period as a Christian time with limited artistic capabilities, the Baratti amphora proves that a high level of skill was still practiced in Late Antiquity and the images on the amphora are decidedly non-Christian. The precise method of doing the decoration is still being discussed, for the vessel contains 132 medallions which appear to have been impressed onto the surface and then had their details incised with a sharp instrument. There are two rows of six medallions on the neck, a row of eight medallions at the base of the neck and then seven rows of 16 medallions each on the body of the vase. The appearance is that of a simple vase studded with cameo-like images throughout its exterior.

The neck appears to contain images of the zodiac while at the base of the neck appear images of the seasons and parts of the world. Below this are festive dancers and musicians in a row on the upper shoulder beneath which is a spirited Dionysiac cortege. The third, fourth and fifth registers on the body appear devoted to images of traditional gods and goddesses; there is no Christian imagery. On the sixth register are again dancers and musicians and, at the bottom, scenes of Cupid and Psyche. De Tommaso interprets the vase as a message of joy and salvation, featuring the traditional gods of Greece and Rome along with Attis, Mithras and Cybele, all united now to bring happiness and blessings to the devotee. Cybele is given particular prominence as mother of the gods and she remained highly popular in Late Antiquity, being a special favorite of the Emperor Julian.

The overall message may be to honor the great gods so that the devotee will achieve eternal happiness, as exemplified at the bottom of the vessel by the Cupid and Psyche figures, expressing the

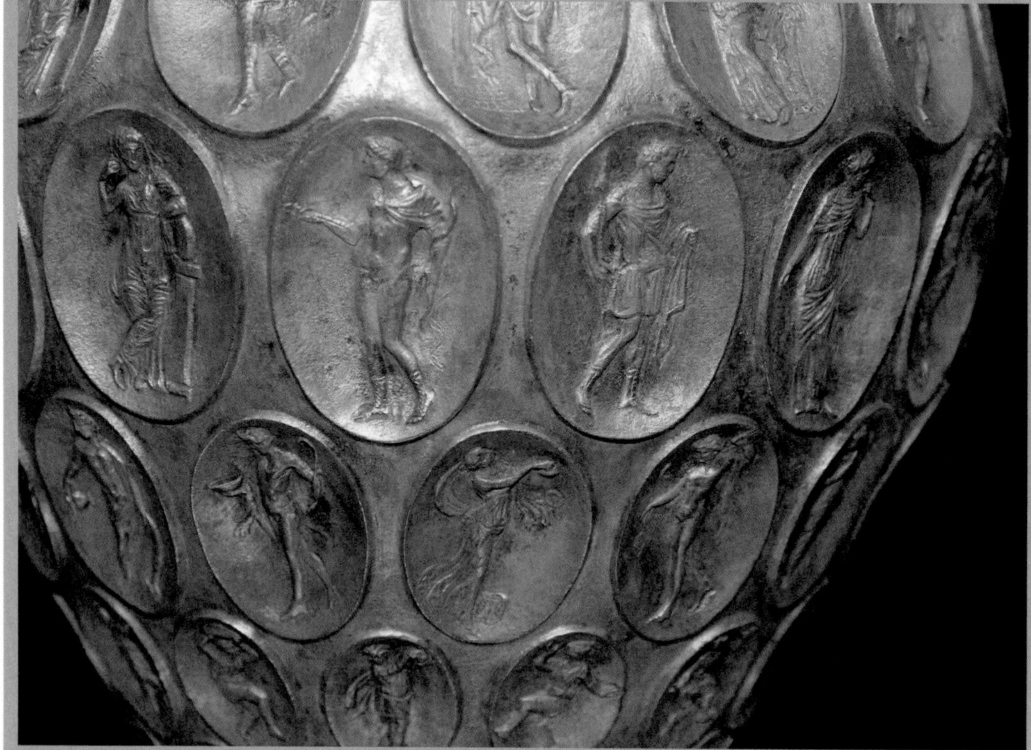

Fig. XIII-31a (keft) and 31b (above) The Silver Amphora of Port Baratti. Detail of the side and neck. Photo Credit: Dan Duncan. Courtesy of Giandomenico De Tommaso.

search of the spirit to find love and happiness. To achieve this harmony one must appreciate the harmonies of the universe, expressed numerically on this amphora. The 12 medallions on the neck may stand for the months. The four seasons also make their appearance along with the four parts of the Earth. They comprise the eight medallions at the base of the neck. The seven registers may parallel the seven stages of initiation in the cult of Mithras and seven is also the number of planets in the system of the cosmos of the Greco-Egyptian astronomer Claudius Ptolemaeus. The 16 figures per register may parallel the subdivisions of the universe of Ptolemaeus and the 132 total figures may represent the total regions of the world in antiquity. De Tommaso believes that, although one may question the identify of some of the figures, the vessel is intended to offer a hope for salvation through a particular cult, perhaps associated with Cybele, working in unison with a variety of other traditional divinities. The work may have been lost in an ancient shipwreck and was perhaps originally destined to be part of the collection of a wealthy devotee

CRITICAL THINKING EXERCISES

- 1. Why did the Tetrarchy fail?
- 2. Constantine the Great is sometimes depicted as a transformative Christian hero and sometimes as a ruthless and opportunistic murderer. What evidence is there for each view and how can they have been applied to one man?
- 3. The *Basilica Nova* is often considered to be the last great monument erected in the area of the Roman Forum. To what extent was it influential and unique?
- 4. Rome went from being the center of Roman power in the third century CE to a city rapidly diminishing in importance in the fourth century and finally to a town in the seventh century. Explain what happened to cause such a steep decline in only a few centuries.
- 5. Were the Vandals always destructive as they have been depicted in history? What was their role in the downfall of Rome?
- 6. When do Christian churches begin to dominate the religious landscape of Rome? How early does Christianity play a major role in Roman affairs?
- 7. The fourth through sixth centuries CE are known as a time of remarkable natural disasters. Is this really true or is it an ancient fabrication. If there were mega-disasters, what were they?
- 8. How successful was Justinian at rebuilding the ancient Roman world and what did he accomplish in revitalizing Italy?
- 9. Religion in the later Empire was a mixture of traditional and Christian practices. To what extent is this reflected in the Mildenhall Treasure and the Baratti Silver Vase?
- 10. In your opinion, when did the Roman Empire come to an end? Is there a particular date? Did it all happen everywhere at once?

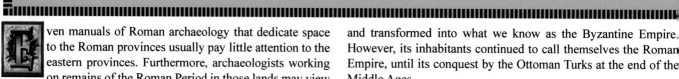

Chapter XIV
Greece in the Roman Period—The Evolution of a New Culture

Even manuals of Roman archaeology that dedicate space to the Roman provinces usually pay little attention to the eastern provinces. Furthermore, archaeologists working on remains of the Roman Period in those lands may view themselves as regional specialists first of all, with the consequence that they tend to be in dialogue with regional specialists of other periods more than with Roman archaeologists working elsewhere in the Empire.

This can lead to paradoxical situations. For instance, no handbook of Roman archaeology fails to mention the Arch of Titus, but few, if any, discuss the archaeological evidence of the Jewish War (such as the remains at Masada), which it commemorates. Likewise, religious monuments of the western provinces, even ones concerned with indigenous deities, are normally mentioned, while Egyptian temples of the Roman Period or the Temple in Jerusalem, built at the time of Augustus, are not. In the Classical Greek lands the Roman Period was traditionally neglected or considered as an appendix to the glorious preceding periods. As recently as 2011 the long-time director of the German excavations at Olympia could write in a book on the site that there was little of interest from the Hellenistic Period onward, after the end of the independent Greek city-states.

This lack of attention to the eastern provinces would probably surprise a Roman of the Imperial Period. He would stress the cultural unity that allowed him to feel at home from the Levant to Britain. It is true that the *lingua franca* of the eastern provinces remained Greek and that other languages also survived (such as Aramaic and Egyptian). Latin was known mostly in the army or through the study of Roman law. This linguistic situation was less of a hindrance than might be thought today. For centuries an educated Roman had been expected to be well-versed in the Greek language and literature, and a more practical mastery of the Greek language was widespread lower down the social scale at Rome and elsewhere in the Latin-speaking provinces. Furthermore, by the Imperial Period a Roman was by no means necessarily someone born and raised by the Tiber or the descendant of such a person. More and more provincials, including eastern ones, gained Roman citizenship. It was not until Emperor Caracalla's *Constitutio Antoniniana* edict of 212 CE that citizenship was given to all free inhabitants of the Roman Empire.

St. Paul is said to have proclaimed: "*civis Romanus sum*" (I am a Roman citizen) and thereby availed himself of the right to be judged at Rome. At the end of the second century, not only could the emperor, Septimius Severus, be North African, but the Imperial family could have strong ties to Syria through his wife, Julia Domna, the daughter of the hereditary high priest of Emesa (modern Homs). Thus, the inhabitants of the eastern provinces were just as much Romans as those of the western ones. Finally, the eastern provinces were, generally speaking, the most developed and richest part of the Empire. They also managed to survive the crisis of the fifth century, when the western half of the Empire collapsed. Although the eastern half lost important parts (Syria and Egypt to the Arab conquests in the seventh century and most of the Balkans to Slavic penetration), the Eastern Roman Empire lasted and transformed into what we know as the Byzantine Empire. However, its inhabitants continued to call themselves the Roman Empire, until its conquest by the Ottoman Turks at the end of the Middle Ages.

Elsewhere in this handbook reference is made to the eastern provinces of the Empire. This chapter focuses on examples of the archaeological record of the eastern provinces, taking advantage of work carried out in recent decades that allows a picture of the Roman Period there to be drawn up. Research into the Roman Period in the modern country of Greece (comprising the Roman provinces of Achaea and parts of several others) illustrates how one region, with an ancient cultural heritage with which the Romans identified, reacted to incorporation into the Roman Empire. Outside that region but in a culturally related and neighboring province, Ephesos gives insight into how a city functioned in the Roman Empire. Another eastern province, Egypt, shows the particularly complex situation of a country that was the seat of a 3000-year-old civilization, exotic to the Romans, and also hosted one of the major centers of the Greek East, Alexandria. Thus, the eastern provinces were an integral part of the Roman world. The Roman Period there forms an important slice of their history, and the tale of the impact of their incorporation into the Roman Empire is likewise an integral and important part of Roman history.

INTRODUCTION TO GREECE IN THE ROMAN PERIOD

Greece is probably the country in the eastern part of the Roman Empire whose Roman archaeology is best known. This is ironic, because, as we have seen, the Roman Period was long the unwanted stepchild of archaeological research there. Greek and foreign archaeologists focused much more on other periods—first the Classical Period with the Archaic Period that led up to it; then, with the discovery of the Minoans and Mycenaeans, the Prehistoric Period, and finally, the Byzantine Period. Rodney Young, the distinguished Near Eastern archaeologist and president of the Archaeological Institute of America, once defined Roman archaeology in Greece as "what you have to dig out of the way to get down to interesting things." But times and opinions have been changing.

Modern thinking sees investigating social evolution and the development of a given territory as the proper task of archaeology. We no longer seek to highlight a succession of moments of glory (such as "the Golden Age of Athens") while passing over other dark times. Roman archaeology in Greece has come into its own now and it is no longer possible to think of the Roman Period as a time of foreign oppression—it is rather an important period of transformation that permitted the transmission of Classical culture to the Byzantine world.

A new culture more suited to the conditions of a province in a worldwide Empire emerged from the Classical heritage of the independent city-states of Classical Greece. The Romans obviously had interests in Greece, which evolved over time. At first they were drawn into the area as one of the neighboring players in Hellenistic politics. After the conquest of Greece in the second century BCE and the civil wars of the first century BCE that preceded the establishment of the Roman Imperial system, the Greek lands became a part of the peaceable interior of the Empire. For the Romans, Greece was the land of sacred myths and the home of a culture with which they identified and from which they borrowed so much, even though they disdained the Greeks' supposed effeteness and tendency toward fractious (often democratic) politics. It was not, however, merely a question of the Romans promoting their interests, but also of the Greeks employing strategies to further their own ambitions in the realities of the times. A look at Roman Greece overall and at some of its important sites will allow us to see some of the curious interaction that took place.

THE BACKGROUND

Greece entered into the world of Roman political activity because of a conflict of interests with Macedonia in Illyria toward the end of the third century BCE. Rome encroached more and more, until it finally incorporated Greece into the Roman state in 146 BCE (Fig. XIV-1). At first the entire Hellenic peninsula was a single province with its capital at Thessaloniki in Macedonia. This was largely a land of cities, although some of the western and northern regions were only recently or lightly urbanized. The cities of the province varied in their official status, mostly because of their behavior during the wars of conquest and then during the subsequent civil wars. Some were formally free, allied cities, while others had lesser rights or paid tribute. There were also cities that had the status of Roman colonies. Between the reigns of Augustus and Vespasian, in the later first century BCE and the later first century CE, Greece was reorganized several times, until in the final arrangement the Peloponnese and the southern mainland constituted a separate province called Achaea under Senatorial control, Macedonia remained a major province under direct Imperial control extending as far south as Thessaly, and Epirus (modern northwestern Greece and southern Albania) made up a third province, which was also under direct Imperial control but of lesser rank. Crete was joined with Cyrenaica in North Africa to form another province, which was Senatorial with its capital at Gortyn not far from the southern coast of Crete. The Greek islands off the Aegean coast of modern Turkey belonged to the province of Asia, one of the most important ones under Senatorial control.

During the first century BCE, Greece was involved in several wars and never knew any long period of peace. In the First Mithradatic War (89-84 BCE), Mithridates VI, the king of Pontus, near the Black Sea, attempted to expel Rome from the East. Many Roman citizens, who had settled in Greece, were massacred and a number of cities (including Athens) were laid waste. Destruction layers from the general Lucius Cornelius Sulla are a fixed point in the archaeological record there, known to every archaeologist working in this period of time. Even when wars took place farther east, Greece was still unsettled by the passage of the armies through their land. Finally, the civil wars that marked the end of the Roman Republic in the first century BCE were fought to a large extent on Greek soil.

The reign of Augustus marked the beginning of a period in which Greece was little involved in the high politics of the Roman Empire. Among Augustus' activities in Greece was the foundation of two cities: Nicopolis and Patras. The first, located near the site of his victory over Cleopatra and Marc Antony and named "Victory City" to commemorate it, was formed by the synoecism or fusion of formerly separate settlements of a large part of northwestern Greece. It was created as an allied city (*civitas foederata*) and thus was a Greek city considered to have most favorable status. Patras was, on the other hand, a Roman colony created for military veterans. In Macedonia other cities were refounded as colonies at this time.

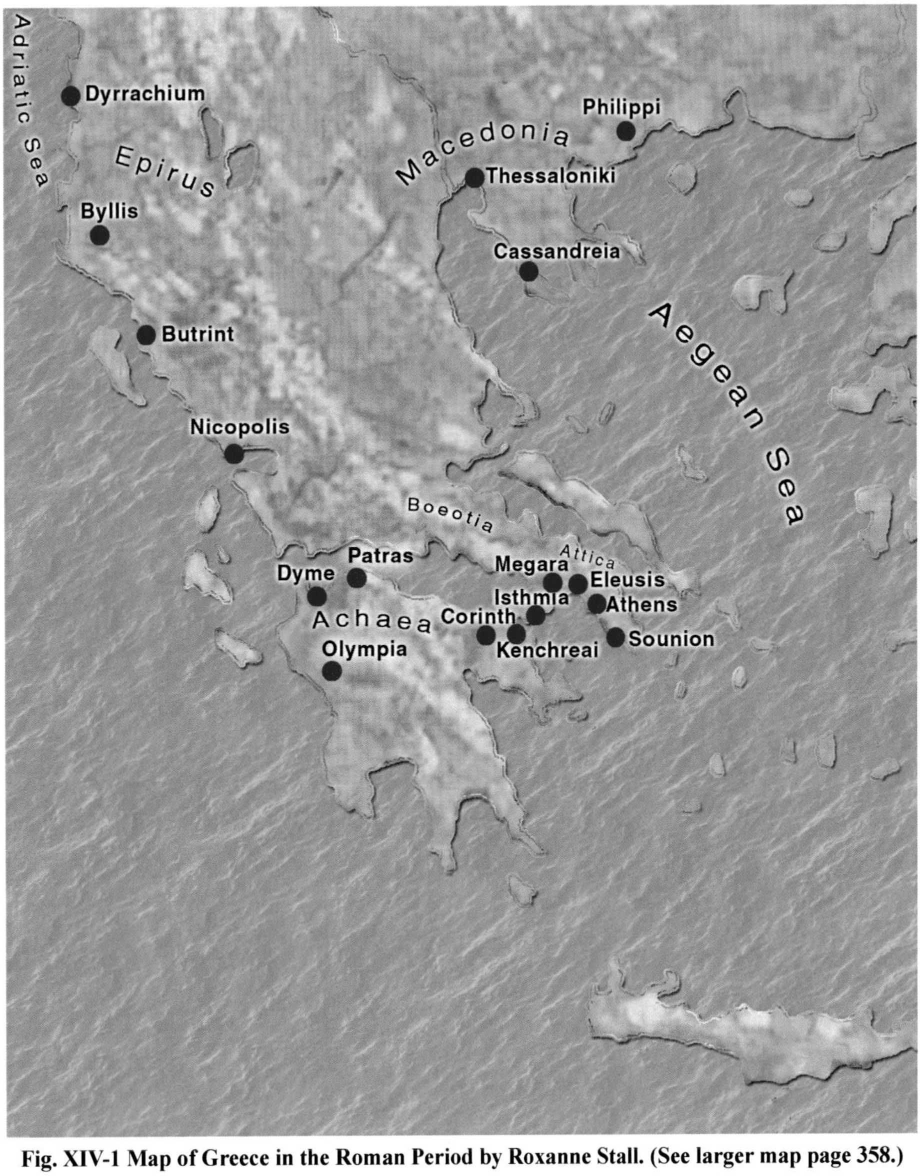

Fig. XIV-1 Map of Greece in the Roman Period by Roxanne Stall. (See larger map page 358.)

Fig. XIV-2 Plan of ancient Athens showing major monuments and walls. Courtesy of John Camp and the American School of Classical Studies in Athens / Athenian Agora Project. (See larger map page 359)

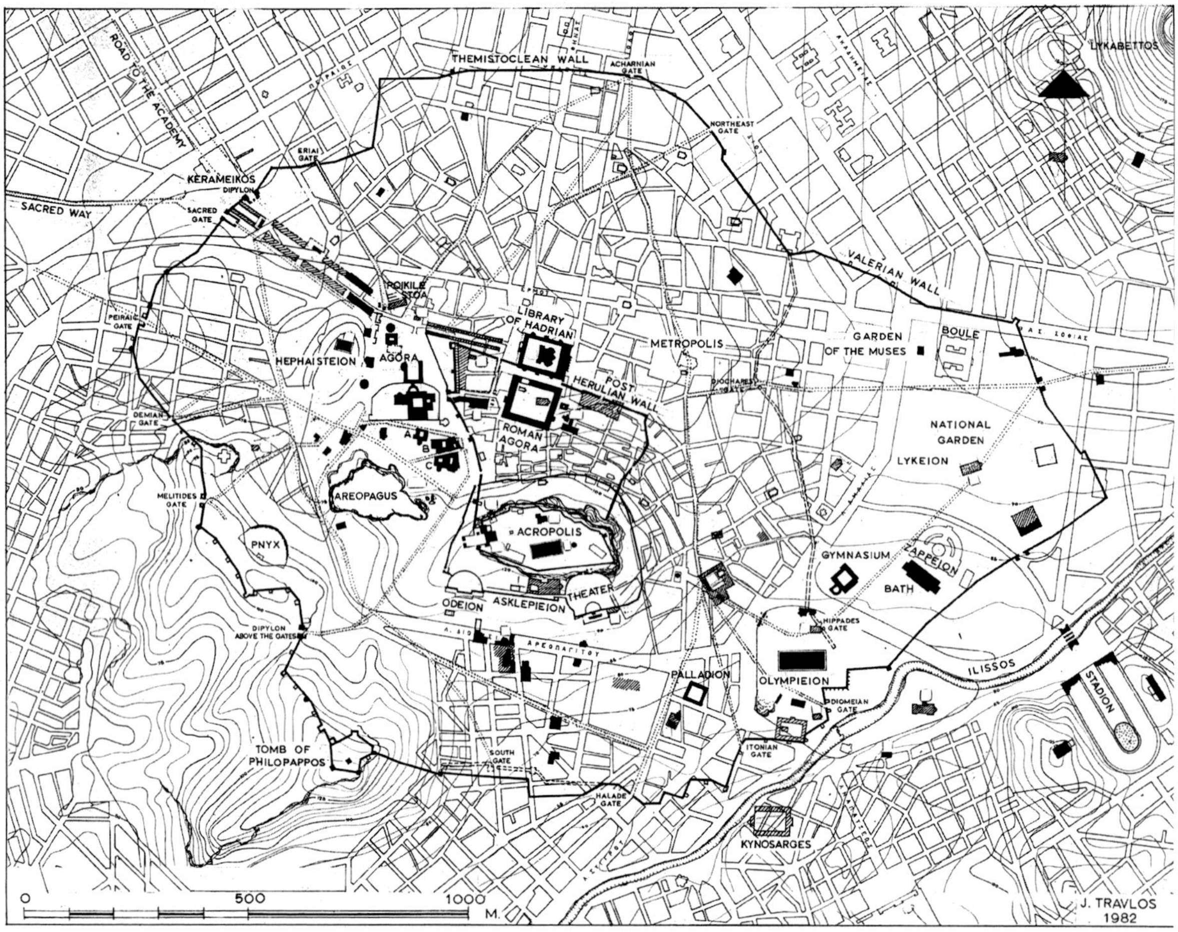

Among later emperors, Nero expressed special interest in Greece. After the great fire of 64 CE in Rome, he removed many works of art to decorate his rebuilt capital. Then he traveled through Greece in 66 and 67, participating in various games, including a specially proclaimed session of the Olympic Games. He also ordered the cutting of a canal across the Corinthian Isthmus. This project proved to be too great a task but its completion became one of the achievements of 19th-century engineering.

Hadrian, ruling from 117 to 138 CE, was the greatest philhellene emperor. He made several trips to Greece, and showed a strong interest in renewing Greek institutions. He also undertook various building projects, including the completion (after seven centuries) of the huge temple of Olympian Zeus in Athens near the Acropolis, a sizable library complex (actually an ancient cultural center for Athens) and an arched gateway marking the passage from old Athens to his new city.(Fig. XIV-2,10)

In the late second and third centuries CE, Greece was threatened several times by Germanic hordes who penetrated from beyond the borders of the Empire. In this atmosphere of increasing insecurity, the defenses of the cities were renewed, as was the defensive wall across the Isthmus of Corinth. Archaeologically the most important of these invasions came in 267 with the Herulians, who sacked various cities in the heart of Greece, including Athens. This event and the measures taken afterward mark another horizon in the archaeological record.

Under Diocletian and Constantine at the end of the third and beginning of the fourth centuries came the first reforms of the provincial administration of Greece, as a part of the reorganization of the whole Empire, since the first century. The three former provinces were replaced by Macedonia with its capital at Thessaloniki, Thessaly with its capital at Larissa, Achaea with its capital at Corinth and Epirus vetus with its capital at Nicopolis. Crete, which previously had been joined administratively with Cyrenaica in modern-day Libya, became a province unto itself. During Constantine's reign, these five provinces together with the provinces farther north on the Balkan Peninsula constituted the Illyrian prefecture, whose first capital was at Sirmium (slightly to the west of modern Belgrade).

In the later fourth century Greece was touched by the wars against a Germanic tribe known as the Goths, which soon separated into two tribes, the Visigoths and the Ostrogoths. In 375/376 CE the Visigoths crossed the Danube under pressure from the Huns. At first they sought protection but soon began to act as invaders, who were joined by individuals disaffected from the more oppressed sectors of the local population. During the next 20 years and in spite of attempts by the Roman authorities to contain them, the Visigoths made various incursions, reaching as far as the Peloponnese under their king and former soldier in the Roman army, Alaric.

The end of the Roman Empire in Greece is difficult to define. A major factor in this is the question of the legal continuity between Rome and Constantinople, with the continuity in life and culture this represents. In fact, the Byzantine Empire stood in direct succession to the Roman Empire and always referred to itself as such rather than using the name modern historians have bestowed upon it, which derives from Byzantium, the name of the city existing on the site of Constantinople at the time of the foundation of the new capital.

Probably the greatest break occurred between the end of the sixth and the seventh centuries with the Slavic invasions, a point which arouses modern Greek nationalistic attention. Written sources indicate that large parts of Greece, including most of the Peloponnese, were lost to Byzantium until the ninth century and were occupied by Slavs. Some cities on the coasts, such as Thessaloniki and Athens, and islands remained in Byzantine hands and served as starting points for the re-Hellenization of the rest of Greece later in the Middle Ages. The archaeological record confirms this picture, with important breaks or changes in material culture in various places and the near-disappearance of coins in the Peloponnese between the mid-seventh and ninth centuries.

THE GREEK COUNTRYSIDE IN THE ROMAN PERIOD

How prosperous Roman Greece was has been a much debated question. Until recently, it was possible to draw a picture of the condition of the primary sector of the economy of Roman Greece only though the written sources. These present various problems. First of all, none of them derives from specifically economic texts, which of course did not exist in antiquity. Then, the texts often have political or moral intentions or use literary effects contrary to a dispassionate and factual discussion of the question. They may repeat commonplace ideas that may no longer have been true (if they ever were). Furthermore, ancient written sources invariably reflect the concerns of the higher and more urban sectors of society. The picture drawn on this basis, especially for Achaea, was one of a devastated, under-populated and poor countryside following the troubles of the first century BCE and lasting for a long time afterward.

A rarely posed historical question concerns landownership and changes in it between the Hellenistic and Roman Periods. Traditionally it was thought on the basis of the mention of various calls for land redistribution and the cancellation of debts that landownership must have been concentrated in fewer hands in the Hellenistic Period even before the arrival of the Romans. More recently there has been a tendency to believe that the argument for a massive restructuring of landownership goes too far. The main effect of the coming of the Romans is considered to have been a strengthening of the position of the local elites that were favorable to the Romans and favored by them and a consequent worsening of the position of the poorer citizens now that there was no need to maintain armies made up of smallholding citizens.

By the 1990s there were results from a sufficient number of survey projects in Greece for archaeology to be able to shed light on the question of the condition of the countryside in Roman times. They range from systematic projects that investigate a region intensively to less intensive but still systematic projects and finally to unsystematic projects that can still offer useful information and comparisons.

A similar picture emerges in the data from every one of the sufficiently detailed projects. Between the late Classical and early Hellenistic Period the Greek countryside was characterized by many dispersed small sites, generally interpreted as farms. In the late Hellenistic and early Roman Periods there is a drop, often drastic, in the number of sites occupied. After this initial drop the number of Roman sites remains essentially unchanged for centuries, even if there are signs of recovery in some regions in the second or third centuries CE. Finally, in Late Antiquity, there is a return to a situation similar to that before the late Hellenistic/ early Roman drop.

In order to determine what this sudden drop in the total number of sites means, we must first consider the continuity in the occupation of the sites. High levels of continuity are consistent with stability in landownership. On the contrary, a low level of continuity together with a good percentage of newly founded sites can indicate a change in the ownership and use of land. It is precisely this that occurs in Greece in the Hellenistic and Roman Periods. These archaeological survey results suggest that the influence of the Romans and their conquest of Greece caused a major upheaval and a redistribution of economic resources.

In interpreting the archaeological data site by site, it is also necessary to look also at the size of the sites that disappear or survive. Compared to the Classical Period, the Roman Period sees a distinct decrease in the percentage of sites of 0.3 hectares (one full hectare is c. 2.47 acres) or less in extent and an increase in larger ones. It is reasonable to attribute the former to the centers of smallholdings on which live owners who cultivate them intensively. Therefore, a reduction of this category is to be supposed, presumably in favor of the two extremes of the social range connected with the nucleated (clustered) settlements—the poorest, who could not survive without the solidarity of their neighbors, and the richest, who wanted to enjoy the pleasures of city life.

It remains to examine the larger sites, which could be either aggregations of nucleated smallholders or else the centers of large properties. Here the characteristics of the sites help. First of all, places with architectural elements of a certain level (columns, walls made of stone blocks, towers) can be termed "elite sites" or sites of considerable social pretension. Villa sites, which combine these elements along with others such as mosaics and wall paintings to create stately homes, are clearly identified with the elites, and form the centers of large agricultural estates. An example is the villa at Loukou in the Peloponnese, attributed to the patron of the arts and philosopher Herodes Atticus because of the discovery of portraits of him and his family. This villa even had its own aqueduct to supply water. It is only one of several villas that this wealthy Roman Senator of Greek origin with connections to the Imperial family is known to have possessed. Thus, it is possible to see that a certain number of large sites associated with the elites dominated a relatively empty countryside. This ostentation was a new development in Greece, where economic inequalities had tended to be masked rather than flaunted in earlier times.

The archaeological evidence offers, therefore, an independent confirmation of the picture drawn from the written sources of the early Roman Period in Greece: a shift from a number of holdings adequate to maintain a citizen of modest means in favor of a smaller number of larger estates. Furthermore, the archaeological data show the validity of these conclusions for a wider area than the written sources allow. The same picture appears, in fact, in places that are different in their environment and political conditions. It must have been determined by large-scale transformations in the social and economic conditions and not by local factors. This is how contemporary archaeology attempts to draw a picture of how an ancient society really lived and what its day to day experience was like; if we use archaeology in an holistic manner we can ask and possibly answer a variety of questions, which is much more insightful than simply using archaeology to unearth beautiful objects and display them.

It remains to ask how land was used in Roman Greece. Normally greater resources are demanded from an area that becomes a subordinate part of an Imperial entity. This demand can be satisfied in two ways: through agricultural intensification (that is, through maximizing gains from traditional cultivation with a greater use of labor) or through specialization in cultivations of high value. The written sources speak, however, of the abandonment of agricultural land and desolation, and we have seen that a settlement scheme was established in Greece that does not fit with intensive use of the land. Furthermore, marginal land that had been used in the Classical Period was no longer cultivated in the late Hellenistic and Roman Periods, when there was a concentration on the best land. Finally, where it is possible to observe, there is a drop not only in the smaller rural habitation sites but also in the dispersed distribution of artifacts in the countryside, of the sort that could indicate the presence of villagers coming out to work the land. These data suggest the creation of large estates capable of supporting their owners in a suitably high style even without being exploited fully, perhaps with a greater reliance on animal husbandry i.e., the breeding and raising of livestock.

To sum up then, it appears that the Roman intervention favored concentrating economic resources in the hands of a wealthier layer of society that represented their interests in Greece. The evidence also shows that the expropriated and even the remaining smallholders preferred or, more likely, had to live in the nucleated settlements, which provided the possibility of alternative employment, supplied ties of solidarity among peasants, and offered charity from the powerful. The low level of exploitation of the land during the first centuries of the Roman Empire can also be explained by the lack of pressure to supply armies. Greece was also relatively free from the demands of the state welfare system in Rome (the *annona*). So the central Roman power preferred simply to satisfy the sector of local society through which it ruled.

For Late Antiquity we are not so well informed through written sources as before, nor is there the same sort of archaeological synthesis available. Nevertheless, various studies give a picture of surprising prosperity.

It has been noted that the very sparse occupation of the countryside between the late Hellenistic Period and the early Roman Period contrasts not only with the previous scheme of the Classical and early Hellenistic Periods but also with the late Roman Period. The reports on various survey projects underline the reappearance at that time of a settlement pattern similar to what there had been before the arrival of the Romans. It has also been remarked that many Classical-Hellenistic sites were reoccupied in Late Antiquity.

Aside from the survey projects, there is other evidence for a renewed interest in the countryside from c. 300 CE. In Attica, for example, traces of occupation exist in various areas, from Sounion in the east to the border with Megara in the west, as well as in caves and hilltop sanctuaries and in the mountains between Attica and Boeotia.

Various explanations have been advanced for this renewed Late Antique settlement activity in the Greek countryside. In some cases the reasons have nothing to do with the economy. For instance, the interest in hilltop sanctuaries could have come about because of the pressure from Christianity and the desire to continue pagan cults without being obvious. It seems that the reoccupation of some key points controlling access to the Attica plain from Boeotia depend on the desire to defend the territory. Nevertheless, there can be no doubt that the majority of the Late Antique sites were occupied or reoccupied for economic, and specifically for agricultural reasons. This is often considered to be related to the changed political situation of the late Empire. First of all, the foundation of Constantinople opened new possibilities and a need for the exploitation of the countryside. On the one hand, Constantinople offered an important new market for the products of the eastern Mediterranean, which must have been a direct stimulus to production. There is some evidence that the southern Argolis (in the eastern Peloponnesus) was interested in the production of oil for export. On the other hand, the market of Constantinople would have attracted trade toward itself, leaving other regions to cope with their requirements more autonomously, so that Constantinople acted also as an indirect stimulus. It is also possible that barbarian attacks and occupation of some western areas, which like North Africa had previously been large exporters, may also have created more opportunities for local production.

The examination of the ceramic record offers another view of the economic condition of Roman Greece with respect to survey projects. In many parts of the Roman Empire, major standardized productions of fine ware were established. In a first wave, the inspiration came from Italian *sigillata*; then in the later first century CE the model came from North Africa. It is undoubtedly significant that there was no example of this phenomenon in Roman Greece, where at most there were productions of local importance in import substitution (e.g., at Athens and apparently at Patras) but no substantial fine ware production. This contrasts with the province of Asia, which supported several centers of production of widely exported, standardized fine ware.

Some parts of modern Greece gave rise to the large-scale export of amphora-borne goods in Roman times. The eastern Aegean Islands, which had been important exporters of wine in the Hellenistic Period, maintained a presence on the markets in Roman times with well known amphorae, and Cretan wine containers are widely attested from the early Imperial Period onward. These areas can be considered peripheral—the eastern islands belonged to the province of Asia, which also had important centers of export on the mainland, and Crete was less associated with the Greek mainland than with North Africa, where the other part of the province to which it belonged was located. No such production is known for the core of Roman Greece. Centers for the production of lamps that developed their own traditions can be cited for Corinth and Athens, favored no doubt by a general tendency for a more dispersed production of these fragile objects that did not lend themselves particularly well to being packaged for transport. As everywhere, the normal range of domestic vessels was produced locally. The picture drawn from the ceramic evidence for Roman Greece is, therefore, one of a less dynamic region than, for instance, its Asian neighbor.

CITIES IN ROMAN GREECE

The countryside in Roman Greece seems to have been relatively empty, suggesting a preference for living in nucleated or concentrated settlements. What was urban life like in these settlements? Two aspects were particularly important: the relationship between the cities and the country and the role of the cities in the new provincial and Imperial structure.

In considering the relationship between cities and country, it is necessary to see what evidence there is for greater nucleation as the preferred residential choice. Urban survey, the best tool for the purpose, gives contradictory results—in some areas urban sites decline with the rural ones, while in others cities continue and prosper. Evidently there is more regional variation than was seen for the countryside alone. Other, more indirect indicators, such as building activity or the survival of rural sites closer to urban ones rather than more distant ones, suggest that urban centers exerted a strong attraction and influence.

What factors made life in a nucleated settlement attractive in the early Roman Period? It should be borne in mind that the Greeks showed a marked cultural preference for nucleated life even during the Classical Period, which was the one that saw the greatest dispersion into the countryside in order to intensify agricultural production on smallholdings. With the decrease in smallholding under the Romans, that stimulus disappeared, and the benefits of access to neighbors' solidarity, other forms of gainful employment and charity from the rich became more important. Nevertheless, cities maintained strong ties with the surrounding countryside—the elites were present in their villas, and cities showed a considerable interest in marking their boundaries.

Although city-states survived as the basic political entity of Roman Greece, some archaeological evidence indicates that it is a radically different situation from the independent city-states of the preceding period. There were, for example, infrastructural elements, such as aqueducts and roads, that would have been unthinkable earlier because they could not be defended and perhaps ran through the territory of more than one city-state—these became possible with the creation of the overarching province within the Empire.

Often the incorporation of a territory into an empire brings a radical administrative reorganization. This was not the case when Greece became a part of the Roman Empire, as it already possessed a structure using the city-state as the basic unit of administration, which the Romans favored. In Greece the direct interventions were mostly lighter. New foundations concerned mostly the western periphery (e.g., Nicopolis and Patras), which was less urbanized and affected by the wars of conquest and the civil wars of the late Republic. An important exception was the destruction of the ancient and renowned city of Corinth in 146 BCE and its refounding as a Roman colony a century later. New cities are easily recognized archaeologically by their structures and by the *centuriation* (the laying-out of a grid pattern) of the land around them. New cities could also involve the destruction of older settlements in the surroundings, whose population was moved to the new urban center. City-states also gained or lost territory on occasion according to their choices during the conquest and later in the civil wars.

After the last major interventions of the Augustan Period, the concerns of the cities were essentially administrative: getting the amounts to pay the necessary taxes, running an efficient market, maintaining a sufficient population, keeping up the territory adequately. With wars against neighboring cities no longer happening, a favorite scheme was to appeal to the emperor for favor on the basis of ancient glories. Athens in particular had recourse to this ploy, but other cities such as Sparta used it too. An unimportant place in the Peloponnese recalled that it was the home of Evander, who was supposed to have emigrated to Italy and founded a village on the site of the future Palatine at Rome. Mantineia took advantage of being the reputed ancestral homeland of Antinous, Hadrian's favorite. There is also ample evidence, especially epigraphic, of members of the provincial or Imperial elites (e.g., Herodes Atticus) acting as patrons for various communities with which they had ties. Another way of meeting demands was by sacrificing some autonomy and joining a local league of cities or even participating in a synoecism (merging of cities into a single new one).

The result of such choices, and also of the individuals' decisions to move from a less attractive to a more attractive location, was a trend toward a smaller number of larger urban entities. Cities by the sea tended to survive better than inland ones. A good position on the road network was also an advantage. Sometimes a glorious past was enough for the inhabitants or outsiders to guarantee the continued existence of a settlement that had declined to a small size. Among the surviving cities of Roman Greece, there is a great range—Corinth, the capital of Achaea, for example, grew to a completely different order of magnitude with respect to the small city-states.

In evaluating the relationship between the cities and their territories, it is necessary also to consider the role of religion. One aspect was the use of extra-urban sanctuaries to mark the limits of cities' territories and borders, which ancient cities continued to do even into Roman times. Thus, one can say that the countryside may have lacked people but not gods. Another aspect was removing sacred objects, which served to destroy or transfer local loyalties—there are examples of this in Roman Greece, particularly during the wars of conquest or in cases of synoecism. A new and widespread phenomenon was the Imperial cult, which was carried out both on important sites in city centers and in the Pan-Hellenic sanctuaries. It was the vehicle of great rivalry among the elites, as well as a manifestation of loyalty from the community, which was useful in obtaining or maintaining benefits and privileges. The connection of the Imperial cult and civic life was so strong as to justify the physical transferal of temples to the centers of the cities.

Therefore, we can see in the cities as in the countryside a restructuring stimulated by the new position of Greece as a Roman province. The population preferred to live in nucleated settlements. Among cities there is a tendency toward amalgamation. The past and the differentiation from the Roman (that is, from the Other) are used to create a sense of identity to present to the Greeks themselves and to the Romans.

ATHENS IN THE ROMAN PERIOD

In the first years of Roman domination, until 86 BCE, the economic condition of Athens was relatively good. Through the will of the Romans, Athens controlled Delos from 166 BCE. This island served as a free port at a principal node of the trade network, while Athens served as the mainland base for the traders on Delos and therefore took on a more cosmopolitan character. Another sign of Athenian prosperity at this time was the acceptance of its coinage as the standard throughout much of Greece alongside the Macedonian coinage.

Between 86 BCE and the reign of Augustus the situation worsened. The sack by the Roman general Sulla during the war against Mithridates VI, the king of Pontus, whose puppet ruler Aristion controlled Athens, was obviously a turning point in the economic history of Athens. It gave rise to the often repeated picture of the disastrous conditions in the city. Furthermore, the Cycladic Island trading center of Delos lost its commercial role, and the silver mines at Laurion, on which the Athenian coinage depended, became exhausted. Sulla granted Athens a relatively favorable status among the Greek cities, however. There was also a certain commercial reawakening because of the presence of a considerable number of Roman merchants. On the other hand, the element that later became almost exclusively responsible for the prosperity of the city was already playing a role at this time—the prestige of Athens' past, which attracted foreigners to its schools and religious festivals.

During the early centuries of the Empire, Athens became more and more a university and cultural center (Fig. XIV-2). Foreigners came either for advanced study with the professors of philosophy or to enroll in the *ephebia* (originally the program for the military training of the youth, which was transformed into an elite school). The famed Eleusinian religious mysteries also drew many visitors. Under the emperor Augustus an extensive building program was carried out at Athens, which cannot be considered a sign of the city's prosperity since the funds necessary were not found locally but rather came from abroad, especially from Imperial sources. Indeed, the lack of initiative on the part of Athenians shows how scant the local possibilities were. In particular under Hadrian and also with Herodes Atticus the artificial stimulus of the spending of outside sums for building programs left the city decidedly more resplendent but probably not more prosperous.

For later centuries we have less information from written sources about the economic situation of the city, and we depend therefore more on the archaeology. During the first two thirds of the third century it is reasonable to expect that Athens suffered something of the political and monetary troubles that afflicted the Empire in general. It is true that the university and the *ephebia* continued to exist and to attract foreigners. On the other hand, the exportation ceased of carved marble sarcophagi, which until then had been the only important export product that we can now trace. For Athens specifically, the crucial event of this century was the invasion by a Germanic tribal group known as the Herulians, who left a large part of the city in ruins; this attack must have been a great blow. The picture drawn traditionally for the period between the Herulian invasion in 267 and that of the Goths under Alaric in 396 was of a slow recovery. According to this idea, various buildings were rebuilt and then destroyed again by the Goths. An opposing hypothesis considers that there was little reconstruction before the Gothic invasion and consequently little destruction under them, an idea that is more in agreement with the written sources, which speak of Athens being taken by Alaric without a fight or sacking.

The most important monument that can be attributed without a doubt to the period immediately after the Herulians is the so-called post-Herulian wall (Fig. XIV-2), which enclosed a very reduced area and was built carelessly, thus not suggesting any great prosperity in the city at the time. After 267 the university continued, although the professors were no longer paid from the Imperial purse and fewer foreigners came. The *ephebia* ceased. During the fourth century the university recovered, due in part to provisions made by Constantine in favor of the professors. In the fifth century there was a period of relative prosperity, with the construction or reconstruction of various buildings. These include the so-called Palace of the Giants in the Agora, which was another

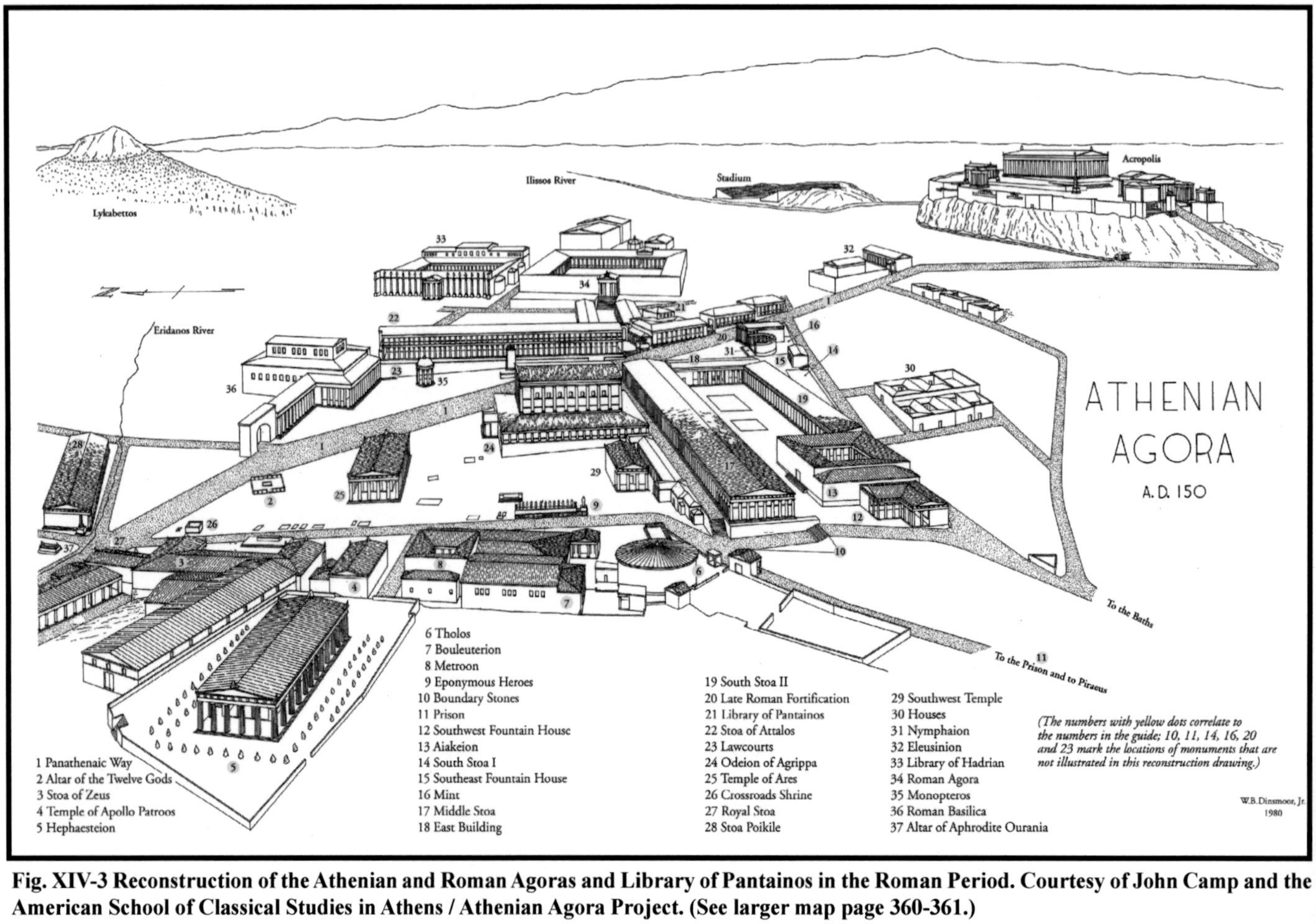

Fig. XIV-3 Reconstruction of the Athenian and Roman Agoras and Library of Pantainos in the Roman Period. Courtesy of John Camp and the American School of Classical Studies in Athens / Athenian Agora Project. (See larger map page 360-361.)

Fig. XIV-4 (left) Hunt of the Calydonian boar. Scene on a Pentelic marble sarcophagus. Imperial Roman, 150-170 CE. From Ayios Ioannis, Patras. Location: National Archaeological Museum, Athens, Greece. Photo Credit: Vanni / Art Resource, N.Y.

Fig. XIV-5 (below) View of the Roman agora showing water clock known as the Tower of the Winds, first century BCE, by Andronikos. Courtesy of John Camp and the American School of Classical Studies in Athens / Athenian Agora Project.

mperial initiative according to recent research and which recycled significant portions of the Roman Odeon Fig. XIV-3). This period takes in the last flowering of the philosophical schools at Athens, especially of the eo-Platonists. This mini-boom came to an end in 529, when the emperor Justinian ordered the schools closed. Between this and the Slavic incursion of 582 Athens ceased to be a cultural center.

After 582 Athens continued to exist and prosper o some extent as one of the few places in Greece not occupied by Slavs. During the Middle Ages and then n the Ottoman Empire, Athens was, however, an nsignificant place and only re-acquired importance n the 19th century, when the town of a few thousand nhabitants was chosen as the capital of the new Greek state.

Thus, we can see some constant factors in Athens' history in the Roman Period through Late Antiquity. It soon lost its importance as a commercial center, first in the first century BCE with the decline of its dependency Delos and even more after the reign of Augustus. Instead, it reinvented itself as a cultural center taking advantage of its prestigious past. This manifested itself first of all in its educational institutions—primarily in the philosophical schools making up the university but also until the time of the Herulian invasion in the *ephebia*. Another manifestation of this spirit can be seen in the revival of ancient sculptural traditions, the so-called Neo-Attic style, which re-elaborated the themes and styles of the Archaic and Classical past, and also more indirectly in the carved marble sarcophagi—both productions that ceased in the third century (Fig. XIV-4). Another constant element was the dependence on outsiders for its building programs, particularly its reliance on Imperial sources. These two constants, recalling the past and depending on outsiders, were

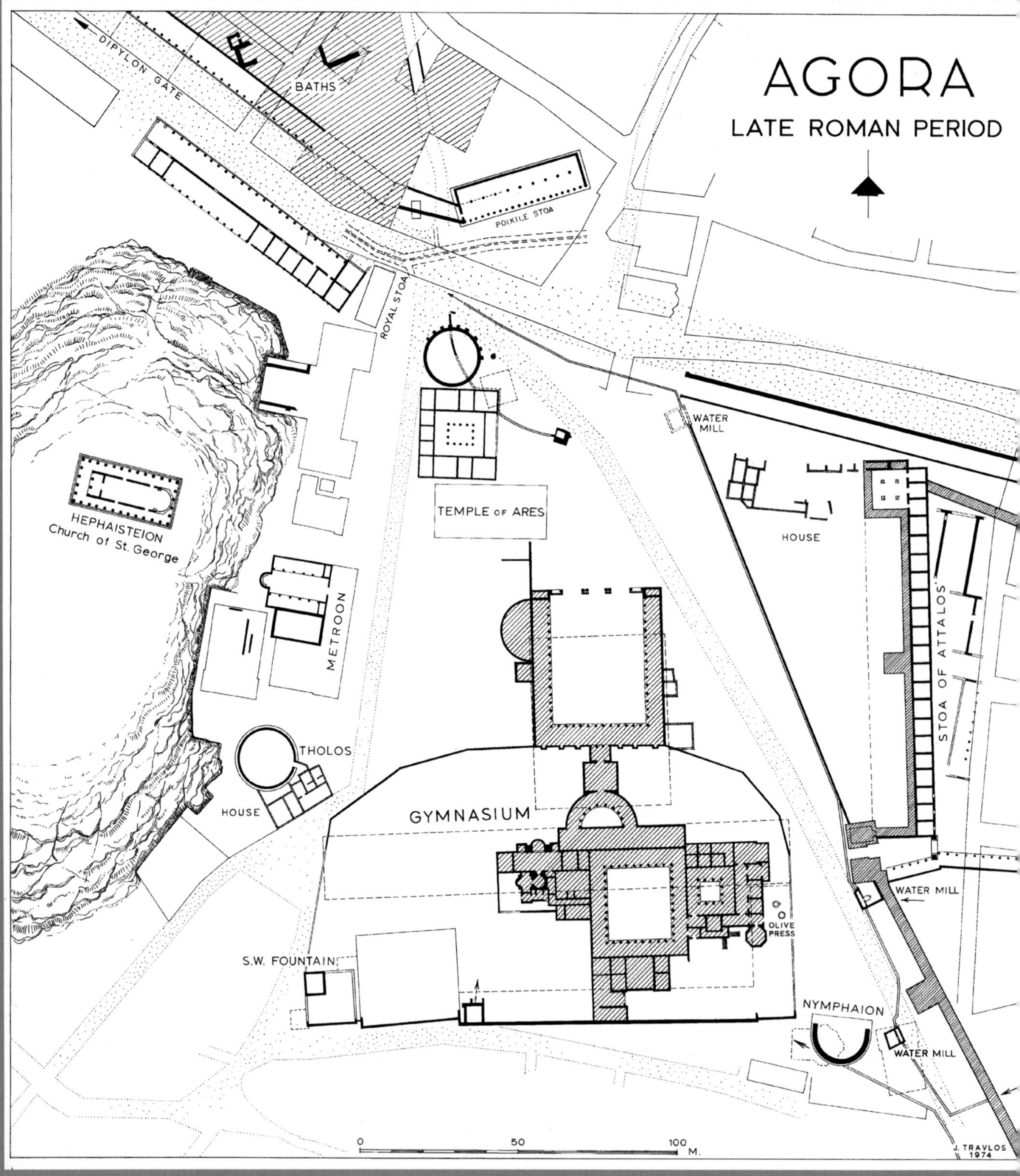

Fig. XIV-6a Plan of the Athenian Agora in the later Roman Period, c. 400–700 CE, including the Temple of Ares and Gymnasium in the area of the Odeon. Courtesy of John Camp and the American School of Classical Studies in Athens / Athenian Agora Project.

connected in that outsiders were interested in Athens because of the prestige of its past and Athenians emphasized their past glory in order to attract foreign interest.

The transformation of Athens from a city-state to a provincial center of the Roman Empire can be followed well in its monuments and town planning, both in the design of the single monuments and the relationship between them and in the choice of the types of monuments built. In the design there is usually a dialogue between the Greek tradition and the new imported Roman ways. In noting the choice of the monuments one realizes the importance given to buildings concerned with culture and one also sees the elimination of the ancient spaces dedicated to democratic political life. This reveals the direction Athens took under the Romans.

The Roman Agora is something decidedly Roman and is also well documented archaeologically (Fig. XIV-3, no. 34; Fig. XIV-5). It occupied the site of a probable open-air market. As far as the still existing structure is concerned, we learn about its foundation essentially from the dedicatory inscription on its entry gate or propylaeum: it was built with funds contributed by Julius Caesar and then by Augustus following an embassy from Eukles of Marathon and was inaugurated during the archonate (magistracy) of a certain Nikias. As this name does not appear on the extant list for the years from 18 to 12 BCE and the years before then can be excluded because of bad relations between Augustus and Athens, and Nikias does not bear the further title of priest of Drusus, which the archons had from the year of his death in 9 BCE, we can surmise that the inauguration must have taken place in 11 or 10 BCE. A possible reason for the Roman Agora's construction may have been the desire to create a space for the merchants displaced from Delos. In terms of Athenian town planning, the intention seems to have been the removal of commercial activities from the ancient Agora. In this we see something similar to what took place in the Imperial Fora at Rome with respect to the Roman Forum.

As a building the Roman Agora represents as much an infusion of external ideas as the money that financed it. It consists of a square enclosed by high walls with porticos around it. There are clearly traditional features, especially in the Gate of Athena Archegetis (Athena the Leader) and in the propylaeum or entry gate to the east. Nevertheless, the overall scheme is foreign to Athens and quite close to Rome's Forum of Caesar, which was built at the same time.

The construction of the new Roman Agora is closely connected with the rebuilding program carried out in the ancient Agora under Augustus and the Julio-Claudians (Figs. XIV-3, 6a, 6b). In general, it was changed from an essentially open space to one surrounded by monuments—therefore from a space that was suitable for use for gatherings of people primarily for political purposes but also for commercial ones to a sort of museum celebrating the glories of the city. This calls to mind the way in which the Roman Forum lost its function at the same time as a location for spirited politics and trade and became a place for representation and the celebration of glorious memories. In Athens a large role was given to culture and to the association between the Imperial house and the ancient tutelary or patron divinities of the city. In this way the Agora expressed well the new reality of Athens in the Roman Empire.

The Odeion of Agrippa was the most imposing of the new monuments in the Agora (Fig. XIV-3, no. 24). It was a high structure dominating the rest of the Agora. Its original construction appeared to coincide with Agrippa's visit between 16 and 14 BCE. In this phase it had a very daring covering with a width of 25 m. without internal supports. It was also innovative in that its lighting illuminated the stage from the back, the earliest known example of this feature. The entrances were at the lower level from the Agora to the north and at the upper level from the Middle Stoa to the south. The building was decorated with marble incrustation and had Corinthian capitals. This was another structure with parallels in Italian architecture but none in Athenian architecture. The taste that placed the building squarely on the north-south axis of the Agora at the center of the southern part of the former square was also Italian. One can consider the Odeion of Agrippa at the same time a splendid tribute to Greek culture represented by Athens and a clear indication to the Athenians that they should no longer dedicate themselves to the democratic politics but rather to the cultural activities that the Romans appreciated.

The Temple of Ares (Fig. XIV-3, no. 25) is to be found in a similar position in the northern part of the former square, in this case along the east-west axis. It was placed there at the end of the first century BCE, but it is a fifth-century building near in date and style to the nearby Hephaisteion or Temple of Hephaistos and may have been built by the same architect. It is also often identified with the Temple of Ares from Acharnai in the Attic countryside. One can see from marks incised on each block that it was accurately dismantled, moved from its original location, and reassembled in the Agora. It incorporates with certainty the sima from the Temple of Poseidon at Cape Sounion. There is strong evidence that the temple was dedicated to the Imperial cult in its new position—there is a dedicatory statue base to Augustus' grandson Gaius (and adoptive son) as the "New Ares" and the attribution of the epithet "New God Ares" to Tiberius' son Drusus.

Another monument, which is associated at least hypothetically with the Imperial cult, was also brought into the Agora from elsewhere at about the same time—the Southwest

Fig. XIV-6b Aerial view of the Athenian Agora. The Temple of Hephaistos appears at the upper left and the vertically placed building at the center is the Stoa of Attalus.

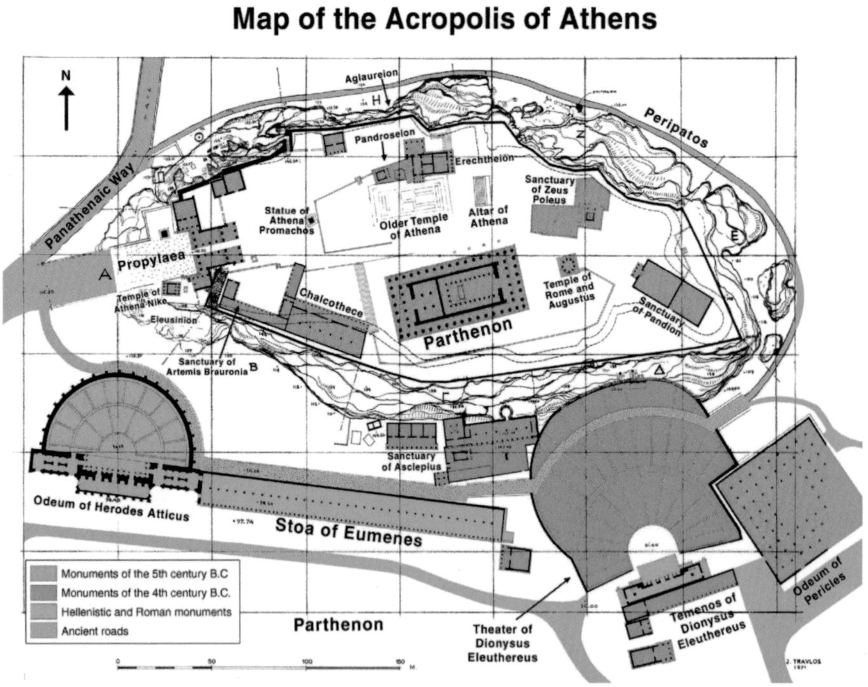

Temple (a Doric temple, originally dedicated to Athena at Cape Sounion in the Classical Period; Fig. XIV-3, no. 29), which was probably dedicated to the deified empress Livia, wife of Augustus.

There are yet other traces of the Imperial cult in the Agora from this period. There were, for example, 13 altars mentioning Augustus in a way used for divinities (in the genitive or dative case) rather than for

Fig. XIV-7 (left) Reconstruction of the Athenian Acropolis. The small round Temple of Augustus is located behind the Parthenon. Photo Credit: © DeA Picture Library / Art Resource, N.Y. (See larger plan page 362.)

Fig. XIV-8 (below) Odeion of Herodes Atticus (Tiberius Claudius Atticus Herodes , c.101-177 CE), erected to the memory of his wife, Regilla, who died in 160. Also shown is the Theatre of Dionysos and the Odeion of Pericles, along with other major buildings of the Acropolis area, Athens, Greece, Location: Private Collection. Photo Credit: Gianni Dagli Orti / The Art Archive at Art Resource, N.Y.

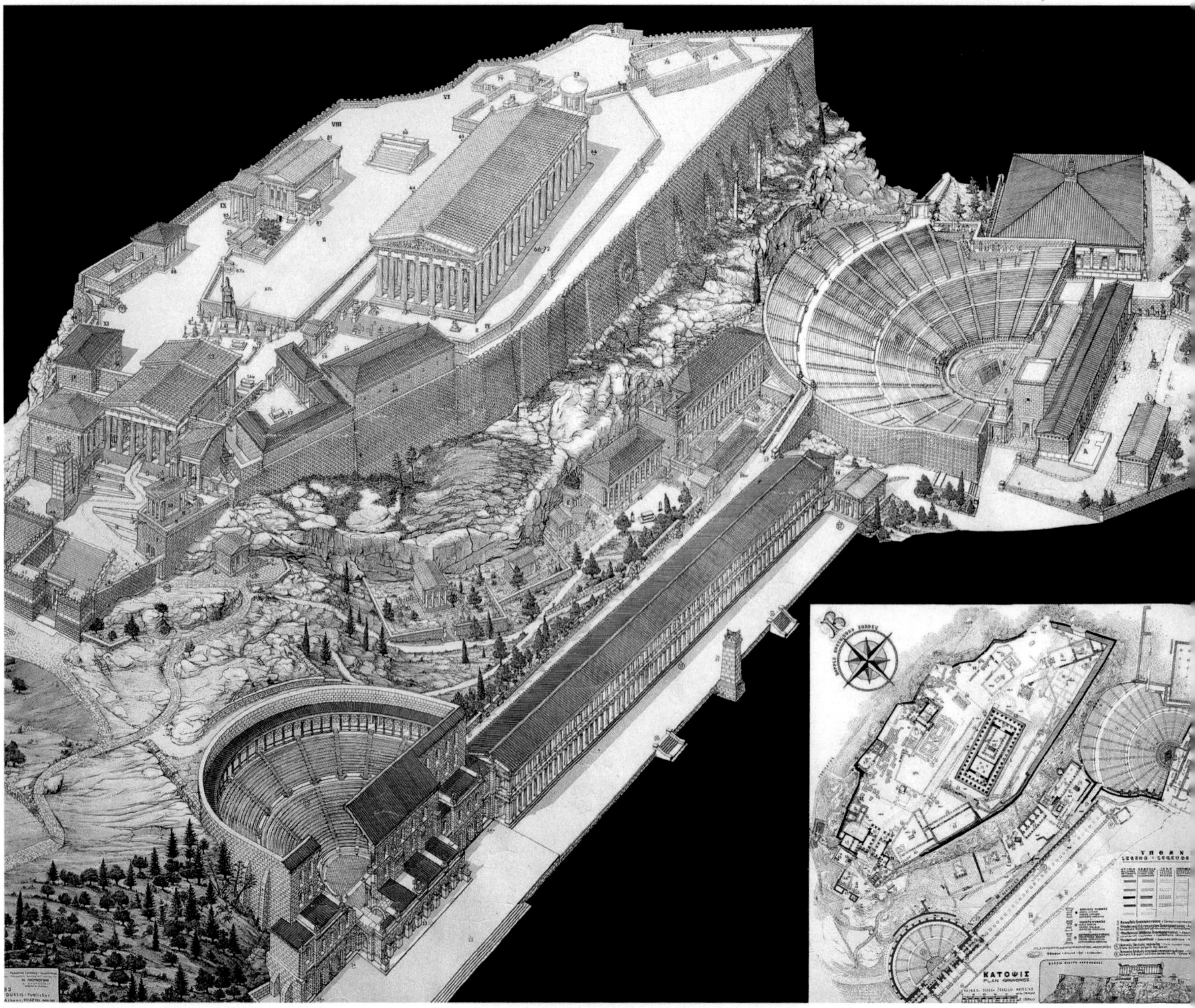

mortals (in the accusative—"The Athenians honor so-and-so"). It is also possible that the addition of two rooms behind the Stoa of Zeus Eleutherios (Fig. XIV-3, no. 3), which is situated along the northwest corner of the Agora, should be connected with the Cult of the Emperors identified with Zeus the Liberator.

Although the Acropolis in Roman times was maintained substantially in the form inherited from the past, there was, however, a secure manifestation of the cult of Augustus there. It was the Temple of Rome and Augustus erected it in front of the Parthenon and therefore in a position whose symbolic importance is obvious. It was erected by the will of the Athenians themselves—perhaps as a gesture of thanks for the donation of the funds to complete the Roman Agora (Figs. XIV-7, 8). The other contribution to the Acropolis at the time of Augustus was the rededication of an existing monument, the pillar in front of the Propylaeum, in honor of Augustus. The pillar was originally erected for King Eumenes II of the Hellenistic Kingdom of Pergamon and his brother Attalos, who were winners at the Panathenaic Games in 178 BCE, and subsequently it bore the statues of Marc Antony and Cleopatra in the guise of New Dionysos and New Isis.

After a period of little building, there was some renewed activity at the time of Trajan. Perhaps the most important phenomenon for town planning was the introduction of porticoed streets as a means of tying together heterogeneous elements behind a uniform and monumental façade. Its introduction marks the first use at Athens of this feature of architecture that was common to the entire Empire, particularly in the east. In one case, the street between the ancient Agora and the Roman Agora forms part of the architectural complex known as the Library of Pantainos, identified from an inscription found there (Fig. XIV-3, no. 21). It can be dated to the years 98-102 because of the Imperial titulature in the dedication that Pantainos made to Athena Polias, Trajan, and to the city (Trajan had in fact already received the title of Germanicus but not yet Dacicus, that is he had celebrated a triumph over Germanic people but not the Dacians). The street leads from the ancient Agora with an oblique stoa creating an open area between Pantainos' complex and the Stoa of Attalos ending in an arch. After that, another stoa leads directly to the Gate of Athena Archigetis on the Roman Agora (Fig. XIV, no. 34). The complex consisted otherwise of a nucleus made up of a central courtyard with a peristyle and a room behind that must have held the books, a third stoa along the Panathenaic Way, and rooms behind the stoas that were probably used as shops.

Fig. XIV-9 (above) Ruin of the Philopappos monument, c. 116 CE, Athens, Greece, erected by the Athenians in honor of benefactor of Athens, the exiled prince of Commagene, Julius Antiochus Philopappos, who settled in Athens, became a citizen and assumed civic and religious offices. Courtesy of John Camp and the American School of Classical Studies in Athens / Athenian Agora Project.

Fig. XIV-10 (below)Temple of Zeus Olympios in Athens. Photo Credit: Noelle Soren. University of Arizona School of Anthropology Archive.

Another monument that had less influence in the development of town planning but is nonetheless a landmark in modern Athens is the mausoleum of Gaius Julius Epiphanes Philopappos (died 116 CE), better known today as the Philopappos Monument (Figs. XIV-2, 9). It brought together elements that derived from his heritage as the grandson of the last king of the Hellenistic kingdom of Commagene, as a Roman Senator and as a citizen of Athens, where he lived and was a benefactor. The position itself, on a very visible height, recalls his ancestral burial site at Nemrud Da in his homeland in southeastern Anatolia. His ancestors are commemorated also in the iconographic program of the decoration—to his right there is his grandfather and originally to his left was Seleucos, a maternal ancestor and former officer and successor of Alexander the Great. Underneath a relief shows Philopappos in a consular procession recalling the relief on the Arch of Titus at Rome. The style and the working of the sculptures derive directly from Attic prototypes. Altogether, the monument gives testimony to the cosmopolitan atmosphere that reigned in the upper classes of the Empire at the time, for whom Athens was an essential reference point.

The philhellene Roman Emperor Hadrian was responsible for a second building boom at Athens, not only with single monuments but also with the imposition of an axis that characterized the town planning. On the one hand, a new quarter of town was built and on the other a conscious Romanization of the center of Athens was carried out.

One pole of activity under Hadrian was the new area in the eastern part of town. Hadrian's Arch is normally considered to mark the passage from the old city to the new one, as an inscription on it indicates. The most famous of his realizations was the completion, many centuries after its beginning, of the Temple of Zeus Olympios, which held a series of statues dedicated to the emperor (Fig. XIV-

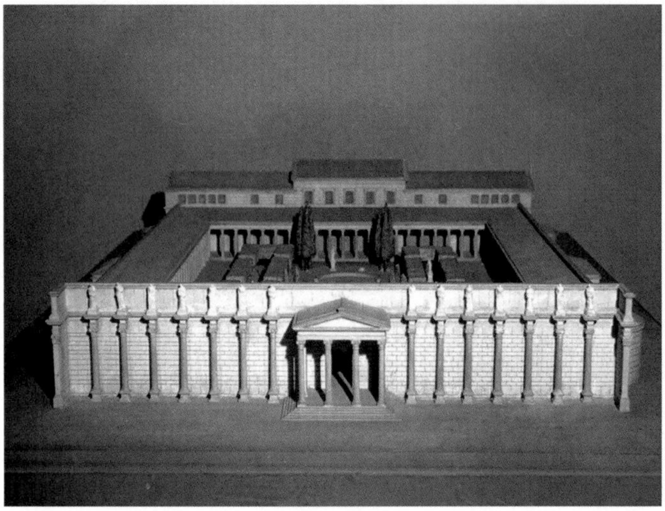

Fig. XIV-11a Model of the Library of Hadrian in central Athens, Greece. Courtesy of John Camp and the American School of Classical Studies in Athens / Athenian Agora Project.

Fig. XIV-11b View of the surviving border wall of the Library of Hadrian. Courtesy of John Camp and the American School of Classical Studies in Athens / Athenian Agora Project.

10). Nearby one can mention the pan-Hellenion, a Doric temple within an enclosure, dedicated to the cult of Zeus and Hera on the part of all the Greeks.

Hadrian managed also to transform the center of town. Here the main initiative was the so-called Library of Hadrian, which was actually much more than a simple library (Fig. XIV-3, no. 33; Fig. XIV-11). Architecturally it is closely related to the nearby Roman Agora and the Imperial Fora at Rome (especially the *Templum Pacis* built by Vespasian). It presented a large square delimited by high outer walls. Behind the massive blocks that recall the Hellenic tradition, it can be observed that the structure was realized in concrete in the Roman tradition. The interior was surrounded by porticos, behind which are *exedrae* and lecture rooms. The center contained gardens. The great difference from the Imperial Fora in Rome was the absence of a temple, which was always located along the central axis at Rome, while here there was the actual library, perhaps in *homage* to Athens' central position in Greek culture. In the plan of the city, the Library formed a pair with the Roman Agora and was aligned with the basilica built at the same time on the north side of the ancient Agora, which is also a typically Western building (Fig. XIV-3).

The works carried out by Herodes Atticus at the time of Antoninus Pius and Marcus Aurelius completed the adornment of Athens but they had less impact on the town planning. His first work was cladding the old Panathenaic stadium with local Pentelic marble, decided when he was the magistrate chosen to organize the Games. On the western side he erected a Temple to Tyche (Fortune), which had a concrete podium. Opposite it, on the other side of the stadium, there was his sepulcher with an Attic sarcophagus and an archaizing inscription in keeping with the taste of the time and the man himself. The other Athenian complex owed to Herodes Atticus is the Odeion, which he built in memory of his wife and probably as a replacement for the Odeion of Agrippa, which collapsed at that time and was rebuilt on a reduced scale (Fig. XIV-3, no. 24; Figs. XIV-6, 12). The roofing scheme of the Odeion of Herodes Atticus is considered to be innovative. The building, now in the open air, is still used for summer-time performances.

As in many other places, including Rome itself, the walls of the city became a concern after the middle of the third century CE, after centuries of neglect. Not long ago research established that the fortifications that the written sources say were built under the emperor Valerian (Fig. XIV-2), who reigned between 253 and 260, consisted of the rebuilding of the famous walls of Themistocles going back to the fifth century BCE, with the difference that they included the new Hadrianic area. As is well known, these fortifications did not resist against the Herulians.

Some time after the devastation that the Herulians caused, probably during the reign of Probus (276-282), who issued the most recent coin found in layers associated with the structure, what is now called the post-Herulian wall was erected. Because of the many coins later than Valerian that were found in association with it, it can no longer be attributed to Valerian as it was in older scholarship. The construction consists of two faces built of stone, using marble and poros limestone according to what was at hand nearby, with a cement fill containing building rubble. The line of the post-Herulian wall takes in a drastically reduced area with respect to the walls of Themistocles and Valerian, and in particular excludes the ancient Agora (Fig. XIV-2). This wall remained in use for some time—there are even repairs from the time of Justinian—although eventually it was thought feasible to revamp the more extensive line of walls. The essential fact is that the post-Herulian wall marks a deep break in the urban continuity—for the first time in a thousand years the Agora was no longer the public square of Athens. Indeed, it lay in ruins, aside from some minimal repairs, for more than a century after 267, until the beginning of the fifth century.

At the beginning of the fifth century, probably with Imperial help, Athens experienced a recovery. The most important building of this time is the Palace of the Giants, which occupies the southern part of the ancient Agora (Figs. XIV-6, 12). Archaeologists named it for its reuse in its façade of statues of giants recycled from the second phase of the Odeion of Agrippa, which had stood on the site. Because of its size and other characteristics, the Palace of the Giants must have been an official residence, probably intended for visits by the emperor and high officials. It consists of a large external courtyard and an internal *nucleus* including a bath complex around a peristyle. At a later stage the whole building was surrounded by a wall to separate it from utilitarian structures that were growing up in the area, including a series of mills that used an aqueduct that came down the Panathenaic Way.

Higher up, on the northern slopes of the Acropolis, there are other houses of this period. They have been interpreted as houses of professors, both because their size and richness shows that they must have belonged to important citizens and because they contain rooms suitable for receiving students to hear the lessons, which written sources say were given in the professors' houses. Another consideration is that they underwent disasters about 530—in some cases pagan statues were hidden and the houses were abandoned; in others the houses appear to have survived but in decay and without maintenance. This accords well with what we hear from the written sources of the prohibition of the teaching of philosophy in 529.

The fifth century also saw the foundation of the first churches at Athens that can be identified archaeologically. These were the conversion of the Agoranomeion (the market supervisor's building) in the Agora, without architectural changes, and the new construction of a tetraconch or four-apsed building in the Library of Hadrian. It is probably significant that they were both structures with no previous associations with the pagan religion.

Fig. XIV-12 Giant sculptures from the large residential building in the Agora, Athens, Greece. The sculptures were salvaged from the Odeion of Agrippa (built 15 BCE) and used to adorn the new structure, built c. 400 CE. Photo Credit: Gianni Dagli Orti / The Art Archive at Art Resource, N.Y.

As we have seen, life at Athens continued, however reduced, without an interruption. Archaeological indications are, for example, an olive press and supports in a complex to the east of the Stoa of Attalos in the Agora. In the seventh century, Christianization had reached a point in which it was possible to convert pagan religious buildings, e.g., the Hephaisteion overlooking the Agora, into churches without offending Christian sensibilities or encountering pagan resistance.

ELEUSIS

Athens' main sanctuary, Eleusis, located some 20 km west of the city, played an important part in the city's success as a

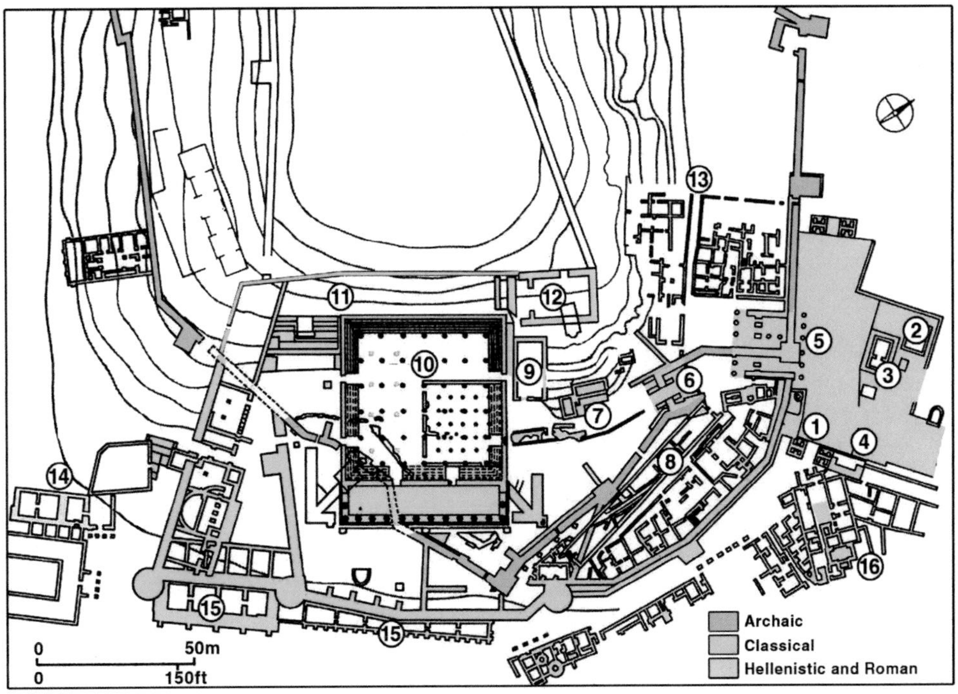

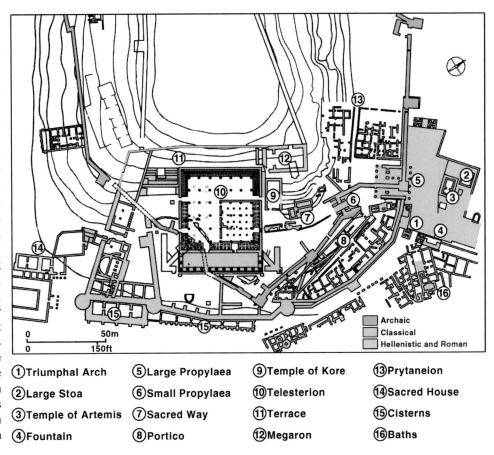

①Triumphal Arch ②Large Stoa ③Temple of Artemis ④Fountain
⑤Large Propylaea ⑥Small Propylaea ⑦Sacred Way ⑧Portico
⑨Temple of Kore ⑩Telesterion ⑪Terrace ⑫Megaron
⑬Prytaneion ⑭Sacred House ⑮Cisterns ⑯Baths

Fig. XIV-13 Plan of the Sanctuary of Eleusis, Greece by Roxanne Stall. (See larger plan page 363.)

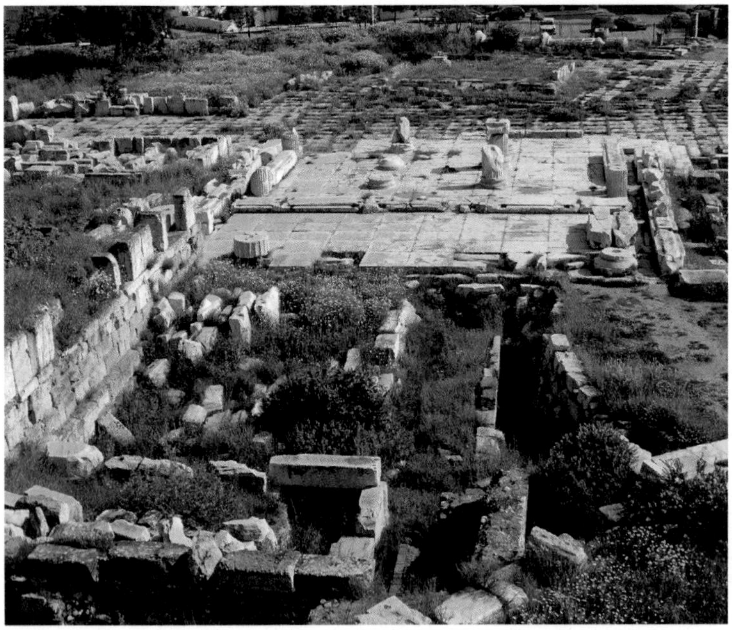

Fig. XIV-14 Sanctuary of Demeter and Kore. Site of the Eleusinian mystery celebrations. View from southwest over the Great Propylaea, with the Temple of Artemis above it and the Small Propylaea to the right and the *Prytaneion* in the raised area at the left. Photo: D. Dagli Orti. Location: Eleusis, Greece Photo Credit: © DeA Picture Library / Art Resource, N.Y.

cultural center. In fact, the sanctuary reached its greatest splendor during the Roman Period, to a large extent because of the interest of emperors and important Romans (Fig. XIV-13). The cult, dedicated to Demeter and Kore, went back to the earliest days of Greek civilization. The rites are little known, precisely because they were mystery rites with a strict obligation for the initiates to keep the secret. They seem to have to do with agricultural fertility and the recurrent rebirth of nature and individual salvation.

The Roman monuments of nearby Eleusis begin with a bridge built on Hadrian's orders a few kilometers before the sanctuary in order to guarantee access at any time of the year. To enter the sanctuary one passed from a courtyard with the Temple of Artemis and two copies of the Arch of Hadrian at Athens through the Great Propylaeum from the time of Marcus Aurelius (inspired by the fifth-century propylaeum of the Athenian Acropolis), and the Small Propylaeum (Fig. XIV-14). This latter is the earliest Roman building at Eleusis, not classicizing like the others but rather in the eclectic Hellenistic taste typical of the mid-first century BCE.

In the sanctuary, the most important building is the Telesterion, where the mystery rites were held. The Roman building, erected after a Germanic incursion of the second third of the second century CE, was the most recent of a series of buildings beginning with a Late Bronze Age Mycenaean structure that is considered to have been the royal residence in which the cult first took place and which was gradually taken over by it. Essentially, the Roman Telesterion follows the lines of the Classical one built by Pericles, with the extension of the cut in the rock by a few meters and a new series of columns on bases made of reused material. Around the central area in which the mysteries took place, the building has a series of steps, probably for standing or seated spectators. Above the Telesterion there are two temples of the Roman Period, both datable in the second century CE, in which it is proposed to recognize the cult of two empresses who were called "new Demeter" according to the written sources—Sabina, Hadrian's wife, and Faustina, the wife of his successor, Antoninus Pius (Fig. XIV-13 nos. 9 and 12).

CORINTH AND ITS TERRITORY

Corinth's position has given it a natural strategic importance throughout history. It is located at the foot of the Acrocorinth, a height that dominates the Isthmus of Corinth (Fig. XIV-15). The isthmus provides the land route between the Peloponnese and the Greek mainland. By means of a short transshipment, Corinth also connected the sea route between the Aegean and the West. Therefore, Corinth became one of the major city-states of ancient Greece. It was a Roman provincial capital and retained a certain importance throughout the Middle Ages and up to modern times. The town on the site of the ancient city was destroyed by an earthquake in 1858, and a new settlement was built closer to the coast. Thus, the archaeological area was largely unencumbered in 1896, when it was assigned to the American School of Classical Studies at Athens for investigation. Since then, research in the center of the city and some outlying areas, including the port at Kenchreai and the Sanctuary at Isthmia, has been one of the main endeavors of the ASCSA.

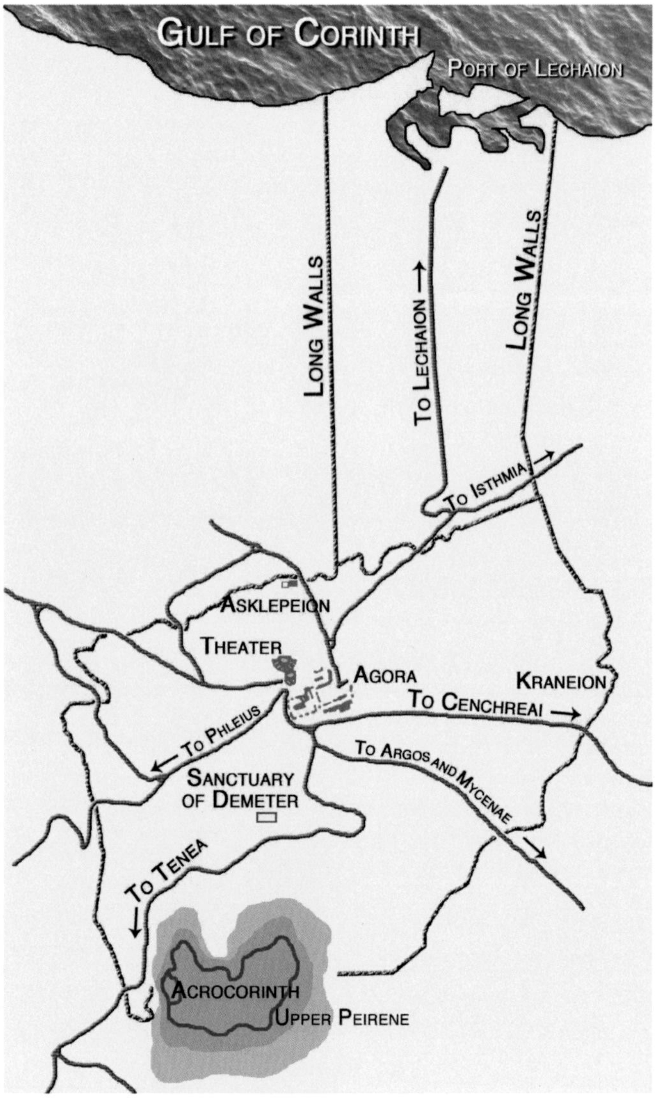

Fig. XIV-15 (right) Plan of the ancient Corinth area by Cherylee Francis.

Fig. XIV-16 Kenchreai, eastern port of the ancient Greek city of Corinth. Photo Credit: Gianni Dagli Orti / The Art Archive at Art Resource, N.Y.

Corinth followed a different strategy from Athens. While Athens exploited its past to survive in its present, Corinth was much more up-to-date and forward-looking. Of course, Athens never experienced a break in the continuity of its life, in spite of sacks and incursions, while Corinth was abolished in 146 BCE and was refounded a century later as a fresh political entity (a Roman colony) with new inhabitants. The Roman colonists and their descendants may have wanted to recall the heritage of Corinth's ancient past, but they lived in a city that was to a large extent built anew under the Romans.

In a historical debate that was very active in the second half of the 20th century on the nature of the ancient city (and indeed on all pre-industrial cities), one side proposed the idea of the consumer city as a parasite on the countryside and the other countered with the idea of the service city, which provided services for a primary economic sector (agriculture) that was prosperous enough to have a surplus to spend on acquiring them.

Corinth offers a prime example of what a service city would have looked like. As all centers of city-states, it provided its territory with administrative, cultural, religious and commercial occasions. Furthermore, as the capital of a province, it did the same at the provincial level. In addition, the Pan-Hellenic sanctuary of Isthmia located on its territory attracted people from all over to attend important games in years between the Olympics held at Olympia. Finally, it commanded an important position for trade—within Greece it controlled the overland route between the Peloponnese and the rest of Greece, and more importantly it was a key point for exchange between the western and the eastern Mediterranean. This was because it possessed two good ports: Lechaion on the Corinthian Gulf and Kenchreai or Cenchreai on the Saronic Gulf (Figs. XIV-1, 15, 16).

Anyone wanting to avoid the dangerous passage around Cape Malea in the southern Peloponnese could unload his merchandise at one port and transport it across the Isthmus of Corinth to the other. The importance of this activity can be seen in the size of the installations at Lechaion and the richness of the remains at Kenchreai but even more so in the Diolkos, a track for hauling heavy loads across the Isthmus, and in the attempts to cut a canal across the Isthmus. The Diolkos was made during the Archaic Period of Greek history and was so important that it remained in use until the ninth century CE. There can be no doubt that Corinth earned a large part of its income from this traffic across the Isthmus, with all the secondary services that it offered to travelers. It is certainly not a coincidence that the Roman colony of Corinth was founded in 44 BCE with a good number of freedmen, who knew how to take advantage of the position of the city and left it with their entrepreneurial stamp.

At the ports, there is little to be seen at Lechaion other than its position. Investigations in the early-20th century, however, showed that it had a considerable harbor structure. On the other side, at Kenchreai, excavations took place later in the century. There a mole, storerooms and some sanctuaries were discovered (Fig. XIV-16). In fact, one of the most spectacular finds for Late Antique art history was made in the Sanctuary of Isis on the north mole—a series of packages with panels of glass *opus sectile*. This was a technique that featured materials such as glass or marble cut into decorative patterns to make a design. Unlike mosaic *tesserae* or little cubes, pieces of *opus sectile* were of considerable size, sometimes reaching 10 to 20 cms across.

At Kenchreai's Isis sanctuary, the *opus sectile* formed a decorative program intended to cover a wall of c. 150 m2 with an idealized landscape. Evidently the packages had just arrived

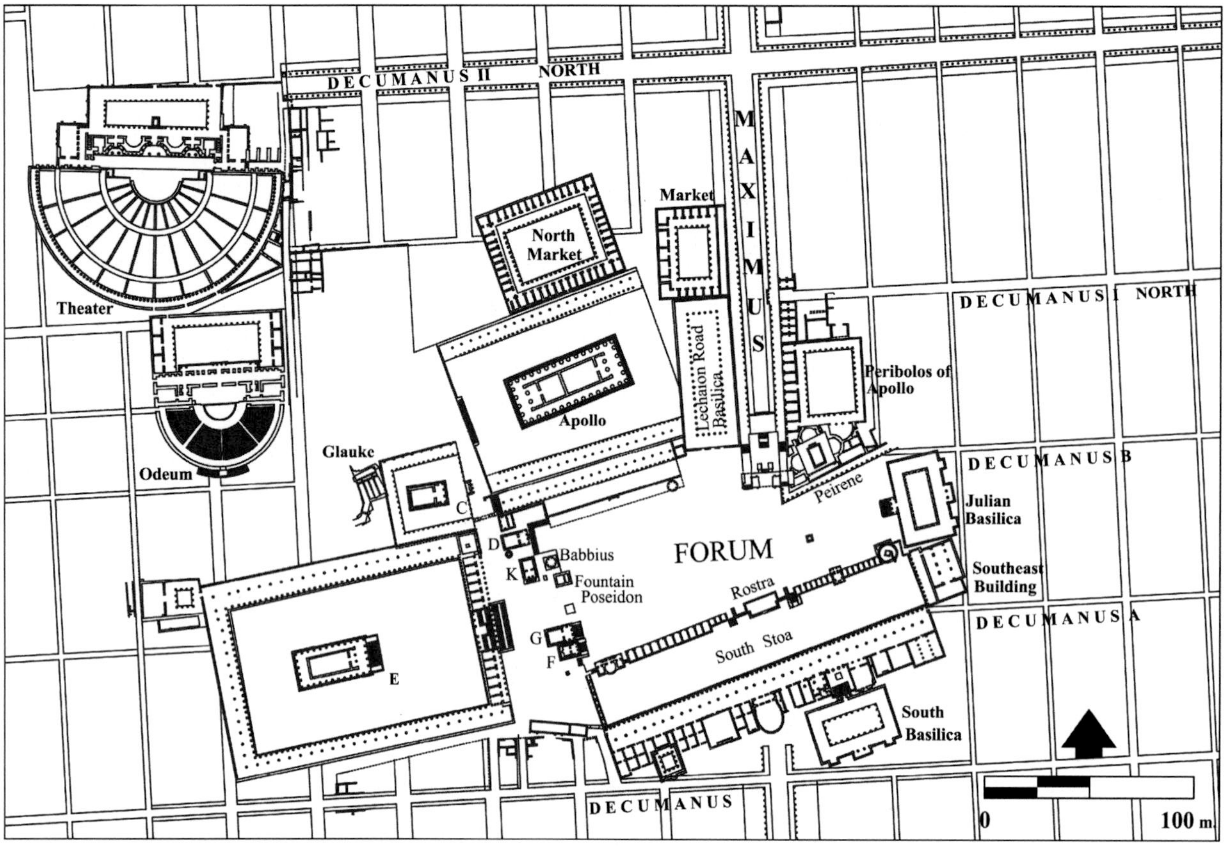

Fig. XIV-17a Reconstruction of Roman Corinth, Greece, including the Temple of Apollo and theatre complex. Photo Credit: © David Gilman Romano, Corinth Computer Project. (See larger graphic page 364.)

when an earthquake destroyed and buried the sanctuary, probably the one known to have devastated the area in 375 CE. They are therefore not only a testimony for the wealth of Kenchreai, but also one of the latest examples of pagan resistance to Christianity. On the other side of the harbor there are remains of storerooms built of Roman-style concrete work and a sanctuary identified hypothetically with one dedicated to Aphrodite.

At the Isthmus there are the remains of the Diolkos already mentioned and of attempted cuts to make a canal. The Diolkos was a path with double grooves about 1.5 m apart. It was not so much suitable for transporting ships, as is sometimes supposed (although small ships and war ships, which were narrower than most trading vessels, may have used it), but rather for floats on rollers guided by the grooves. This was a form of transportation especially suited to heavy loads, such as marble and timber, the former transported mostly to the west and the latter to the east. The canal was finally realized at the end of the 19th century using the course laid out under the emperor Nero in the 60s CE. From his time there remains a shrine dedicated to Hercules, who was particularly concerned with hydraulic engineering projects.

The center of Corinth is located under the height of Acrocorinth, one of the strategic points for military control of Greece, from which Corinth drew importance in campaigns before and after the Romans.

Climbing the hill from Lechaion, one arrives at a first bath complex in the suburbs, a type of structure in the Roman tradition with which the city was well supplied. This dates to the end of the second or the beginning of the third century CE.

The Lechaion road leads to the Agora as a porticoed street (Figs. XIV-17a, b). To the left, shortly before reaching the Agora, there is another bath complex. This has been identified as the one donated in the Augustan Period by Eurykles, the tyrant of Sparta. Beyond an enclosure (*peribolos*) sacred to Apollo is located the monumental fountain of Peirene. It has various phases, the most important of which dates to the second century, when the fountain was used as the termination point of an aqueduct donated by Hadrian. On the other side of the street there is a basilica, another type of building (for commercial and administrative meetings) of Roman tradition with which the city is well provided. The basilica is separated from the Agora by a monument known as the Façade of the Prisoners or Captives (not shown on the plan but visible before the basilica on the reconstruction of Fig. XIV-17a). The entrance from the street to the Agora is by means of an arch, visible on the reconstruction.

The area of the Agora is especially vast. Unlike Athens it is unencumbered, aside from a row of monuments and buildings along the line of the terrace that divides the upper part in the south from the lower one in the north. There are two rows of *tabernae* or shops, one on the north side to the west of the Façade of the Prisoners and the other on the west side, and additional ones on parts of the terrace wall. The east and south sides of the Agora were dedicated mostly to public buildings. The building at the southeastern corner, the successor of the Tiberian Period to one of the earliest buildings of the Roman colony, has been identified as an archive and perhaps a library. It was rebuilt together with the nearby Basilica Julia. The most important structure along the terrace wall is the bema, the tribunal or *rostra* from which the governor of the province held audiences. St. Paul was said to have been heard here, called to judgment by the Jewish community of Corinth.

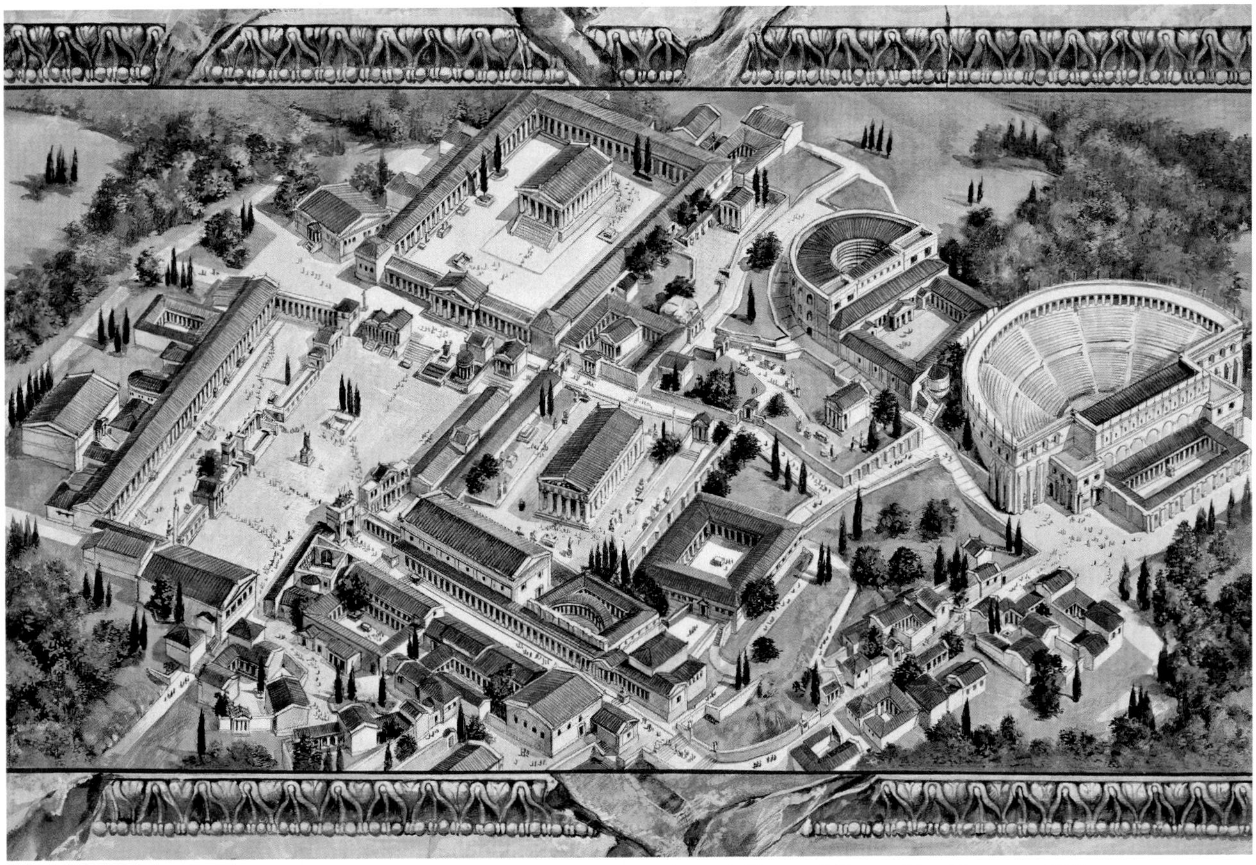

Fig. XIV-17b Plan of Roman Corinth. Photo Credit: DeA Picture Library / Art Resource, NY

In the South Stoa, various rooms were found dedicated to administrative offices. The most prestigious is the Agonotheteion (second room from the right, next to a hall with two rows of columns), the seat of the official in charge of organizing the Isthmian Games, the highest local political office. Another room gives access to a third basilica known as the South Basilica. Before the beginning of the wide road leading south to Kenchreai, there is the *Bouleterion*, the seat of the local council. It is distinguished by an apsidal back wall. To the west of the South Stoa are more baths. In front of the row of shops along the west side of the Agora is located a series of small temples, among which is a monument dedicated by Gnaeus Babbius Philinus, a freedman, one of the oldest of the colony, as well as a temple to Poseidon of the second century located just below the Babbius monument.

Other public buildings are grouped around the Agora. One of the few remains from Archaic Greek Corinth is the Temple of Apollo, restored in Roman times and perhaps rededicated to the *Gens* Julia (the Augustan Imperial family); the structure still dominates the hill to the north of the Agora (Figs. XIV-17a and 17b). It has been suggested that another temple, known archaeologically as Temple E, was involved with the Imperial cult. The central area of the city had additional market areas and a monumental fountain (Glauke Fountain).

Somewhat farther away is a theatre from the Greek Period which was renovated with new scenic structures, first a simpler one in the Augustan Period and then a more complex one in the second century. Toward the end of the first century CE an odeion was added nearby. Finally, Corinth was one of the few Greek cities and the only one on the mainland to have an amphitheatre for gladiatorial contests.

Within the territory of Corinth there was also an important sanctuary, the Pan-Hellenic one of Poseidon at Isthmia, which obviously attracted visitors (Fig. XIV-18). We have already seen that the superintendent of the Isthmian Games was the highest official figure in the colony of Corinth, with an office in the

Fig. XIV-18 Temple of Poseidon, Isthmia, Greece. Photo Credit: Vanni / Art Resource, N.Y.

Agora. The way that local elites used cults in exercising power has already been discussed. There seems to be a contrast here with the situation elsewhere (e.g., Athens and Eleusis), in that a generation passed after the refounding of Corinth before the management of the sanctuary was assigned to the colony.

At Isthmia the Corinthians of the Roman Period inherited as the main building a Doric temple at the end of the first-half of the fifth century BCE, stylistically very close to the Temple of Zeus at Olympia. It underwent substantial restorations during the fourth century BCE but preserved its essential traits for the rest of its long history. The colossal Greek altar shows signs of abandonment during the period of the Roman obliteration of Corinth—there are cart tracks across it. In Roman times two successive altars were built farther away from the temple. In the Roman Period the shrine to a hero, The Palaimonion, was added to the sanctuary. This occupied a first, small courtyard, while a larger one was erected around the temple. Outside the enclosure of the sanctuary is located the Roman Stadium, where the Isthmian Games took place. This replaced the Greek stadium near the Palaimonion. Lower down the valley there are a theatre and a Roman bath complex.

After the devastation by the Goths under Alaric and the closure of the pagan sanctuaries ordered by the emperor Theodosius in 396, the buildings underwent a very drastic spoliation in order to get blocks with which to build the Hexamilion, the fortification that was built across the Isthmus to defend the Peloponnese.

Corinth reacted to incorporation in the Roman Empire in a different way from Athens and leaves the impression of a more dynamic community. As in other places, cases of Imperial favor are not lacking—the aqueduct built on the orders of Hadrian is a prime example—but Corinth does not appear to have depended on them. Likewise, there was some recollection of the glorious past of the earlier Greek city, especially in the two large temples in the city center and at Isthmia, but that is not what set the tone. Corinth was characterized mainly by its commercial and administrative structures.

THESSALONIKI

Thessaloniki is a relatively recent city in Greek terms. It was founded in 315 BCE at the wish of the Macedonian king Cassander, who promoted the synoecism of 26 nearby communities (Fig. XIV-1). At first it was important as a commercial center. Thessaloniki's favorable geographic position as a port with access through the Vardar Valley to the Balkan hinterland, which has played a role repeatedly in the city's history, was a significant factor in this. It also benefited in Roman times from its position along the Via Egnatia, the road linking the Adriatic coast to Asia Minor. Within the Roman Empire, Thessaloniki served as a provincial capital and occasional Imperial residence. In the Byzantine Empire and then the Ottoman Empire, to which Thessaloniki belonged until 1912, it remained a major city, in many respects second only to Constantinople. Today, Thessaloniki forms the second-largest metropolitan area in Greece.

Thessaloniki's enduring role as a major city means that much of its archaeological record was destroyed and built over throughout the centuries. Furthermore, archaeological research there was not favored by the city's long incorporation into the Ottoman Empire, which was less interested in archaeology than the Greek state, and the lack of surviving Archaic and Classical structures also failed to inspire early interest in exploring the city's history. Much of what is known of Thessaloniki's archaeology derives from rescue excavations carried out in recent decades on the occasion of urban renewal or building projects.

Since its foundation, Thessaloniki's fabric has shown a substantial continuity. The most tangible sign of this consists of the city walls, which were rebuilt in the late fourth century, under Theodosius II (379-393), mostly on the line of the Hellenistic defenses—the exception was on the side toward the sea, where the city had expanded during the late Hellenistic and Roman Periods. These walls were maintained with various reconstructions until the 19th century. Most scholars have considered that the orthogonal street plan of the Roman city went back to Hellenistic times although it has been suggested that the Roman orientation deviated by a few degrees from the Hellenistic one. It is also usually thought that the Roman Agora was built over the Hellenistic one. Recently it has been maintained that this is not the case, but, at the least, the location remained constant from the early-Imperial Period to the seventh century.

Although its Roman phase is less well known than that of Corinth, Thessaloniki is comparable in that it also became a provincial capital under the Romans. Its continuity contrasts with Athens, where the center of town moved away from the Agora and the line of the walls was reduced and then probably re-expanded.

The heart of ancient Thessaloniki was the Agora (Fig. XIV-19). The Roman Agora is a square surrounded by columns, going back to the early-Imperial Period. On one side is an odeion. A *cryptoporticus* or underground passageway connected the upper part with the lower. Following earthquake damage at the beginning of the seventh century, the Agora was abandoned. It is undoubtedly significant that, on the contrary, the nearby church of St. Demetrius was repaired—evidently the ancient structure had lost its function and could be dispensed with, while the new ecclesiastical structure was needed.

Fig. XIV-19 View of the Roman Agora in Thessaloniki, Greece. Photo Credit: Erich Lessing / Art Resource, N.Y.

Thessaloniki is best known for its Late Antique monuments. These fall into two groups—a palace complex and churches. The Imperial complex is an important example of Late Antique palace architecture. The churches also form one of the most significant groups of extant early church buildings outside Rome. Unfortunately none of these monuments is well dated and all have various structural phases, and that presents difficulties in evaluating them.

Fig. XIV-20 (left) Reconstruction of the *tetrapylon*, colonnaded street and rotunda, part of the residence of Galerius at Thessaloniki. C. 300 CE. Drawing by Cherylee Francis.

Fig. XIV-21 (below) War scene with elephants, from the Arch of Galerius, , built c. 300 CE to commemorate Emperor Galerius' victories over the Persians. Thessaloniki, Greece. Photo Credit: Gianni Dagli Orti / The Art Archive at Art Resource, N.Y.

Scholars are united in attributing the eginning of construction of the palace omplex to the emperor Galerius, one of the etrarchic or four co-rulers of the Empire, who hose Thessaloniki as his residence at the nd of the third and beginning of the fourth entury CE. It is less clear whether he finished he complex, and indeed the argument has een made that Constantine, who also lived at Thessaloniki in 322-323 before founding his ew capital at Constantinople, may have been esponsible for completing it. The complex vas located in an area in the eastern part of he city that had not been built up previously. t consisted of three parts along an axis, with a ippodrome to the east of it. The palace itself stood on flat land near the sea. It included a vestibule on the main street, a large courtyard surrounded by rectangular and apsidal rooms, nd an octagonal building. The Octagon, ossibly intended as the throne room, may ave been finished under Constantine.

The Arch of Galerius was in the center of the axis, on the main street of the city (Fig. XIV-20). It was a quadrifrons or four-fronted arch with a central cupola. The relief decoration is considered to be a forerunner of Byzantine art. It is placed on four registers running around the pillars rather than located along a single visual plane (Fig. XIV-21). The figures in the foreground are sculpted vigorously, with a tendency toward frontality of pose, while those in the background are rendered with incised lines. This last feature was known previously on monuments from the western provinces and became characteristic of Late Antique art.

The third element of the complex, higher up from the Arch, is the Rotunda (Fig. XIV-22). This is normally interpreted as the mausoleum

Fig. XIV-22 (left) Rotunda of Galerius, c. 300 CE. Location: Agios Georgios (Rotunda of St. George), Thessaloniki, Greece. Photo Credit: Scala / Art Resource, N.Y.

Fig. XIV-23 Basilica of Agios Demetrios. This five-aisled Byzantine church was originally built in the fifth century CE on the alleged site of the martyrdom of Saint Demetrios, patron of Thessaloniki. It has been extensively restored in the seventh century CE and in 1917. Location: Thessaloniki, Greece. Photo Credit: Vanni / Art Resource, N.Y.

for Galerius, although it was not used for this purpose, as he was buried at Romuliana, his birthplace at what is now Gamzigrad in modern-day Serbia. An alternative interpretation sees it as the intended mausoleum for Constantine, uncompleted because he decided to be buried at Constantinople after moving there. The lack of a crypt would be expected in pagan mausolea preceding Constantine but not in Christian ones from his time onward, It probably speaks for the thriving nature of the city that the complex was built on previously unused land and that its later abandonment seems to have had no ill effect on Thessaloniki.

Churches were installed gradually in the fabric of the city. In the case of St. Demetrius, the patron saint of the city, we know that the church reportedly stands on the site of his martyrdom, a bath complex to the north of the Agora. The current building (badly damaged in a fire in 1917, shortly after it was returned to Christian worship after centuries of use as a mosque) is a basilica with five naves separated by columns (Fig. XIV-23). It is generally considered to go back to the fifth century CE, possibly replacing a smaller structure; it underwent extensive restorations in the seventh century. The Rotunda was transformed into a church dedicated to St. George, but the date when this took place is still debated. The building may have been finished but undecorated and left without a function at the time of Constantine's departure for his new capital in 323, then damaged in the earthquake of 363 and finally transformed into a church by the emperor Theodosius to atone for his massacre of 7000 Thessalonians in 390.

The mosaic decoration of the Rotunda's dome presents elements recalling Classical taste, especially the architectural backdrops to the scenes in the lower zone, which it has been argued would better fit the experimental spirit of late fourth century Christian art rather than the already codified art of the fifth and sixth centuries. Another Late Antique church is Panagia Acheiropoietos, a basilica with three naves of probable fifth-century date, for which parallels have been drawn with the church architecture of Syria and Anatolia. Further early churches are known archaeologically—for instance, the transformation of the octagonal building in the palace and a basilica preceding the church of Agia Sophia, the cathedral built on a domed plan in the Byzantine tradition.

Thessaloniki survived the Slavic onslaught with no break in continuity, undoubtedly in part because of its mighty walls. Thus, it remained a center of Hellenic culture throughout the Middle Ages and became the second city of the Byzantine Empire and later a major city of the Ottoman Empire.

OLYMPIA

Olympia is a different sort of site from the ones considered so far. Rather than a city, it was a great Pan-Hellenic sanctuary and then in Christian times a simple country town. Thus, it represents first a major focus of interest in Greece in the Roman world and then gives some insight into the life of a rural community. After the end of the Late Antique settlement the site was abandoned. The modern town of Olympia grew up only after the beginning of the German excavations in 1876, which have continued with interruptions to the present day, and the resulting establishment of the site on the tourist circuit.

Olympia was the oldest Pan-Hellenic sanctuary, included in Roman times and for most of its history before that in the territory of the city-state of Elis (Fig. VIII-17; Fig. XIV-24). It was also perhaps the most fortunate sanctuary during the Roman Period. Of the four canonical ones, only Olympia and Delphi survived uninterruptedly, while Nemea was abandoned in favor of Argos and Isthmia was revived after a break. The Olympic Games brought professional athletes and many visitors in the summer every four years. The sanctuary was also the recipient of special favors from high personages. The emperors Augustus, Tiberius and Nero all made visits.

Herodes Atticus, the second-century Greek philanthropist with connections to the Imperial house, provided it with a water supply. There is some indication in the ceramic record, however, to suggest that receipt of outside benefactions put Olympia at a disadvantage when they were not forthcoming, as for example around 200 CE, when there is no record in the written or archaeological sources of significant activities financed externally. In a context dated to c. 200 that has been analyzed statistically there are few imported pieces of any sort, and in the seriation (chronological order) of the fine ware discovered in all the old German excavations anywhere on the site there is also a break at that time. The dearth of imports suggests an economic crisis, which may be ascribed to the lack of external patrons after the site had depended on them for generations. This hypothesis will gain strength if future research shows that the crisis was specific to Olympia rather than a more widespread phenomenon.

In Roman times the heart of the sanctuary continued to be the complex known as the *Altis*. Here there were three peripteral temples (that is ones surrounded by colonnades) with their altars—the great Temple of Zeus and the *Metroon* or Temple to the Mother of the Gods (both dating from the Classical Period) and *Heraion* or Temple to the goddess Hera from the Archaic Period. The *Altis* also contained a large number of statues and other monuments, as

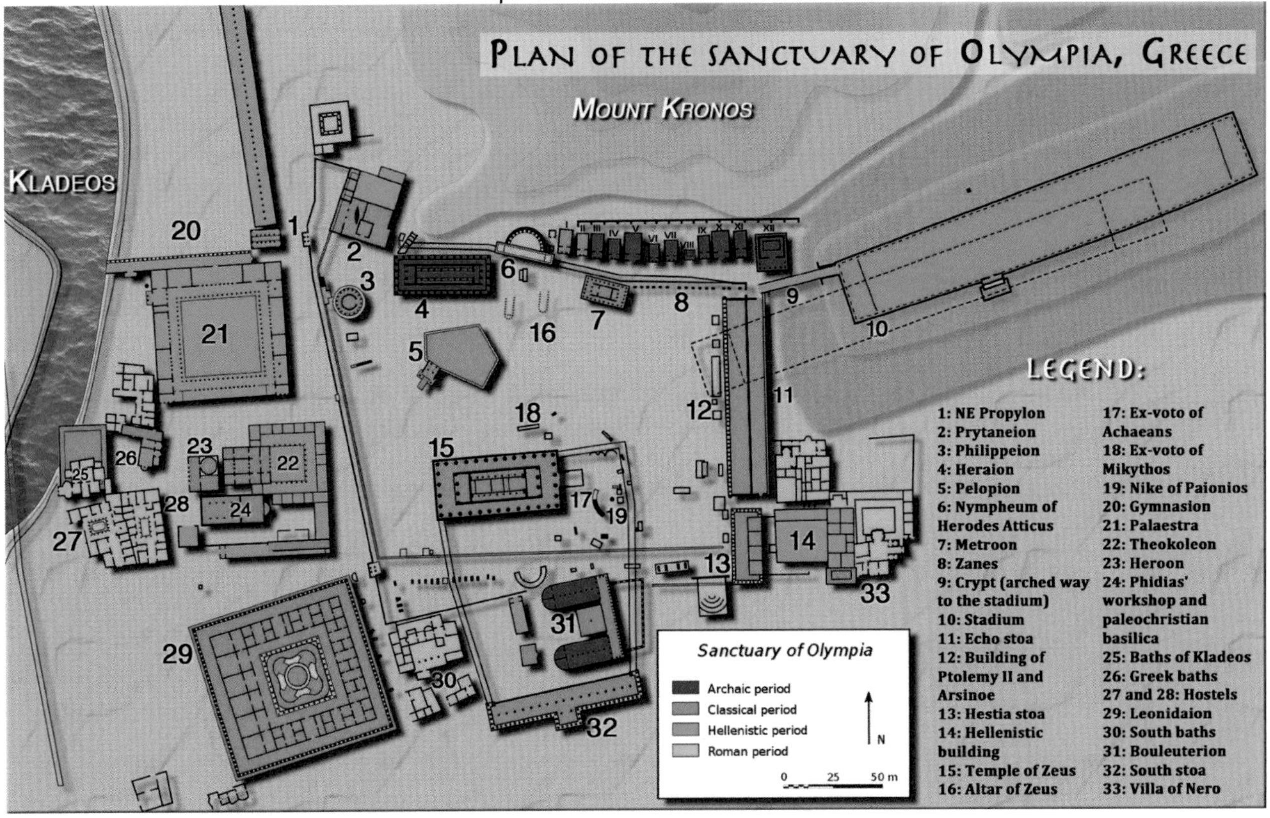

Fig. XIV-24 Plan of the site of Olympia, Greece by Cherylee Francis. **(See larger plan page 365.)**

well as a row of treasuries along its northern edge on the lower slope of the hill of Kronos, going back to the Archaic, Classical and Hellenistic Periods. The *Altis*, the area most closely related to cult functions, shows a great continuity with respect to pre-Roman times. Architecturally, the greatest change is the construction of an enclosure wall with monumental entrances, which was carried out at an unknown moment of the first or perhaps the second century. For the users of the sanctuary the most significant modification was probably the rededication of the Metroon to the Imperial cult, which is indicated by the discovery of statues of the members of the Imperial family there. Otherwise, evidence of the Roman Period in the *Altis* consists largely of repairs, including repairs to the roof of the Temple of Zeus in the time of Diocletian around 300 CE.

Outside the *Altis*, repair and maintenance were undertaken periodically in Roman times, for instance in the nearby stadium. The focus of activities in the Roman Period was, however, on the infrastructure surrounding the *Altis*, in order to bring the hygienic standards up to date and to improve the capacity to receive visitors.

It is symptomatic that Olympia presents one of the first baths of the Campanian type of the first-century BCE known in Greece or indeed outside Campania. The Greek Hypocaust Baths in the western part of the site was state of the art, with new elements such as the *testudo* (a metal basin for heating water) and a hypocaust system (Fig. IX-28). At one time it was argued by researchers at Olympia that the type originated there c. 100 BCE and spread to Campania. Now there are indications of a date for the Olympia Hypocaust Bath around 40 BCE, especially from the reuse of architectural elements from buildings destroyed in an earthquake then. Thus, Olympia appears to be an early adopter of a bit of technology from the West.

Later, many so-called baths were built at Olympia. Some were certainly stand-alone bath buildings, while others belong to complexes. The Kladeos Baths, located near the Greek Hypocaust Baths and dated to around 100 CE, are undoubtedly autonomous. They have a *frigidarium* or room-temperature bath, *tepidarium* or lightly heated bath and *caldarium* or hot bath, as well as a *laconicum* or dry sweating room and an individual bath. The South Baths and the East Baths are about 100 years more recent. The former is another stand-alone bath building, while the latter is a part of a building known erroneously as Nero's House or villa. Somewhat later in the Imperial Period a bath element was added to the North Building, which appears to be a pavilion for banqueting that contained a base for pitching elaborate tents. The Leonidaion Baths, a small but well-designed bath building made of bricks and concrete with vaulted roofs (i.e., in a quintessentially Roman fashion), were constructed no earlier than c. 200 CE right on the roadway of the Sacred Way that the procession took from the political center of Elis to the sanctuary. Thus, throughout most of the Roman Period of the sanctuary there was a great interest in providing bathing facilities at Olympia.

Herodes Atticus' gift to Olympia in the mid-second century of an aqueduct, which solved the site's problem of water supply, certainly favored the use of bath complexes. The so-called *Nymphaeum* of Herodes Atticus—actually dedicated in the name of his wife, Regilla—constitutes the termination of the aqueduct. It is a sumptuous structure standing above the sacred enclosure by the treasuries. The decoration consists of a program of portraits of Herodes' family and the Imperial house.

Tradition called for visitors to the Olympic Games to lodge in tents, and that undoubtedly continued to be the case in the Roman Period. Other possibilities were created, however. There are two structures near the Kladeos that are considered hostels of the mid-Imperial Period. Another building of this sort is the Leonidaion, identified though the description of Olympia by Pausanias in the second century CE. The name and the original structure go back to the fourth century BCE. The central courtyard and the rooms around its four sides were rebuilt extensively in brick. The parallels for the rooms are to be found in the villa architecture of Italy in the first century BCE and the first century CE. The arrangement of the garden in the open area of the courtyard with curvilinear elements in a basin recalls the garden of the lower courtyard in the *Domus Flavia* or Palace of the Flavian emperor Domitian on the Palatine in Rome (Fig. IX-12). Therefore, it is likely that the reconstruction can be dated to the Flavian Period, perhaps to the reign of Domitian.

The Southwest Building was the object of particular research by a team from the German Archaeological Institute in the 1980s and 1990s. Its position is very prominent—on the southern side of the Sacred Way (just to the south of the Leonidaion and the Leonidaion Baths) just beyond the crossing of the Kladeos River, not the place for just any structure. The Southwest Building has been interpreted as the headquarters of the athletes' association. The hypothesis rests on two elements. One is architectural—the presence of a room in the front part of the building that was richly decorated with marble cladding on the walls but had a sand floor suitable for gymnastic exercises (in this case probably for show rather than real training). The other is epigraphic—the discovery of a bronze inscription listing the names of winners at Olympic Games. The examination of the walls shows two clear building phases. The first used *opus mixtum*, a facing of *opus reticulatum* (a net-like pattern of small pyramidal blocks) within a frame of brickwork, over a concrete core. The second, more extensive phase completing the building employed the usual brick masonry of the Roman Period at Olympia.

Opus reticulatum and *opus mixtum* are the normal masonry at Rome and its surroundings in the first and second centuries CE, but elsewhere they are rare and associated with the emperor or the Roman state. The *opus mixtum* in the Southwest Building is of very high quality, with the best parallels to be found in the reign of Nero. Furthermore, the pottery found in the layers associated with the first phase can be dated to the middle of the first century, while the pottery and glass found in the layers associated with the second phase can be dated to the end of the century. Combining this evidence with the written sources, it is suggested that the building was offered by Nero as the headquarters of the athletes' association at the time of his visit in 66, that it remained incomplete after his fall in 68 and that it was finally finished a generation later.

There are two questions to ask about the end of the pan-Hellenic Sanctuary at Olympia. When did it take place? Did it mark a significant break in the history of the site, i.e., was it the end of antiquity there?

The first question has two alternative answers. Traditionally the order by Theodosius I for the closure of the pagan cult sites in 391 was considered to mark the official end of the Sanctuary at Olympia, although there is no written source referring specifically to Olympia. The hypothesis of an end to the sanctuary's use nearly 130 years before Theodosius' edict gained ground among the excavators in the decades after World War II. The key element here is a wall built of *spolia* or reused building materials that cuts off the Temple of Zeus inside the fortification from its altar outside. The wall re-used elements of most of the buildings and altars of the sanctuary. This had earlier been known vaguely as the "Byzantine" wall, but it was re-interpreted as having been built as an answer to a supposed Herulian threat in 267, although there is no evidence for a Herulian threat concerning Olympia. In the meantime an examination of the wall has clearly established a Late Antique date for it and not a third-century one, although the purpose of the wall is still debated. The inscription listing Olympic victors discovered in the Southwest Building covers most of the fourth century, up to 385, with athletes from many parts of the Greek world. Thus, the sanctuary's main cult continued, and not merely as a local festival, at least up to the eve of the Theodosian decree. The closure of the sanctuary cannot have come before then, although there is no evidence to prove that the pagan cult ended just then rather than somewhat later.

There is also no indication that the years around 400 witnessed any sharp break. No evidence has been discovered of destruction of buildings. All the archaeological indications of a Christian presence at Olympia date to the fifth or sixth centuries. In the ceramic record it appears that the supply of fine wares to Olympia declined gradually from 300 to 600, with nothing particular to note around 400. Thus, the late-fourth and early-fifth centuries appear not to have been traumatic for the site and cannot be seen as the end of antiquity at Olympia followed by a situation best considered medieval.

Two phases have been seen in the Late Antique settlement. The first, lasting from some time in the early- to mid-fifth century until the settlement was destroyed by an earthquake toward the mid-sixth century (perhaps the one attested for 551 CE), was located around the church built into the workshop of Pheidias to the west of the *Altis*. The houses in this phase consisted of several large rooms, including one identifiable as the kitchen by the presence of a hearth, built-in *pithoi* (large ceramic storage jars) and a working area. The so-called Herulian wall belongs to this phase. The area that it encloses takes in the Temple of Zeus. It, the church and the private dwellings were all made of *spolia*. The second phase of the settlement was focused to the east of the Temple of Zeus with houses for the first time in the *Altis*. It is also the first time that the *spolia* used in construction included pedimental sculpture (as a part of the infill between rectangular blocks placed vertically). The houses now were densely packed complexes of small rooms. The church was reconstructed on a smaller scale, but the fortification wall was partly built over. Nearly 200 inhumation graves have been discovered associated with the houses of the Late Antique settlement and not kept separate from them, as they would have been in earlier times.

The economy of the Late Antique settlement is generally agreed to have been based on viticulture and wine-making. Iron implements and large *pithoi* used for those activities have been identified, and 14 vats for wine production are attested. In one wine press establishment, the must flowed from the press through reused lions' head sculptures into waiting vessels.

Aside from agriculture, the inhabitants of the Late Antique settlement engaged in various handicraft activities. The best evidence is for pottery production. Waste associated with a kiln and three associated vats, which appear to have been in use from the fifth century until the late-sixth, has been reported. Lamp molds provide further evidence of ceramic production. There are also indications of iron and bronze working and textile production.

The Late Antique settlement had some trade links with the Mediterranean world. Coins give an indication of circulation, and the small finds show that Olympia kept up with trends in fashion. The best evidence comes from pottery imports, however. The small percentage of amphorae suggests a modest level of trade. On the other hand, the impressive geographic range of the imports

ig. XIV-25 Late Antique earthquake destruction / fallen columns from the Temple of Zeus at Olympia. Photo credit: Noelle Soren. University f Arizona School of Anthropology Photo Archive.

amphorae from Africa, the Levant, the Aegean; fine wares from Africa and Asia Minor; lamps from Africa) speaks for solid links.

All this paints the picture of a flourishing country town. It appears to be a community largely reliant on itself but also provided with a range of external contacts. It is far from the world-renowned sanctuary previously existing on the site. The life led there, from its handicrafts and material culture to its trade, continued recognizably in the ancient tradition, however.

The Late Antique settlement ended between the late-sixth century and the very beginning of the seventh. First there is a horizon of hoard deposition toward the end of the sixth century. Although there is no evidence (for instance, destruction layers, unburied skeletons or scattered arrowheads) to indicate that anything materialized, there must have been a threat or series of threats, such as the Slavic/Avar incursions mentioned in written sources for this time, to provoke this activity. This horizon is followed by a reduced occupation of the settlement, attested by finds of single coins up to the reign of Phocas (602-610). Nothing later of any class of material has been found at Olympia itself. About 1 km to the north of the site of the sanctuary and Late Antique settlement, however, a Slavic cremation cemetery was discovered, which used a pagan rite of burial in ceramic urns. The finds, which can be dated from the second quarter of the seventh century until at least the late eighth, can be compared to finds in the area from the lower Danube to the middle Dnjepr and have little or nothing in common with Late Antique or Byzantine material culture. The real break with antiquity at Olympia comes, then, c. 600. Up to that point there is continuity, even if it is in very changed circumstances. Afterwards there is as complete a break as one could hope to see archaeologically.

A modern interdisciplinary approach to the understanding of Greece in Roman times shows varying responses to incorporation into the Roman Empire and life as a part of it. Athens appealed to the past and used its traditions to become a cultural center. Corinth faced its future squarely and maximized its geographical advantages. Thessaloniki became a provincial capital and crossroads between Italy, Anatolia and the Balkans. Olympia evolved from a Pan-Hellenic sanctuary to a thriving country town.

CRITICAL THINKING EXERCISES

•1, Did every Greek community respond to Roman domination in the same way?

•2, How did Greek communities vary in their response to Roman domination?

•3, How did the Athenian Agora, the major gathering place of the city, transform during the Roman Period?

•4, Which Roman Emperors were the biggest Philhellenes and how did they show this?

•5, What was the relationship of wealthy landowners in Greece to the poorer people in the cities and countryside.

•6, How does the study of pottery help to explain a great deal about Greek daily life in the Roman Period? Give specific examples.

•7, What role did Greek athletic and religious centers play in the Roman Period?

• 8, How did Roman Greece come to an end? Did some places show greater continuity than others?

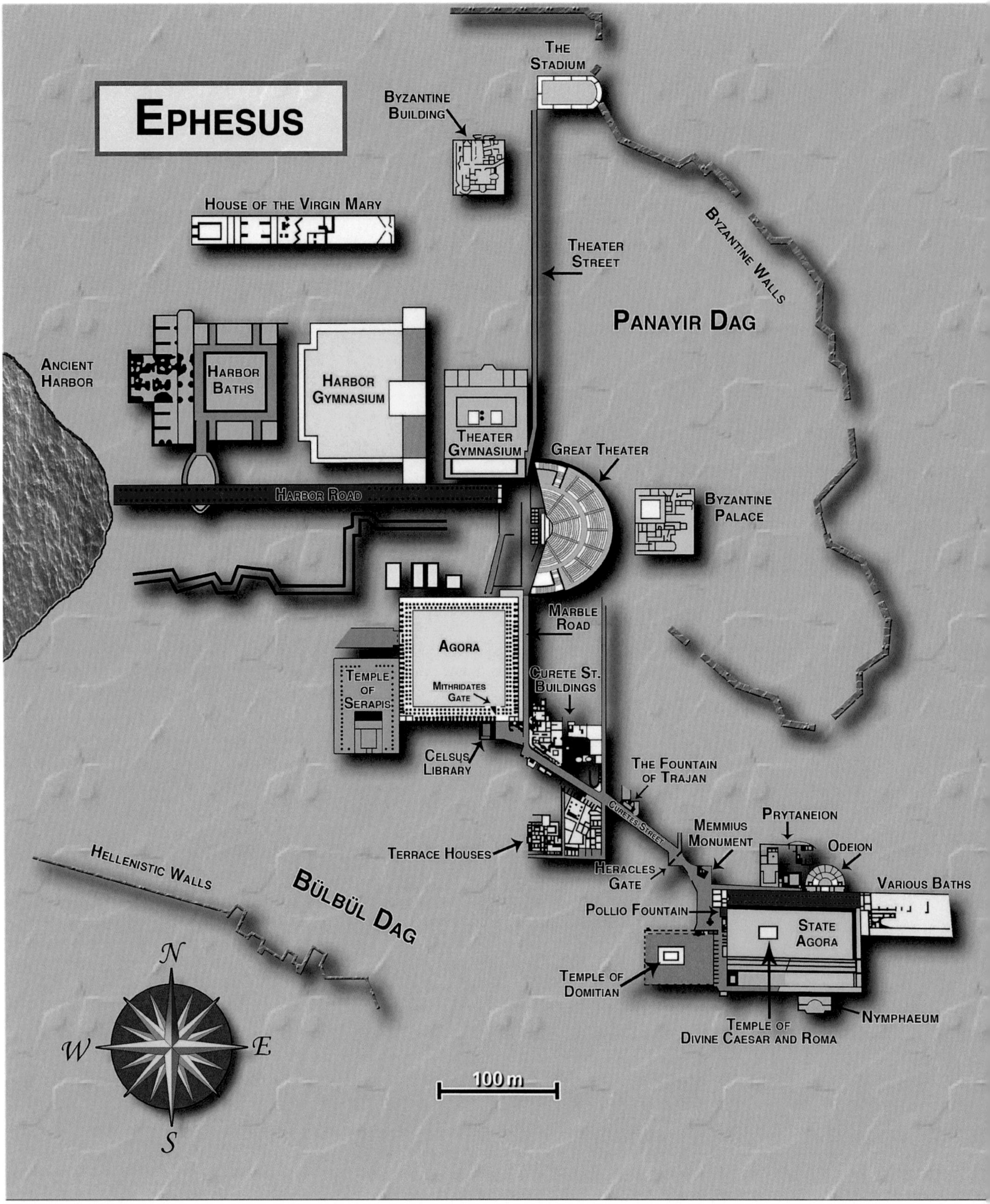

Fig. XV-1 Plan of the city of Ephesos in Turkey by Cherylee Francis.

Chapter XV

Ephesos–How a City Functioned in the Roman Empire

Although beginning students of Roman art and archaeology tend to focus on two cities: Rome and Pompeii, the Empire in general and the eastern part in particular was a land of cities, and other urban centers offer insight into the functioning of Roman cities in the Imperial Period. Here we want to take a more detailed look at how one city functioned in the Roman Empire. Ephesos offers the opportunity of examining both the Romanization of a community with a centuries-old tradition and the transformation of a provincial city in Late Antiquity. It became the capital of the Roman province of Asia and one of the major cities of the eastern part of the Empire. Before that it had been a leading city of the Greek world for centuries. It continued to be important throughout Late Antiquity and even into the early Byzantine Period. One great boon about the location of the ancient city is that Ephesos was never built over by a modern city. It is therefore free of all overburden and allows archaeologists to directly probe the Late Antique and Roman settlements. This has led to extensive excavations, first by the English in the 19th century and for more than a century by the Austrians.

The province of Asia, of which Ephesos was the capital, consisted of the part of modern Turkey facing the Aegean and also of the islands offshore. It came into the possession of the Roman state in 133 BCE by bequest from the last king of Pergamon, Attalos III. From then until the establishment of the Augustan peace, the province was afflicted by various wars: first, the internal unrest at the time of the constitution of the province, and then the wars carried out under the leadership of Mithridates of Pontus in the attempt to expel the Romans from the East, and finally the Roman civil wars. From the time of Augustus, it became a province of consular rank under Senatorial control, and was one of the most prestigious.

Asia has legitimately been considered the counterpart of Achaea in Greece. Like Achaea, Asia was a land of ancient Hellenic cities and culture. The province included the territory of Ionia, one of the major branches of the ancient Greek people. Homer, the Greek national poet, was Ionian, for instance, and Smirne (modern Izmir) and Chios, both in the province of Asia, claimed to be his birthplace.

There were differences, of course. Asia had always had stronger Eastern influences, which affected the expression of Hellenic culture into Roman times. There were elements of the population overlaid by the Greeks that had indigenous roots, and the area had belonged to the Persian Empire. In the Roman Period, it is, however, in the economic sphere that one sees the greatest difference, as Asia became more dynamic. Various centers of Hellenistic wine production continue to export their products during the early Imperial Period in amphorae that have been recognized in the ceramic record in many parts of the Empire—Rhodes, Kos, and Knidos. To these can be added a new production area for wine with a distinctive container in the hinterland of Ephesos, lasting from the early Roman Period to Late Antiquity, as well as others of Late Antique date. It is also significant that the province contained two centers of standardized, widely exported red fine ware in the Roman tradition during the early and middle Imperial Period (Pergamon and Tralles) and another center that produced an equally important Late Antique fine ware inspired by the North African tradition (Phocaea).

GEOGRAPHICAL SETTING

A major element conditioning the city's development throughout its history is its topography (Fig. XV-1). The site lies in the lower valley of the Küçük Menderes (ancient Kaystros) river. It is organized around three hills; two toward the west are closely connected (Panayırdağ and Bülbüldağ) while the third (Ayasoluk) is located to the east. The coastline has advanced throughout the history of Ephesos, beginning with the intensive farming of the hilly interior in the early first millennium BCE, which gave rise to significant erosion. In the Archaic Period an arm of the sea passed to the north of Ayasoluk. By the early Hellenistic Period it had silted up to a point between Ayasoluk and Panayırdağ. At the beginning of the Roman Imperial Period the sea had retreated to the base of Panayırdağ. Under the Roman Empire it was possible to maintain a passage to the harbor to the west of Panayırdağ. By the Middle Ages the site was landlocked, and the coast now lies about 5 kilometers to the west of it. These factors must be borne in mind in considering the historical and archaeological evidence for the settlement of the area.

ORIGIN OF EPHESOS

Ephesos originated in the late Bronze Age, when the Mycenaean Greeks took an interest in the western coast of Asia Minor. This is attested locally by the discovery of a Mycenaean grave on Ayasoluk. A plausible hypothesis sees Ephesos (specifically a settlement on Ayasoluk) as Apaša, the center of a buffer state between the Mycenaean sphere and the Hittite area. At the end of the Bronze Age, with the disintegration of Hittite and Mycenaean power after 1200 B.C., groups of Greeks (known as Aeolians and Ionians) settled on the Aegean coast of Asia Minor, founding new city-states. The Greek foundation myth for Ephesos recalls that Androklos, a son of the Athenian king Kodros, founded a settlement called Koressos and reached an agreement with the local population and its great sanctuary of a goddess whom the Greeks assimilated to their Artemis. Throughout ancient Greek recorded history, Ephesos became famous as the city of Artemis or in Roman times her equivalent Diana.

At Ephesos Artemis was considered to have been born on Ephesian territory at Ortygia, where a group of semi-divine worshippers of Zeus called the Kuretes raised such a clamor that Hera was unable to interfere with her birth. The Archaic Greek, specifically Ionian, settlement reflected in the Androklos story is generally supposed to have been on the northern part of Panayırdağ. Traces of another Archaic-Classical settlement, identified with a

Fig. XV-2 (left) Reconstruction of the fourth c. BCE Temple of Artemis, Ephesus, Turkey. Photo Credit© DeA Picture Library / Art Resource, N.Y.

Fig. XV-3 (below) Artemis (Diana) of Ephesus. Second c. CE. Location: Museo Archeologico Nazionale, Naples, Italy. Photo Credit: Scala / Art Resource, N.Y.

village called Smyrna, have been found farther to the southwest under the later Tetragonos Agora, at the time directly on the coast. Graves discovered along the later street called the *Embolos* perhaps belong to yet another settlement in the upper part of the valley between Panyırdağ and Bülbüldağ.

Greek legends connect the Sanctuary of Artemis with the Amazons (mythical female antagonists of the Greeks who were also associated with various other places in Asia Minor), perhaps preserving some memory of pre-Greek relations in the region. The location of the earliest Artemision or Temple of Artemis is uncertain, although most scholars assume that it was on the same site as later, between Ayasoluk and Panayırdağ. It is well documented historically that Kroesos, the wealthy king of Lydia in what is now central Turkey, resettled the Ephesians near the Artemision, presumably on Ayasoluk, when he conquered them around 560 BCE but nothing of it has been discovered archaeologically.

ARTEMIS AND THE ARTEMISION

The Archaic and later Artemision became one of the great sanctuaries of the Greek world and also the oldest significant archaeological testimony of Ephesos (Figs. XV-2,3). The Artemision was so important that it survived in use into Roman times. Re-evaluation of the earliest layers on the site and their dating suggests that a *peripteros* or sacred enclosure was built in the first-half of the seventh century BCE rather than in the eighth, as had been thought. Later in the seventh century a larger temple and retaining walls facing a nearby stream were built. Both the *peripteros* and the succeeding temple were considered as monumental buildings in their day. However, a gigantic building—a *sekos* or unroofed enclosure with a covered double colonnade containing a temple-like structure that used the early seventh-century *peripteros* as its foundation—was erected in the early sixth century and dedicated by Kroesos, the king of Lydia c. 560 BCE.

The so-called Temple of Kroesos burned in 356, supposedly on the very night when Alexander the Great was born. However, it was rebuilt at a higher level largely according to the previous plan. This Late Classical temple remained in use until the end of antiquity. So famous were the sixth-century temple and its successor that they were counted as one of the Seven Wonders of the World. The size of these giant temples, 10 times that of the earlier *peripteros*, as well as the richness of their decoration, impressed the Greeks. The *columnae caelatae* or culpted lower parts of the columns, some of which survive and re in the British Museum were famous, and the extremely ornate olumn bases were widely imitated across the Greek and later Roman world (Fig. XV-2). Finally, the technical innovations that were required to build on such a scale on increasingly swampy land nd to transport and employ such large blocks of stone prompted dmiration and wonder.

The Artemision's architecture was a reflection of the nstitution's power. Its ceremonies involved sacrifices and processions for the broader public and a mystery cult for initiates, both of which contributed to great popularity. It held the right of sylum for those who fled to it, a jealously maintained privilege. As place under the protection of an important divinity where great iches were deposited, it became a banking center. Furthermore, it vas the owner of extensive landed property.

Some of the non-Greek aspects of the appearance of the Ephesian Artemis have provoked discussion, particularly the rows of pendulous bulbs on the lower part of her torso in various, mostly Roman, representations (Fig. XV-3). These are traditionally nterpreted on the basis of Christian writings as multiple breasts. Two hypotheses reject this idea, pointing out that no nipples are hown even when other details are represented realistically. The irst idea suggests that the bulbs are scrota from sacrificed bulls ttached to the cult statue as a symbol of fertility. Although this hypothesis has found some popular favor, scholarly opinion has remained skeptical because there is no literary or archaeological evidence for the sacrifice of bulls in the rites for Artemis Ephesia. The second hypothesis sees a connection between the bulbs and the leather bags that are common as divine attributes in Anatolian prehistory.

THE CITY OF LYSIMACHOS

The main settlement site for Ephesos inherited in the Roman Period goes back to c. 300 BCE, to Lysimachos, one of Alexander the Great's bodyguards and successors, who brought the Ephesians from their city near the Artemision and the inhabitants of several small cities in the region to a new city on Bülbüldağ and Panayırdağ, which he named Arsinoeia in honor of his wife. The reason for this move was not only the increasingly waterlogged condition of the settlement of Kroesos, which could not drain properly because of the silting of the arm of the sea in this area, but also presumably because of Lysimachos' desire to diminish the hold of the sanctuary hierarchy on the city and to increase his own influence and power. The new name did not last, but the new town did, first as New Ephesos with respect to the old settlement and then simply as Ephesos, whose massive ruins attract hordes of international tourists today (Figs. XV-1, 4).

Little of Hellenistic date remains visible or has been investigated archaeologically because of the great overburden of the

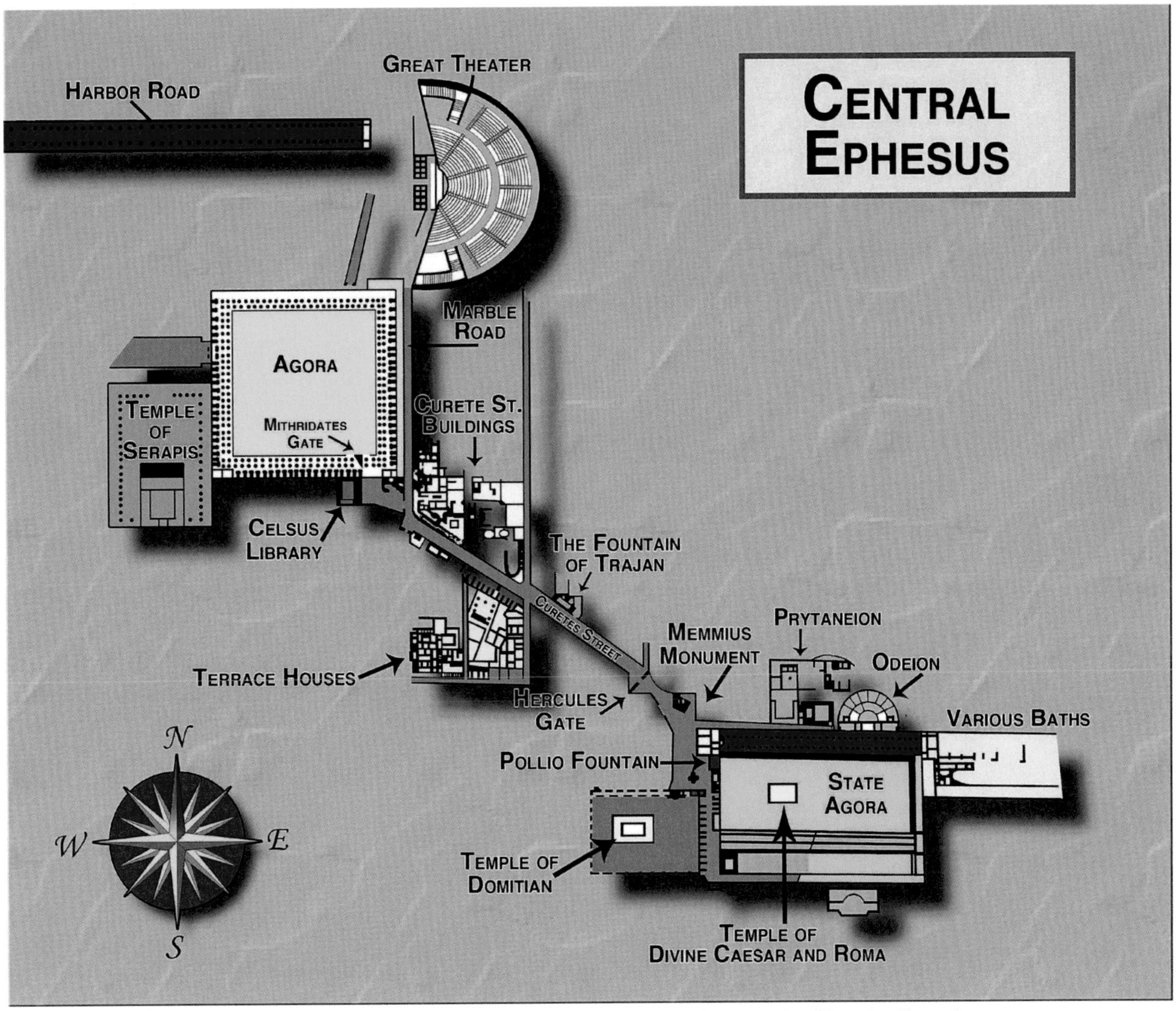

Fig. XV-4 General plan of the main areas of the city of Ephesos by Cherylee Francis.

Fig. XV-5 Upper area of the Street of the Curetes featuring the Monument of Gaius Memmius at Ephesos and looking down to the Library of Celsus. Photo Credit: Noelle Soren. University of Arizona School of Anthropology Archive.

Roman city. The city wall enclosing all of Panayırdağ and the northern slopes of Bülbüldağ was one defining element until Late Antiquity. It is also clear that the town was laid out on the Hellenistic principles attributed to Hippodamos of Miletos of a regular grid plan of rectangular blocks, in what has come to be known as Hippodamian planning. Recent surveying work in the upper city on a plateau between Panayırdağ and Bülbüldağ is designed to clarify the course of the city wall and the street plan in that area, which could be the center of the Hellenistic city. Other Hellenistic remains have been found in the area behind the harbor, particularly under the Tetragonos Agora. The lower part of the *Embolos* later occupied by the Terrace Houses was rather sparsely occupied in late Hellenistic times. What is certain is that the Hellenistic city had a lesser extent than the Roman one.

One reason that the regular street plan needs clarification is that much of the archaeological investigation has been centered on an exception to the system, known as the *Embolos* at least in Late Antiquity and sometimes as the Street of the Curetes in the archaeological literature. It is an important street that runs diagonally to the regular system, following an older course along the valley between Panayırdağ and Bülbüldağ and making up part of the processional route from the Artemision around Panayırdağ, through the city and back.

EPHESOS BETWEEN HELLENISTIC KINGDOMS AND THE ROMAN REPUBLIC

Ephesos, like other Greek city-states, maintained a certain local autonomy but always belonged to one of the territorial states that were established after Alexander the Great. After the time of Lysimachos it changed hands between two Hellenistic dynasties, the Seleucids and the Ptolemies, until the Romans, who had taken control of the area, assigned it to the pro-Roman king of Pergamon in 188 BCE.

The city came under direct Roman rule in 133 BCE, when the last king of Pergamon's Attalid dynasty willed his kingdom to the Roman people. Sacred land, such as that of the Artemision, remained sacrosanct as before. Ephesos and other cities were granted the special status of *civitates liberae et immunes*, meaning that they remained autonomous and did not have to pay tribute to Rome. Royal lands became the property of Rome. While Rome was involved in wars and troubles in Italy and the West, Ephesos along with Rome's eastern possessions were left largely in the hands of tax-farmers and others who wanted to enrich themselves at the provincials' expense. Because of the dissatisfaction with this exploitation, Mithridates' war against Roman domination in 89 BCE gained widespread support in Asia Minor. Death was decreed at Ephesos for all Italians living in the province, and massacres ensued known to ancient historians as the Ephesian Vespers. Because of this, the victorious Roman general Sulla punished the city with a heavy fine and the loss of freedom, which was restored only decades later. Ephesos was also involved in the struggles of the Roman civil wars of the later first century BCE, particularly as a place of residence of Mark Antony.

The monument to Gaius Memmius, a grandson of Sulla, which was situated on an important location at the top of Curetes Street, is one of the rare surviving late Hellenistic structures at Ephesos, although it has been extensively rebuilt in modern times (Figs. XV-4, 5, 6). Apparently it had the form of a four-sided triumphal arch. The monument, which features portraits of members of the family, commemorates Sulla's victory, seen as a liberation from Mithridates.

Fig. XV-6 Detail of the Monument of Gaius Memmius at Ephesos. Photo Credit: Noelle Soren. University of Arizona School of Anthropology Archive.

Another Hellenistic structure is the Octagon somewhat lower down the *Embolos*, just below the Terrace Houses on the left. Its decoration dates it between 50 and 20 BCE. It contained the skeleton of a woman of 15-16 years of age. The monument's date and the skeleton's age make it likely that this was the burial place of the famous Cleopatra's younger sister, Arsinoe IV, who was held prisoner at Ephesos and murdered there in 41 BCE.

By the end of the first century BCE Ephesos had a heritage of a millennium of history. It had long been one of the major cities of the Greek-speaking world. It also drew upon non-Hellenic traditions. There were a still relatively new town with its harbor on Panayırdağ and Bülbüldağ and the venerable sanctuary below Ayasoluk. Politically the city had been part of the Roman province of Asia for more than a century but when and how did the city become Roman?

THE BEGINNING OF ROMANIZATION

Often the remains of everyday material culture, which for the archaeologist is most frequently represented by pottery, can provide insight into such questions, as they involve the intimate sphere of life. The pottery record shows that Ephesos continued in a Hellenistic tradition into the reign of Augustus. That is, until then people cooked, served and ate their food as their ancestors had done. Then they began to import tablewares from Italy (Italian *sigillata* platters, plates and cups and thin-walled drinking vessels). At the same time local potters started producing Italian-influenced vessels (in particular Eastern *Sigillata* B). There is good evidence from the name on potters' stamps that the Arretine workshop of C. Sentius was involved in the local production of Italian-influenced pottery. This tendency lasted for a couple of generations, until the mid-first century CE, by which time a local tradition incorporating some Italian elements was once again consolidated and largely ended the need for imports. One can see a similar phenomenon in the field of illumination, where the Ephesians adopted the Roman style of mold-made oil lamps and soon created their own tradition with specific types. There was also a certain penetration of western amphora-borne produce in the Ephesian market at this time. These importations and imitations indicate a desire to adopt some semblance of Roman habits in daily life, from meals to household furnishings.

Fig. XV-7 Government area (State Agora) of Ephesus, Turkey. Location: Ephesus, Turkey. Photo Credit: Erich Lessing / Art Resource, N.Y.

parts of the city between Panayırdağ and Bülbüldağ and at the western foot of the former were destined for these purposes, leaving the slopes as the main residential areas.

EPHESOS UNDER THE JULIO-CLAUDIANS

The architectural transformation of the city began under Augustus and his successors, the Julio-Claudians. Various entities and individuals, of whom inscriptions inform us, were responsible for the building operations.

The most notable intervention was the creation of the so-called administrative district at the upper end of the *Embolos*, which can be described as a complex of buildings offering the amenities of an Italian town (Figs. XV-4, 5). We know from historical sources that Augustus allowed the *conventus civium Romanorum* (the association of Roman citizens) to erect a temple for the worship of *divus Iulius* (the deified Julius Caesar) and Roma (the personification of Rome), perhaps during his stay at Ephesos. Archaeologists have traditionally interpreted this to be a precinct with two chambers behind the north side of the so-called State Agora. Recently it has been proposed to identify the precinct with a Temple to Artemis and an Augustus sculpture which was found there, and to attribute the temple on the longitudinal axis of the State Agora, which is datable to the third-quarter of the first century BCE, with cults to *divus Iulius* and Roma (Fig. XV-4).

The State Agora, 160 m long and 58 wide, is located on a terraced space that was crossed by the processional route of the cult of Artemis. It had apparently existed already in the late Hellenistic Period but reached its final form only in the late Augustan Period. Along the south side of the agora was a double colonnade in the Doric style. The original arrangement of the east and west sides is not well known, although colonnades like the one on the south are likely. The agora was bordered to the north by the two-story, triple-aisled Basilica Stoa in the Ionic style, erected in 11 CE by the great Ephesian benefactor C. Sextilius Pollio and his family. Pollio and his family also provided the city with an aqueduct sometime between 4 and 14 CE. Presumably because of these benefactions Pollio's stepson was allowed to erect a funerary monument to him on the west side of the agora (Fig. XV-4). A *chalcidicum* (annex) was added at the western end of the stoa under Nero. Behind the stoa was the *prytaneion* (an assembly or town hall where banquets and receptions might also be held) built under Augustus, as well as the precinct already mentioned. The city's sacred fire was kept in the *prytaneion*, which also became the seat of the Kuretes, which came to be the main group of priests of Artemis (Fig. XV-4).

Outside the administrative district another focus of Augustan and Julio-Claudian building activity was the Tetragonos Agora

Historical sources also point to the Augustan Period as the real beginning of the Roman Period at Ephesos. Augustus spent part of 29 BCE at Ephesos, directly involved in Ephesian affairs. During his reign he regulated the affairs of the city and the sanctuary, returning to the latter usurped lands but also re-establishing the traditional boundaries of asylum, which had been extended by Mithridates and Mark Antony to include part of the city, causing problems of public order. Ephesos also became the seat of the governor (proconsul) of the province of Asia, the highest ranking province among those governed by the Senate in the division of provinces that Augustus carried out. This standing gained Ephesos the title of Metropolis of Asia. Perhaps most important of all, the *pax Augusta* permitted the prosperous development of the city.

From the Augustan to the Antonine Periods important parts of the population became legally Roman and thus harbored a double identity. To some extent, especially in the earliest times of Roman rule, there were Roman citizens at Ephesos because of immigrants from the West. An early component consisted of Imperial freedmen, who had been liberated from slavery by their masters. These individuals were Roman citizens and had ties to Rome but may have been of Eastern origin. As part of the typical Roman policy of co-opting local aristocrats, leading Ephesian citizens gained Roman citizenship during the first and second centuries CE. Some Ephesians were admitted to the equestrian and Senatorial orders and pursued careers at the level of the Empire, as well as at Ephesos. Inscriptions inform us of the activities of Ephesians in all these areas.

Archaeologically we are best informed about the development of the public and monumental side of the city, on which investigation has concentrated over the last century. The flatter or commercial agora at the bottom of the *Embolos*. The agora in its earliest form goes back to Hellenistic times. A new and larger agora was built in the late first century BCE, although it was almost completely re-erected on the same plan, apparently after an earthquake in 23 CE. It consists of a square surrounded on all four sides by double-aisled colonnades. In 43 a statue to the Emperor Claudius was dedicated in the agora, and under Nero a basilica was added behind its west side. The main feature surviving from the Augustan Period is the south gate, built in 3 BCE by the Imperial freedmen Mazaeus and Mithridates in the form of a triumphal arch with three passages (Figs. XV-4, 7, 8, 9).

Aside from the Tetragonos Agora, it seems that the coastal plain in general was also built up in the earliest Imperial times. Here stands the theatre, used as other theatres in the Greek world not only for dramatic performances but also for political and other assemblies of the people (Figs. XV- 4, 7, 10). Its date is not clear—some scholars suppose an original phase of the time of Lysimachos, while there is more solid evidence for a late Hellenistic phase, but construction lasted into the early Roman Period, concerning particularly the *scenae frons* (the backdrop to the stage). By this time it could hold over 20,000 people. The gymnasium opposite the theatre may date to the Augustan Period. The stadium, or running track, beyond the theatre in the Koressos district (Fig. XV-1), could well have existed already in Hellenistic times but was renovated and expanded, probably under Nero at the expense of a freedman called C. Sterninius Orpex, in typical Roman fashion on vaulted terraces.

At the Artemision some as yet unpublished buildings could perhaps have served the Imperial cults mentioned in inscriptions.

Fig. XV-8 (above) Library of Celsus and main entry to the Tetragonos or Commercial Agora of Ephesos. Photo Credit: Noelle Soren. University of Arizona School of Anthropology Archive.

Fig. XV-9 (left) South gate of the Tetragonos Agora, built in 3 BCE by the Imperial freedmen Mazaeus and Mithridates in the form of a triumphal arch with three passages. Photo Credit: Noelle Soren. University of Arizona School of Anthropology Archive.

Fig. XV-10 (below) View north from the Theatre of Ephesos over the Arkadiane. Photo Credit: Noelle Soren. University of Arizona School of Anthropology Archive.

EPHESOS FROM DOMITIAN TO THE ANTONINES

Between the reigns of Domitian and Hadrian, Ephesos experienced another building boom. Rather than concentrating on specific parts of the city, it was concerned with filling in the urban fabric in the administrative district, along the *Embolos* and in the harbor and theatre area.

One of the leading figures in Ephesos at the time of Domitian and Trajan was Tiberius Claudius Aristion, a Roman citizen of Greek origin to judge by his name. He is recorded in various offices, among which are three times Asiarch (highest official of the provincial assembly), priest of the Imperial cult and gymnasiarch (official in charge of the gymnasia). A temple of the Imperial cult was an important addition to any city, as having a province's official temple for an Imperial cult (a *neokoros* temple) was a privilege for which cities vied greatly. It was a great boast of Ephesos that it had two *neokoros* cults (as well as another couple of ephemeral ones to emperors who then suffered *damnatio memoriae* or damnation of their memory). This one was perhaps first dedicated to Domitian and then transferred to his father, Vespasian, after Domitian's *damnatio* or perhaps always dedicated to all the Flavian emperors (Figs. XV-4, 11a, 11b).

The temple complex was located to the west of the State Agora on a terrace with a vaulted substructure and faced with a colonnade displaying barbarian caryatids (female supporting figures), a motif known also at Rome and Corinth. A monumental fountain in front of the west wall of the State Agora, featuring an apse with a sculptural group of the Odyssey, was also built under Domitian as part of the same program. Aristion was also responsible for a *nymphaeum* or colossal fountain toward the middle of the *Embolos*, a two-story structure decorated with a statue of Trajan that marked the end of an aqueduct, and for other fountains elsewhere in the city (Fig. XV-12).

Games of Olympic rank were associated with the Imperial cult. This led to important modifications of the harbor area, in which they were held. The Harbor Baths, a complex containing baths, a gymnasium and athletic grounds were built just east of the harbor (Fig. XV-1). Between these baths and the older Theatre Gymnasium, an open area surrounded by triple-colonnades, known as the *Xystoi*, was also laid out. In connection with these buildings and as part of the continuing attempt to maintain the harbor and provide it with a dignified approach, the harbor facilities themselves were renovated. Quays were built for the enclosed basin some 4-6 m deep. A gate was also erected under Trajan or Hadrian at the center of the harbor façade in the form of a triple triumphal arch.

Because of the lack of an inscription it is not known to whom was dedicated the so-called Serapeion, a precinct west of the Tetragonos Agora featuring a podium temple (Figs. XV-4,13 Temple of Serapis). It has been noted that the same group of sculptors from the inland city of Aphrodisias, renowned for

Fig. XV-11a (top left) and 11b (above) Two-story portico bordering the Temple of Domitian at Ephesos. Photo Credit: Noelle Soren. University of Arizona School of Anthropology Archive.

Fig. XV-12 (bottom left) Fountain of Trajan shown in partial restoration at Ephesos, including all recovered architectural parts but leaving out most of the column shafts. Photo Credit: Noelle Soren. University of Arizona School of Anthropology Archive.

ts traveling teams of fine sculptors, was ised here and in the Harbor Baths to do he decoration. The precinct's good water upply suggests that the divinity involved ad healing properties. The complex is asily accessible from the Tetragonos Agora and other surrounding buildings. Thus, it has been suggested recently that his is the Asklepieion, honoring the great ealing god Asklepios, well attested in pigraphy in the early second century, and suitable location for the Mouseion, a nedical school also known epigraphically nd perhaps directed by Trajan's personal hysician, T. Statilius Crito. Visitors might ome to such a place to seek cures for ingering illnesses, dedicate offerings to he god and seek remedies which involved nedicine, prayer and special practices such s hot or cold water bathing, exercise and nud treatments.

The Library of Celsus is one of the nost magnificent monuments of Ephesos Fig. XV-8). As the inscriptions in Greek nd Latin indicate, it was built as a memorial to Tiberius Julius Celsus Polemaeanus by his son, Caius Julius Aquila. The father, probably from the city of Sardis, was a Roman Senator, Consul in 92 and Proconsul of his home province of Asia in 106/107. The son followed in the footsteps of the distinguished father and was consul in 110. The library, located at the bottom of the *Embolos* by the Tetragonos Agora, presents a two-story façade with four projecting pavilions on each level. The interior is a rectangular space with three stories of colonnades around it. Beneath an apse on the main axis is the burial chamber for Celsus himself, making the building a heroon in the Hellenistic tradition. The building is an example of Baroque architecture with projecting and recessed columns. The façade, about 90% of which was recovered, was full of niches that contained female sculptures embodying attributes of the honored Celsus, such as Wisdom, Virtue, Good Will, and Knowledge. It has been estimated that the building housed some 12,000 scrolls.

The second *neokoros* temple was dedicated to Hadrian. Recently it has been argued persuasively that the temple for this cult is to be identified as a temple in the Corinthian order rivaling the Artemision in size, situated near the harbor on reclaimed land. Here Hadrian would have been assimilated to Zeus Olympios.

Another building, located on the north side of the *Embolos* toward the middle, was dedicated to Artemis, Hadrian and the people of Ephesos and donated by Publius Quintilius Valens Varius (Figs. XV-14, 15). It is notable for its rich sculptural decoration and central arcuated lintel. However, its function

Fig. XV-13 (top) The Commercial Agora and the Theatre—north view from the Bülbüldag Hill at Ephesus, Turkey. Location: Ephesus, Turkey Photo Credit: Erich Lessing / Art Resource, N.Y.

Fig. XV-14 (middle) Street of the Curetes and the Temple of Artemis and Hadrian and the People of Ephesos, seen from the Terrace Houses. Photo Credit: Noelle Soren. University of Arizona School of Anthropology Archive.

Fig. XV-15 (right) Temple of Artemis and Hadrian and the People of Ephesos. Photo Credit: Noelle Soren. University of Arizona School of Anthropology Archive.

and history remain the subject of debate, although there seems to be some connection with the Baths of Varius behind it. Its traditional identification as the Temple of Hadrian should probably be excluded.

The Gate of Hadrian framed the intersection of the street leading to Artemis' birthplace of Ortygia with the bottom of the *Embolos*. This tripartite gate in the Corinthian order recalls the Arch of Hadrian at Athens.

Under Hadrian and the Antonine emperors (Antoninus Pius, Marcus Aurelius and Commodus) several generations of the Vedii, a family originally from Italy, were responsible for many benefactions in the city, which filled in the last remaining free spaces for monuments. The first important member of the family, Publius Vedius Antoninus, is mentioned as a magistrate in the dedicatory inscription on the so-called temple to Hadrian on the *Embolos*. In some cases, such as a sundial in the theatre, it is not certain which member of the family is responsible. However, the most important builder is undoubtedly Publius Vedius Antoninus' grandson, the long-named Marcus Claudius Publius Vedius Antoninus Phaedrus, who reached the rank of Roman Senator. He built the *bouleterion* or council house behind the basilica of the State Agora (Fig. XV-4; it is also interpreted as an odeion or covered music hall and may have served both functions) and a gymnasium in the Koressos district (Fig. XV-1). The latter is considered a typical bath complex of Asia Minor, with the four main rooms for bathing disposed along the longitudinal axis, secondary rooms around them and an *ambulacro* and a *palaestra* behind them. A notable feature of the complex is the Imperial room, a marble-encrusted exedra or recessed area on the *palaestra* containing statues of Antoninus Pius, Androklos and the donor.

A son-in-law of Phaedrus, Titus Flavius Damianos, was also an important benefactor, perhaps with money from his wife's family, as well as a philosopher. His most important work was a covered walkway joining the Artemision and the city. Excavation and geophysical survey work in the 1990s revealed that this consisted of a marble hall near the Artemision, a brick stoa with massive foundations (5 m deep pylons with joining foundation walls) leading by the most direct route to the Koressian Gate and a connection part way along to the Magnesian Gate in the upper city.

THE DONATION OF CAIUS VIBIUS SALUTARIS

It is not surprising that a need was felt to define and restate the Ephesian identity in a city that had become integrated into the Roman Empire as a provincial capital. This was the sense of a benefaction donated in 104 to the city by Caius Vibius Salutaris, a member of the Ephesian aristocracy of Roman equestrian rank. It should be remembered that the stipulations of his donation were not only desired by Salutaris but also accepted and ratified by the city authorities, who made the terms public with inscriptions displayed in prominent positions in the theatre and the Artemision, i.e., in the most important places concerned in the donation. Salutaris established both the distribution of sums of money to various groups of citizens in a way that reaffirmed the categories to which they belonged and also regular processions (as often as twice a month) carrying statues he provided along the processional route.

The statues numbered 29, one of gold and the others of silver, representing Artemis nine times (including a gold statue), the reigning emperor Trajan, his wife Plotina, Augustus, Lysimachos, Androklos and another early hero, as well as personifications of the institutions of the Roman state and Ephesos. The procession was accompanied in the city by the ephebes (youths preparing to take up their duties as citizens), and stopped in the theatre, where the statues were placed on pedestals to sit with the people during their meetings. The processional route has been read as tracing the history of the city, especially for the benefit of the ephebes, from its Roman present through its Hellenistic refounding back to its Ionian foundation and beyond that to the birth of Artemis. The last is seen in this version as the event from which the Ephesians drew their primary sacred identity.

EPHESOS IN THE MIDDLE IMPERIAL PERIOD: THE TERRACE HOUSES ON THE *EMBOLOS*

By the end of the Antonine Period Ephesos had completed its great early Imperial development. The city was endowed with an extensive infrastructure of public buildings of various sorts as well as temples and monuments. It had also passed the peak of its economic prosperity. There was little building activity for about a century afterward, and much of that was concerned with repair and maintenance. However, there are still important attestations of life in the city during this period.

The residential areas of the city have not generally been at the forefront of investigation at Ephesos (Figs. XV-4, 14, 16, 17). However, the principal location where living quarters have been excavated, Terrace House II, on the south side of the *Embolos*, has provided the most significant example outside Pompeii and its surroundings of a residential complex with its decoration of paintings, mosaics, marble cladding and other furnishings still well-preserved. This is one of two Terrace Houses, which are actually not single houses but rather two blocks, each made up of various houses (called residential units in the literature). Because of the importance of the finds and especially because the most important phases have been radically re-dated to the middle-Imperial Period, it is worth taking a more detailed look at the Terrace Houses.

Fig. XV-16 View inside a Terrace House II courtyard at Ephesos. Photo Credit: Noelle Soren. University of Arizona School of Anthropology Archive.

Fig. XV-17 Muses in panels. Wall painting from Terrace House II, Ephesus, Turkey. Location: Ephesus, Turkey. Photo Credit: Erich Lessing Art Resource, N.Y.

The first to be excavated was the one to the east, Terrace House I. In spite of some indications of stratigraphic observations in the preliminary reports, it was a clearance operation proceeding from the north to the south (i.e.,, from the *Embolos* uphill) with digging at various levels contemporaneously and the constant threat of material from above collapsing onto the excavation. The excavators produced a chronological framework from the Augustan Period to Late Antiquity by matching phenomena in the Terrace House to data recorded in written sources, such as earthquakes and invasions.

When work shifted to Terrace House II and continued with similar methods, the excavators assumed that the chronological framework elaborated in Terrace House I was applicable there as well. Other factors besides the preference accorded to outside considerations in interpreting the excavation led to what can now be recognized as a mis-dating of the phases of Terrace House II. There was a misunderstanding of stratigraphic relationships (that is, how the layers related to each other). The archaeologists failed to distinguish clearly between burnt layers and layers containing debris deposited secondarily from a burn. There was also confusion in dating a floor between coins found below it or on it (coins found below a floor give a date after which the floor was made, but coins found in abundance on a floor may give the date after which the floor below went out of use). All of this caused serious problems for the understanding of the chronology of this sector of the site.

The ignorance of current progress in pottery studies also hampered the understanding of the excavation, in that, for example, typical mid-Imperial wares were considered Late Antique or Byzantine long after they had been defined elsewhere. Finally, it was decided to publish the art historically attractive wall paintings and mosaics before the architectural study of the buildings or even the excavation itself was complete. The scholars charged with these art historical studies were naturally not in a position to question what the excavators said and took their evidence as true. They assembled comparative material from elsewhere in the Empire in order to agree with the dates of the finds from Terrace House II, but unfortunately they also made reference on occasion to each other for chronological support, creating vicious circles. As a result of the concatenation of all these factors, Terrace House II was for several decades considered an example of Imperial architecture surviving with renovations and refurbishments into the seventh century CE and its furnishings as important documents of Late Antique art.

Interdisciplinary studies have now demolished this vision of Terrace House II. The study of its structural history has shown that most of the block was rebuilt in the last of four major construction phases, after which it was abandoned, probably as the result of damage from recurrent earthquakes. Destruction layers found in new excavations, as well as in reliably identified ones in the documentation of the old excavations, have yielded pottery of third-century date (such as late Eastern *Sigillata* B and African red-slip ware C) and no characteristic Late Antique wares. Reading the graffiti scratched into the wall paintings also helped define the chronology of the walls and their paintings, as a number of them record expenses paid in coins that were no longer minted after the time of the mid-third century Roman Emperor Gallienus and quickly disappeared from circulation. The reconsideration of the paintings in the framework data on Terrace House II shows that there was an Ephesian workshop with its own provincial painting style comparable to what has been observed in Roman houses at Ostia and Rome. Its work can be traced in various residential units in Terrace House II and manifested itself with greater or lesser quality according to circumstances such as the importance of the room. The re-dating of the Terrace House II paintings makes much more sense historically, rather than considered an anomaly among Late Antique paintings.

Terrace House II was therefore built in the Tiberian Period on three terraces. The block corresponds to the regular plan rather than the course of the *Embolos*. Thus there are shops of various depths in the wedge-shaped space along the *Embolos*. Originally there were six residential units in the block, two per terrace, each with an entrance from one of the side streets climbing up the hill from the *Embolos*. The plans of the units derive essentially from the Hellenistic tradition, with formal rooms overlooking a colonnaded courtyard, with secondary rooms grouped around them. However, some elements recall Italian precedents, for example the principal room on the main axis, called a *tablinum* in Roman terminology. Perhaps because of the slope the units extended to upper stories. The houses were furnished with sculpture (both in shrines and as decoration), mosaic floors with geometric and figural motifs, marble wall cladding in some of the most important reception rooms, and wall paintings. The last are articulated horizontally in three sections and can present figural motifs, architectural imitation and simpler schemes such as scattered flowers. The figural motifs drew upon Greek literature and mythology: for example, portraits of the philosopher Socrates and the poet Sappho, representations of the Muses, scenes of Herakles battling snake-legged Acheloos, the river god, over the hand of Deianeira and of the water nymph Nereid and the sea god Triton.

From such similar beginnings each unit developed differently over the several centuries that Terrace House II existed. Thus, what was a single unit on the western side of the middle terrace was ultimately divided into two. Here one can see that the owners attempted to maintain a certain level through having wall paintings of a good quality. In the case of units 4 and 6 in the eastern part of the block, it is possible to speak of a dependence of the former with respect to the latter, as unit 4 on the middle terrace lost space to unit 6 on the lower one and especially because the heating system for the latter could be operated only from the former. Very likely unit 4 was assigned to the administrator and unit 6 to the owner and his family.

Residential unit 6 is especially interesting because we are acquainted epigraphically with an owner, Caius Flavius Furius Aptus. He was a leading citizen of Ephesos in the later second century, who was involved in the cult of Dionysos. His descendants were presumably still in possession at the time of the abandonment as his statue and inscription had not been removed. This unit contained both a large marble-decorated reception room (whose wall panels were stacked up awaiting remounting at the time of the abandonment) and a private basilica. Thus, the qualification of the unit as the city palace of an important landowner is justified.

GLADIATORS'S CEMETERY

Gladiatorial games derived from the Roman-Italic tradition rather than from anything Greek, and their presence in the Greek East can be considered a feature of Romanization. Indeed, they are attested there, for the most part from the second century CE, in Roman colonies and places with important populations of Roman citizens or those desirous of underlining their loyalty to Rome. It has been known for some time from inscriptions that Ephesos held gladiatorial contests. First the theatre was adapted for these shows, to judge from graffiti, and later the stadium. Recently a cemetery for gladiators, something rarely attested, has been discovered at Ephesos. It is located on the northeast side of Panayırdağ along the processional route, part of the larger cemetery area of the city, and it is securely identified by inscriptions and reliefs showing gladiators. The style of the representations and the form of the letters, all that scholars can go on, indicate dates in the second or third centuries. In some cases, where the bones have been preserved and can be associated with inscribed stones, physical anthropologists have seen that the deceased suffered wounds typical of gladiatorial combats in general and of the specific specialties mentioned. Many skeletons show healed wounds, as well as ones from which the gladiators died.

EPHESOS IN THE LATE ANTIQUE AND EARLY BYZANTINE PERIODS: FROM THE TETRARCHS TO JUSTINIAN

The emperor Diocletian, as we have seen, brought relief to the troubles of the Roman world in the later-third century CE. He inaugurated a new form of government under two senior and two junior emperors, the Tetrarchs. He also reorganized the provincial administration, with much smaller provinces. Ephesos remained the seat of the governor of Asia, now limited to the coastal strip of western Asia Minor.

Ephesos saw building begin anew in the Tetrarchic Period, and further growth spurts can be traced throughout the fourth and fifth centuries and into the sixth. For most of this time the builders were local magistrates or private benefactors. One of the earliest building schemes consisted of repairs to the Artemision under Diocletian, which were made necessary by an attack of the Goths in the 260s during the reign of Emperor Gallienus. Respa, Veduc, and Thuruar, leaders of the Goths, had sailed across the strait of the Hellespont to Asia Minor and set fire to the Temple of Artemis at Ephesos, inflicting grave damage before moving on.

Some other later restorations were rebuildings of existing structures, even if they give rise to new names: e.g., the Harbor Baths rebuilt as *Thermae Constantianae* (the Baths of Constantius) by order of Emperor Constantius II c. 350 or the Bath of Varius restored in the late fourth century by a pious lady called Scholasticia (Fig. XV-18). Much of the inherited infrastructure was maintained into the fifth century in spite of various earthquakes. In some cases the function changed, however. For example, the Library of Celsus was transformed into a monumental fountain with the use of *spolia* (re-used architectural material). Both *spolia* and fountains are encountered often in the excavation of Late Antique Ephesos. Another feature of the city in Late Antiquity was the emphasis placed on the streets compared to the squares. The entire route through the city from the harbor to the State Agora was paved in marble (once again *spolia*) to represent the nobility of Ephesos. Of

'ig. XV-18 Baths of Scholasticia. View from the *Caldarium* or hot oom over the baths to the Library of Celsus. Photo Credit: Noelle oren. University of Arizona School of Anthropology Archive.

:ourse, the most notable development was the Christianization of he city.

The *Embolos* remained one of the leading streets of Late Antique Ephesos but with a changed character. A gate, called the Ierakles Gate by the excavators because of the relief decoration n its pillars, was erected at the top of the street, closing it to ehicular traffic (Fig. XV-19). This took place at the latest in the ifth century and perhaps earlier. A parallel development saw the treet gradually lined with colonnades that had statues underneath hem built to honor emperors, magistrates and worthy citizens. nscriptions were also displayed. The new *Embolos* thus became he prime location for the city and its elite to represent itself, a sort f museum and hall of honor.

The long street between the theatre and the harbor, which must go back at least to Hellenistic times, was known in Late Antiquity s the Arkadiane, i.e., the street of Arcadius (CE 383-408), undoubtedly because the emperor of that name had something to do with a renovation of it (Fig. XV-20). This street also was lined with colonnades. It was marked at the harbor end by the entrance gate of early Imperial date and at the theatre end by a new gate made of *spolia*. In the fifth century it is recorded that it had street lighting.

The Arkadiane contrasts with the *Embolos* in that it had a distinctly commercial nature. The inscriptions that are securely Late Antique in date mostly have to do with merchants. Furthermore, there is only one important Late Antique sculptural element, the Tetrastyle Monument placed at the center of the Arkadiane at the major intersection, probably in the second quarter of the sixth century. Because it features four columns it has often been interpreted as a monument to the four evangelists. Recently it has been pointed out that such a monument would have no parallel in any other Late Antique city and that it would be the only such monument not dedicated to an emperor and his family, which makes it likely that this is also an Imperial monument.

Fig. XV-19 (above) Gate of Herakles in the Street of the Curetes. Location: Ephesus, Turkey. Photo Credit: Erich Lessing / Art Resource, N.Y.

Fig. XV-20 (left) Ancient harbor, Arkadiane street, and the Harbor Baths and Gymnasium. North view from the Bülbüldag. Location: Ephesus, Turkey. Photo Credit: Erich Lessing / Art Resource, N.Y.

As we have noted, the squares lost importance with regard to the streets, so that the Arkadiane took over much of the commercial function of the Tetragonos Agora and the *Embolos* that of the State Agora as the center of public life. It is perhaps emblematic that scholars have not been able to agree which agora was rededicated as the Theodosian Forum, as an inscription whose find spot is unfortunately unknown recalls. However, for some time at least the agoras were not abandoned, as repairs were carried out to both of them in the fourth century or possibly the early fifth. At some point in Late Antiquity the State Agora was partly taken over by private housing.

CHRISTIAN EPHESOS

Ephesos is vividly alluded to in Acts 19-20 in connection with St. Paul's extended ministry in the city. Apostle Paul is believed to have spent two and a half years in Ephesos during his third missionary journey (55-58 CE), allegedly culminating with stirring up a crowd in the theatre which answered him with the cry "Great is Artemis of the Ephesians!" A jeweler in the crowd named Demetrios was supposed to have riled up the crowd against Paul because he feared a drop in sales of his images of Artemis for visitors. The *grammateus* or town mayor is supposed to have quelled the riot, but some religious authorities believe Paul was imprisoned in the so-called Prison of St. Paul in Ephesos until a riot forced him to leave the city rapidly. Eventually the belief in Christ and the veneration of his Blessed Mother replaced the worship of Artemis and the other deities.

Christian traditions recall that Paul's disciple Timothy founded a community. From the fact that the Ephesian Christians later defended the calculation of the date of Easter to coincide with Passover it has been supposed that the Christian community was drawn to a large extent from the well-documented Jewish community at Ephesos.

Some, particularly in the Catholic church, believe that the Virgin Mary was brought to Ephesos by John, to whom Christ had entrusted her. Others, including the Orthodox, claim she lived out her life at Jerusalem and that John came to Ephesos alone. The much visited House of Mary near Ephesos has no tradition older than the 19th century.

Another story concerning Ephesos and Christianity is mentioned in the late sixth century by Gregory of Tours, the chronicler the Frankish kings. It states that Mary Magdalene died in Ephesos, after living there with the Virgin Mary and John the Evangelist, the author of the fourth Gospel. Other early medieval writers reject this tale, but it has proven popular over the centuries with the Catholic Church. Saints of a later date, venerated also by Muslims because they are mentioned in the Koran, are the Seven Sleepers of Ephesos, who supposedly hid in a cave at the time of the intense Christian persecution under Diocletian about 304 CE and fell asleep to awake nearly 200 years later under the Christian Emperor Theodosius II!

However, the archaeological evidence of Christianity at Ephesos dates only to Late Antiquity, after the triumph of the church and none of the early traditions can be verified. One sign of Christianity is the elimination of pagan elements from the city. Thus, we see the dismantling of temples (e.g., the one in the State Agora), the defacing of statues of Artemis and the erasure of her name in inscriptions. There was the careful burial of the "multi-breasted" statues of Artemis found in the *prytaneion*, presumably by pagans hopeful of better days. In other cases Christians wanted to leave more positive traces. A man called Demeas recalls in an inscription that he caused the statue of the demon Artemis to be cast down from above a gate and replaced by the symbol of truth: a cross. Christian symbols are incorporated into new structures as well. It was the abundance of these signs of Christianity that allegedly astounded the Sleepers who went into the city upon awakening.

The first of the two most important churches was the cathedral, the Church of Mary. It occupied the western part of the south colonnade of the Olympieion and consisted of an *atrium* in the form of a peristyle, a transverse narthex or entry hall and a main hall with a nave ending in an apse and two aisles. The date of this church's construction is debated. The Acts of the Council of Ephesos of 431, which is remembered for declaring the Virgin to be the Mother of God, say that the meetings were held in the Church of Mary, and scholars traditionally held that the building must have existed by then, which would make it the earliest church dedicated to the Virgin Mary in the world. Evidence from archaeological investigations seems to exclude such an early date, and other explanations were sought, such as the hypothesis that the council was held in the colonnade before the building of the church and that the Acts, which were written much later, simplified the matter. Now it appears that there is a possibility that the church may be old enough to have been the venue of the council.

The other great church at Ephesos is the Church of John on Ayasoluk. The Byzantine emperor Justinian replaced an earlier church, itself built over the martyrion (shrine at the martyr's tomb) beginning in 535/536, when the bishop of Ephesos was a cleric influential at court. It is a massive domed structure on a Latin cross plan that would have been richly decorated with paintings and mosaics. It has been suggested that in plan and overall effect St. John's would have recalled St. Mark's at Venice. The Artemision was heavily plundered of its stones for the construction of the church, which was in turn largely demolished for the construction of the 14th-century mosque of İsa Bey at the foot of Ayasoluk. During the Middle Ages it was widely believed that sick pilgrims visiting this spot could be treated by exposing themselves to dust blowing up through a hole in the floor around the grave of John. This magic healing property of the church attracted many visitors.

THE END OF ANCIENT EPHESOS

Where to put the end of antiquity is always a difficult question, and the answer will vary from place to place according to local circumstances, as we have seen. In the eastern part of the Roman Empire the problem is especially great because of the strong degree of continuity that manifested itself there. There was no break in the succession of the eastern emperors, who considered themselves the legitimate heirs of Augustus. Nor has Ephesos been abandoned until today, although the settlement gradually became concentrated at Ayasoluk to the exclusion of the site chosen by Lysimachos, and the once powerful city declined to the level of a minor town.

The seventh century does, however, mark an important turning point. Ephesos may have lost its status as a capital when the Late Antique system of provinces was reorganized into new units called themes, although it is generally supposed that it became the capital of a theme. First the Persians and then the Arabs made a series of devastating incursions into Asia Minor. Ephesos is recorded as having been sacked in one of the Arab campaigns. From the archaeological point of view it is significant that at some time in the early seventh century the city was provided with new walls that included only the western slopes of Panayırdağ and the harbor area, leaving both agoras and the *Embolos* outside. The abandonment of what had been the core of the city for centuries indicates a major shift in urbanism. It was probably in the seventh century as well that the episcopal seat was transferred to St. John's on Ayasoluk, which was also fortified and became the major settlement for Ephesos. However the Ephesians of the time may have felt, the scholar observing from the distance of today perceives that a different reality had come into being in the seventh century.

OTHER CITIES IN THE EAST

Ephesos gives a particularly good opportunity to see how a city in the eastern provinces reacted to the coming of the Romans and functioned within the Imperial framework, because it is not overlain by a later city and because of the long history of research there. It was, however, one city among many in the Roman East.

lexandria, the capital of Egypt and second city of the Empire, vas built over by a great city in the 19th and 20th centuries, but ne ancient city is gradually becoming better known, through ne rescue excavations carried out since the 1990s by the French entre d'Études Alexandrines and through the excavation over ecades by the Polish mission of Kom el-Dikka, a large area near ne center of the city.

Antioch, the capital of Syria, was another major city in the East, vhich is best known archaeologically for its Late Antique mosaics. erusalem with its radical transformations from the religious center f the Jews to a new pagan city at the time of Hadrian and to the hristian holy city under Constantine is a fascinating study. There re also many lesser towns with their contributions to make to the istory of urban development in the Roman East.

A special case concerns the residences of the emperors n the eastern part of the Empire. In the troubled times of the hird century after the end of the Severan dynasty, the emperors pent much time in the East and established residences there, lthough there was no fixed abode or new capital until the time of onstantine. These residences tended to be in the Balkans, which was the region from which most of the emperors of the time came and which also formed an important link between the East and Italy. We have seen, for example, that Galerius chose Thessaloniki as his residence and built an Imperial complex there, which was probably also used by Constantine early in his reign. Sirmium (Sremska Mitrovica, just to the west of Belgrade) is another place where various emperors sojourned. Diocletian resided as emperor at Nicomedia (modern İznik, on the Asian coast opposite the Balkan Peninsula). Finally, in 330 Constantine inaugurated a new capital on the Bosporus, Constantinople, specifically designed to rival the old capital at Rome—this launched the city, now İstanbul, on its career as an Imperial capital that lasted until the abolition of the Ottoman Empire in the 20th century. The main surviving late-Roman monument there consists of the city walls built in 413-414 by Theodosius II, which protected the city for centuries. There are, of course, also churches going back to the sixth century, foremost among them Hagia Sophia, which however have more to do with the subsequent history of Byzantine and Ottoman architecture than with the Romans.

ROMAN CAIRO

Unlike many cities in what was the eastern part of the Roman Empire, Cairo, the metropolis of medieval Islam and the sprawling capital of modern Egypt, is not usually associated with Roman archaeology, although the existence of some Roman remains has been known for centuries. Now recently published, innovative work carried out in the 1990s and 2000s at Old Cairo has shed new light on the Roman phase of Cairo's history and its importance for the further development of the city.

The greater Cairo area occupies a key geographic position. It lies at the junction of the Nile Valley with the Delta, the place where the long, narrow valley opens onto the broad, flat land through which the river flows in branches and canals before reaching the Mediterranean to the north. A natural east-west route of communication also passes through there. This geographic importance is reflected in the early capital of Pharaonic Egypt slightly upstream from Cairo at Memphis and of course in the Pyramids at Giza on the west bank of the Nile, opposite Cairo, which lies on the east bank.

There are some traces of occupation of the area of Cairo from all epochs of antiquity. For the early Roman Period there are indications, particularly in the written sources that a legion was stationed there. Nevertheless, the archaeology concerns two periods in particular—the reigns of Trajan and Diocletian.

The archaeological work took place during a project to lower the groundwater level in Old Cairo, known in antiquity as Babylon. In the process, numerous boreholes were sunk and shafts dug. A surprising amount of data was obtained by careful archaeological observation and recording under undoubtedly difficult conditions. These data, pieced together like a puzzle with the information from archaeological investigations done earlier in the 20th century and from restoration efforts on various monuments in the zone, allowed a good picture of the stratigraphic sequence of Old Cairo to be formed, starting with the natural conformation of the territory. This consisted of a relatively narrow band of land bounded on the west by the Nile, which ran farther to the east than nowadays, and on the east by limestone hills.

Trajan's reign marked a defining moment in the making of the topography of Old Cairo and indeed of the city as a whole. As part of his general interest in improving the infrastructure for shipping, Trajan promoted the creation of a canal between the Nile and the Red Sea at the Gulf of Suez. In this he was following the lead of the Pharaohs of the Late Period and the Persian kings before the conquest of Egypt by Alexander the Great, a time when there was special interest in contacts with the lands to the east of Egypt. This early canal seems to have fallen out of use during Ptolemaic times, before the Roman conquest. The canal, called the *Amnis Traianis* (Trajan's River), took advantage of a prehistoric branch of the Nile and natural depressions. Apparently, water was allowed to fill the canal during the annual flood of the Nile and was then blocked to avoid its receding. Merchandise was loaded onto special barges for transportation along the canal. The entrance to the canal from the Nile was at Cairo, where a monumental harbor was built under Trajan. Its main feature was a series of quays built of closely fitted limestone blocks held together by clamps, a type of construction that finds parallels in the harbor built for Rome at Portus near Ostia also during the reign of Trajan.

During the reign of Diocletian, a fortress was built around the entrance to the canal, part of a program that saw also the fortification of the great Pharaonic temple at Luxor in southern Egypt. The fortress finds parallels with structures of the time. It is a rectangle with the southwest corner (along the river) cut off diagonally. The walls present rounded towers at the gates and at regular intervals along the walls. Barracks and other buildings lined the canal inside the fortress. The entrance to the canal and its exit from the fortress were marked by round towers. There is also evidence for a bridge across the Nile at this point, by way of the island of Roda.

The reign of Diocletian with its persecution of the Christians was particularly significant for Egypt, so much so that still today the Coptic Christian calendar takes as its first year his accession and the time of troubles. Historical references suggest that the fortress at Cairo may have been a center of anti-Christian persecution under Diocletian. This could explain why various churches still existing today were built in the fortress—the Greek Orthodox Church of St. George over one of the round towers of the northern gate and various Coptic churches. This made Old Cairo a center of Christian devotion in Egypt.

Cairo was not a city in Roman times—the capital of the Ptolemies and their Roman successors (both oriented toward the Mediterranean) was at Alexandria on the northern coast. A city grew up there only after the Arab conquest in the seventh century. Nevertheless, the structures going back to the time of Trajan and Diocletian guided the growth of the medieval and modern city. The continued existence of the canal in early Arab times was probably a factor in the choice of Cairo as the capital of the new power, when the rulers of the country looked to the east. The layout of Old Cairo itself respected the walls and street plan of the fortress. The canal and the road flanking it constituted a major artery to the north that conditioned the expansion of the city, from the Mosque of Amr (built by the Arab conqueror of Egypt and the oldest in Africa) just north of Old Cairo to the various new enclosures that succeeding rulers built each farther to the north than the one before. The last remnant of the canal was filled in only in 1896 as a health hazard.

The case of Cairo is instructive in two ways. Methodologically, it shows how much historical information can be produced by painstaking archaeological work, even under unpromising conditions. It also reveals how important the archaeology of the Roman Period can be in understanding even a place without obvious great Roman monuments.

A ROMAN TOWN IN SYRIA

Fig. XV-21 Philip the Arab (ruling 244-249 CE). Roman bust. Braccio Nuovo, Museo Chiaramonti, Vatican Museums, Vatican State. Photo Credit: Scala / Art Resource, N.Y.

Philip the Arab is a Roman emperor familiar to only the most ardent Roman historians (Fig. XV-21). Although he ruled only from 244 to 248 CE he was responsible for constructing the immodestly named city of Philipopolis in the Hauran region of southern Syria. Philip had come from this region, being born in the small town of Shahba around CE 200 to a prominent family that had managed to obtain equestrian rank as Roman citizens.

His older brother, Julius Priscus, was the Praetorian Prefect of Mesopotamia under emperor Gordian III and fought heroically against the Persians in 242. He also served as Procurator of Mesopotamia and Macedonia and was an important judge in Alexandria. Philip was less famous initially but more ambitious to be emperor. After concluding a treaty with the Persians and struggling against Germanic tribes along the Danube, he appointed the Senator Trajan Decius to fight against the Germans and in 248 that commander revolted and defeated Philip in a battle near Verona. Philip and his 10-year-old son and heir died.

This left unfinished Philip's plan to place Philipopolis over his native Shahba, a site of some 800 square meters designed to be surrounded by a huge defensive wall and an internal gridded plan featuring a major north-south and east-west street, each lined with colonnades. The meeting point of the two streets was marked with a *tetrapylon* or 4-sided arch. Such colonnaded streets and *tetrapyla* were typical features of the Late Antique Near East and North Africa. Roman theatres were not common in the Hauran, especially one made of black basalt, a local stone that reflects the fact that a small volcano may be found near the town. So the example at Philopopolis is important if not spectacular. This building and the large bath complex and aqueduct show that Philip was trying to give his native town all the comforts of Rome.

The town had native elements also in its architecture. The *kalybe* is the name given locally to a native open-air temple known in this region and often having a tripartite division: a large central space with smaller chambers to the side, perhaps for statuary to be exhibited (Fig. XV-22). The central chamber may be reached beneath an arched lintel. Philipopolis still needs a great deal of study which will help to reveal this unusual site as more of a cross between the Roman and the indigenous Syrian than any other site in the Hauran. Was Philip planning to relocate the center of Roman power to the East in order to better supervise the campaigns against the Persians and to keep areas such as Palmyra pacified? If so, he would have anticipated Constantine's idea by almost 80 years. Unfortunately, he did not live long enough for us to find out

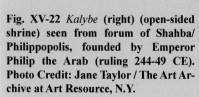

Fig. XV-22 *Kalybe* (right) (open-sided shrine) seen from forum of Shahba/ Philippopolis, founded by Emperor Philip the Arab (ruling 244-49 CE). Photo Credit: Jane Taylor / The Art Archive at Art Resource, N.Y.

CRITICAL THINKING EXERCISES

- •1. How and why was Ephesos created in western Anatolia?
- •2. Discuss the significance of the cult of Artemis to Ephesos.
- •3. What role did Lysimachos play in establishing the city?
- •4. How did Ephesos become Roman? How did this transform the city?
- • 5.What made Ephesos such a major city in the middle Roman Empire?
- • 6.Ephesos is revered as a major center in the development of Christianity? What is the evidence for Christianity in the city and what role did the Virgin Mary and Saints Paul and John play here?
- • 7.How did Romanization affect other towns in the eastern Mediterranean?

Appendix I
The Importance of Roman Pottery

Many works of Roman art and architecture are masterpieces of considerable stylistic and historical importance, but these treasures that are collected, selected and shown in the museums of the world were not what most Romans possessed. Their daily lives were taken up with mundane objects of little intrinsic value, particularly quantities of pottery for a multitude of uses. For many years on excavations most of the pottery was quickly discarded, but far from being an obstruction to today's excavator, it has become one of his most valuable tools to understanding ancient Rome.

Pottery specialists are capable of producing analyses that contribute to answering many questions of interest to modern scholars that were neglected by ancient authors. To appreciate the importance of the humble sherd and what it can tell us about the ancient Romans it is useful to get an overview of Roman pottery. There is nothing magic about what pottery specialists do. Rather they develop an expertise with pottery equivalent to what allows dog-fanciers to identify various breeds or enthusiasts of cars or women's clothing to recognize and date different brands and styles.

Fig. App. I-1 Dish with niello decoration from the Mildenhall treasure or Roman silver tableware, Mildenhall area, Roman Britain, fourth century CE. The restrained decoration is carried out simply in engraved lines filled with niello (silver sulphide) which provides a black contrast to the silver. It has a diameter of 55.6cm and weight of 5.023 grams. Location: British Museum, London. Photo Credit: Erich Lessing / Art Resource, N.Y.

Usually, pottery is neglected in academic studies, because even the finest Roman pottery is mass-produced in series with limited aesthetic pretensions and normally rates at best a cursory mention in handbooks of Roman art and archaeology. Pottery was used in the Roman world much more widely than it is now, which we do not fully appreciate because today we use plastic for many of the same functions. For the field archaeologist, however, pottery is critical because it is omnipresent, not recyclable and almost indestructible, at least in the form of sherds. Every archaeological site has thousands upon thousands of pottery sherds, generous quantities of broken bricks and tile and a variety of other scraps that, because of soil conditions or general hardiness of material, have survived through the centuries.

THE ROMAN HOUSEHOLD

Fig. App. I- 2 Glass cup signed by Ennion. first-half of first century CE. Roman, early Imperial Period. Height 2 7/16 in. (6.2 cm); diameter 3 13/16 in. (9.7 cm). Gift of J. Pierpont Morgan, 1917 (17.194.225). Location: The Metropolitan Museum of Art, New York, N.Y., U.S.A. Photo Credit: © The Metropolitan Museum of Art. Photo Credit: Art Resource, N.Y.

The typical Roman household would have had a wide variety of vessels in various materials at its command, of which pottery would have been the most common but by no means the only one. Even moderately well-off families normally possessed silver plate for tableware, and gold plate also existed (Fig. App. I-1). The workshops producing ceramic tableware often imitated prototypes in precious metals. This can be seen in the forms because sharp articulations are not natural for pottery but are common for metallurgy. Relief decorations on pottery can also be compared to those on metal work. It has been suggested that even the dominant colors for fine tablewares copied metal—black might be used for silver (remembering that the ancients allowed silver to develop a black patina rather than keeping it shiny) until the late first century BCE and red, which became the dominant color in the later-first century BCE, could be used to imitate gold. Glass was also used widely during the Imperial Period—glass blowing was developed in the first century BCE—not only for drinking vessels but also for dishes (Fig. App. I-2). Bronze appears in vessels for use in the kitchen and pantry and sometimes for lamps as well as at table.

Fig. App. I-3 Pottery mortarium, an essential kitchen utensil for grinding. From London, first century CE. Location: British Museum, London. Photo Credit: © The Trustees of the British Museum / Art Resource, N.Y.

Fig. App. I-4 Black Gloss boss-centered dish (*phiale*) with relief decoration. Roman. 250-180 BCE. The *phiale*, with its distinctive bossed center, was a shallow dish used primarily for pouring libations during religious rituals. This mold-made example imitated contemporary silver vessels: the interior shows Sol, the god of the sun, and his chariot. It is inscribed: LUCIUS CANOLEIOS L.F. FECIT CALENOS, "Lucius Canoleius of Cales, the son of Lucius, made (this)." Cales (Calvi) in Campania, near Naples, was settled by Romans in 334 BCE. This vessel shows an early use of Latin in a predominantly Greek-speaking part of Italy. Pottery, diam. 18 cm. Inv. GR 1928,0117.71. Location: British Museum, London. Photo Credit:© The Trustees of the British Museum / Art Resource, N.Y.

Marble could be used for small mortars (*mortaria*), while volcanic stone was employed for grinding grain to flour (Fig. App. I-3).

It is useful to think of pottery by functional groups, each of which has its own history of studies. Those with decorations or with epigraphic material have been studied for centuries, while others have attracted scholarly interest more recently.

AMPHORAE

Amphorae are readily defined as two-handled jars for long-distance shipping of wine, oil, fish sauces and other liquid or semi-liquid products, usually shipped by water (Fig. App. I-12). Unlike other pottery, amphorae were merely the containers for goods and not the merchandise themselves. Thus, they give us a more direct look at some of the important foodstuffs of the Roman world. After use in transportation amphorae could be recycled for secondary purposes ranging from storage to the burial of infants and paupers. As utilitarian objects, amphorae were little subject to changes in fashion, although specific shapes could be recognized as typical of certain contents or origins, much as people today expect different beverages from Coca-Cola or champagne bottles. At various times and places makers' marks were stamped into amphorae before firing or other information was added in paint, ink or scratches, for instance at customs control points.

LAMPS

Lamps are intended for illumination, with a reservoir of olive oil burned with a wick (Fig. VII-27; App. I-13)). Lamps could vary widely in their shapes, as long as they had a reservoir and a wick hole, and also in the presence or absence of decoration. One tradition of lamp production decorated the *discus* with scenes of gladiators, lovemaking or gods and goddesses among others. There were even lamps featuring best wishes for the New Year. These objects changed readily to follow the dictates of fashion. Lamps are usually local or regional products, probably because they do not lend themselves to compactness in transport, although they do appear sometimes outside their regions of production.

FINE WARES

The sort of pottery most likely to be imported, other than amphorae, is fine tableware. It can present decorations of various sorts and varies with changing fashions. Fine ware is generally understood as vessels in standardized forms with a glossy coating or at least a slip of good quality, destined for serving and consuming food. Its production requires specialized equipment such as complex kilns and possibly molds, and it usually is widely distributed from a limited number of production centers. Roman fine ware can be divided into two groups, both of which share a special glossy, semi-vitrified slip. The first is black-gloss ware, which continues traditions going back to pre-Roman times and lasts until the mid- to late first century BCE (Fig. App. I-4) The production of black-gloss ware was widespread around the Mediterranean, where it was made in numerous workshops of local or regional importance. There are, however, some kinds of regional black-gloss ware that exported standardized forms widely throughout the western Mediterranean basin and occasionally to the eastern. For example, Campana A ware comes from the area of Naples and uses a Greek repertoire of ceramic forms. The so-called Atelier des Petites Estampilles or Workshop of the Little Stamps (actually more than one workshop in Rome and its surrounding area) produced a completely different range of forms derived from metal prototypes. This more Romanized repertory was taken up by the Campana B circle in Etruria and northern Campania and also by Campana C located in Sicily.

ig. App. I-5 (right) *Arre-ne ware* or Italian *sigil-ata* bowl recovered from 'apua, Italy, with reliefs f the Seasons. Later first entury BCE. Location: ritish Museum, Lon-on, Great Britain. Photo 'redit: Harper Collins 'ublishers / The Art Ar-hive at Art Resource, N.Y.

ig. App. I-6 (lower right) aulish red-slip pottery owl, Roman, made at a Graufesenque, south-rn France, c. 20-40 CE. ritish Museum, Lon-on, Great Britain. Photo 'redit: © The Trustees of he British Museum / Art esource, N.Y.

The concentration and tandardization of fine wares eached its height in the Augustan Period with the reation of what is generally now called *sigillata* (red-gloss ware). *Sigillata* was produced initially in a small number of places n the Tyrrhenian area of entral Italy (most famously Arezzo, giving rise to an old-fashioned term *Arretine ware*, o which the name Italian *sigillata* is now preferred). t had a repertoire of forms distinctly inspired by metal work (Fig. App. I-5). For several generations Italian *sigillata* had a great success, with exports traveling as far as northwestern Europe and even India. It seems that there was a widespread desire to set a Roman-style table.

Already in the first century CE, however, Italian *sigillata* began to run into stiff competition in the provinces. In the eastern Mediterranean various centers, that either had already produced red-gloss wares or were newly founded at the time, adopted Romanized forms and developed them further. *Sigillata* production centers were created also in Gaul and Hispania. The Eastern, Gaulish and Hispanic *sigillata* challenged Italian *sigillata* even on its home soil but were never able to gain enough of a foothold to eliminate it (Fig. App. I-6). Finally, however, this is exactly what African red-slip ware did (Fig. App. I-7). Between the late first century CE and the first-half of the

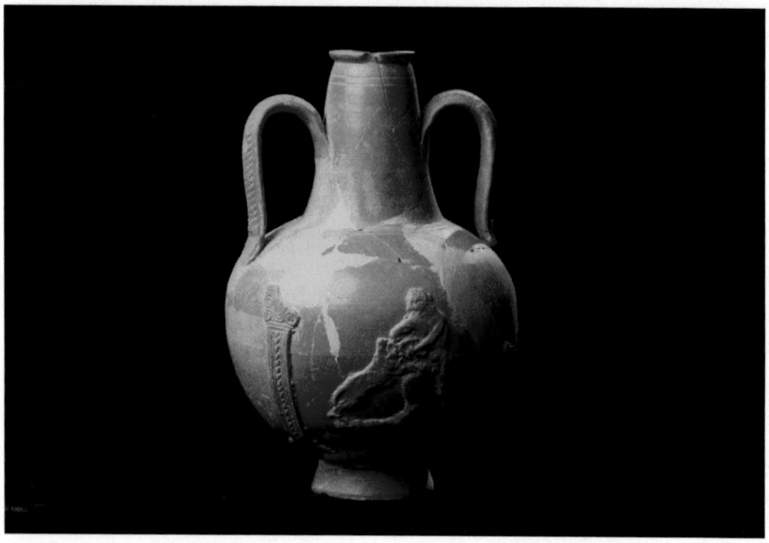

Fig. App. I-7 African red-slip Ware *gladiator* vases, with relief appliqué decoration, from central Tunisia. Early third century CE. Photo Credit: Dan Duncan.

second century African red-slip ware replaced Italian *sigillata* in Italy and the western Mediterranean except for regional imitations in marginal areas. It maintained its position of dominance until the end of the ancient tradition of pottery in the seventh century CE, and it was even able to invade the eastern Mediterranean as well from the third century, although it never took over that market completely.

These developments in fine ware pottery supply did not happen randomly. They were the result of major developments in Roman socio-economic history and need to be understood in that light. The rise of the widely exported, standardized fine-ware productions (first black-gloss ware and then especially Italian *sigillata*) corresponds both to the Roman conquest and domination of markets in the whole Mediterranean world and much of western Europe and also to the establishment and development of the slave mode of production in the heartland of Tyrrhenian central Italy. Epigraphic evidence from stamps on the vessels tells us in fact that much of the Italian *sigillata* was produced in workshops operated with slaves. Why were these highly efficient operations not able to hold their own against provincial competition? In general the question needs to be seen in the context of the larger one of why Italy passed from being a massive exporter of goods in the last two centuries of the Roman Republic and the first century of the Empire to being almost exclusively an importer after that, a situation with possible parallels in America today.

Limiting the considerations to pottery, one can observe that there seems to have been some attempt to relocate production centers nearer the markets. Thus, Pisa at the mouth of the Arno River gained in importance at the expense of Arezzo inland. Subsidiaries were set up at Lyon in Gaul to serve the military market along the Rhine in particular, and there were probably others elsewhere, such as in Asia Minor. In the case of Lyon the subsidiaries were not a long-term success, while other *sigillata*-producing centers in Gaul were. The key seems to lie in that the other centers, such as La Graufesenque near Millau in southern Gaul, made use of a simpler social structure than the Italian-style nes—the potters were mostly free locals who probably integrated heir livelihoods with farming as a sideline. It has also been peculated that African red-slip ware and the related cooking ware nd lamps were the results of seasonal activities on estates taking dvantage of otherwise dead periods.

COMMON AND COOKING WARES

Ordinary household vessels (common or coarse ware) were nade for a whole range of uses, such as storing foodstuffs and other substances, preparing them for consumption, and serving nd consuming them (Fig. App. I-8). Most tend to be locally made even on sites where other wares are imported. Even at such an active port as Ostia only a small percentage of these vessels are found to have been imported, and elsewhere practically none is. This is undoubtedly because this kind of pottery is precisely what any competent potter could turn out.

Cooking wares are ceramic vessels used in the kitchen for cooking and must be able to withstand the thermal shock caused by the fire. They too were also mostly locally produced but can be imported. Imported wares are especially common in towns well integrated into maritime trading networks. Ostia offers undoubtedly one of the most extreme cases, with wares from Campania in southern Italy in the first century BCE and first century CE, and then from the first century CE throughout the Imperial Period significant quantities of cooking vessels from North Africa and some from the Aegean are found. There seems to have been a concentration on importing specific forms, so that a kitchen in the port city of Ostia would have contained pieces from different places. The reason imports could gain a hold is that producing a good cooking vessel offers more scope for special skill and ingredients in the clay mix than coarse ware, so that imports could distinguish themselves from local products in quality. If sturdier or better imported cooking ware pots were available relatively inexpensively in a coastal town they would have been used.

Fig. App. I-8 (above) Local ribbed common ware pottery for everyday use (cup, bowl, pitcher etc.). Mostly first-half of first c. CE, early Roman Imperial era. Location: Israel Museum (IDAM), Jerusalem, Israel. Photo Credit: Erich Lessing / Art Resource, N.Y.

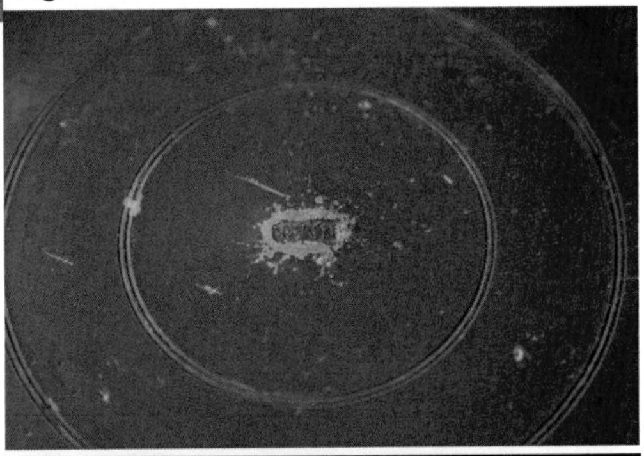

Fig. App. I-9a, 9b (right) *In planta pedis* (sole of the foot) type pottery stamp labeled SEXAFRI. Italian *sigillata* dating after c. 15 CE. Photo Credit: Dan Duncan.

TYPOLOGY AND CHRONOLOGY

As early as the Renaissance scholars looked at the representations that can be found on some Roman lamps and fine tableware for illustrations of such subjects as everyday life or the Classical divinities. Decorations on the upper part or *discus* of lamps were literally cut away from the rest of the lamp and displayed in various early collections, showing that the interest concerned the images rather than the objects themselves (Fig. VII-27).

In the late-19th and early-20th century ancient stamps that were found on fine tablewares, lamps and amphorae also attracted scholarly attention (Fig. App. I-9a & b). Since then ceramic epigraphy, the study of potters' stamps and other epigraphic material, has developed into a specialized branch of study, which can provide information such as the provenience of pottery (that is where it was made) and the organization of workshops. The need to publish stamps for the great corpus of Latin inscriptions that was being prepared under German auspices led to the creation of typologies still in use today for amphorae and lamps. Fine-ware typologies began to be formulated at the same time, although these were done for the presentation of excavation reports rather than for epigraphic collections.

A typology is a series that groups together items with similar characteristics and

Fig. App. I-10 a (above) & b (below)

distinguishes them from others with different ones. People instinctively make typologies when they have the task of sorting things and they make piles putting like with like. Typologies are not necessarily associated with dating, although those most useful to archaeologists are.

Once types have been defined, it is possible to see which ones appear in independently dated contexts, such as the destruction layer of Pompeii from the eruption of Vesuvius in 79 CE, the occupation layers of the short-lived camps occupied in Germany during the Augustan campaigns in that area or the destruction layers of the July 21, 365 CE earthquake on southwest Cyprus (Figs. App. I-10 a-e). In this way, when they appear elsewhere, these types serve as chronological markers that the archaeologist can use to date his site. For example, if a dated type is found under a floor of a building, the floor was installed no earlier than the type's date although possibly much later (pottery specialists prefer to judge on the basis of groups of datable sherds in a context rather than single ones).

In this way, Roman pottery has become the most important chronological tool on archaeological excavations. Normally, archaeologists

n orient themselves only with the help of the finds ntained in the stratigraphy (layered occupational units) ey excavate, and these consist mostly of potsherds. Most ople are unaware that the interpretation of archaeological es often depends almost entirely on the analysis of humble tsherds, especially for those sites outside Rome and a few her major cities. This is because on those sites there is less ance of historical records or epigraphic evidence offering lp with chronology.

One example will serve to show how this is done. ecently, the study of pottery proved instrumental in termining the date of a series of buildings in eastern vitzerland. The buildings in question are three towers the western end of the Walensee that were recognized r some time as dating to the time of Augustus and hose short period of occupation was considered to have me connection with the conquest of the region under s direction. However, the generic Augustan date-range oposed allowed conflicting interpretations of the towers'

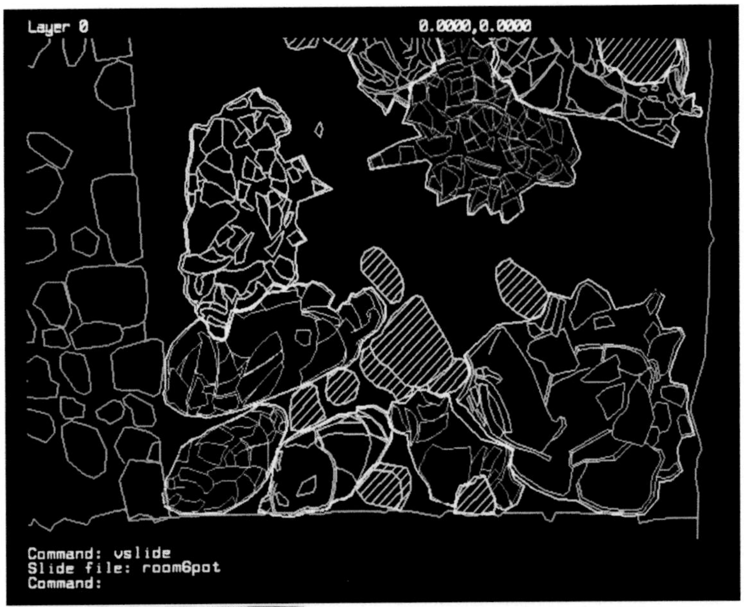

Fig. App. I-10 a-e Common ware pottery found in the archaeological excavations at Kourion has been carefully drawn, photographed, restored and rephotographed, then placed back in the position in which each shattered pot was found in 1985. The house was believed to have been destroyed on July 21, 365 CE c. 5:30 a.m. in the major Medterranean earthquake described by the writer Ammianus Marcellinus. The finds form a useful typology and dating index with which to compare finds from other sites in the imediate area and beyond. Photo Credit: Noelle Soren. University of Arizona School of Anthropology Archive. Computer drawing by John and Peggy Sanders.

Fig. App. I-10 c (top), 10d (left) and 10e (below

recise role: did they serve in the preparation of e Roman campaign in 15 BCE or were they tended to secure an important north-south oute after the conquest?

In a re-examination of the pottery the thin-alled ware (drinking vessels) proved decisive: showed that the occupation of the towers ates to between 20 and 10 BCE. Furthermore, e range of pottery, which includes a surprising umber of amphorae from various sources, dicated a military origin for the assemblage. he closest parallels are to be found at the fort t Dangstetten just north of the Rhine from the Valensee, from which they must have been upplied and for which they must have been utposts. Other finds, such as some of the metal ilitary equipment, support the conclusions rawn from the pottery. Thus, the towers are to e seen in the context of the Alpine conquest f 15 BCE and can take their place among the arliest stone-built Roman structures north of he Alps, erected at a time when the Roman rmy in the region normally built with earth and vood.

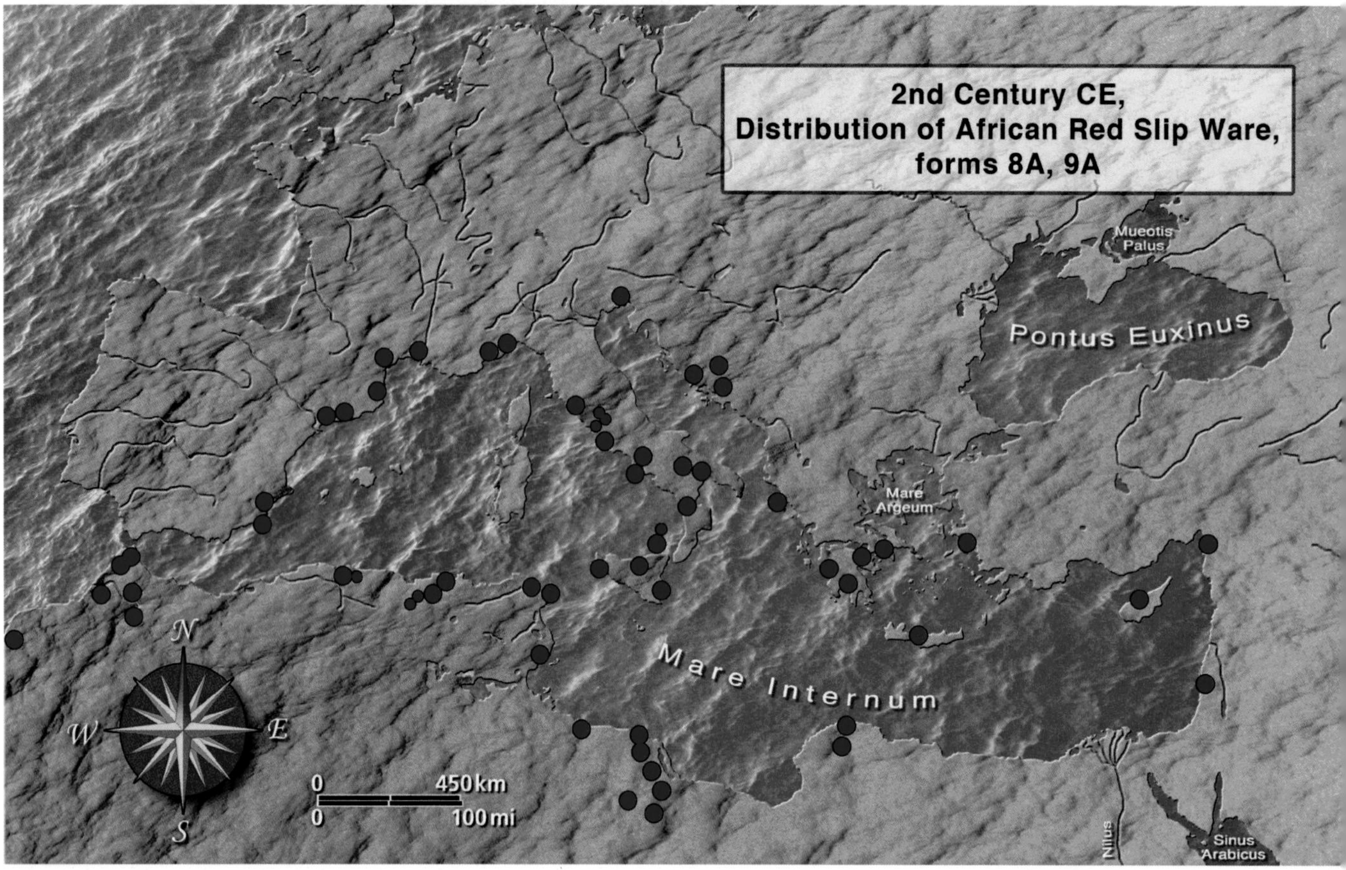

Fig. App. I- 11 Pottery distribution map by John Hayes for find spots of African red-slip ware bowls forms 8A and 9A in the second centur CE. Courtesy of John Hayes / British School at Rome.

POTTERY AS A SOURCE OF SOCIO-ECONOMIC INFORMATION

The interest among Roman historians in the ancient economy in the second half of the 20th century and the realization that written sources alone can never provide a sufficient basis of evidence marked the study of pottery, which became a major source of information on this subject. It is normally pottery that gives us the clearest window onto socio-economic questions that are of great interest to modern scholars but were of none at all to the Romans. Examples of the kinds of questions which have come under intense scrutiny are: with what region(s) did a site trade or have contact, and to what extent was a site integrated into regional and interregional networks of exchange? Traditional methods for studying pottery are based on recording the presence or absence of wares or types and then comparing them with other relevant material. Sometimes the results are expressed in the form of distribution maps (Fig. App. I-11). Pottery has also been used to generate statistics in the same way that socio-economic studies are done today. This approach means pottery specialists can no longer just select certain interesting pieces and neglect or even discard the rest of the group. Now they must take a larger view of entire classes of pottery and consider whole pottery assemblages.

ARCHAEOMETRY

Pottery studies have also benefited from the development and application to archaeology of methods of analysis derived from natural science, which has given rise to a branch of study called archaeometry. Along this line, petrographic and mineralogical observation of thin sections and chemical analysis of sherds hav already been used for several decades to determine and defin fabric groups (i.e., groups with similar compositions of clay) making their recognition and proveniencing (locating their point o origin) an integral part of pottery studies. Thus, information can b drawn even from typologically non-diagnostic body sherds. Thi means that even if we cannot specifically identify what kind o vessel the sherd came from, we can still get scientific informatio from it such as where it was made or where it was traded from Residue analysis of the contents of vessels is becoming equall important in the discussion of how pottery was used.

EPIGRAPHY

Another way in which the pottery specialist can use sherds t provide valuable information is through epigraphic studies, that i looking at inscriptions or stamped writing on the piece. Frequentl pottery is found with stamped decoration and sometimes the nam of the pottery workshop or *officina* is given (Fig. App. I-9). Th publication of a new corpus of potters' stamps on Italian *sigillat* has already begun to have effects. Its compiler was able, fo instance, to shed light on the history of one of the most importan workshops, that of Ateius. The researcher identified a number o Ateius stamps from a dump of kiln waste in Pisa that he coul date to the last decade of the first century BCE on the basis of th typology of the vessels attested. These types and stamps were littl known outside Arezzo. Apparently Ateius shifted his activity t Pisa just before the turn of the millennium. A slightly later dump o Ateius kiln waste at Pisa contained stamps produced with a wor die corresponding to stamps found at Arezzo made with it whe

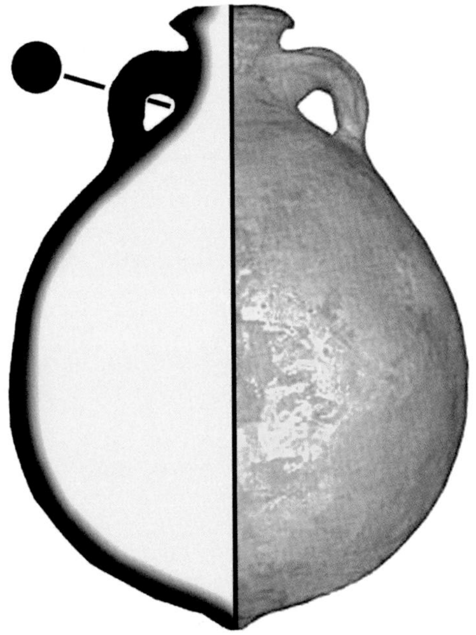

'ig. App. I- 12a Dressel 20 type of Roman amphora. Drawing by Cherylee Francis.

fresh. Other stamps from the Pisan dump are attested on many other sites. This work tells us that it was from a base at Pisa that Ateius was able to gain a large share of the market for Italian *sigillata* and to found provincial branches, such as one known at Lyon in the south of France.

Fig. App. I-12b Dressel 20 stamp reading SAXOFERREO from an amphora produced at a site now called Huerta de Belén near the town of Palma del Río, where remains of a kiln site with this stamp were found. Courtesy of Ili Nagy, Archer Martin and the American Academy in Rome, no. 1055.

Another example of the exciting possibilities created by ceramic epigraphy: the case of the globular amphora known as type Dressel 20 (Fig. App. I-12a). Survey work along the Guadalquivir River and its tributaries in southern Spain has identified the workshops that produced these amphorae and stamped them on the handles. They carried olive oil and were important to the Roman state for welfare distributions to the people of Rome and also for supplying the army in the northwestern provinces of the Empire. Therefore, they were purchased in extraordinarily arge numbers. Because of this research, if archaeologists find, for example, a stamp reading SAXOFER (with possible variants), they now that the amphora bearing it was produced at a site now called Huerta de Belén near the town of Palma del Río, where remains of kiln site with this stamp were found (Fig. App. I-12b). In this case the stamp gives us the ancient name of the place "Saxum Ferreum," vhile at other times stamps contain personal names or initials (presumably of landowners) or sometimes both place names and personal ames.

The Dressel 20 amphora can also carry other special epigraphic information. If the oil that the amphora contained entered into the velfare distribution system, it had to go through various control points on its way to Rome, so the amphorae were marked accordingly vith *dipinti* (painted notations) in specific positions on them labeled conventionally with Greek letters in a simple code: α–weight of he amphora when it is empty, β—the name of the shipper (beginning in the third century CE after the landed estates were confiscated; indicates not the shipper but the provincial financial authority), γ—the weight of the contents, δ—various information including the onsular date and the names of the officers controlling export, ε—some kind of optional mark perhaps concerning loading. Once in Rome the oil was decanted and the amphorae discarded behind the river harbor facilities in the south of the city. The discarded amphorae eventually constituted a large hill known today as the Monte Testaccio (discussed in Chapter VI) offering favorable conditions for preserving *dipinti*. In the case of the SAXOFER stamps, an example has been discovered bearing the consular date for 149 CE, which allows amphorae with this stamp to be placed chronologically with precision as well as geographically. In this way, typological details, such as the precise articulation of the rim of the amphorae dated by this stamp, also become diagnostic for dating. It is not surprising that this sector of the ancient economy is becoming one of the best known and most popular with specialists.

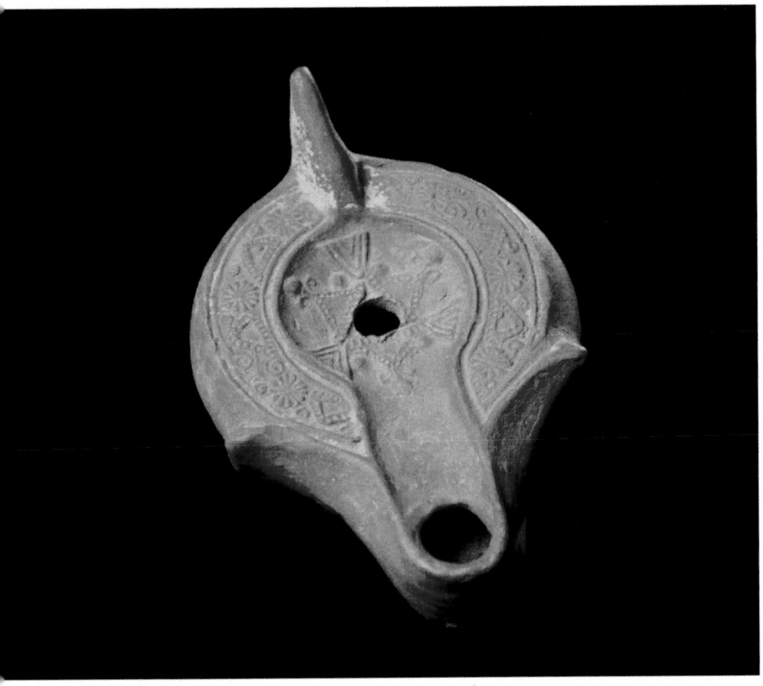

Fig. App. I-13. Roman lamp. University of Arizona School of Anthropology Collection. Fourth century CE. Christian lamp manufactured in Carthage. Photo Credit: Dan Duncan.

LAMPS

It is not only the pottery present on a site that can reveal important information about socio-economic patterns but even what is not there. For example, the Greco-Roman–style of oil lamp can be said to have appeared when lamps began to have a bridged nozzle (rather than a mere pinched spot on the rim) allowing the wick to be maneuvered more easily (Fig. App. I-13). This element, which distinguishes the Greek lamp from its predecessors in Eastern lands, was developed in the Greek motherland during the seventh and early-sixth centuries BCE. Its use depends, of course, on the availability of oil beyond what was needed for eating and for making medicinal ointments and perfumes. It quickly spread throughout the Hellenic world, including the Greek cities of southern Italy and Sicily. Apparently lighting with oil lamps was adopted as a sign of "Greekness" that Greeks everywhere wanted to adopt.

It is notable that the other populations of southern and central Italy, including the Etruscans and the Romans, who adopted other aspects of Greek culture enthusiastically, did not use such lamps for centuries. One reason may be that they had a plentiful supply of wood and pitch suitable for torches but no surplus of olive oil. In this respect it could be significant that the Romans adopted oil lamps on a large scale toward the end of the third century BCE, when they had devastated their forests for ship-building in the Second Punic War and begun to practice more intensive, market-oriented farming, including olive oil production. From that time onward oil lamps were as typical of the Romans as they had long been of the Greeks.

In present-day Switzerland, as elsewhere in the northern provinces of the Roman Empire, the appearance of oil lamps is closely connected to Roman military occupation. The civilian population normally continued to use indigenous methods of illumination, such as candles and torches, except occasionally in some places neighboring the long-standing province of Gallia Narbonensis or where there was a significant element of Roman citizens. Even villas that made a show of "Romanness" in their construction and decoration with mosaics and wall paintings do not appear to have used oil lamps normally. Lamps became rare when the army left the area in the mid-Imperial Period and increased again in Late Antiquity, when it was again of military importance. However, as lamps went out of practical use, they were placed more frequently in graves and had a symbolic function. In considering the scarce use of oil lamps in Switzerland, it must be remembered that olive oil is not native there. Both in Italy in the earlier period and then in Switzerland, the adoption of oil lamps depended on the interaction between the availability of olive oil as fuel and the lamps' symbolic value.

THE ROMAN ARMY

The history of the Roman army is another area that can be elucidated by the study of pottery. It is possible to make inferences about troop movements between provinces merely from the study of cooking vessels. At York in England, for example, a utilitarian ware, consisting mostly of cooking vessels, with no connection with the local native pottery, appears in military contexts such as the legionary fortress and the associated settlement and rarely elsewhere. Ebor Ware, as it is known from the name of the fortress, was produced from the Flavian Period onward. However, in the Severan Period (193-225 CE) a series of forms occurs with no antecedents in the ware or parallels anywhere in Roman Britain. A number of these vessels are casseroles with rounded, sometimes rilled or grooved, bottoms intended for use on stands in braziers. This contrasts with the normal cooking technique in Britain and the northwestern provinces, which was done in flat-bottomed pots placed directly in the hot ashes of an oven, but it corresponds precisely to the North African mode of cooking, where indeed a similar repertoire of cooking vessels is found. Other cooking vessels with a distinctive triangular rim lack parallels in the Romano-British or North African traditions but correspond well to the repertoire of modern Languedoc in the Roman province of Gallia Narbonensis.

Evidently York in the Severan Period had a considerable number of people who wanted such exotic vessels and knew how to use them. These consumers must have been soldiers, and, as it is highly unlikely that independent potters would have moved spontaneously to Britain to find their fortune, the producers must have been brought in by the army. Epigraphic evidence indicates some presence at the time of military men of African origin in Britain, including the emperor Septimius Severus himself, who came from Leptis Magna in what is now Libya and had British connections with the military. Taking the ceramic evidence together with the epigraphic testimony, it is most probable that special detachments of men from other legions or auxiliary regiments were brought from North Africa and southern Gaul. They were sent to Britain to augment the strength of the legions that were unable to recruit sufficient numbers locally. Such reinforcements were known as vexillations (from the Latin term *vexillatio* for the special flag that identified them). The potters making the special cooking pots would have been producing for the benefit of the vexillations.

OLBIA IN PROVENCE

The eating habits of other individuals besides the soldiers of the Roman army can also be suggested by the study of pottery; in fact it is possible to document the entire evolution of cooking at an ancient site. Excavations in the Greek colony at Olbia in Provence on the south coast of modern France revealed an assemblage of pottery datable between the mid-fourth century BCE and the mid-first century BCE. The scholar studying it hoped to see not only how food consumption changed there over the centuries but what cuisine dominated and when. In this region with so many influences, would the pottery suggest that the diet was Greek, Celtic, Ligurian or Roman?

During these centuries Olbia was in contact with its Greek homeland through its nearby mother city Massalia (now Marseille) and with the rising power in the region, Rome. The mediocre and uniform pottery recovered includes very few exceptional or luxurious pieces, which suggests the frugal exploitation of local resources rather than an elaborate grand cuisine. The maritime Greeks and the Romans both had grain-based diets according to literary sources, with wine as the principal beverage. This was very different from the diet of the Celtic and Ligurian populations that were located inland from Olbia, which was based on boiled and grilled meat and on dairy products, with beer as the normal beverage. The prevalent grain among the Greeks was barley in the form of thick porridges, while the Romans used thin wheat porridges. The Greeks supplemented their porridges with bread, with legumes such as chick peas and with fish and occasionally meat. Their principal fat for cooking was olive oil.

The Romans combined their porridges with vegetables like turnips and beans and apparently made more use of meat and lard than the Greeks did and less use of bread and fish, which were introduced under Greek influence. The archaeological evidence (in particular from Athens and Cosa, a colony founded by Rome) shows what vessels were used for cooking, presenting and consuming food. The Greek vessels for cooking consisted of round-bottomed pots, as well as lidded vessels for stewing fish and

ig. App. I- 14 Roman thin-walled cup from the area of Arezzo with vertical scorings on the side. robably early first century CE. University of Arizona School of Anthropology Photo Archive. hoto by Dan Duncan.

ying pans. Their tableware included a range of serving vessels ecause the round-bottomed cooking pots could not be used for ıat purpose. The main element among the Roman cooking vessels vas a flat-bottomed cooking pot, which could be used for serving s well. In the third century BCE a vessel for stewing fish and baking dish for bread came into use. Both the Greek and the oman tableware became more diversified in the second century CE, including more individual rather than collective vessels and specially new drinking vessels (hemispherical cups derived from netallic prototypes in Greece and thin-walled beakers among the omans) (Fig. App. I-14).

Olbia remained clearly attached to Mediterranean ways hroughout the period in question, importing pottery from various ources and following the developments of the wider Greco-oman world. There is no discernible Celto-Ligurian influence t Olbia at all, while, on the other hand, the Celtic and Ligurian ites, which maintained their traditional diet and continued to use he pottery suitable for it, do not show patterns like that of Olbia. he only exception is the consumption of wine by the upper-levels f Celtic and Ligurian society as an act of prestige. Furthermore, lbia stayed faithful to its roots, the Greek maritime tradition in ooking, with only a timid appearance of Roman baking dishes. Vith the diversification of tableware forms in the second century CE, the Olbians imported products from central Italy and dopted Roman-style thin-walled drinking vessels rather than the emispherical ones used in Greece. Thus, the study of the pottery shows that at Olbia the model to follow in the Mediterranean sphere changed from Athens to Rome in the second century BCE, even while Rome was being influenced by Greek usage.

ROMAN POTTERY IN GREECE

Pottery assemblages have been used also in the Greek homeland to evaluate the Roman impact. Athens, an urban center with no break in continuity, imported some Italian olive oil and wine as early as the second century BCE, but the pottery assemblages show no sign of any other western influence, even well into the first century BCE. At another long-established Greek city, Argos, the situation is similar, although there is no great importation of western amphorae-borne products such as the wine and olive oil. In both places there is finally an upswing in imports from Italy in the second quarter of the first century CE, some time after the region came under Roman rule. It appears that there was an interest in acquiring Romanized fine tableware, either Italian *sigillata* or increasingly eastern *sigillata* influenced by Italian prototypes. Both Athens and Argos maintained their repertoires of common domestic pottery and cooking vessels derived from the Hellenistic tradition.

Aside from tablewares, lamps constitute the other functional group in which Roman models came to dominate. The Greek city-state of Corinth contrasts with the other two cities, because it was refounded as a Roman colony with a new population of freed slaves, veterans and others with a western orientation. Here the pottery assemblages were, not surprisingly, Romanized a generation earlier than at Athens and Argos, and imports from Italy penetrated much more deeply. Thus, pottery assemblages in Roman Greece indicate that populations with an unbroken tradition did not abandon their traditional cookery but were willing to adopt Roman ways in the more display-oriented spheres of the presentation and consumption of food and illumination.

DISTRIBUTION MAPS

There has been considerable research into plotting the distribution of various wares and drawing conclusions from the maps thus produced. One of the pioneers of modern pottery research, John Hayes of the Royal Ontario Museum, made an important study of African red-slip ware and produced a series of maps showing the sites on which this kind of tableware is found at various times (Fig. App. I-11). Hayes noted that distribution in the first century CE was concentrated in Tunisia and Italy. In the succeeding centuries it became much more widespread, first in the western Mediterranean and then also in the eastern Mediterranean and beyond. This expresses very effectively how the market for

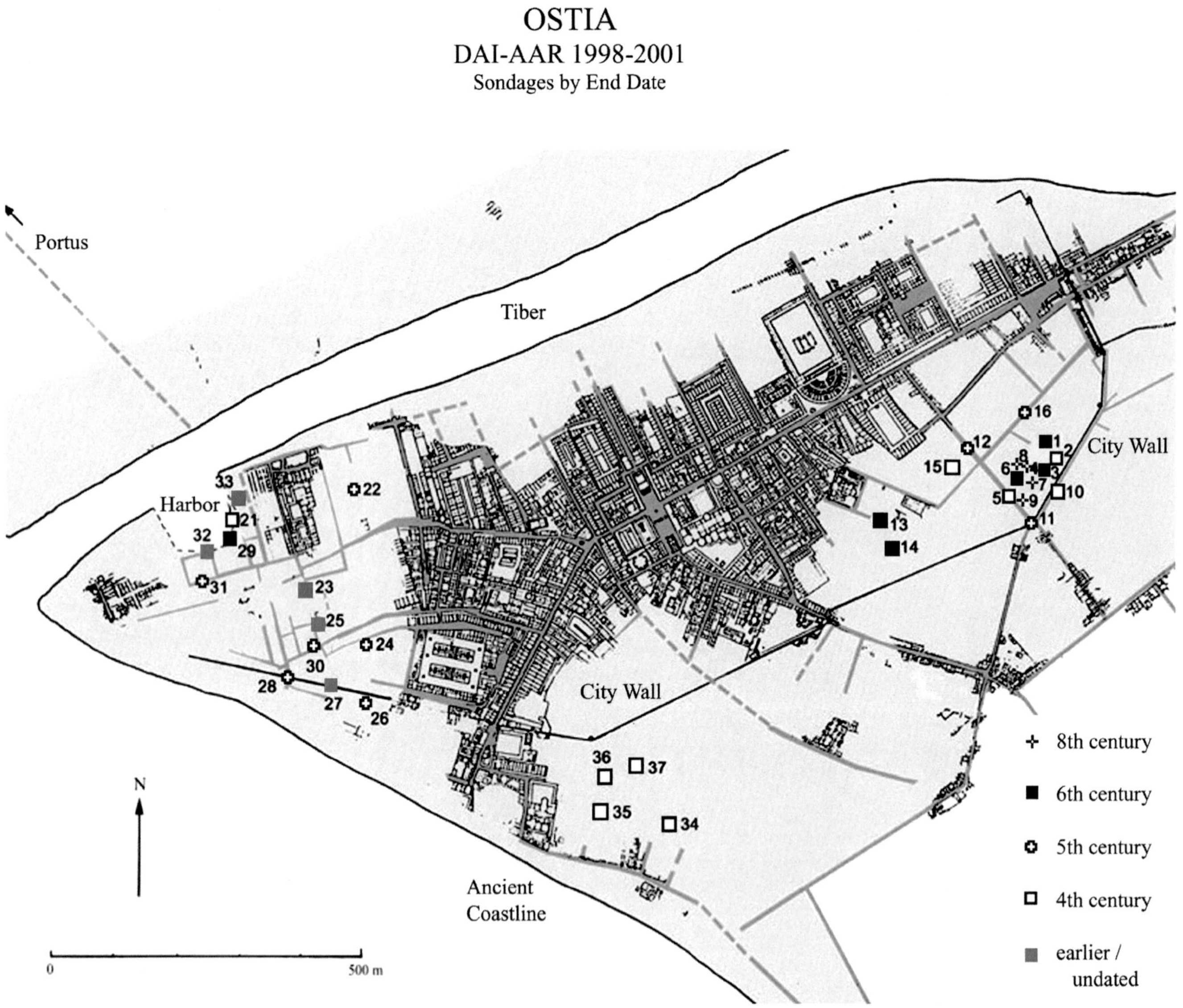

Fig. App. I- 15 Plan showing the soundings (sondages) made at Ostia which produced pottery of the fourth through eighth centuries CE and gave indications of the shrinking of the extent of the city in Late Antiquity. Image credit: Archer Martin.

African red-slip ware expanded to dominate most of the Roman world.

Distribution maps of pottery can also be used to good purpose in the interpretation of a single site. A map plotting the end dates of the pottery sequences for soundings carried out by the American Academy in Rome and the *Deutsches Archäologisches Institut Rom* (the German Archaeological Institute in Rome) at Ostia shows the gradual shrinking of the inhabited area of the city from the fourth to the eighth centuries CE (Fig. App. I-15). The latest frequentation of the seaside villas outside the walls in the south is in the fourth century. The fifth century sees the last evidence for most of the soundings outside the wider area of the episcopal basilica in the east area of the city. The final date for the evidence from the remaining soundings, aside from those in the immediate surroundings of the basilica and one site near the harbor, is in the sixth century. The latest dates are for the basilica itself in the eighth century.

QUANTITATIVE ANALYSIS

Pottery specialists armed with computers and statistical data produce studies of how sites relate to one another by examining what pots are present and not present and in what quantities. This is what they are after when they make comparisons between subsets of an assemblage or different assemblages from site to site.

Ephesos (in what is now western Turkey) and Olympia (in southern Greece), for example, are both sites in the eastern part of the Empire that imported Italian *sigillata*. However, a comparison of their patterns of supply of the ware shows what differences could exist within the so-called Eastern market (Fig. App. I-16). Expressing the chronological range of the different types of Italian *sigillata* at each site as a cumulative curve in which the number of examples of each type is distributed over the decades during which it was produced (e.g., 10 examples of a type produced from 1 to 100 CE give an example per decade throughout the century), it appears clearly that the importation of Italian *sigillata* at Ephesos was concentrated in a short period, the last decades of the first century BCE and the first decades of the first century CE, while at Olympia importation of Italian *sigillata* took off only toward the mid-first century CE and then lasted for a century. This result is borne out not only by the consideration of the vessel types of *sigillata* found at the two sites but also by the potters' stamps, which both indicate not only a later date for Olympia but also a different supplier source within Italy.

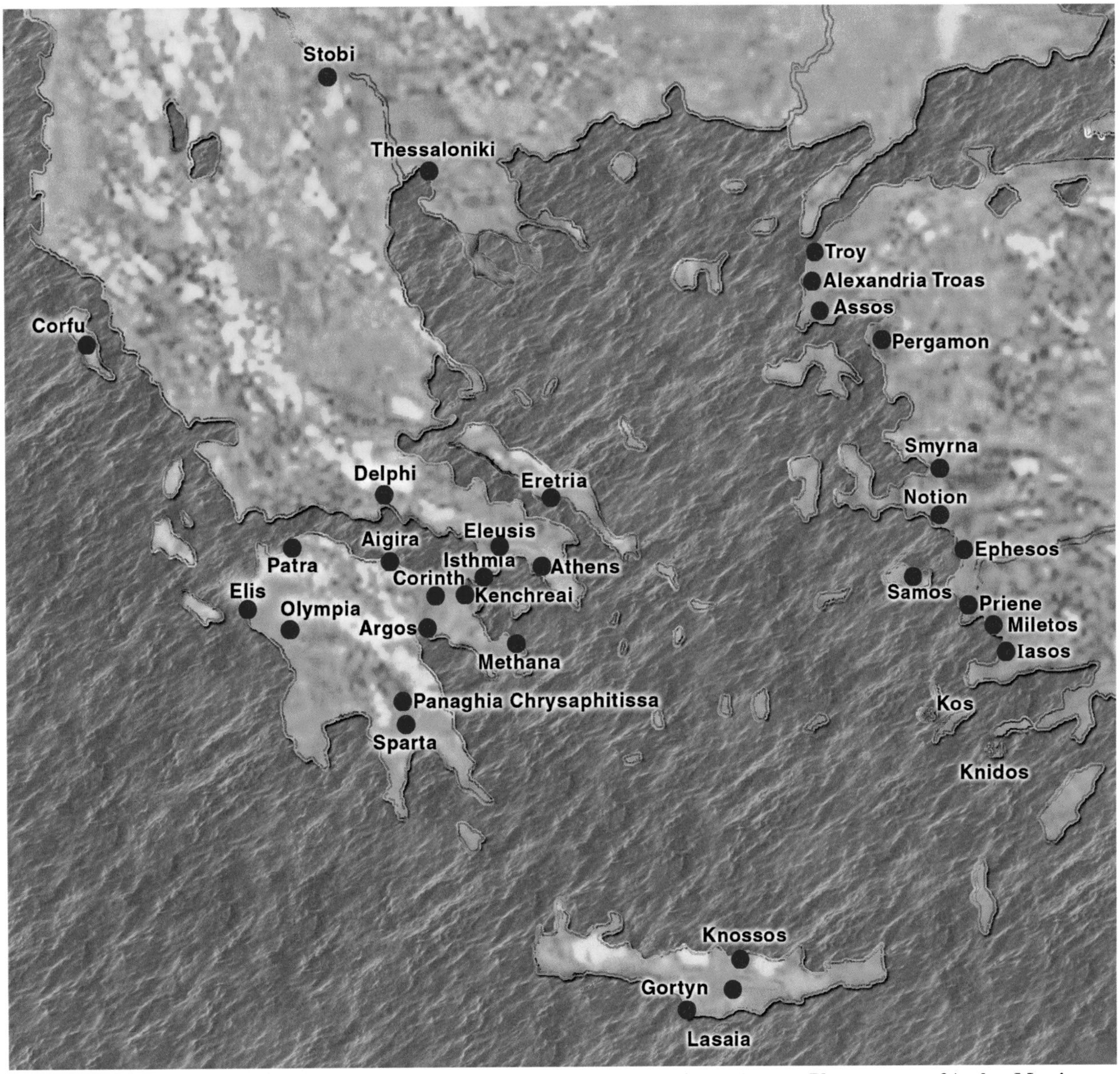

Fig. App. I- 16 Plan showing the distribution of Italian *sigillata* at sites in the Aegean. Plan courtesy of Archer Martin.

A statistical comparison of the amphora supply at Ostia found in stratified deposits from the first to the fifth century CE excavated by the joint project by the Deutsches Archäologisches Institut and the American Academy in Rome shows various shifts in supply. By provenience Italy, then the Iberian Peninsula and finally North Africa are the dominant suppliers over this period, which confirms a trend already observed by archaeologists at Ostia. In breaking down the supplies carried by the amphorae into wine on one hand and olive oil and/or fish products on the other, an interesting reversal of tendency appears: in the first century CE about 2/3 of the amphorae attested can be attributed to wine but in the later horizons only 1/3. This gives rise to considerations about the possibility of wine not carried in amphorae, presumably from the hinterland of Ostia, making up a greater part of the supply in the later periods, as a drastic fall in the consumption of wine with respect to oil and fish sauce is unlikely.

Fig. App. I-17 (right) Map showing Ostia, Rome, Chianciano Terme and Lugnano in Teverina and the Tiber River, four sites recently studied and compared with regard to pottery trade by Archer Martin.

The statistical composition of assemblages by functional groups can reflect the degree of a site's integration into the network of overseas and river transportation. A study for example examined fifth-century CE deposits at Ostia (a major shipping center for the entire Mediterranean), Rome (a major destination of trade and center of consumption), Lugnano in Teverina (a villa in Umbria on the navigable stretch of the Tiber upstream from Rome) and Chianciano Terme (an ancient spa in southern Tuscany on a non-navigable tributary of the Tiber) (Fig. App. I-17). Thus, care was taken to compare sites of the same period but

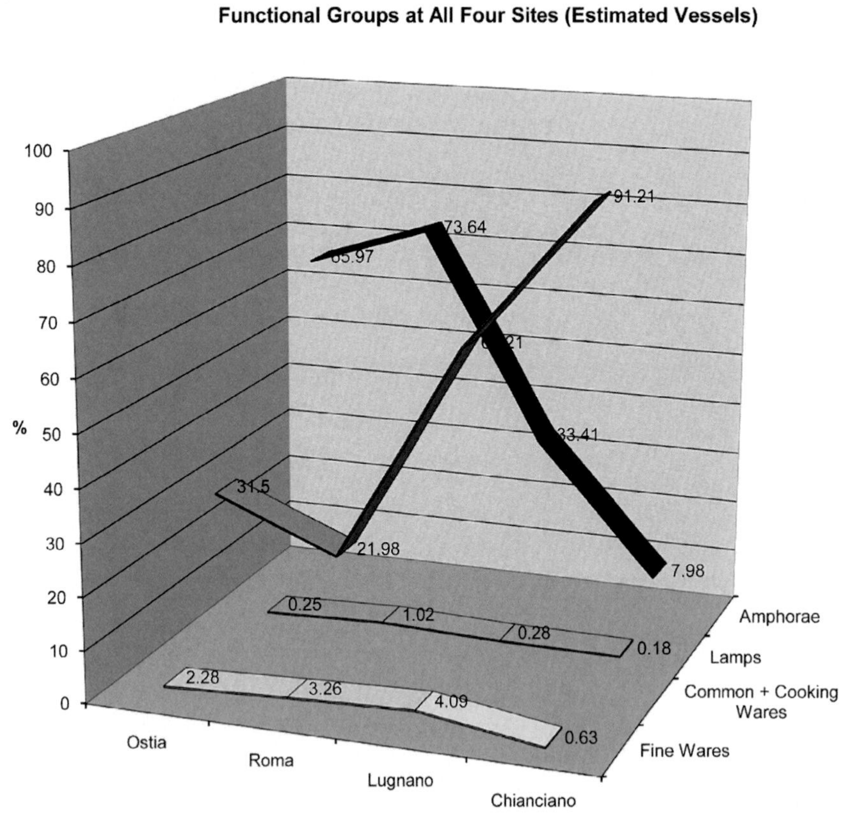

Fig. App. I-18 Three dimensional chart of a typ commonly used by pottery specialists, showing th relative popularity of types of Roman pottery an oil lamps at the sites of Chianciano Terme, Lugna no in Teverina, Ostia and Rome. Courtesy of Ar cher Martin.

different geographic position (Fig. App. I-18). Amphorae made up between 2/3 and 3/4 of the total at Ostia and Rome, about 1/3 at Lugnano and a negligible percentage at Chianciano. The amphorae in question came from many parts of the Mediterranean at Ostia and Rome, from a more limited range of sources at Lugnano with a greater importance of regional containers and almost exclusively from within the local region at Chianciano. The fine tablewares were almost wholly imported at Ostia and Rome but to a large extent made up of import substitutes or imitations at Lugnano, while at Chianciano there were very few pieces of fine ware, all of which were imported. These data suggest that the production and marketing of import substitutes required both a certain barrier to imports to allow the activities to grow up and a minimum of regional circulation to make them worthwhile to make. Imported cooking wares were able to gain a significant presence at Ostia but much less of one at Rome and none at all upstream. Other domestic wares and lamps were only occasionally imported on all the sites studied. This sort of analysis promises to provide a tool for judging a site's position with regard to the trade network where it is otherwise not clear.

More recently, another similar study of contexts at Ostia and Pompeii datable between the second century BCE and the first century CE showed the importance of the chronological dimension in making comparisons. There the percentages of the amphorae in the assemblages were comparable to those of the outliers among the fifth-century contexts, although both were important ports. Evidently the volumes carried on the trade networks of the late Republican and early Imperial Periods were lower than in the fifth century, so that even well integrated sites had percentages of amphorae that would be low in later times. It is not surprising that the state of almost continual warfare and endemic piracy in the late Republic was not conducive to long-distance trade, and in fact the percentages of amphorae in the contexts considered rose noticeably during the Augustan Period and the first century CE, when more peaceable conditions were established.

PETROGRAPHIC ANALYSIS

As has been remarked, the most importan contribution of archaeometry so far t pottery studies concerns the determination o provenience, which is of course of fundamenta importance in evaluating such matters a trade relations. For example, wine amphora were produced throughout Tyrrhenian centra Italy in the late Republican and early Imperia Periods. A petrographic study or analysis o the mineral content in their fabrics compare samples excavated in Switzerland with one from central Italy. This study has contributed t distinguishing the central Italian wine amphora from non-Italic amphorae, as well as identifyin subgroups among the Italic amphorae. Amphora from Tyrrhenian central Italy, from Albinia in th north at least to the Gulf of Naples in the south are characterized by the presence of volcani elements derived from the Pleistocene volcani complex of central and southern Italy and ca thus be readily distinguished from example made elsewhere. Variation of these volcani elements allows distinctions to be made within the group. In some cases the groups can be distinguished chemically, but in others the mineralogical examination of thin sections is necessary to separate chemically similar groups (Fig. App. I-19).

X-RAY FLUORESCENCE

Chemical analyses can be carried out using a technique called X-Ray fluorescence, in which the pottery sample is exposed to X-Rays. Simply put, the photons of the X-Ray excite and eject the electrons of the pottery material that is being tested. A certain amount of light is emitted and then analyzed by a device called a spectrometer. The component parts of the pottery sample possess different levels of energy that can be calibrated and assessed, allowing them to be identified.

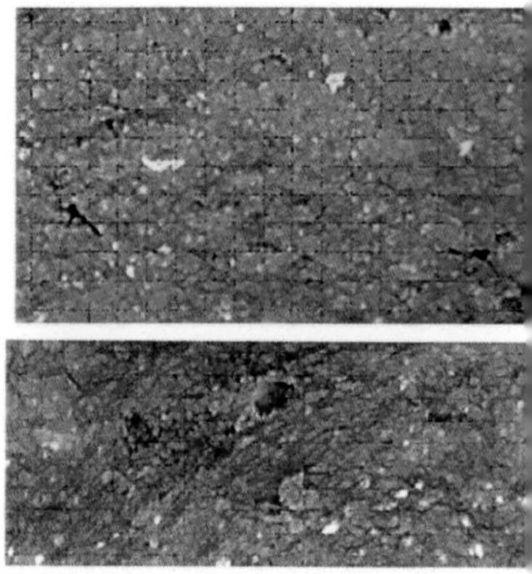

Fig. App. I-19 Examples of pottery thin sections on common ware from Chianciano Terme. These sections allow pottery specialists to distinguish differences in the composition of ceramics from various localities and even within the same localities

This process was used on 132 samples of Italian *sigillata* from the Rome area in order to investigate the ware's production and circulation around the capital. The results were compared with the data bases for known production sites at Arezzo and elsewhere in northern Etruria and at Vasanello and Scoppieto in the Tiber valley north of Rome. As a result it is now possible to define six groups on the basis of their chemical composition: one that can be attributed to Arezzo, allowing for some doubt in a few cases that belong at any rate to northern Etruria; five groups that can be located in central Italy (southern Etruria, northern Latium, the iber valley and perhaps Rome itself), including the products of 'asanello and Scoppieto. The combined study of potters' stamps lays an important role in this study, verifying the attributions nade for archaeological or epigraphic reasons of potters' names production centers. For instance, a stack of burnt vessels from stia stamped by Sex. Annius, which gave rise over the years) speculation that there was *sigillata* production there, is now nown to belong chemically to the Arezzo area (where the name is nown) and cannot be local Ostian kiln waste. In short, there is no vidence for a production center for this potter at Ostia. In other ases pieces stamped with the same potters' names can be shown to elong to different chemical groups, requiring archaeologists and pigraphers to come up with possible explanations: for example, nat a workshop set up a branch elsewhere or that independent otters happened to have the same name.

DENTITY STUDIES

Economic questions were the dominant concern among ottery specialists in the second-half of the 20th century and have y no means disappeared. In recent years, however, a new interest as emerged—the investigation of identity through pottery.

It has already been seen that large parts of the Roman world vished to use Italian tableware, that is Italian *sigillata*, or wares sing the Italian repertoire of forms during the reign of Augustus nd in the early-first century CE. This can be seen as a choice of lentity—people wanted to present themselves as Romans when ney dined.

Occasionally it is possible to see the opposite choice, as seems) be the case at the site of Schedia in the Egyptian Delta about 0 km southeast of Alexandria. There *sigillata* is not unknown—a ertain amount of Eastern *Sigillata* A (a product of the area of ntioch that adopted the repertoire of Italian *sigillata*) is attested, s well as a few pieces of Italian and other sigillatas. There are even are locally made imitations of *sigillata* forms. The overwhelming najority of the vessels in local fine ware continue, however, to resent the previous Hellenistic repertoire of forms. Evidently the nhabitants of Schedia were aware of the trend in the wider world ut chose to maintain their tradition, much as people today in ural districts of Egypt, like this one, eat in the traditional manner vith their hands while sitting on the floor, in contrast to the urban opulation that has adopted the Western-style of using cutlery round a table. The people of Schedia accepted the Mediterranean orm in tableware only in Late Antiquity, by which time North African products were the model.

UTURE GOALS

In the future pottery scholars will be focusing on new ways o use pottery and other material culture holistically to understand nore about the daily life of the Romans. Pompeii is a productive ite for this kind of research, according to J. Theodore Peña of he University of California—Berkeley. Unlike most sites in he Roman word where one simply recovers material culture rom trash middens and other discard contexts, Pompeii offers n opportunity for synchronic study, since it was buried in the eruption of Mount Vesuvius in 79 CE. Therefore, it contains not nly discard contexts but also provisional discard complexes, that s, places where people piled up refuse anticipating its eventual lefinitive discarding. Pompeii also has pottery (and other artifacts) hat are recovered in what are called use-related contexts, that is n locations where pottery was being used or where it was being tored in anticipation of eventual use. So the great strength of the vidence from Pompeii is that it offers a much richer picture of portable material culture in the midst of its use rather than simply in what is normally the end of its life history.

Another area of pottery research that is providing ample fodder for research is examining the technology of pottery manufacture and understanding how it is connected to the organization of pottery production. For example in Italy there has been great interest in understanding the technology and organization of the terra *sigillata* pottery industry, that fine ware that grew up in and around Arretium, now the Tuscan town of Arezzo, in the third-quarter of the first century BCE. To further study the wares of Arezzo, Peña has analyzed the pottery chemically and then set out to find the specific clay bed that was employed by the potters working there. The clay bed proved to be of such fine quality that the potters working at Arezzo were effectively able to use the clay immediately as it came out of the ground, that is without needing to resort to the practice of levigation to remove a coarse component in order to obtain a finer-bodied clay that was appropriate for the manufacture of this very high quality tableware. At the same time Peña was also able to observe that this particular clay deposit was overlain by a deposit of peat, which turned out to be the only major peat deposit in peninsular Italy. In northern Europe, where peat is quite abundant, it is regularly used as a fuel for firing pottery, and probably in Arezzo those who were obliged to dig through the peat to get to the fine clay could also use the peat for fuel. Comparative evidence from the early-Modern Period shows that the use of peat for a fuel is substantially more economical than the use of other traditional fuels such as wood. This suggests that this combination of efficiencies was available to Arezzo potters.

Therefore, the possibility of obtaining clay of fine texture that they could use to make a high-quality ceramic body with no additional input of labor and the availability of an economical fuel source probably created a situation within which producers at Arezzo were able to capitalize on access to major markets like Rome. This may be why the terra *sigillata* industry emerged there. These discoveries show the ability of modern technicians and scientists with an interest in archaeology to break new ground by asking questions that are different from those posed by earlier generations, taking advantage of new techniques of analysis. Yet it was surprising that despite all of the interest among scholars in the Arretine terra *sigillata* industry that no archaeologist had ever undertaken the basic step of consulting the geologic map and then following through on what that map quite clearly indicated to find the clay beds.

CREATIVE THINKING EXERCISES

•1. What are some of the duties of a modern pottery specialist on an archaeological excavation?

•2. What can the study of amphorae tell us about international trade?

•3. How did the Romans illuminate their homes in the evening hours?

•4. Describe some of the different classes of Roman pottery.

•5. How has epigraphy on pottery shed new light on ancient trade habits?

•6. Pottery study can inform us about the customs and preferences of ancient peoples. Give several examples of this.

•7. How is quantitative analysis used to determine specific characteristics about ancient archaeological sites?

•8. What are some of the techniques developed over the past 30 years to allow us to derive more basic information from the collection of pottery on archaeological sites?

Appendix II
Excavating a Roman Archaeological Site

In this volume we have examined something of the art and archaeology of the ancient Romans. In this chapter we investigate how an ancient archaeological site is unearthed and what approaches are used to gain the information that goes into an excavation report. Fortunately, in studying the Romans, we can rely a great deal on literary evidence and sometimes, using coins and inscriptions, we are able to date events with great precision. However, information often has to be derived scientifically through surveying and excavating sites. It is therefore instructive to pause briefly and examine what it means to study archaeology and to investigate a site and extract evidence from it.

Archaeology is the scientific unearthing of the past. Once the domain of treasure hunters, it is today an accepted academic discipline, and the excavator is normally a professor affiliated with a college, university or museum, although he or she may also be part of a private or public firm. An archaeologist specializing in the excavation and interpretation of Roman sites most often has a Ph.D. in classical archaeology, and, like other classical archaeologists, he or she will have studied foreign languages such as ancient Greek, Latin, French, German and Italian at the minimum, and will undergo more language training if necessary in the particular country that contains the Roman archaeology he is studying. The more languages the would-be archaeologist can learn while young or can take as an undergraduate in college, the better off he or she is likely to be and the greater the chances of getting into a good graduate program.

Fig. App. II-1 Deborah Carlson found a niche for herself in nautical archaeology after training as a classical archaeologist. She now investigates shipwrecks around the Mediterranean and directs the Institute of Nautical Archaeology. Courtesy Institute of Nautical Archaeology.

A classical archaeologist should also take general courses in archaeology, art history and history as much as possible during the obtaining of a Bachelor of Arts and a Master's Degree, and then begin to specialize into an area of interest at the doctoral or Ph.D. level. If the student has a strong idea of the field in which he wishes to specialize at the Master's Degree level, the specialization can begin at that time also, but generally it is wiser to obtain a broad-based education in the field before focusing more narrowly on one specific area.

HOW TO BECOME A CLASSICAL ARCHAEOLOGIST

The archaeologist needs a background in history as well as art history and anthropology (the study of the development of man) plus good writing skills and training in English in addition to foreign language training. Additional specialties are welcome too, such as computer studies, surveying, mathematics and the ability to sketch and draw. An archaeologist who has a special ability that others do not have has a distinct advantage—extraordinary language skills, knowledge of pottery, training in computer mapping, or even the ability to teach other subjects such as general art history or film. Surprisingly, knowledge of film and filmmaking can be a real boon, since excavators are often used as television consultants or may wish increasingly to document their own sites for future study or presentations and the visual documentary side of archaeology is an area that is growing rapidly in demand and appreciation.

The reason for all this background training is that the excavator is normally both a professor and someone who spends his free summers and sabbatical leaves in the field excavating an ancient site. Indiana Jones was a good example of this, taken to the extreme, although he never seemed to spend very much time in the classroom at Marshall College and he never used much science in his archaeological method, even the science available to him in 1936. The excavator usually begins as an apprentice, learning his trade both in the classroom and in the field under professionals. Eventually, as he builds up expertise over a number of years and makes connections in his field, he may branch out with the help of his professors to find a position in a university or museum. Positions in archaeology are scarce, as it is an over-saturated field, but the very best students learn to focus on their studies, develop their required skills and set precise and realistic goals (Fig. App. II-1, 2).

BEGINNING AN EXCAVATION

Once established at a university where colleagues can provide further connections and support (known as "networking"), the

Fig. App. II-2 Deborah Carlson's INA team uses underwater balloons to lift columns of the later second century BCE from an underwater shipwreck off the southwest coast of Turkey at Kizilburun.

ɤcavator may be able to develop his own excavation or "dig." It sually takes a minimum of $30,000 to assemble a minimal field ›am, usually beginning with a survey season. When the excavator nally obtains his own site he learns immediately that he is a field eneral who must have or quickly develop leadership capabilities; is most important skills are diplomacy, patience, the ability organize materials, a strong sense of focus, and the ability manage other people. He is regularly required to negotiate ith representatives of the host country to get the all-important xcavation permit—so a degree of fluency in the language of the ountry is extremely useful. He is dealing with staff and student roblems in the first seasons, but over time he learns to select eople who are both qualified and mature and, with a bit of luck, the ifficulties of living together in an isolated environment become educed and the nucleus of a regular staff or team is created.

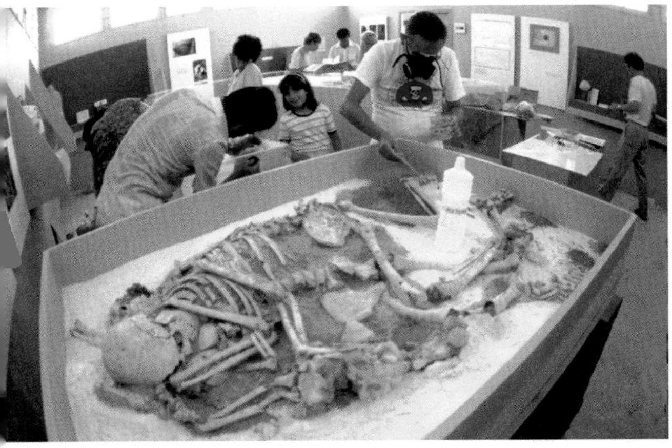

ig. App. II-3 (above) Excavators and specialists led by Walter Birk-y, Human Identification Laboratory, Arizona State Museum, pre-are a new museum built by the excavation team at Kourion, Cyprus 1987. This excavation task included the physical construction of e building, installation of exhibits (going on in the background), nd excavation of the site including lifting, cleaning and chemically oating bodies trapped in an earthquake believed to have occurred in 65 CE. Photo credit: Noelle Soren. University of Arizona School of nthropology Archive.

ig. App. II-4 (right) Gridded plan of the excavations at the local-y Mezzomiglio in the Tuscan town of Chianciano Terme made by he University of Arizona team, arranged in large 10 meter quares to locate the soundings and ruins uncovered. These quares are located by reading the letters of the grid at the ft and the number at the bottom. Each 10m square is subdi-ided into 4 squares of 5m labeled a,b,c,d and read clockwise. lan by Jose Olivas.

Nonetheless, the excavator must worry about many hings he never expected in graduate school that he would ave to think about, including how to deal with errant tudents, how to ensure that nutritious and safe food is vailable, how to acquire living accommodations that are ot excessively primitive and of course how to achieve the verall harmony of the group working together. Qualities ought in a student going on a dig are special skills, an rganized mind, the ability to produce requested work n time, a cheerful attitude, and a willingness to try to et along with other people. Often difficulties result rom group cohabitation in remote areas and/or confined paces, and these can cause significant problems in the ccomplishing of the excavation objective.

In order to describe how an excavation functions it is best to work from an example, such as the excavations conducted at Kourion in the 1970s and 1980s by the University of Missouri-Columbia (Fig. App. II-3). An interview was granted with the Director of Antiquities of the island of Cyprus in the eastern Mediterranean, Dr. Vassos Karageorghis, in 1977, and a formal application was made to the Department of Antiquities. With the permission of the Director, a survey was made of the site by the would-be excavator, David Soren, which consisted of simply walking over the area in conjunction with reading all available previous publications and field diaries about the excavation. It was determined that the site may have been destroyed by earthquakes so a team was posited that consisted of specialists with geological and geo-physical expertise. The Cypriote Department of Antiquities agreed to allow excavation provided that funds could be raised to provide for it, and a time limit of one year was given to raise these funds and begin limited excavation.

Would-be excavators thus frequently find themselves in a Catch 22 situation. They can dig provided they have the money to dig, but in order to raise money to dig they must have in hand a permit to dig. This is usually surmounted by stating that one has a tentative agreement to excavate, and one can then ally with a university grants specialist and plan a strategy to raise enough funding to get into the field with a team as soon as possible.

This was then followed with extensive fund-raising attempts ranging from private donors, appeals to the National Endowment for the Humanities, the National Geographic Society, the American Philosophical Society, the National Science Foundation, participating universities (usually several universities may participate in order to generate seed money) and of course private donors. Grant-writing is difficult and often involves cost-sharing and indirect costs, concepts that many archaeologists find vague and confusing. It is useful to consult the university grants specialist, whose job often depends on the number of successful grant applications that he or she can make.

All of this fund-raising may result in the obtaining of some grant money, enough to accomplish a beginning season, which includes making an overall gridded plan of the site, much like a chessboard, with each square measuring 10 square meters and each square identified by letters and numbers. Such gridded plans are

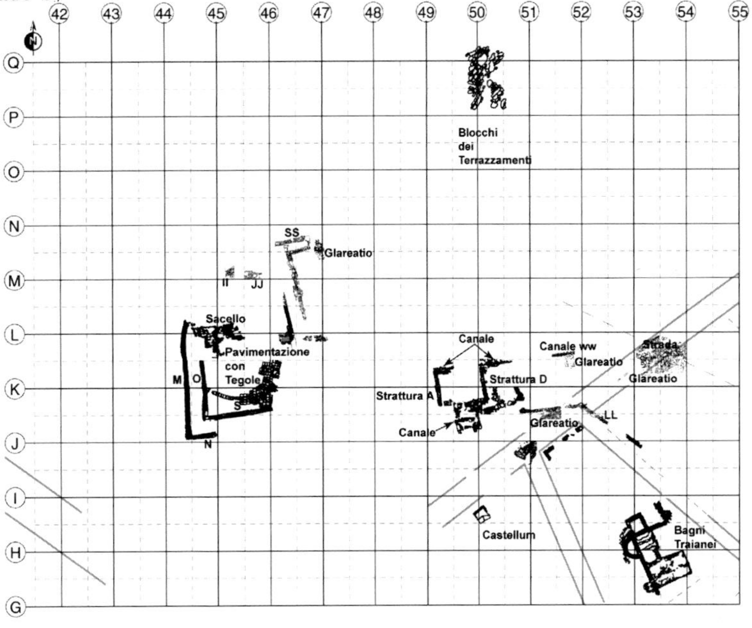

essential and are set up by most excavators before they do anything else at the site, even though the configuration of the grid may vary a bit from dig to dig (Fig. App. II-4).

The gridding of the site is done by a professional surveyor or mapper, who is able to use a measuring instrument known as a theodolyte to get exact elevations of the different topographical areas of the hillside site. By locating a benchmark or precise spot with known elevation through the local government's geological survey office, the recently shot elevations can be tied into the actual height of the land above sea level to give a correct overall elevation for the various parts of the site.

Once the site is put onto a grid and properly surveyed, stakes are placed in the ground at measured locations along the grid to indicate periodically various coordinates of the grid for easy access. These are known as the grid points. By subdividing each grid into four-5 meter squares labeled clockwise a, b, c and d, it is possible to gain even more precision for any important finds that are recovered on the surface by the team members, who fan out and walk about the site in ordered rows following the grid. The grid also provides the key reference location for any finds that come from trenches dug into the earth along the grid points.

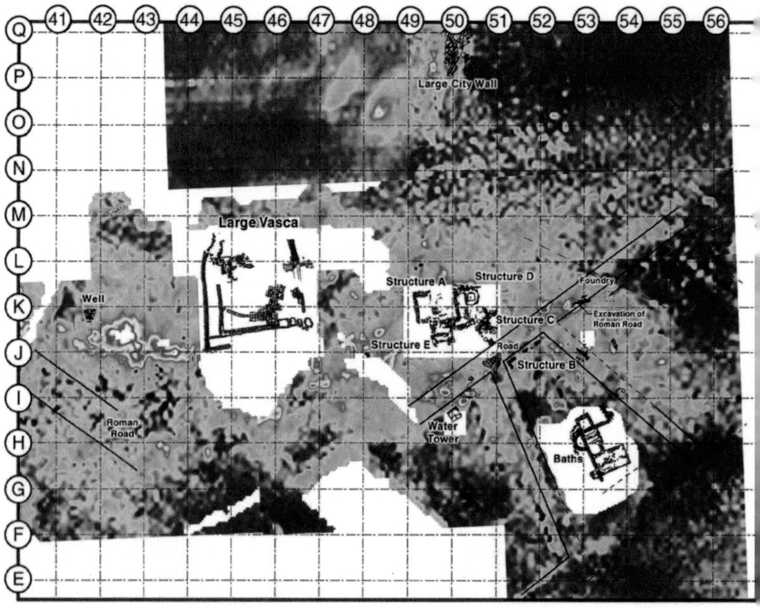

Fig. App. II-5 (above) Anomalies showing in orange-red on an Electronic Distance Meter survey at Chianciano Terme, Mezzomiglio area, Tuscany. Photo credit: Noelle Soren. University of Arizona School of Anthropology Archive. Courtesy of Lewis Somers, Geoffrey Jones, David Maki.

GEOPHYSICAL SURVEYING

Fig. App. II-6 (below) Results of a Twin Electrode Resistivity Survey after filtering data, at Chianciano Terme. Courtesy of Lewis Somers, Geoffrey Jones, David Maki.

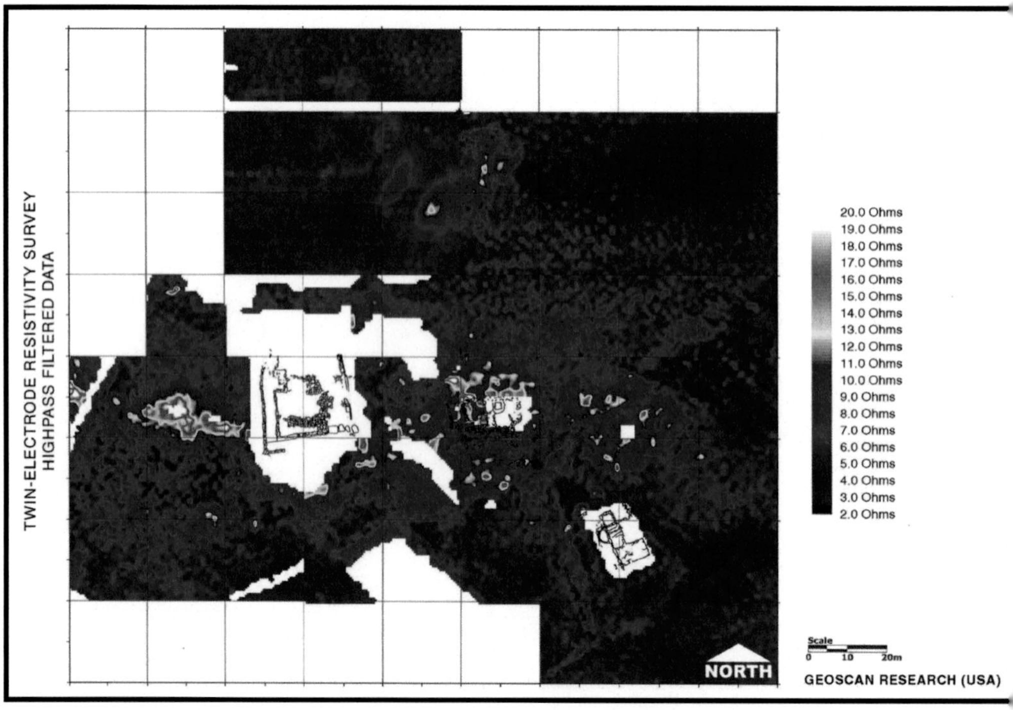

Each site requires a special approach depending on what the excavator hopes to find, the money available and the expertise of the excavator and his staff. In the Mezzomiglio area in Tuscany a site was excavated by the University of Arizona. The project director was not sure exactly where to begin digging, despite having walked over the surface and collected shards to attempt to identify possible starting spots. An inexpensive way to determine what existed on the site without going to the considerable expense of putting in numerous trial trenches is to conduct geophysical survey investigations. One popular technique which was applied on the Mezzomiglio site early on is called an Electrical Resistance Survey (Figs. App. II-5, 6). This was achieved by inserting into the ground a device that resembles a pogo stick but has two tiny probes or prongs at the bottom fastened to a plate which is connected to an electronic measuring gauge. These probes are placed into the ground along the site grid at regular intervals, usually every meter, by having the archaeologist or his assistants jump onto the device to fix it into the ground, wait for a reading, then move the device to the next spot along the grid (Fig Intro-20). The numerical value and precise position of each data point may be automatically recorded in a digital format. The data points can then be downloaded to a computer and used to produce plans of the site showing the likelihood of structures or at least anomalies existing under the surface at a given spot. The probes actually measure the electrical resistance of the soil, architectural features or other objects below.

A number of factors can affect the measurement of the resistance. For example, coarse-grained or dry soils, stone, concrete and brick are highly resistant to the flow of electricity while fine rained, moist or organically rich soils conduct electricity well. he electrical resistance work proved to be the most successful pe of underground surveying done at the Mezzomiglio site in hianciano Terme, because it was able to locate a large medieval ell and to find seven major streets associated with the site that ad not been known before. All of these elements appeared as high esistance anomalies (Figs. App. II-5, 6). Subsequent excavation onfirmed the existence of all of these elements.

Another type of geophysical surveying done at Mezzomiglio a bit more difficult to understand. Magnetic Field Gradient urveying is designed to measure small-scale local variation in e Earth's magnetic field, which may be caused by different aterials at or near the surface of the soil (normally less than 2 eters deep). If the Earth's magnetic field flows very well through particular material in the Earth, that earth is said to exhibit high usceptibility. Organically enriched earth or burned earth is highly usceptible to magnetic field gradient surveys and will register as a ositive anomaly on a gauge. However, less susceptible materials an register as a negative anomaly and may indicate that structures re going to be found if the excavator digs slightly under the urface in a specific spot. Sedimentary rock used for architecture a good example of a desirable negative anomaly. Structures ying just under the soil often have their own positive and negative omponents and are at odds with the Earth's magnetic field so e call these structures bipolar. They are also often referred to as emanent structures. This means that they have eir own particular permanent magnetism r magnetism which remains. Examples of emanent bipolar anomalies that the excavator an discover through the Magnetic Field radient Survey are iron, igneous rock, fired rick or tile, concentrations of ceramics, earths, kilns or burned out buildings. ometimes it is difficult to determine just hat is being detected in a Magnetic Field radient Survey, but if something shows up it an be a good idea to do a test trench to see hat one may encounter. It is also to compare he results of different kinds of above-surface esting systems to see which areas show up in ommon when the results are plotted on the rid. However, this survey yielded very little hat was useful at the Mezzomiglio site.

Ground Penetrating Radar was the inal geophysical survey method used at Mezzomiglio (Fig. App. II-7). GPR, as it s referred to by professionals, transmits an lectromagnetic pulse into the ground, and when it strikes something unusual the pulse s reflected back towards the surface and into receiver antenna. The amount of time the ignal takes to travel into the earth and come back is thus measured and the depth of the nomaly and its location can be revealed. GPR an thus yield both vertical maps showing he depths of anomalies found up to 2 meters elow the surface or regular flat plans showing he locations of anomalies. However, highly onductive soils such as clays cause signal loss and rocky or heterogeneous soils cause signal scattering and faulty readings. The clay-rich soil of Mezzomiglio rendered GPR surveying all but useless.

At Mezzomiglio, earlier excavations had revealed traces of ancient structures that could be easily identified as either late Etruscan or Roman by studying the type of wall construction employed. The surface finds recovered in the initial walking survey showed that the site did not have an abundant supply of fine material culture, which means that there were few coins and little fine pottery found. Thus excavation of the site was not expected to yield a great amount of material and one could suspect that the site may have been looted or cleaned out to a large extent in antiquity. This was an hypothesis based on preliminary evidence and it proved to be true after excavation was achieved.

There was not yet available the $30,000 necessary to do a proper geophysical sub-site scan, but at this point the archaeologist, David Soren, had to decide whether or not to accept the site to excavate. This is the moment of truth because sites may be offered for a limited period of time by the particular Italian *soprintendenza*, especially with regard to foreign archaeologists, and therefore the archaeologist must weigh all the factors and then accept the site or pass on it. If one is going to invest the many years and money required to study an area, one needs to know that the site shows promise of unusual discoveries of a material or intellectual nature. Simply excavating one more typical Roman bath or a cistern or

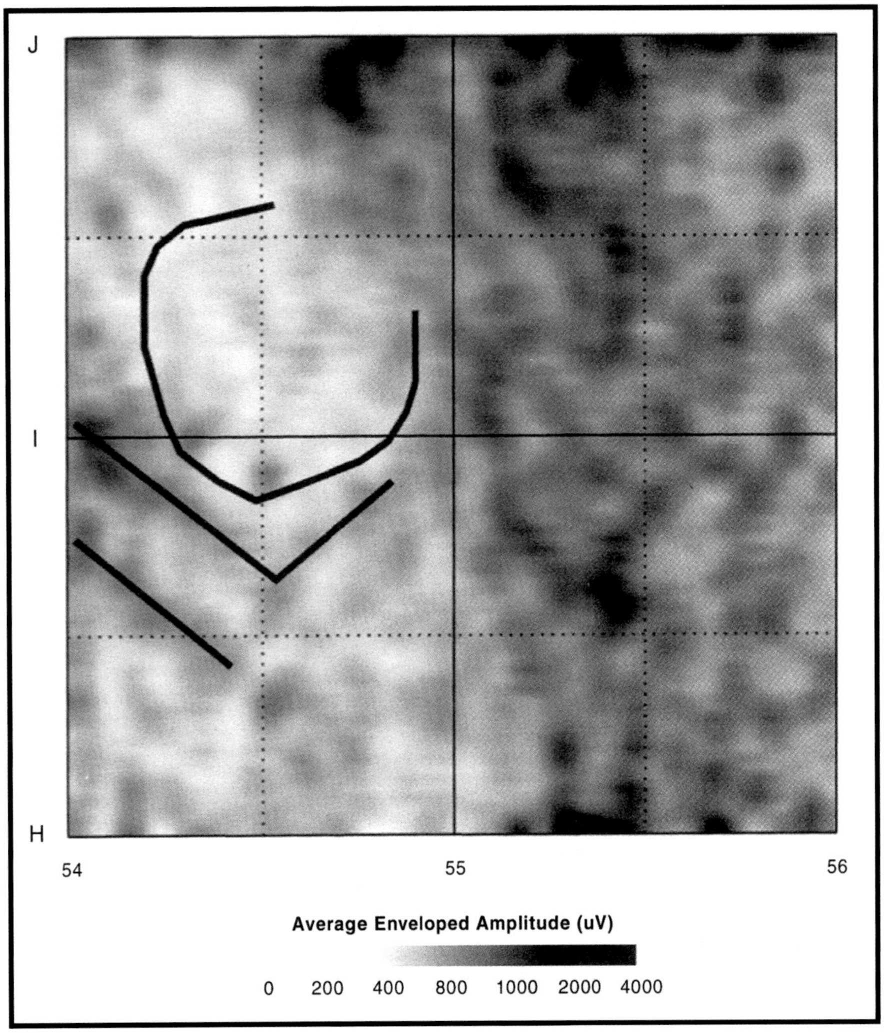

Fig. App. II-7 Ground Penetrating Radar (GPR) survey results from Chianciano Terme, with graphical interpretation. Courtesy of Lewis Somers, Geoffrey Jones, David Maki.

a shapeless field of ruins may not reveal much about Roman culture and will not either further the discipline or the archaeologist's career, nor will it excite possible investors, granting agencies or university administrators, all of whom are inclined to support sites with unique or at least significant potential for spectacular or significant results.

SELECTING THE SITE

In the case of the Mezzomiglio locality, the local Italian archaeology club members who had done preliminary work there, reported that whenever they tried to excavate the site, water gushed forth almost immediately (Fig. App. II-8). The American excavator knew that this area was noted for natural springs and felt that the site had the potential to be an ancient spa of a type little documented archaeologically and that it might be important for the history of Roman architecture. Furthermore, the preliminary research had shown that the famous springs of Chiusi or *fontes Clusini* frequented by the Emperor Augustus and the poet Horace were known to have been in this general area. If the springs might be found, it would be archaeologically significant. Money could be raised to attempt the excavation and journals and publishers would be interested to transmit the results to scholars. Therefore the risky decision to go ahead with the project was made.

Fig. App. II-8 Water gushes forth regularly from a natural spring under the ground and puddles on the site of Mezzomiglio at Chianciano Terme. Photo credit: Noelle Soren. University of Arizona School of Anthropology Archive.

At this point accords were signed with the Department of Antiquities or *Soprintendenza per i Beni Archeologici* as it is known in Italy and an *ispettore* (the current title is *funzionario archeologo*), an Italian official working for the *Soprintendenza* and assigned to supervise this region, was asked by the director of the *Soprintendenza* to oversee all excavations done and to sign off on the permit. Now the excavator's difficulties truly began, for the rest of the year had to be devoted to writing grants and assembling the team. Competition for grants is fierce, especially in hard financial times, when the granting agencies for arts and archaeology reduce their stipends, and help from local foundations and even private individuals had to be enlisted through speeches to local civic groups and fundraising lunches and dinners. To excavate reasonably well in Italy for five to six weeks in the summers now costs a minimum of $30,000 each year, depending on the size of the team and the amount of laboratory analysis that is desired. The excavator knows that once this money is raised for one season, he must then start all over again for the next year almost immediately after the completion of the digging season. This creates a seemingly unending and wearying process, which, when coupled with the regular academic university year of lectures and committee meetings, is particularly time-consuming. Sometimes the excavator ends up without sufficient money, and he must open his excavations to the general public to get money and workers. This can be done by charging a fee for participation or signing up with a national organization that sends people on excavations for a commission. Such efforts may bring a little needed cash but often also can bring in untrained and sometimes overenthusiastic or ill-suited people. Excavators generally prefer to work with a team they have personally trained and prepared for the summer work, selected from their own graduate level students and perhaps some qualified undergraduates as well.

ASSEMBLING THE TEAM

Assembling the team is the next challenge. The excavator must make an educated guess as to what kinds of specialists he will need to take with him. After the first season he will have a much better idea of whom to bring, but each excavation will require different personnel, depending on what is unearthed. Initially, when digging is to be a part of the program, it is useful to

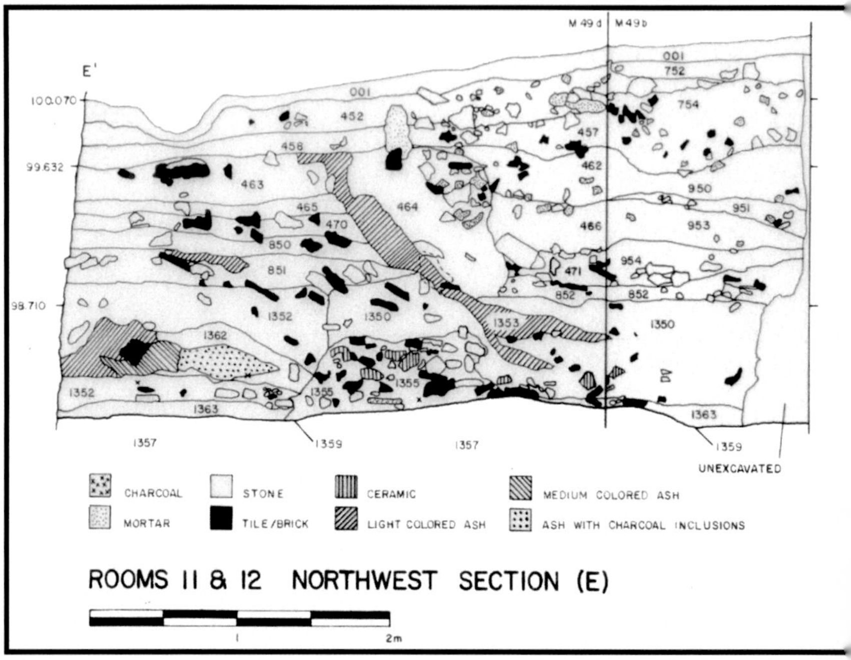

Fig. App. II-9 Drawing of the complex stratigraphy found in the infant cemetery in Lugnano in Teverina showing the quick filling up of the area and the placing of infant burials within Rooms 11 and 12 of a destroyed villa there which was reused for burials.

ave a stratigrapher, someone who is well versed in studying the arious layers of soil and debris which, when piled one on top of e other, tell the story of the area (Fig. App. II- 9). Often this is e excavator himself who, after years of experience on sites, has reasonable idea of how communities rise and fall in his area and hat this looks like in the soil. At Mezzomiglio, which was built n a hillside, it is known that the hill gradually slid and slumped ntil it covered over the site and buried it under 10 feet of sand nd clay. Because this particular site is full of natural springs and ven mini-geysers, as well as acres of impermeable clay and sand, geologist had to be brought in, as well as an hydrologist to study e nature of the water in the area and to compare the modern pring water with the springs that may have been there in antiquity. omparisons of modern natural phenomena in an excavation area ith the ancient natural characteristics is often highly instructive nd can give valuable information about the mineralogy of the area, e nature of soils, what grows in the soils and how drainage was ccomplished, particularly if the overall climate has not changed reatly since antiquity.

Geologists give invaluable help by knowing the composition f the soil, recognizing traces of fires and identifying the various tones used in building the site. Paleo-osteologists are also of great nportance, not only for identifying uman and animal bones but also or drawing conclusions about the ncient diet of the local people and o find out what they were butchering nd eating. Animal bones may also ive indications of religious rituals in ractice, particularly when they are ecovered from cemeteries.

At Lugnano in Teverina, Jmbria, not far from Mezzomiglio, cemetery entirely of infants killed n a malaria epidemic in the mid-fth century CE featured animal one offerings of a raven's talon nd a toad and nine puppies that had een sacrificed and had their jaws ipped apart (Figs. XIII-24, 26). One uppy had been cut in half in an ttempt to rid the community of the hen unknown epidemic that caused regnant mothers to abort their etuses and have them buried in this emetery. Such conclusions, if they re unusual, may be challenged by ther scholars. Therefore, the careful rocessing and analysis of bones with respect to their archaeological ontext is essential. This is why the xcavator must work closely with very member of his team to see hat they are well informed about he context and find spots of what as been discovered as well as the bjects themselves. In working with pecialists who are interpreting data, he veteran excavator knows that ontextual understanding is critical. It is not enough to find a worked bone but rather it is necessary to study that bone in relation to other finds from this area and to the architecture of the area itself. For this reason, regular meetings among all specialists present are extremely helpful.

A palynologist is another essential member of any team, studying the ancient plants, particularly burned seeds, and reconstructing what is called the paleo-environment or the climate of the area in the time of the Romans (Fig. App. II-10). Sediment from the site is gathered up in bulk amounts and processed by flotation (water separation) to filter out small, buoyant plant parts from the non-organic debris. The sediment is poured into a large tub of water and the floating debris is skimmed off using a tea strainer with a fine mesh of about 1mm. The remains are dried indoors in a folded newspaper and then bagged for the field laboratory where each group of plant remains is studied under a binocular microscope magnifying it 8 to 50 times. The result at Chianciano Terme was the recovery of quantities of charred wood from trees or shrubs plus fruit or seeds of wheat and barley, olive pits and grape seeds.

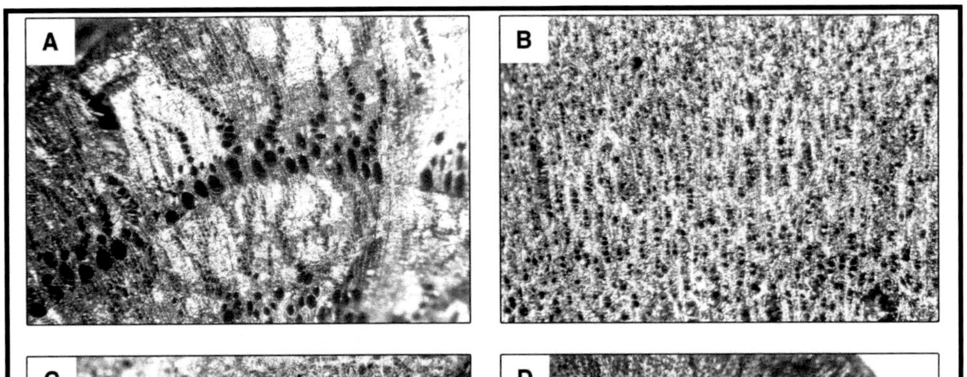

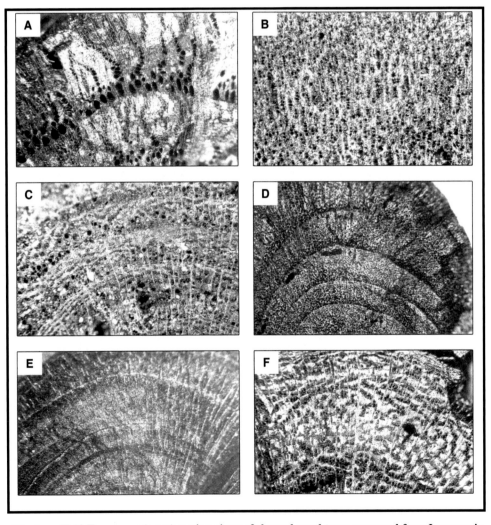

Fig. App. II-10 Transverse (cross) section views of charred wood types recovered from Lugnano in Teverina excavations. Upper left: oak (*Quercus cerris*), upper right: olive (*Olea europaea*); middle left: elm (*Ulmus laevis*); middle right: honeysuckle (*Lonicera caprifolia*); bottom left: cypress/juniper (*Cupressus/Juniperis*); bottom right: genista (*Spartium junceaum*). Processed by Karen Adams, Crow Canyon Archaeological Center.

Fig. App. II-11 (above) Archaeologists Claudia Giontella and Claudio Bizzarri consider how to treat fallen and burned oak beams from administrative building D at Chianciano Terme. Photo credit: Noelle Soren. University of Arizona School of Anthropology Archive.

Fig. App. II-12 (below) Burned wooden beam of oak (*Quercus cerris*) being excavated from Structure D at Chianciano Terme. Photo credit: Noelle Soren. University of Arizona School of Anthropology Archive.

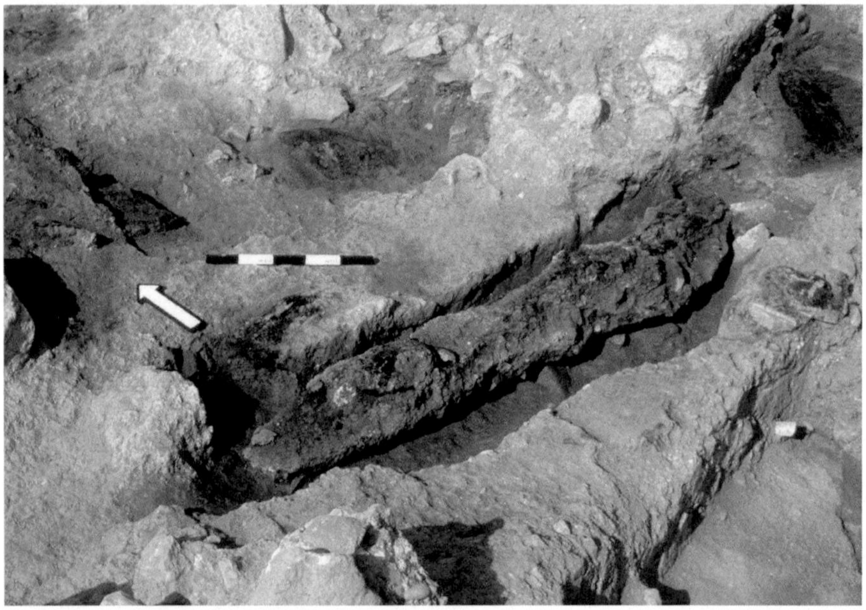

WOOD AND CARBON 14

At Mezzomiglio the uncommonly good preservation of various kinds of wood included wooden columns and beams, as well as wattling used for walls, was remarkable. Most of the wood was found preserved within a series of collapsed and burned buildings (Figs. App. II-11, 12). Once the wood was identified, insight was gained as to what the Romans were using to build wooden structures in this area, an opportunity rarely afforded the excavator because wood is so perishable; in this case oak for the structural supports along with hornbeam and beechwood for the wattling were found along with roof tiles sealed under a severely burned layer of ash. The palynologist was able to prepare the wood for further study, including examinations of the preserved rings of the wood so that an attempt might be made to date the sample by using dendrochronology or tree-ring dating invented in 1913 by Dr. A.E. Douglass of the University of Arizona.

To date, no sufficient number of rings has been preserved at Mezzomiglio in the burned wood to allow a complete chronology to be worked out and compared to other known assemblages for the Mediterranean. All trees have rings that grow annually and may be of greater or lesser size depending on climate conditions or the age of the tree. Peter Kuniholm, formerly of Cornell College, has been the most active American in recent years in attempting to put together a tree-ring chronology for the ancient Mediterranean with considerable results, but the sequences are far less secure than those found in the desert southwest and in Arizona in particular, where reasonably accurate sequences of datable tree rings date back 2000 years ago.

It was also possible to study the burned wood from Mezzomiglio by exposing it to radiocarbon testing at the University of Arizona's Geochemical Isotope Laboratory. Fragments of burned oak beams and wattles were submitted to the laboratory. First discovered in 1949 by J.R. Arnold and W.F. Libby, this technique can be difficult to comprehend for the non-scientist, although its principles are fairly simple. Neutrons enter the Earth's atmosphere and encounter nitrogen, which creates a carbon isotope, a variant form of the carbon. This particular isotope is known as Carbon 14 because it contains 14 neutrons in its *nucleus* while it should have 12 when it is not being bombarded by the alien neutrons. The carbon under siege becomes unstable and very slowly decomposes, and Libby argued that the Carbon 14 would take 5568 years to half-dissolve, which is known as its half-life. As the neutrons depart, they can be measured, thus giving Carbon 14 dates. In radiocarbon dating, then, one is basically measuring Carbon 14 in its slow process of becoming normal, stable Carbon 12.

Organic samples must not be contaminated by handling or by the presence of other organic materials, and they should come from well-sealed stratigraphic contexts. Usually the laboratory will provide one date for the carbon sample, which will be its best approximation of the date when the tree was cut down. The carbon dating for one wood sample from Mezzomiglio proved to be 1720 +/- 85 years. This means that the wood dated to between 230 and 423 CE with a likelihood of accuracy of 68.3%. The laboratory was able to say with a much higher 95.4% accuracy rate that the wood dated between 128 and 474 CE, but that broad date range was of limited help to the excavator, who already knew that information from his own excavation of the area and the discovery of abundant coins and datable pottery. In order to improve the likelihood of accuracy the excavator had to provide the laboratory with additional samples, which each came back with slightly different ıtes, although the overall result suggested a possible date in the ıird or fourth century for the cutting down of the wood.

To the Roman archaeologist, coin hoards, pottery and oil ımps are usually better indicators of date, but radiocarbon dating useful when there is no other datable material. The wide range dates however prohibits its use as a specific dating tool. Another ·oblem is that radiocarbon dates must be calibrated, which means ıey need to be adjusted because the amount of Carbon 14 in ving things does not remain constant over the centuries due to variety of factors, including solar activity and changes in the arth's magnetic field, but used judiciously, radiocarbon dating is helpful tool for the excavator.

Hard science is providing other possibilities for dating ·chaeological sites but these have been only in limited use on oman sites for now. In the future, when they are less costly and ıore accurate, they will likely replace the radiocarbon approach. endrochronology will become a great boon to the Mediterranean ·chaeologist when the European sequences ın be firmly established.

XCAVATING THE SITE

With the team in place and provisions ıade for processing all the material culture, xcavation can begin, but all finds must be atalogued at the end of each working day y the registrar, whose duty it is to keep a omputerized program that will allow easy ːtrieval of information about the objects xcavated. To accomplish this, a special object ıay be given a number that is either directly ritten on the piece, or else it may be stored specially prepared plastic bags or trays that ave been tagged to allow long-term storage.)rdinary finds, such as a mass of potsherds, ıust also be stored with accurate labels) document their provenience. ınything that cannot be related to precise find spot is less useful but ıay still give some idea of objects ıade or traded at the site.

The excavation usually begins vith probe trenches, which might ormally occupy one of the five-ıeter-square areas of a grid. These may be enlarged if something significant is found (Fig. App. II-13). Each excavator has a size of trench that he likes to use, but at Mezzomiglio the five-square-meter approach has been successfully employed. Each trench has a supervisor and several workers. The supervisor is usually a student who has had several seasons of training in field archaeology and has demonstrated an ability to process finds in an organized manner, keep good records, perform basic mapping carefully, and interpret recovered data accurately. Such a supervisor will have several beginning students under him or her and will train them to become the supervisors and eventually the excavation directors of the future. Almost every director of excavation has begun in this time-tested manner over the past 50 years. It used to be possible to buy one's position as director of an excavation, and there have been numerous examples of enthusiastic amateurs digging up ancient sites in a less than scientific manner, sometimes even with university affiliations that have been purchased, but the past half-century has all but put a stop to this behavior, and the scientific knowledge required to accomplish modern archaeology has also brought this practice to a halt. Still, major donors to excavations may come onto a site and insist on participating in a major way, or may want other family members to take part, and this is generally not a good thing.

To the general public the thrill of digging and the joy of making a great discovery are the essence of archaeology. Tourists to archaeological sites such as Mezzomiglio always ask the same question in a variety of languages: "Find anything interesting?" But the real archaeologist knows that answers may come as much from what is done after the excavation of a site as during. For example, when pottery is recovered from a site the pottery specialist or ceramologist must be brought in (Fig. App. II-14). Sometimes, as in the case of Archer Martin, he will be what is termed a material

Fig. App. II-13 (center) Probe trench into a large Roman pool at Chianciano Terme known as the *vasca*, revealing the drain of the pool and an overflow pipe. Photo credit: Noelle Soren. University of Arizona School of Anthropology Archive.

Fig. App. II-14 (right) Examples of common and cooking ware pots found in fifth century CE debris from the sacred spring of Chianciano Terme. Photo credit: Noelle Soren. University of Arizona School of Anthropology Archive.

Fig. App. II-15 Common ware two-handled pot from Chianciano Terme. Drawing by Paola Mecchia. Photo credit: Noelle Soren. University of Arizona School of Anthropology Archive.

culture specialist, which means that he cannot only identify and date much of the pottery and ancient oil lamps and glass found, but he can also make observations about roof tile fragments, coins, kinds of ancient marbles, iron nails, architectural fragments used in bath buildings, and so on.

Coins are obvious dating materials since they will have images on them including portraits of Roman Emperors and inscriptions, but often these coins are found in such poor condition that only a tiny portion of them is visible and a coin specialist is needed to determine what the date of the coin might be. Usually the material culture specialist will want to make the original pencil drawings himself, since that is an act of interpretation. A drawing shows the exterior of the pot and a cutaway section of the piece (Fig. App. II-15). This gives a ceramic specialist enough information to make observations about the piece, especially when the so-called fabric (material composition of the piece) is known.

Draftsmen are important staff members. One of their tasks may be finishing the pencil drawings of the finds for publication. A mapper, who may also be the supervisor, must draw each trench after it has been completed or before something important has been removed. Like the drawing of the finds, this work is then digitized on a computer and ends up included in the final plan for the site.

If inscriptions are found another specialist, an epigrapher, can be brought in to read the Latin or Greek. Etruscan language is much more rarely found and is not completely understood although a good deal of it has been deciphered and specialists may be brought in even in this area.

It is very important for the director of the project to bear in mind that digging is only a part of the work in terms of man-hours and it may be necessary for him to rein in his diggers. Diggers can be very gung-ho, and even directors can be tempted to excavate a bit more in order to answer some question or simply in the hopes of something coming up. It is often said that there are 20 man-hours of post-excavation work for every man-hour of digging. So it is the post-excavation team that suffers the consequence of such behavior long after the excavation team has moved on. The lack of a final publication and sometimes even of preliminary reports, something that happens more often than students may realize, is frequently to be attributed to an inadequate balance in this regard.

FINAL PRESENTATION OF THE SITE

After all of this has been accomplished and repeated over a period of years, the excavator must close down his excavation and present his site. He may decide to create an archaeological park, but this is rarely done because of the tremendous expense of consolidating walls, paying for the continued maintenance of the site and obtaining the full support of the local community as well as the government. It can run into the millions of dollars, so most archaeologists rebury their sites and simply document what was discovered by issuing periodic reports at first and finally a volume or two about the work accomplished, including attempts to describe how the site was created, developed and destroyed over the centuries. This is known as the presentation of the phasing of the site. These days it often includes color reconstructions done on a computer that attempt to show what the site may have looked like in its various phases or at least in those phases for which it is possible to obtain enough data to suggest its appearance (for example, Fig. VII-21). It may even include flyover videos to illustrate better how the site looked in antiquity.

There are two schools of thought on visual site presentation. Some archaeologists feel that to attempt to present a restored image of a site for which all the details are not known is to create a site and to risk popularizing inaccuracies. Other archaeologists feel that a picture is worth a thousand words and prefer to attempt to show the viewer his best interpretation of what the site was like, while noting in print what has been conjectured. In this latter manner, future archaeologists at the site can adjust the model presented until it more closely resembles what was actually there.

COMPUTER MODELING AND THE EXCAVATION

Constructing a model of what the site or a particular building looked like in antiquity requires collaborative working by the architect who has produced a precise plan, the computer modeler and the excavator. It is the job of the excavator to attempt to put together all the structural evidence for the site and its buildings and convey this information to the modeler. Working side by side patiently, they develop the look to their structure or site that the excavator feels is closest to the truth (Fig. XIII-12a). A particular problem for fallen buildings is determining their original height and the existence, height and positioning of windows, columns and roofs. Usually these must be hypothesized based on knowledge of ancient techniques and surviving examples at other sites, but sometimes enough of a structure or site survives to allow the attempt at restoration.

In order to determine the particular viewpoint for an architectural reconstruction drawing a number of factors must be considered. Areas of a building where one has good knowledge of the physical look of the structure can be included in the perspective chosen. Areas where one is unsure about what the structure looked like may be partially hidden from view by strategic placement of the perspective and angle. At Mezzomiglio a reconstruction drawing of the large immersion pool used a particular vantage point in order to hide a drain which it was thought might have been covered with sculpture in antiquity (Fig. App. II-13 shows the original drain). So little was left of this drainage area that the director wanted to avoid suggesting what it was like (Fig. Intro-18 shows the reconstruction avoiding it). In reconstructions, it is essential to emphasize accuracy and eliminate fantasy as much as possible.

Excavators with an interest in attempting computer site reconstructions should follow several requirements. First, hire professionals familiar with the digital reconstruction process if you are not capable of doing it yourself. That means one should find a digital imaging specialist, who is also a good technical artist, preferably with some archaeological experience. Such specialists can be expensive and hard to find, and this may lead to the hiring of untrained students for this position, which can be time-consuming or at worst disastrous, but if funds are tight this may produce good results also.

It is paramount that the surveying data and technical drawings used to make the reconstruction are at a high level of accuracy. Calculations need to be checked and rechecked by technicians in the field and lab. Surveyors need to calibrate their equipment regularly and technical artists need to check their work for accuracy and scale. Surveyors should use the Theodolite and elevation scope and the computer specialist should use a CAD program such as AutoCAD with a digitizer to draw up the site plans. Although there are many CAD programs, AutoCAD is powerful and versatile and is internationally used. For the actual animation or reconstruction program, Lightwave 3D or 3D Studio Max were used at Mezzomiglio, since both produce high quality animation and graphic images suitable for the film industry. The digital imaging specialist should have tools such as Adobe Photoshop and Illustrator or Macromedia Freehand. These programs will assure that the final output of all images will be of high quality and one will be able to produce images for posters, slides, negatives, videotape, television and other forms of print media that may become necessary. Unquestionably the most important factor in achieving the computer reconstruction is communication. Regular meetings of the excavator and the computer specialist over the digital imaging, technical drawing and architectural details produce the best final results.

VIRTUAL REALITY

A future trend is to reconstruct the site as completely as possible within a computer and then allow the viewer to view this model in

Fig. App. II-16a Virtual reality cave at the University of Arizona AZ-Live Laboratory showing visitors guiding themselves through the multi-dimensional experience. To the right are reconstructed images of the ancient spa at Mezzomiglio locality, Chianciano Terme. Photo Credit: Marvin Landis and AZ-Live.

Fig. App. II-16b Visitor about to enter the virtual reality Trajanic bath complex at Mezzomiglio locality of Chianciano Terme. Photo credit: Marvin Landis and AZ-Live.

a special Virtual Reality Box (Fig. App. II-16a, b). In such a space, which now exists at the University of Arizona Computer Center and at about a dozen sites around the country, it is possible to don a pair of goggles and hold what is known as a joystick and enter into an ancient archaeological site such as the Mezzomiglio locality of Chianciano Terme along with other viewers. The principal viewer can move the joystick around depending on whether he wishes to go up and down steps, in and out of buildings, up and down corridors or even into the immersion area of the large open air pool while others can observe his progress but experience it fully. The effect is to surround and enclose the viewer with the architecture of the site, to put him into the site as vividly as if he were moving through the place in antiquity. The experience can be so realistic that viewers regularly experience nausea and dizziness from the speed of movement or the incredible heights that their eyes tell them are there. Indeed one can use the joystick to give the kind of dramatic overhead view of the site that a flying bird might have. Of course once the goggles are removed, there is nothing three-dimensional left to see and the imagery simply appears out of focus. This total immersion into a site will likely become a standard way to experience and understand an excavation in the not-too-distant future, as it is infinitely superior to viewing photographs or reconstructions on the printed page.

Excavators employing this system find it instructive to have students who are going to visit the site or excavate it experience it visually in three-dimensions first. In this way one can have the feeling of actually being there and even the advantage of flying in a helicopter over the site. Then, after this, reading about the site is much easier and details about the various parts of the excavation are clearer.

Today, it is not necessary that an excavator be a hard scientist but he or she needs to know enough about science to figure out what specialists to call in. The growing primacy of pottery for interpretation of archaeological sites is a result of its enormous presence on every site and the scientific advances being made over the past 50 years. The phenomenon is helping to produce a great divide among excavators—the "old-timers" who dig and classify in the traditional manner of classical archaeologists of the 20th century and the new breed of investigators, fueled by the phenomenal possibilities of science, who are determined to squeeze every possible nuance of meaning from an archaeological site that science will allow.

However, there is still one problem for the new generation before they leave the old-timers in their archaeological dust. The new technologies cost a lot of money. While it used to be possible to mount a dig for a small amount of money, now the hiring of specialists from an extraordinary array of disciplines and the lab fees for analysis that they routinely demand and receive, is making excavation so expensive that the excavator must annually choose how much science he can afford through grants and contributions from his university and the private sector. To a large extent, our scientific knowledge about the sites we unearth will depend on a new generation's sensitivity to the ever-widening possibilities of areas such as pottery studies, as well as to the ability of that generation to come up with plenty of cash!

CRITICAL THINKING EXERCISES

• 1. What are the qualities and characteristics necessary for a classical archaeologist to have?
• 2. Imagine that you have received a grant to create an excavation somewhere in the ancient world. Where would you prefer to excavate, how would you set up the excavation, and what sort of staff would you assemble.
• 3. How would you prepare to assess your site before you excavate it? What sort of techniques might you bring in to use and what sort of specialists?
• 4. To what extent would modern technology help with your proposed excavation?
• 5. After your excavation, how will you interpret your data and process your finds?
• 6. How will you actually lay out your site to excavate?
• 7. After the work at the site is over, what plans would you propose for presenting your site to the public, both in terms of publication and in physical display of the ruins?

GLOSSARY

-A-

***bacus*:** Flat base or plinth at the top of a column. Derived from the Greek word *abax,* which is a flat tablet originally covered with sand in which one might draw.

croterion (pl. ***acroteria*):** Decorative figures on the roof of a temple.

***edes*:** A small shrine in a military encampment that housed the standards of the regiment; generically any temple.

***gger*:** An artificial slope with a ditch or *fossa* in front of it. Also, one of two open rooms at the back of the *atrium* of a Roman house.

la (pl. ***alae*):** A wing or small room attached to the antechamber of a burial chamber.

***lta*:** A back alley or lesser street.

***lveus*:** The tub in a Roman bath; it could seat up to 8-10 people.

***naglypha*:** A relief (stone panel with raised decoration).

***nnona*:** See *Cura annonae*

nnular vault: Curved barrel vaults

ntefixes: Terracotta endcaps for the wooden rafters of a building.

***podyteria*:** Rooms where bathers could disrobe on entry to a Roman bathhouse. They were fitted out with waiting benches and lockers where clothing could be checked.

***potheosis*:** Deification; the transformation of an ordinary human into a god.

rchitrave: The frontal crossbeam of a temple above the capitals of the columns.

***rcosolia*:** In a catacomb, large burial chambers topped with an arch and often painted.

***rcus*:** Official term decreed by the Roman Senate for a triumphal arch celebrating accomplishments of the emperor.

***renaria*:** Corridor tunnels in a catacomb off of which the individual tombs were located.

***rretine Ware*:** See Italian *sigillata.*

***trium*:** Central open court of a large Roman home.

***uguratorium*:** Building in a Roman military camp where sacrifices could be made or omens read before a battle.

***ula*:** Large hall.

-B-

arrel vault: The simplest type of vaulted ceiling, a curved ceiling over a straight walkway, like a tube or tunnel cut in half.

***asis villae*:** a term used to refer to the foundations of Roman villa often made of concrete but sometimes using polygonal masonry or other types of support.

***ildlampen*:** Type of lamp featuring decorative images on an ample and usually ceramic disk.

ucchero ware: A soapy-textured, smooth-feeling ceramic made by the Etruscans.

-C-

aldarium or ***calidarium*:** The principal hot room in the Roman bath (*thermae)*.

apanna (pl. ***capanne*):** A small Iron Age hut.

apital: Top of a column.

***appellaccio tuff*:** A type of granular tuff or volcanic rock .

Cardo (pl. ***cardines*):** Principal north-south running streets.

***Castellum aquae*:** A large circular holding vat where water that was brought into the city via aqueducts could be stored for later distribution.

Castra*:** The plural of ***castrum.

***Castrum*:** A Roman military encampment or fort.

Catacomb: (derived from the Greek words *kata kumbas* meaning "near the hollows"): underground burial chamber.

Catenaries: U-shaped hanging chains of drapery.

***Cella*:** Inner chamber of a Roman temple.

***Centuriation*:** Grid plan for city streets or land surveying.

***Chiasmus*:** In sculpture, an attempt at the portrayal of realistic muscular movement in the human body where the stance uses a counterbalance of tension and relaxation which is carefully distributed over the entire body.

Cisiari*:** Coachmen, named after a ***cisia or two-wheeled carriage.

Cista (pl. ***cistae*):** A chest or container for holding toiletries or other items.

Clandestini or ***tombaroli*:** Italian name for grave robbers who take valuable objects from ancient tombs.

***Cliens*:** Not "clients" in the modern sense but people who owed their livelihoods to the villa or large house owner known as the *patronus*.

***Clivus*:** A street that runs up a hill.

***Cocciopesto*:** A mixture of broken pottery and/or tile and mortar used to compose or to coat a floor or wall to render it waterproof.

***Coemeterium*:** (derived from the Greek *koimeterion* or "sleeping place") Christian term for a burial complex.

***Collegium*:** An association formed for the benefit of its members; a burial *collegium*, for example, would provide funerary services.

***Colonia*:** Colony.

***Comitium*:** Meeting place for a Roman popular assembly.

Compendium **technique:** A painting technique that uses quick strokes to outline the essential details.

***Compluvium*:** The inward sloping roof of the *atrium* of a house

***Crustae*:** Elegant and expensive marbles used for wall facings.

***Cryptoporticus*:** Underground covered corridor.

***Cubiculum*:** Bedroom.

***Cubismus*:** Sculpture style that emphasizes geometric forms over realistic features, common in primitive popular art.

Cuirass: Breastplate of armor.

***Culina*:** Kitchen.

Cunicoli (literally "an underground passage"): Channels cut into a mountain to supply water to an area from a nearby spring. They may also be used for drainage or irrigation of agricultural areas.

***Cunicula*:** Latin term for the Italian *cunicoli.*

***Curator annonae*:** Official in charge of the grain supply for Rome. The office was established by Augustus.

***Curia*:** The Roman Senate house.

Cyzicene *oecus*: A major dining room that surrounded the diners, with ample light, air and water, on at least three sides to create a healthful atmosphere.

-D-

Decumanus (pl. *decumani)*: East-west running streets.

Destrictarium: Private room in a Roman bath where bathers could have their skin scraped down following a soak in the *caldarium.*

Diminution: A design feature of most Greek columns in which they diminish in diameter from bottom to top.

Dolium (pl., ***dolia***): Large storage jar or vessel.

Dolmen: A large stone structure with two upright stones linked by a horizontal capstone lintel.

Dominus: Master of a villa or large house.

Doric column: A simple type of Greek column with a capital featuring an *echinus* and a flat plinth or *abacus*.

Dromos: A long entrance, descending with steps, to a tomb.

-E-

Ear of wheat: the stem and seed rows at the tip of cereal plants such as corn, wheat, barley and rye

Echinus: Convex curving support piece located at the top of a column.

Editor: Official of the games held at the Colosseum who judged their outcomes and awarded prizes (*munera*) to the winners.

Ekklesiasterion: Greek name for the meeting room for initiates located at the rear of a temple area. Also, the meeting place of a Greek popular assembly or *ekklesia.*

Eliothesium: A repository for oils and unguents.

Emblema: A major mosaic set into the all-over decoration of the floor of a room in a place of honor.

Entasis: A design feature of some Greek columns in which they get slightly thicker at the middle.

Equi magni: Equestrian statues.

Exedrae: Large niches or a small hall.

-F-

Fanum: A simple shrine made of wood and perhaps terracotta in the Etruscan tradition.

Fauces (literally "jaws"): a simple vestibule of a home.

Fibula (pl. ***fibulae***): A pin used in ancient times to hold clothing shut.

Filigree: Gold wire used in jewelry making

Fistulae: Lead water pipes used in Roman towns.

Formae: Burials placed into the floor of the catacomb.

Fornix: A small triumphal arch, sometimes erected at the initiative and expense of the *triumphator* in a major battle.

Fossa: A sacred ditch included in the basic design of a Roman city.

Fossores: Professional grave diggers.

Frigidarium (pl. ***frigidaria***): A chamber featuring unheated pools in Roman baths, usually the first room visited.

-G-

Genius: Guardian spirit of a people or household.

Gens: Large family group that formed the basis of a class of people in Roman society.

Gisant: Reclining figure style, such as the reclining image of the deceased on top of Roman sarcophagi.

Granulation: A process of jewelry using little balls of gold

Groin vault: A double barrel vault; two barrel vaults are constructed so that they intersect at right angles to form a groin vault. For a simplified version, see **Pavilion Vault.**

Grotteschi: Term used from the Renaissance through the early 20th century to describe imitations of Roman painting of the Third and Fourth Styles, derived from underground grottoes where visitors might see buried Roman paintings.

-H-

Harena: The Latin word for sand. The term arena used to refer to the Colosseum in Rome is derived from this word since sand covered the surface of the combat area..

Haruspex pl. ***haruspices***): A priest who would base his divination on readings of livers taken from sacrificed sheep. In Etruscan the name for these aristocratic priests may have been *netsvis*

Horreum (pl. ***horrea***): A granary or warehouse.

Hortus: A garden.

Hypocaust: A building technique in which a space is created under a floor through which hot air may be circulated. It is particularly used in Roman baths.

Hypogea or ***cubicula***: Larger family tombs designed for multiple burials, often in a catacomb. A *hypogeum* may also refer to an underground temple as well as a tomb. The term derives from ancient Greek and means "under the ground."

-I-

Impasto ware: A type of ceramics made by the Villanovan people that uses a coarse fabric fired in a reducing atmosphere (oxygen intake is limited) to produce a black surface.

Impluvium: Recessed area in the *atrium* in which rainwater was collected.

Insulae: City blocks.

Ionic column: A Greek column that is thinner and more highly ornamented than the simpler Doric style. Both the base and capital have more ornate ornamentation than the earlier style.

Italian *sigillata*: Red-gloss ware made from around 40 BCE on in various centers in Italy, including Arezzo (hence sometimes formerly called *Arretine ware*).

-K-

Kline (Greek)/***lectus*** (Latin; pl. *lecti*): Reclining couch used in Roman dining rooms for eating.

-L-

Laconicum: Spartan hot bath where the temperatures could be more elevated than in the *caldarium.*

Lararium: A room devoted to the *Lares* or protective gods of a household or family group.

Lares: Protective gods of a household or family group.

Latrinum: A latrine.

Loculi: Little rectangular graves cut in rows along the walls of a gallery in an underground catacomb or tomb.

Lost wax or *cire perdue* casting: A method of casting bronze or other metals. A wax model of the object is sculpted, covered with a thin ceramic shell, and then placed inside a ceramic mold. When molten metal is poured into the mold, the wax melts and the metal hardens into its shape.

Lucernaria: Light and air shafts leading to the surface in underground tombs.

Lucus: A sacred grove

-M-

Macellum: A formal market.

aenianum (pl. ***maeniana***): Interior row of seating within the *Colosseum.*

ansio: An inn for travelers or a time of stay.

egalith: A large stone structure.

etopes: Slabs placed on the exterior of a Doric temple above the architrave in the spaces or openings between the interior roof beams of a building.

ithraeum (pl. ***mithraea)***: Centers of worship built for Mithras, an eastern divinity of disputed origins who provided hope to sailors in peril or more generally to people in hope of a better life. The structures were usually located underground.

odius: Cylindrical container for measuring grain.

undus: Among many varied meanings relating to Earth or the world, it may also be a sacred pit in which to place offerings of the first fruits of a harvest.

-N-

ecropolis (pl. ***necropoleis***) (literally "city of the dead"): Large grouping of tombs constructed by the Etruscans as memorials to their dead.

eo-Verism: Artistic style of the third century CE that blended the traditional Classical Roman emphasis on the realistic portrayal of the human figure with simplified popular and regional art that often featured an otherworldly dematerialized look and a reliance on simplified geometric forms.

ucleus: The top-most layer of mortar in a tile, marble slab or mosaic flooring.

ymphaeum (pl. ***nymphaea)***: Large fountain; the room containing a large fountain.

-O-

culus: Central circular opening in a roof to allow in light or air.

deion: an ancient covered building designed primarily for musical recitals and poetry readings.

ptimates (literally "the best people"): loosely aligned political group of the first century BCE who supported the existing ruling oligarchy. Compare *populares.*

pus craticium: An inexpensive, lattice-type construction style used to build Roman houses and apartment buildings.

pus incertum (literally "unsure work"): A construction technique using a mixture of concrete with a facing of rough-worked or roughly pyramid-shaped stones set in irregular rows.

***pus reticulatum* masonry:** Similar to *opus incertum,* but featured small pyramid-shaped stones set in diagonal rows to make up a wall.

pus scutulatum (literally"little shield work"): The use of small leftover chips of marble and other stones in a mosaic floor.

pus sectile (literally "cut-work floors"): A type of flooring made of sections of marble mortared together and popular in Roman homes from the first to fourth centuries BCE.

pus vermiculatum: A mosaic made up of tiny *tesserae* that involves extremely fine workmanship to create.

ssuarium: A communal grave often used to bury the poor. A simple repository for bones.

-P-

alaestra: Area in the Greek and Roman baths commonly used for taking exercise, particularly in the form of boxing and wrestling.

Palynology: The study of pollen samples and other micro-organic remains to date archaeological finds.

Paradoi: Side entrances for the players to enter a theatre.

Pars fructuaria: The part of a Roman villa where its agricultural produce or sometimes industrial products were made and stored.

Pars rustica: The part of a Roman villa dedicated to the slave workers, animals, and tools.

Pars urbana: The part of a Roman villa dedicated to the living quarters of the wealthy owner and his family.

Patrician: Noble class.

Patronus: Owner of a large villa who employed a group of *clientes* to work for him.

Pavilion vault: A simplified version of the later-developed *groin vault* in which the wooden forms used to frame it are placed along the diagonals and intersect at the apex or crown.

Pediment: A triangular section above the horizontal structure of a Greek or Roman temple.

Periaktoi: The Greek name for rotating side panels in a *skene* (theatrical backdrop) that could be changed for different scenes in a play.

Peripteral temple: A building featuring columns on every side.

Peristyle (*peristylum*): A columnar porch or open colonnade (walkway).

Piscina: A large man-made pool for swimming or for decorative purposes.

Pistrinum: A bakery.

Plebeian: Relating to non-aristocratic Roman people who were not slaves.

Plinth: A base on which a column or sculpture rests.

Pomerium: The sacred boundary around a city that defined it.

Populares: Loosely aligned political group of the first century BCE whose power was based on the people's assemblies and the office of the tribune of the plebs. They were usually in opposition to the *optimates.* Compare *optimates.*

***Pozzo* tombs:** Well-shaped tombs used by the Villanovan people.

Praefurnium: An oven used to heat the room of a *tepidarium* or *caldarium.*

Praetorium: General's house in a Roman military camp.

Principia: The headquarters of the staff in a military encampment.

Pronaos: Entry space or porch for a Greek or Roman temple.

Propylon: Main entrance gate area to an important building complex.

Proskenion: The Greek name for a stage for theatrical performance; the Romans lowered it, made it broader and called it a *pulpitum.*

Putei: Manhole-like openings covered with a slab of rock giving access to the *specus* or water channel of aqueducts. More generally, it may also be a well or pit.

Puticuli: Humble burial place for mass burials; compare *sepulcra.*

Putti: Cupids.

-Q-

Quaestorium: Building in a Roman military camp where supplies and money were distributed to the soldiers.

-R-

Ramping vault: A vaulted ceiling run at an angle for the purpose of covering a ramp or stairway.

Regia: the so-called King's House; the administrative seat of the *pontifex maximus* of Rome.

***Rinceau* patterns:** Decorative patterns featuring spiraling vegetal forms.

Rotulus: Book scroll, or the shape of a scroll in an architectural feature.

Rudus: A layer of small stones, lime, and sand placed above the *statumen* (firm base) in the construction of a mosaic.

Rutellum: A stick used to level off grain once it was placed in a *modius* for measurement.

-S-

Sacellum: Small shrine.

Sacrarium (pl. ***sacraria)***: A place where sacred items were stored.

Scotia: Hollowed out molding found above the *torus* on the base of an Ionic column or other architectural feature.

Sepolcretum: Name given to the Iron Age cemetery of the Roman Forum before the forum was created for civic use.

Sepulcra: Roman term for an elegant graveyard; compare *puticuli.*

Sigillum: A vertically placed stone slab that sealed the burial chamber of a tomb. Generally, any type of seal.

Sinopia: A preliminary drawing made with red ochre earth for a wall painting or a mosaic, tile or marble slab floor.

Skene: The Greek name for a several story high backdrop for a *proskenion* or theatre stage; the Romans called this a *scenae frons.*

Solium (solia, pl.): Simple coffin usually of stone or a bathtub in a Roman bath building.

Specus: A channel carrying water in an aqueduct.

Spolia: Reused pieces of marble or other material in a structure.

Stagnum: Large lake or body of water.

Statumen: A firm base for a mosaic floor usually made of fist-sized stones placed in a sandy mortar that is tamped down and rolled flat on top.

Stretchers and headers building technique: A method for building a wall using blocks placed alternately with the long and then the short sides showing.

Strigae: Barracks for soldiers.

Stylobate: A top step of a temple supporting a group of columns.

Suovetaurilia: A Roman sacrifice of a sheep, pig, and bull that accompanied many important ceremonies of state.

Supranucleus (setting bed): A thin bonding agent consisting of a little lime or perhaps lime mixed with powdered marble and water that held the mosaic cubes in place.

Suspensurae: Small colonnettes placed on a lower floor to support an upper floor and allow heat to circulate between the two floors, frequently used in the *tepidarium* and *caldarium* of a Roman bath.

-T-

Tabernae: Retail shops.

Tablinum: The focal point for the reception of visitors and the display of memorabilia of prominent ancestors in a fancy Roman home, located at the rear of the *atrium*.

Tabulae ansatae: Placards with little triangular projections at either end to call attention to the central information.

Tabulae: Painted panels or pictures.

Temenos: Sacred space.

Templum: Sacred area

Tepidarium: A room in the Roman baths with a hypocaust floor, but the oven was far away and the heat secondary. It provided a transition between the *frigidarium* and the *caldarium.*

Tessera (pl. ***tesserae***): Four-cornered cut cube of marble or other material used to make a mosaic.

Testudo: A tortoise-shaped bronze container placed at the sides of the tubs in a Roman bath to help circulate the hot water.

Tetrapylon (pl. ***tetrapyla***): Four-sided arch highly popular in the third and fourth centuries C.E.

Theatron: The Greek term for the seating area in an outdoor theatre. The Romans called this the *cavea.*

Thermae: Great Roman baths that featured rooms for bathing and exercise.

Tholos (pl. ***tholoi***): A round building usually ringed with columns.

Thyrsus: A staff made of fennel (*ferula*) wood topped with leaves and associated with the followers of the god Dionysus.

Torc: Metal neck ring often worn by Gallic soldiers.

Torus: Rounded molding featured on the base of a column.

Travertine: A hard limestone from the Tivoli area which can give the impression of white marble.

Triclinium (pl. ***triclinia***): Dining room in a large Roman home.

Triglyphs: Vertically channeled stone or terracotta piece placed above the architrave and between the metopes of a Doric temple.

Tympanum: Central triangular area of the pediment.

Tubuli: Openings made of clay piping that circulated the hot air out of the bathing chambers in a Roman bath. Sometimes box shaped tiles are fitted together for this purpose.

Tuff: A porous rock made up of volcanic ash or bits of lava and sometimes also sand, which the Italians call *tufo.*

Type-site: One well-preserved site that typifies a culture.

-U-

Ustrinum: Cremation area where bodies could be prepared for Internment

-V-

Valetudinarium: Military hospital.

Vallum: A flat-bottomed ditch usually associated with Hadrian's Wall in England.

Vault: An arched ceiling over an enclosed space.

Velarium: An awning over the seats in an open air amphitheatre or theatre.

Vestibulum: Vestibule, or entrance to a Roman house or other building.

Via: A major road.

Vicus: A smaller city street or a neighborhood of ancient Rome. There were 265 city vici in the 14 regions of Rome created by the emperor Augustus.

Vilicus: Overseer of a Roman villa.

Villa urbana: Town villa; a villa located within the city limits.

Villa: Complex of buildings, often including a the owner's home, baths, workshops, storage buildings, and housing for slave-workers, as well as the related animals and tools necessary for growing food and manufacturing items.

Viridarium: A particularly beautiful garden.

Volute: A spiral scroll-like ornament.

-W-

Wattle and daub construction: Intertwined twigs mixed with clay and mud used in simple, primitive building construction.

Maps

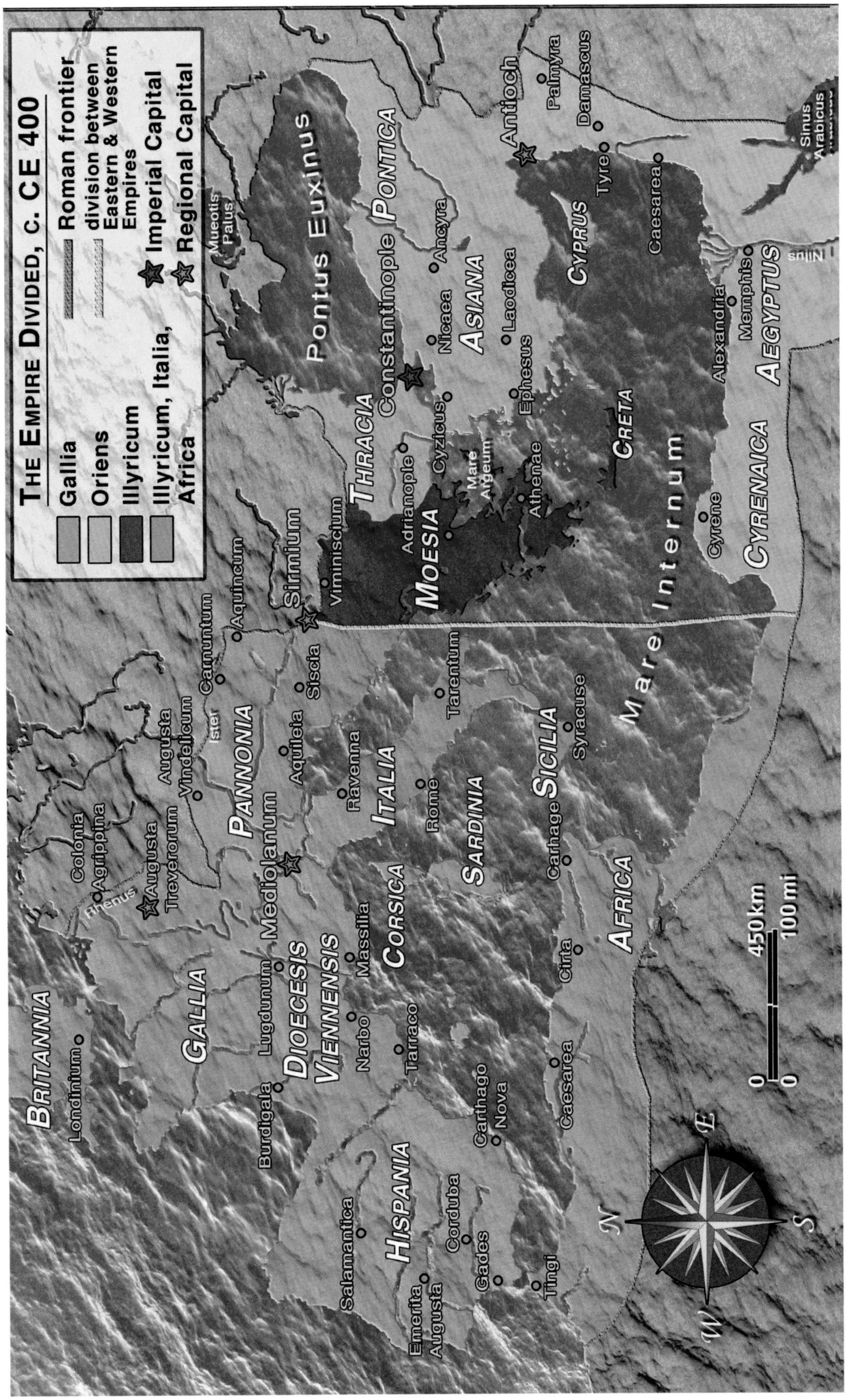

Fig. XIII-1 Map of the later Roman Empire including provincial divisions and locations, by Cherylee Francis.

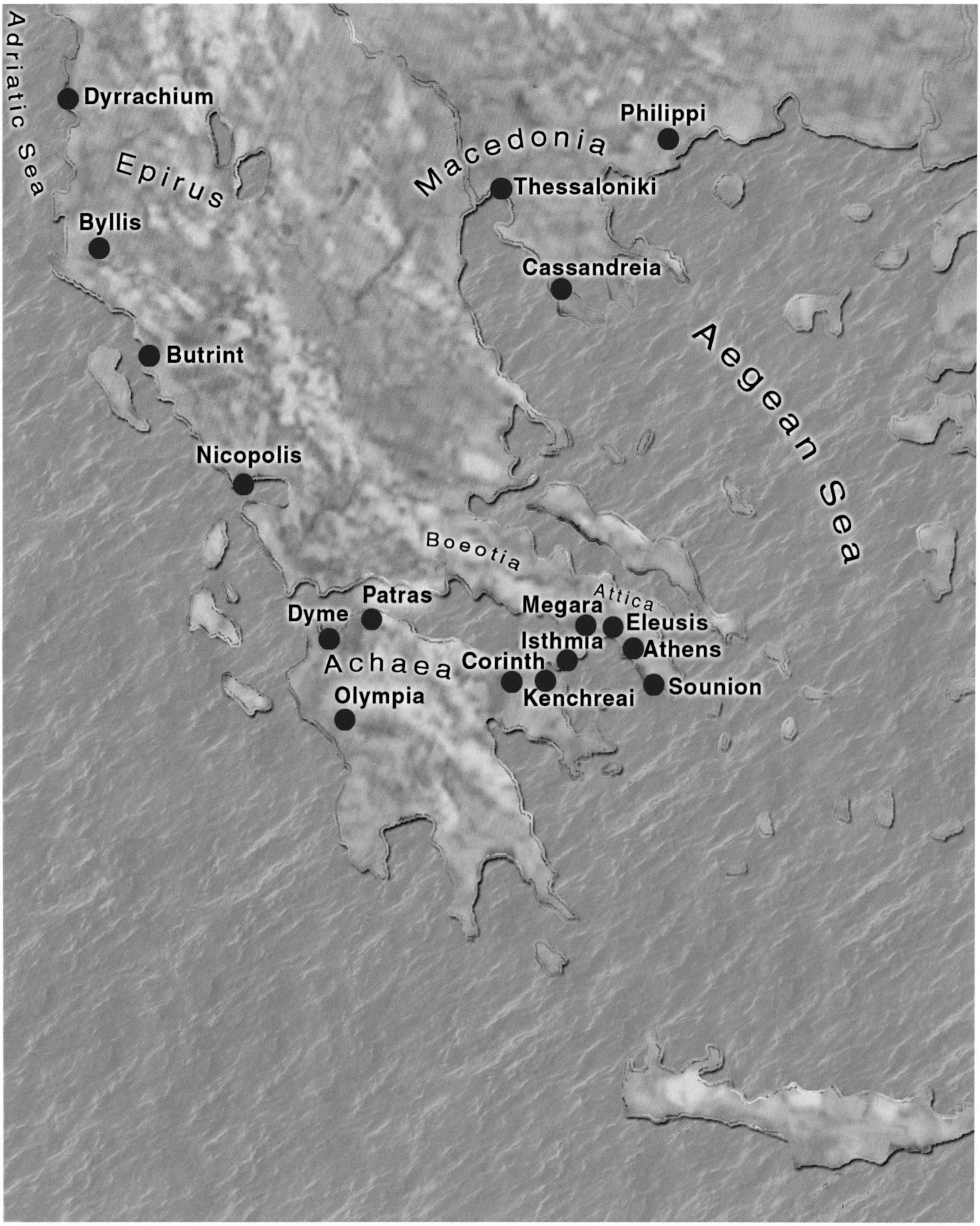

Fig. XIV-1 Map of Greece in the Roman Period by Roxanne Stall.

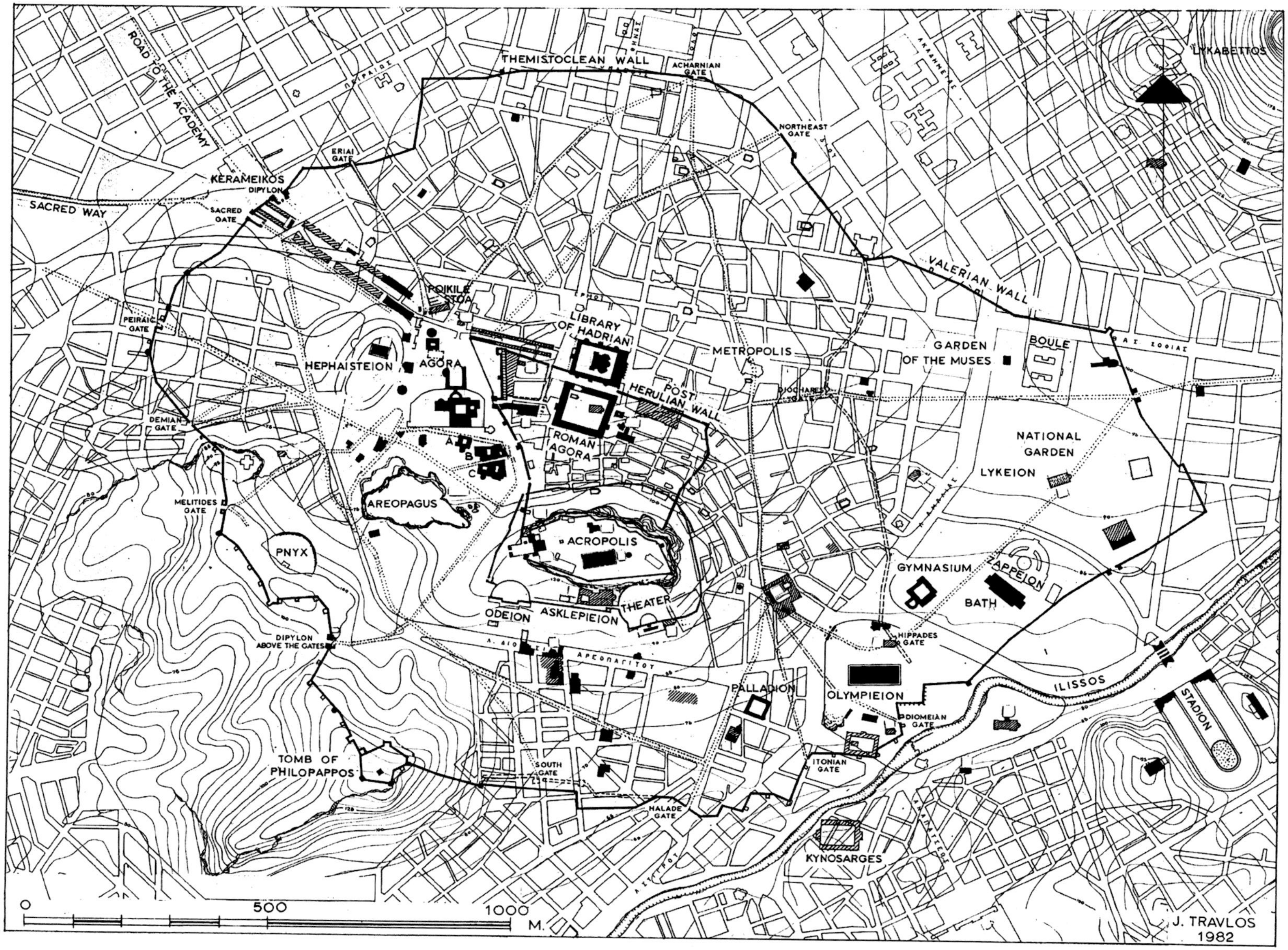

Fig. XIV-2 Plan of ancient Athens showing major monuments and walls. Courtesy of John Camp and the American School of Classical Studies in Athens / Athenian Agora Project.

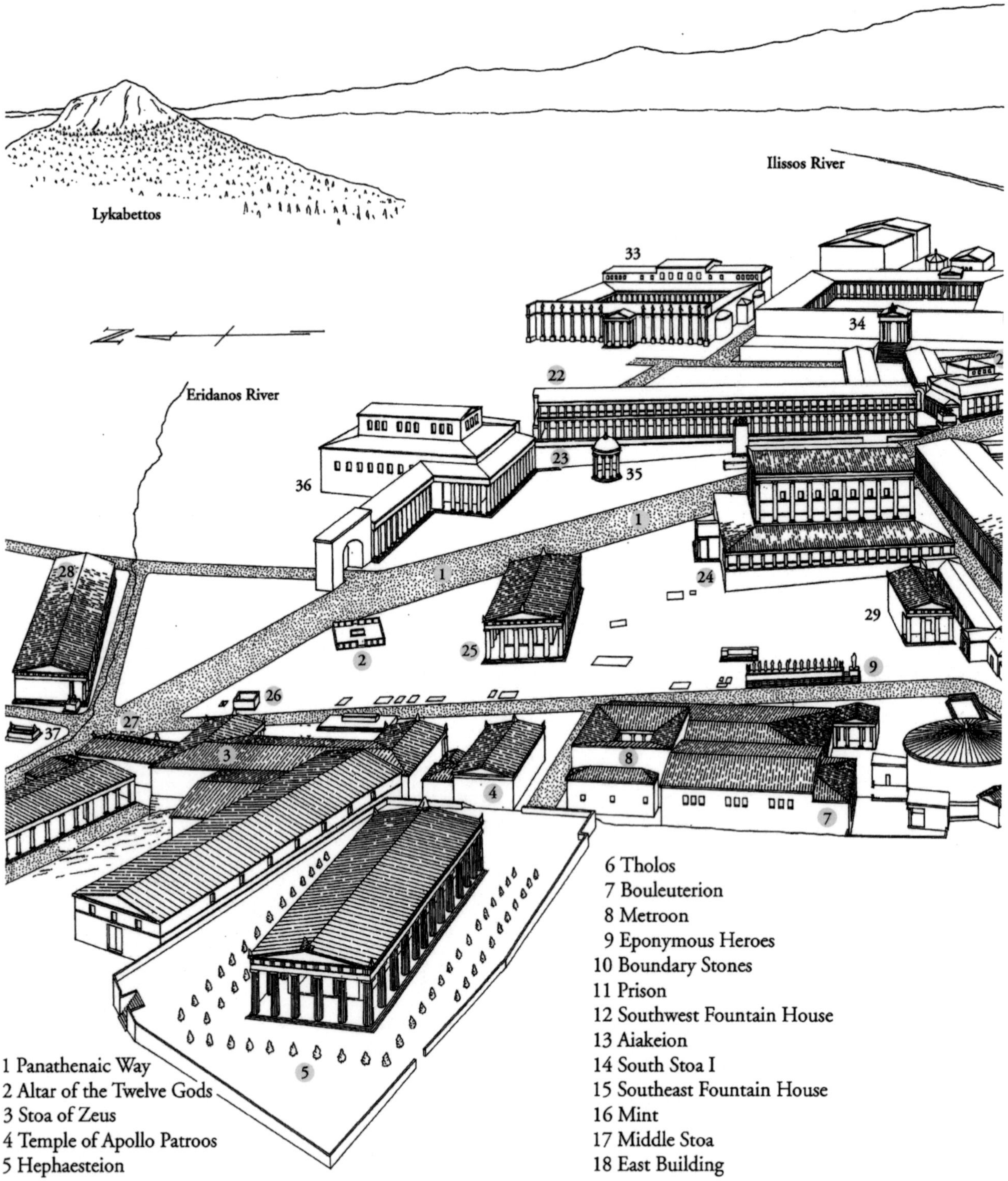

Fig. XIV-3 Reconstruction of the Athenian and Roman Agora and Library of Pantainos in the Roman Period.

19 South Stoa II
20 Late Roman Fortification
21 Library of Pantainos
22 Stoa of Attalos
23 Lawcourts
24 Odeion of Agrippa
25 Temple of Ares
26 Crossroads Shrine
27 Royal Stoa
28 Stoa Poikile
29 Southwest Temple
30 Houses
31 Nymphaion
32 Eleusinion
33 Library of Hadrian
34 Roman Agora
35 Monopteros
36 Roman Basilica
37 Altar of Aphrodite Ourania

(The numbers with yellow dots correlate to the numbers in the guide; 10, 11, 14, 16, 20 and 23 mark the locations of monuments that are not illustrated in this reconstruction drawing.)

W.B.Dinsmoor, Jr.
1980

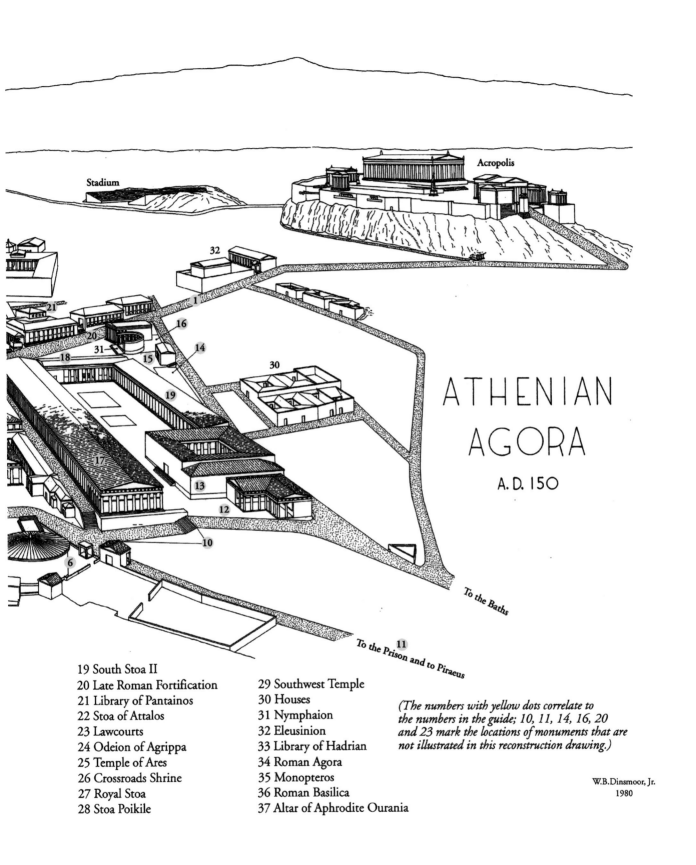

Courtesy of John Camp and the American School of Classical Studies in Athens / Athenian Agora Project.

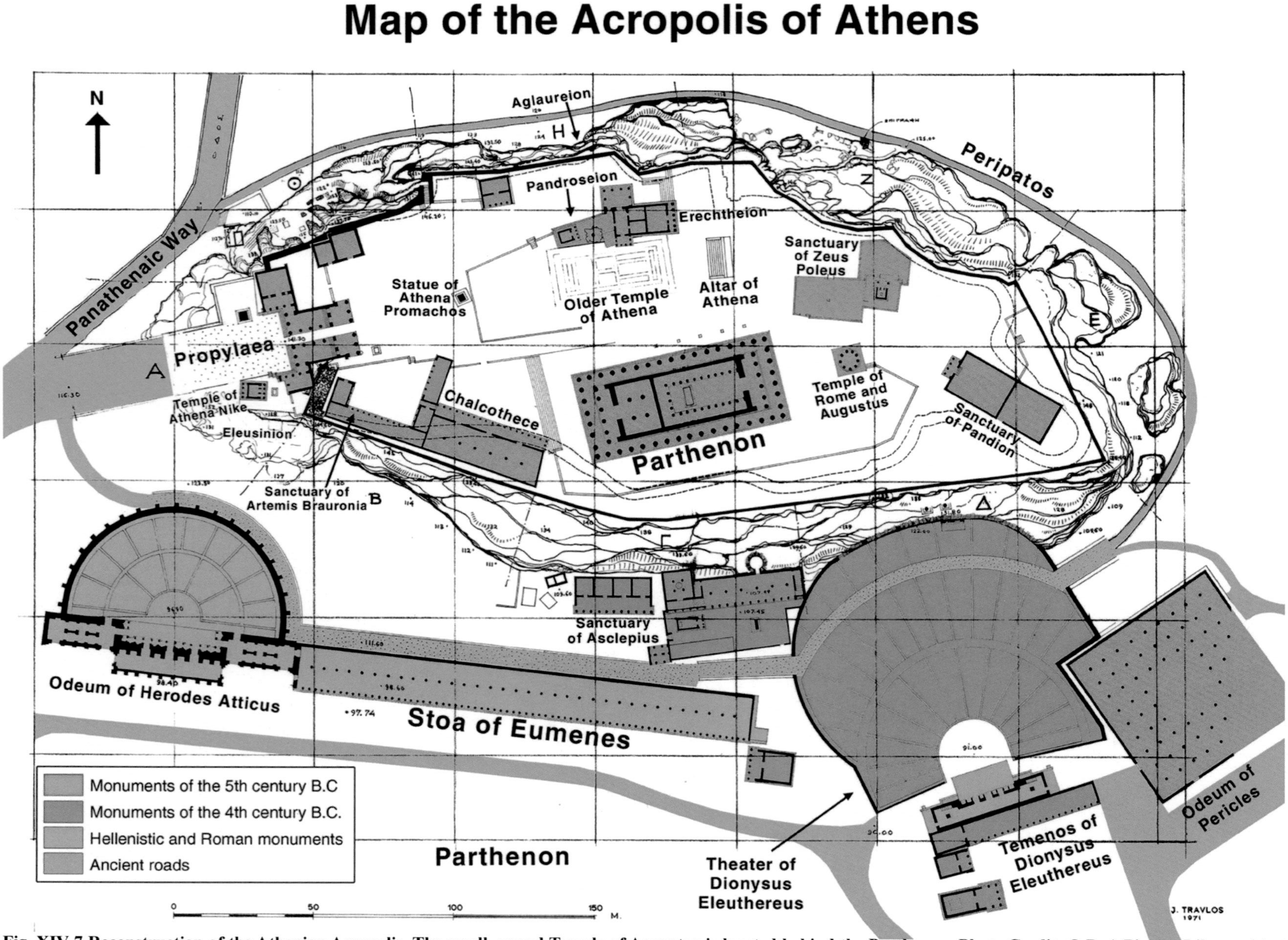

Fig. XIV-7 Reconstruction of the Athenian Acropolis. The small round Temple of Augustus is located behind the Parthenon. Photo Credit: © DeA Picture Library / Art Resource, N.Y.

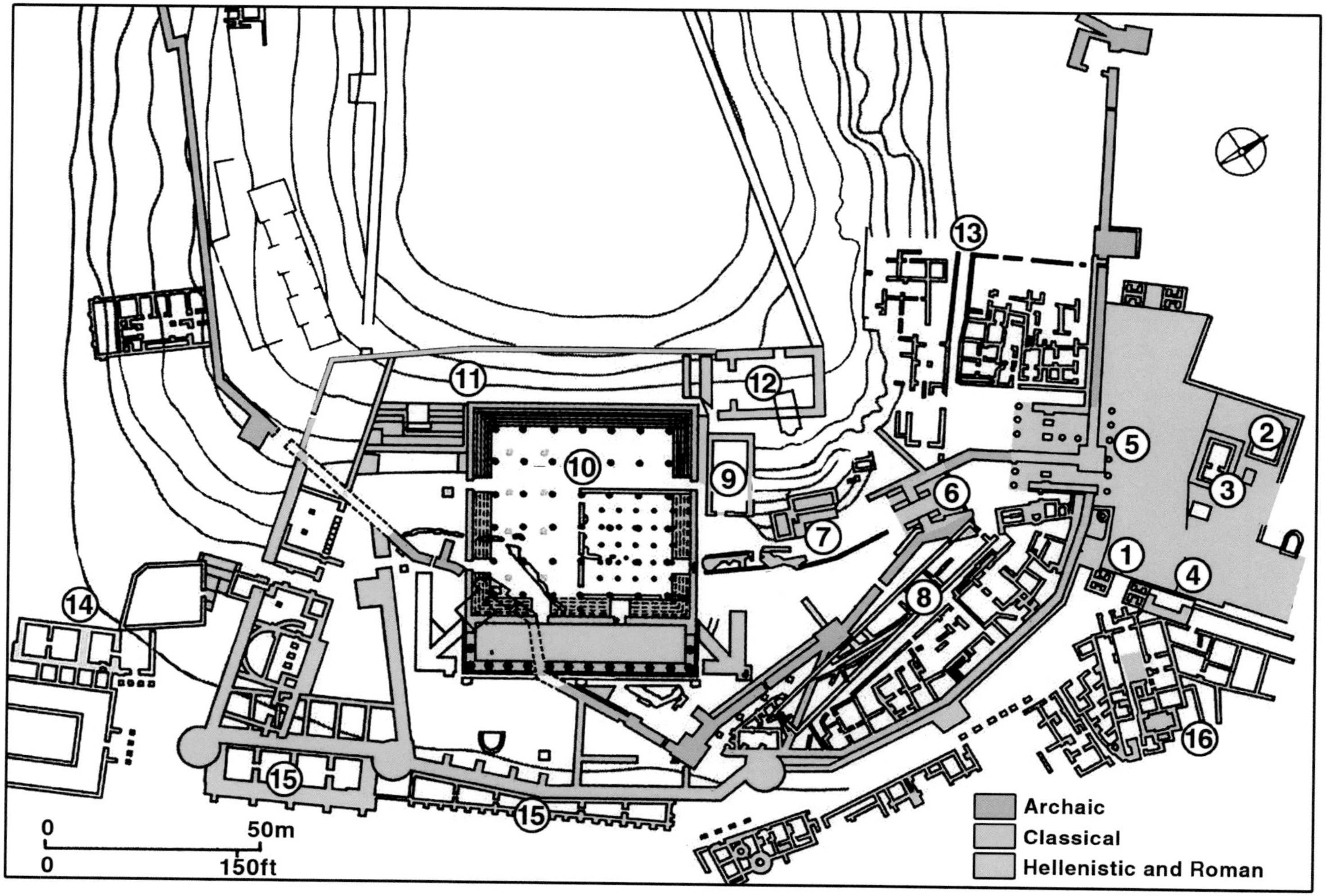

(1) Triumphal Arch
(2) Large Stoa
(3) Temple of Artemis
(4) Fountain
(5) Large Propylaea
(6) Small Propylaea
(7) Sacred Way
(8) Portico
(9) Temple of Kore
(10) Telesterion
(11) Terrace
(12) Megaron
(13) Prytaneion
(14) Sacred House
(15) Cisterns
(16) Baths

Fig. XIV-13 Plan of the Sanctuary of Eleusis, Greece by Roxanne Stall. **(See larger plan page 363.)**

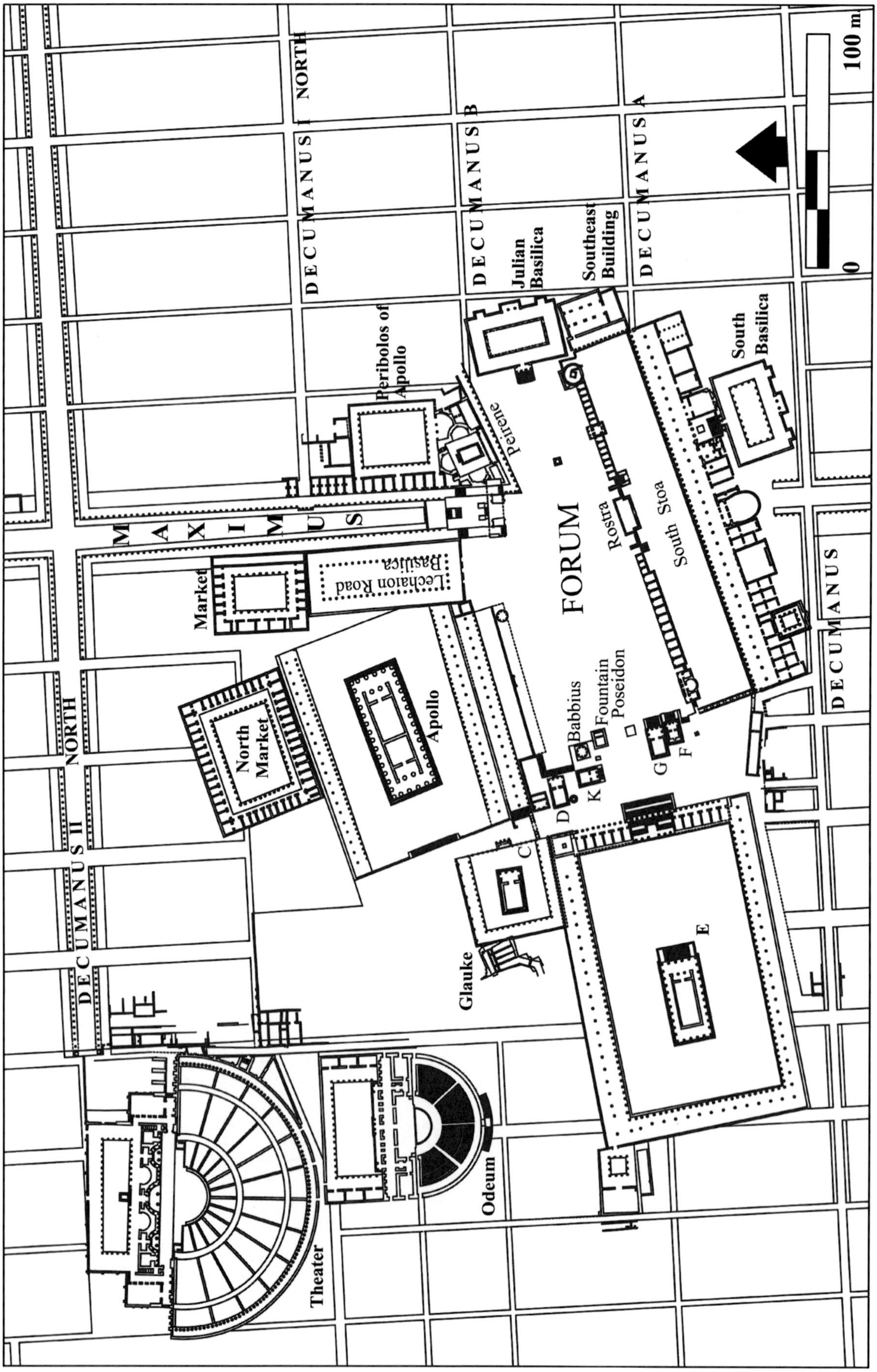

Fig. XIV-17a Reconstruction of Roman Corinth, Greece, including the Temple of Apollo and theatre complex. Photo Credit: © David Gilman Romano, Corinth Computer Project.

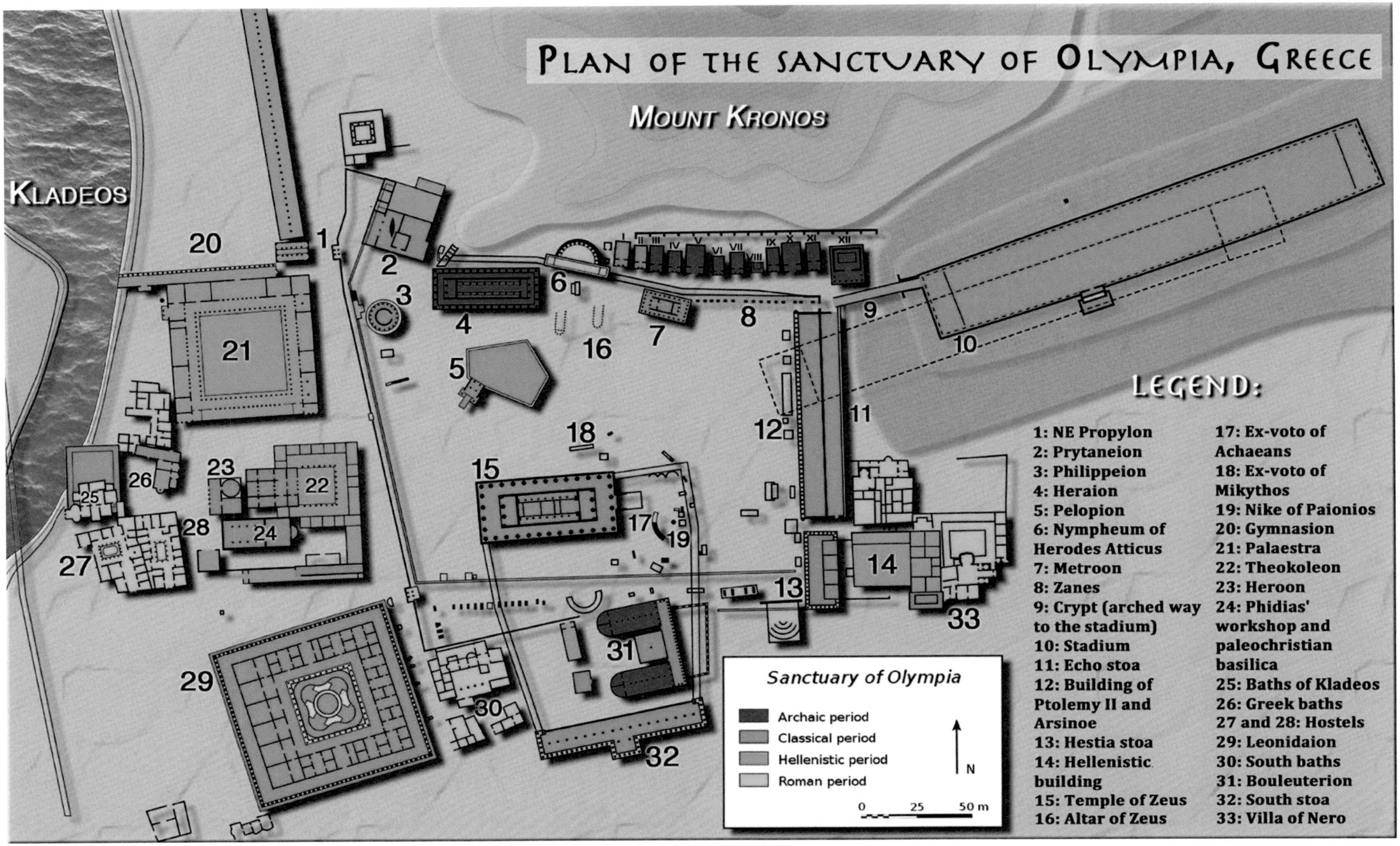

Fig. XIV-24 Plan of the site of Olympia, Greece by Cherylee Francis.

Bibliography

General

Roman Art

Allan, T. 2005. *Life, Myth, and Art in Ancient Rome*. Los Angeles, CA: J. Paul Getty Museum. Andreae, B. 1977. *The Art of Rome*. New York: H.N. Abrams.
Beard, M. and J. Henderson. 2001. *Classical Art: from Greece to Rome*. Oxford: Oxford University Press.
Brendel, O. 1979. *Prolegomena to the Study of Roman Art*. New Haven: Yale University Press.
Brilliant, R. 1994. *Commentaries on Roman Art: Selected Studies*. London: Pindar Press.
Brilliant, R. 1984. *Visual Narratives: Storytelling in Etruscan and Roman Art*. Ithaca: Cornell University Press.
Clarke, J.R. 2003. *Art in the Lives of Ordinary Romans: Visual Representation and Non-Elite Viewers in Italy, 100 B.C.-A.D. 315*. Berkeley: University of California Press
Cornell, Tim, and John Matthews. 1982. *Atlas of the Roman World*. Oxford: Phaidon.
D'Ambra, E. 1998. *Roman Art*. Cambridge: Cambridge University Press.
D'Ambra, E. 1993. *Roman Art in Context: an Anthology*. Englewood Cliffs, N.J.: Prentice Hall.
Elsner, J. 2007. *Roman Eyes: Visuality & Subjectivity in Art & Text*. Princeton, N.J.: Princeton University Press.
Elsner, J. 1998. *Imperial Rome and Christian Triumph: the Art of the Roman Empire A.D. 100-450*. New York: Oxford University Press.
Elsner, J. 1996. *Art and Text in Roman Culture*. Cambridge: Cambridge University Press.
Gabucci, A., S. Peccatori and S. Zuffi. 2002. *Ancient Rome: Art, Architecture and History*. Los Angeles: J. Paul Getty Museum.
Hanfmann, G.M.A. 1975. *Roman Art: A Modern Survey of the Art of Imperial Rome*. New York: Norton.
Henig, M. 1983. *Handbook of Roman Art: A Survey of the Visual Arts of the Roman World*. Oxford: Phaidon.
Holliday, P.J. 1993. *Narrative and Event in Ancient Art*. Cambridge: Cambridge University Press.
Hölscher, T. 2004. *The Language of Images in Roman art*. Cambridge: Cambridge University Press.
Kleiner, F.S. 2010. *A History of Roman Art*. Independence, Kentucky: Cengage.
Ling, R. 2000. *Making Classical Art: Process & Practice*. Stroud: Tempus.
Pollini, J. 2012. *From Republic to Empire: Rhetoric, Religion, and Power in the Visual Culture of Ancient Rome*. Norman: University of Oklahoma.
Pollitt, J.J. 1983. *The Art of Rome, c. 753 B.C.-A.D. 337: Sources and Documents*. Cambridge: Cambridge University Press.
Potter, T.W.1987. *Roman Italy*. London: British Museum Publications.
Ramage, N. and A. Ramage. 2008. *Roman Art: Romulus to Constantine*. 5th ed. Upper Saddle River, NJ: Prentice Hall.
Stewart, P. 2008. *The Social History of Roman Art*. Cambridge, UK: Cambridge University Press.
Stewart, P. 2004. *Roman Art*. Oxford: Oxford University Press.
Strong, D.E., J.M.C. Toynbee, and R. Ling. 1988. *Roman Art*. Harmondsworth, Middlesex, England: Penguin Books.
Walker, S. 1991. *Roman Art*. London: Published for the Trustees of the British Museum by British Museum Press.
Wheeler, M. 1964. *Roman Art and Architecture*. New York: F. A. Praeger.
Winckelmann, J.J. and A. Potts. 2006. *History of the Art of Antiquity*. Los Angeles: Getty Research Institute.
Woodford, S. 1982. *The Art of Greece and Rome*. Cambridge: Cambridge University Press.
Zanker, P. 2010. *Roman Art*. Los Angeles, CA: J. Paul Getty Museum.

Roman Architecture

Anderson, J.C. 1997. *Roman Architecture and Society*. Baltimore: Johns Hopkins University Press.
Boëthius, A., R. Ling, and T. Rasmussen. 1978. *Etruscan and Early Roman Architecture*. Harmondsworth: Penguin Books.
Boëthius, A., and J.B. Ward-Perkins. 1970. *Etruscan and Roman Architecture*. Harmondsworth: Penguin.
Brown, F.E. 1961. *Roman Architecture*. New York: G. Braziller.
Kleiner, D.E.E., *Roman Architecture: A Visual Guide*. New Haven: Yale University Press
Landels, J.G. 2000. *Engineering in the Ancient World*. Berkeley: University of California Press.
MacDonald, W.L. 1982. *The Architecture of the Roman Empire I: An Introductory Study*. New Haven: Yale University Press.
MacDonald, W.L. 1986. *The Architecture of the Roman Empire II: An Urban Appraisal*. New Haven: Yale University Press.
McEwen, I.K. 2003. *Vitruvius Writing the Body of Architecture*. Cambridge, Mass: MIT Press.
Robertson, D.S. 1969. *Greek and Roman Architecture*. London: Cambridge U.P.
Rodgers, N. 2006. *Roman Architecture: an Expert Visual Guide to the Glorious Classical Heritage of Ancient Rome*. London: Southwater.
Sear, F. 1983. *Roman Architecture*. Ithaca, N.Y.: Cornell University Press.
Senseney, J.R. 2011. *The Art of Building in the Classical World: Vision, Craftmanship, and Linear Perspective in Greek and Roman Architecture*. Cambridge and New York: Cambridge University Press.
Stamper, J.W. 2005. *The Architecture of Roman Temples: the Republic to the Middle Empire*. Cambridge: Cambridge University Press.
Taylor, R.M. 2003. *Roman Builders: A Study in Architectural Process*. Cambridge: Cambridge University Press.
Ward-Perkins, J.B. 1981. *Roman Imperial Architecture*. Harmondsworth: Penguin Books.
Ward-Perkins, J.B. 1977. *Roman Architecture*. New York: H. N. Abrams.
Wilson Jones, M. 2000. *Principles of Roman architecture*. New Haven, CT: Yale University Press.

The City of Rome

Adkins, L. and R. Adkins. 1994. *Handbook to Life in Ancient Rome*. New York, N.Y.: Facts on File.
Aldrete, G.S. 2004. *Daily Life in the Roman City: Rome, Pompeii, and Ostia*. Westport, CT: Greenwood Press.
Casson, L. 1998. *Everyday Life in Ancient Rome*. Baltimore: The Johns Hopkins University Press.
Carcopino, J., H.T. Rowell, and E.O. Lorimer. 1940. *Daily Life in Ancient Rome: the People and the City at the Height of the Empire*. New Haven: Yale University Press.
Claridge, A., J. Toms, and T. Cubberley. 1998. *Rome: an Oxford Archaeological Guide to Rome*. Oxford: Oxford University Press.
Clarke, J.R. 2007. *Roman Life: 100 B.C. to A.D. 200*. New York: Abrams.
Coarelli, F. 2007. *Rome and Environs: an Archaeological Guide*. Berkeley: University of California Press.
Connolly, P. and H. Dodge. 1998. *The Ancient City: Life in Classical Athens & Rome*. Oxford: Oxford University Press.
Coulston, J.C. and H. Dodge. 2000. *Ancient Rome: the Archaeology of the Eternal City*. Oxford: Oxford University School of Archaeology.
Cowell, F.R. 1975. *Life in Ancient Rome*. New York: Capricorn Books.

udley, D.R. 1967. *Urbs Roma: a Source Book of Classical Texts on the City & its Monuments.* London: Phaidon Press.
upont, F. 1993. *Daily Life in Ancient Rome.* Oxford, UK: Blackwell.
yson, S.L. 2010. *Rome: A Living Portrait of an Ancient City.* Baltimore: Johns Hopkins University Press.
lwards, C. and G. Woolf. 2003. *Rome the Cosmopolis.* Cambridge: Cambridge University Press.
lwards, C. 1996. *Writing Rome: Textual Approaches to the City.* Cambridge: Cambridge University Press.
oatti, C. 1993. *In Search of Ancient Rome.* New York: Abrams.
ash, E. 1961. *Pictorial Dictionary of Ancient Rome.* New York: Praeger.
chardson, L. 1992. *A New Topographical Dictionary of Ancient Rome.* Baltimore: Johns Hopkins University Press.
obinson, O.F. 1992. *Ancient Rome: City Planning and Administration.* London: Routledge.
carre, C. 1995. *The Penguin Historical Atlas of Ancient Rome.* London: Penguin.
ambaugh, J.E. 1988. *The Ancient Roman city.* Baltimore: Johns Hopkins University Press.
ner, J.P. 1995. *Leisure and Ancient Rome.* Cambridge: Polity Press.

troduction

gnamini, I. 2004. *Archives & Excavations: Essays on the History of Archaeological Excavations in Rome and Southern Italy from the Renaissance to the Nineteenth Century.* London: British School at Rome.
nford, L.R. 2002. *In Pursuit of the Past: Decoding the Archaeological Record: with a New Afterword.* Berkeley: University of California Press.
nford, L.R. 1962. *Archaeology as Anthropology.* Chicago.
ourdieu, P. 1977. *Outline of a Theory of Practice.* Cambridge, UK: Cambridge University Press.
avid, M. 2002. "Fiorelli and documentation methods in archaeology," in. *Houses and Monuments of Pompeii: The Works of Fausto and Felice Niccolini.* Los Angeles: J. Paul Getty Museum.
wyer, E.J. 2010. *Pompeii's Living Statues: Ancient Roman Lives Stolen from Death.* Ann Arbor: University of Michigan Press.
yson, S.L. 2006. *In Pursuit of Ancient Pasts: a History of Classical Archaeology in the Nineteenth and Twentieth Centuries.* New Haven: Yale University Press.
awkes, Jacquetta. 1982. *Mortimer Wheeler: Adventurer in Archaeology.* Littlehampton: Book Services.
ayes, K.J. 2008. *The Road to Monticello: The Life and Mind of Thomas Jefferson.* Oxford; New York: Oxford University Press.
odder, I. 2001. *Archaeological Theory Today.* Cambridge, UK: Polity Press
orden, P. and N. Purcell. 2000. *The Corrupting Sea: A Study of Mediterranean History.* Oxford: Blackwell.
hnson, M. 2010. Archaeological Theory: an Introduction. Chichester, West Sussex, UK: Wiley-Blackwell.Lanciani, R. 2014 (originally published 1897). The Ruins and Excavations of Ancient Rome; a Companion Book for Students and Travellers. New York: Createspace.
IcLaughlin, J. 1988. *Jefferson and Monticello: The Biography of a Builder.* New York: H. Holt.
'Brien, M.J., R.L. Lyman, and M.B. Schiffer. 2005. *Archaeology as a Process: Processualism and its Progeny.* Salt Lake City: University of Utah Press.
nuf, P.S. and N. Cole. 2011. *Thomas Jefferson, the Classical World, and Early America.* Charlottesville: University of Virginia.
reucel, R.W. and I. Hodder. 1996. *Contemporary Archaeology in Theory.* Oxford: Blackwell.
reucel, R.W. 1991. *Processual and Postprocessual Archaeologies: Multiple Ways of Knowing the Past.* Carbondale, IL: Center for Archaeological Investigations, Southern Illinois University at Carbondale.
andall, W.S.. 2014. *Thomas Jefferson: A Life.* New York: Harper.
enfrew, C. and P. Bahn. 2008. *Archaeology: Theories, Methods, and Practice.* London: Thames and Hudson.
owland, I.D. 2014. *From Pompeii: The Afterlife of a Roman Town.* Cambridge, Mass.: Belknap Press.
chiffer, M.B. 1986. *Advances in Archaeological Method and Theory.* New York: Academic Press.
chnapp, A. 1996. *The Discovery of the Past: the Origins of Archaeology.* London: British Museum Press.
hanks, M. and C.Y. Tilley. 1987. *Reconstructing Archaeology: Theory and Practice.* Cambridge: Cambridge University Press.
keates, R. 2000. "The Collecting of Origins Collectors and Collections of Italian Prehistory and the Cultural Transformation of Value (1550-1999)." *British Archaeological Reports International Series (Supplement).* 868.
rigger, B.G. 2006. *A History of Archaeological Thought.* Cambridge: Cambridge University Press.
Vhitley, D. 1998. *Reader in Archaeological Theory: Postprocessual and Cognitive Approaches.* London: Routledge.

hapter I: The First Romans (2000-700 BCE)

lfoldi, A. 1965. *Early Rome and the Latins.* Ann Arbor: University of Michigan Press.
ubet, M.E. 1993. *The Phoenicians and the West: Politics, Colonies, and Trade.* Cambridge: Cambridge University Press.
ietti Sestieri, A.M. 1992. *The Iron Age Community of Osteria Dell'Osa: A Study of Socio-political Development in Central Tyrrhenian Italy.* Cambridge University Press.
ietti Sestieri, A.M. 1988. "The Mycenaean Connection and its Impact on the Central Mediterranean Societies." *Dialoghi di Archeologia* 6, no. 1: 23-51.
lake, E.C. and A.B. Knapp (editors) 2005. *The Archaeology of Mediterranean Prehistory.* Blackwell: Oxford.
arandini, A. 2011. *Rome: Day One.* Princeton, N.J.: Princeton University Press.
lark, G. 1986. "Economy and Environment in Northeastern Italy in the Second Millennium B.C." *Papers of the British School at Rome* 54: 1-28.
ornell, T.J. 1995. *The Beginnings of Rome: Italy and Rome from the Bronze Age to the Punic Wars (c 1000-264 BC).* London: Routledge.
randazzi, A. 1997. *The Foundation of Rome. Myth and History.* Translated by Jane Marie Todd. Ithaca and London: Cornell University Press.
laynes, S. 2000. *Etruscan Civilization: a Cultural History.* Los Angeles: J. Paul Getty Museum.
lolloway R.R., S.S. Lukesh, and N. Nabers. 1978. "The Development of the Italian Bronze Age. Evidence from Trentinara and the Sele Valley." *Journal of Field Archaeology* 5: 133-144.
Iolloway, R.R., 1996. *The Archaeology of Early Rome and Latium.* New York: Routledge.
eighton, R. 2005. "House Urns and Etruscan Tomb Painting: Tradition Versus Innovation in the Ninth-Seventh Centuries BC." *Oxford Journal of Archaeology* 24, no. 4: 363-380.
athje, A. and I. Van Kampen. 2001. "The Distribution of Space and Materials in Domestic Architecture in Early Rome: a Case Study of the Pre-Republican Habitation Levels on the Sepolcreto Arcaico Site at the Roman Forum," in Brandt, J. Rasmus and Lars Karlsson (ed.), *From Huts to House: Transformations of Ancient Societies; Proceedings of an International Seminar Organized by the Norwegian and Swedish Institutes in Rome, 21-24 September 1997.* Stockholm: Paul Åström Forlag, 323-388.
ichardson, E.H. 1964. *The Etruscans, Their Art and Civilization.* Chicago: University of Chicago Press.
idgway, D. and F.R. Serra Ridgway. 1979. *Italy Before the Romans: the Iron Age, Orientalizing, and Etruscan Periods.* London: Academic Press.
almon, E.T. 1953. "Rome and the Latins: I." *The Phoenix* 7, no. 3: 93-104.
almon, E.T. 1953. "Rome and the Latins: II." *The Phoenix* 7, no. 4: 123-35.
estieri, A.M.B. 2008. *The Iron Age Community of Osteria dell'osa: A Study of Socio-political Development in Central Tyrrhenian Italy. New Studies in Archaeology.* Cambridge: University Press.
teingräber, S. 2003. "The Process of Urbanization of Etruscan Settlements from the Late Villanovan to the Late Archaic Period (End of 8th to Beginning of 5th cent. B.C.): Presentation of a Project." *Archaeologiae* 1, no. 1: 81-90.

Toms, J. 2000. "The Arch Fibula in Early Iron Age Italy," in Ridgeway, David (ed.), *Ancient Italy in Its Mediterranean Setting: Studies in Honour of Ellen Macnamara* London: Accordia Research Institute, 91-116.

Whitehouse, R.D. "Bread and Milk. Iron and Bronze Age Economies in South Italy." *Antiquity* 44: 54-56.

Yntema, D.G. 1985. *The Matt-Painted Pottery of Southern Italy. A General Survey of the Matt-Painted Pottery Styles of Southern Italy During the Final Bronze Age and the Iron Age*. Utrecht: Elinkwijk.

Chapter II: The Etruscans (700-500 BCE)

Banti, L. 1973. *Etruscan Cities and Their Culture*. Berkeley: University of California Press.

Barker, G. and T. Rasmussen. 1998. *The Etruscans*. Oxford: Blackwell Publishers.

Bartoccini, R. 1959. *The Etruscan Paintings of Tarquinia*. Milano: A. Martello.

Bell, S., H. Nagy and R. De Puma. 2009. *New Perspectives on Etruria and Early Rome: in Honor of Richard Daniel De Puma*. Madison, WI.: University of Wisconsin Press.

Bonfante, L. and J. Swaddling. 2006. *Etruscan Myths*. London: British Museum.

Bonfante, L. 1986. *Etruscan Life and Afterlife: a Handbook of Etruscan Studies*. Detroit: Wayne State University Press.

Bonghi Jovino, M. 2010. "The Tarquinia Project: A Summary of 25 Years of Excavation." *American Journal of Archaeology* 114, no. 1: 161-180.

Borrelli, F., M.C. Targia, S. Peccatori, and S. Zuffi. 2004. *The Etruscans: Art, Architecture, and History*. Los Angeles: J. Paul Getty Museum.

Brendel, Otto J. 1995. *Etruscan Art*. New Haven, CT: Yale University.

De Grummond, N.T. 2006. *Etruscan Myth, Sacred History, and Legend*. Philadelphia, PA: University of Pennsylvania Museum of Archaeology and Anthropology.

De Grummond, N.T. and E. Simon. 2006. *The Religion of the Etruscans*. Austin: University of Texas Press.

De Grummond, N.T. 2009. *Cetamura del Chianti*. Florence: Edifir Edizioni Firenze.

De Grummond, N.T. and I.E.M. Edlund-Berry. 2001. *The Archaeology of Sanctuaries and Ritual in Etruria*. Porsmouth, Rhode Island: Journal of Roman Archaeology.

Hall, J.F. 1996. *Etruscan Italy: Etruscan Influences on the Civilizations of Italy from Antiquity to the Modern Era*. Provo, UT.: Museum of Art, Brigham Young University.

Haynes, S. 2000. *Etruscan Civilization: a Cultural History*. Los Angeles: J. Paul Getty Museum.

Hencken, H. 1968. *Tarquinia, Villanovans and Early Etruscans*. Cambridge, MA: Peabody Museum.

Hencken, H. 1968. *Tarquinia and Etruscan Origins*. New York: Praeger.

Holloway, R.R. 1986. "The Bulls in the Tomb of the Bulls at Tarquinia." *American Journal of Archaeology* 90, no. 4: 447-52.

Iozzo, M. (ed.). 2009. *The Chimaera of Arezzo*. Firenze: Polistampa.

Jannot, J.R.. 2005. *Religion in Ancient Etruria*. Madison: University of Wisconsin Press.

Lawrence, D.H. 2011. *Etruscan Place: Travels Through Forgotten Italy*. London; New York: Tauris Parke Paperbacks.

Leighton, R. 2005. "House Urns and Etruscan Tomb Painting: Tradition Versus Innovation in the Ninth-Seventh Centuries BC." *Oxford Journal of Archaeology* 24, no. 4: 363-380.

Leighton, R. 2004. *Tarquinia: An Etruscan City*. London: Duckworth.

Martinelli, M., Giulio Paolucci, and Claudio M. Strinati. 2007. *Guide to the Places of the Etruscans*. Florence: Scala.

Pallottino, M. 1975. *The Etruscans*. Bloomington: Indiana University Press.

Pallottino, M. 1966. *The Necropolis of Cerveteri*. Roma: Istituto Poligrafico Dello Stato, Libreria Dello Stato.

Paolelli, R., and G. Sorrentino. 1980. *Let's Meet the Etruscans: Cerveteri*. Italy: S.n.

Pohl, I. 1972. *The Iron Age Necropolis of Sorbo at Cerveteri*. Stockholm: Paul Åström.

Poulsen, F. 1970. *Etruscan Tomb Paintings: Their Subjects and Significance*. Rome: L'Erma di Bretschneider.

Regter, W. 2003. *Imitation and Creation: Development of Early Bucchero Design at Cerveteri in the Seventh Century B.C.* Amsterdam: Allard Pierson Series.

Richardson, E.H. 1964. *The Etruscans, Their Art and Civilization*. Chicago: University of Chicago Press.

Ridgway, D. and F.R. Serra Ridgway. 1979. *Italy Before the Romans: The Iron Age, Orientalizing, and Etruscan Periods*. London: Academic Press.

Scullard, H.H. 1967. *The Etruscan Cities and Rome*. Ithaca, NY: Cornell University Press

Spivey, N.J. 1997. *Etruscan Art*. London: Thames and Hudson.

Steingräber, S. 2006. *Abundance of Life: Etruscan Wall Painting*. Los Angeles: J. Paul Getty Museum.

Swaddling, J., P. Perkins, and S. Haynes. *Etruscan by Definition: The Cultural, Regional and Personal Identity of the Etruscans: Papers in Honour of Sybille Haynes*. London: British Museum, 2009.

Torelli, M. 2000. *The Etruscans*. London: Thames & Hudson.

Turfa, J.M., M. Gleba and H. Becker. 2009. *Votives, Places and Rituals in Etruscan Religion Studies in Honor of Jean MacIntosh Turfa*. Leiden, Boston: Brill.

van der Meer, L.B. 2010. *Material Aspects of Etruscan Religion: Proceedings of the International Colloquium Leiden, May 29 and 30, 2008*. Leuven; Walpole, MA: Peeters.

Warden, P.G. 2009. *From the Temple and the Tomb: Etruscan Treasures from Tuscany*. Dallas: Meadows Museum, SMU.

Chapter III: Etruscans in Rome

Barletta, B. 2009. *The Origins of the Greek Architectural Orders*. New York: Cambridge University Press.

Barker, G. and T. Rasmussen. 1998. *The Etruscans*. Oxford: Blackwell Publishers.

Bell, S., H. Nagy and R. De Puma. 2009. *New Perspectives on Etruria and Early Rome: in Honor of Richard Daniel De Puma*. Madison, WI: University of Wisconsin Press.

Bonfante, L. 1986. *Etruscan Life and Afterlife: a Handbook of Etruscan Studies*. Detroit: Wayne State University Press.

Borrelli, F., M.C. Targia, S. Peccatori, and S. Zuffi. 2004. *The Etruscans: Art, Architecture, and History*. Los Angeles: J. Paul Getty Museum.

Brendel, Otto J. 1995. *Etruscan Art*. New Haven, CT: Yale University.

Camporeale, G. 2004. *The Etruscans Outside Etruria*. Los Angeles: J Paul Getty Museum.

Coulton, J. 1995. *Ancient Greek Architects at Work*. Ithaca, New York: Cornell University Press.

De Puma, R.D. and J.P. Small. 1994. *Murlo and the Etruscans: Art and Society in Ancient Etruria*. Madison, WI: University of Wisconsin Press.

Filetici, M.G. and C.C. de Azevedo. 2011. *Forum Boarium: Guide*. Milano: Electa, World Monuments Fund.

Hall, J.F. 1996. *Etruscan Italy: Etruscan Influences on the Civilizations of Italy from Antiquity to the Modern Era*. Provo, UT: Museum of Art, Brigham Young University.

Holloway, R.R. 1994. *The Archaeology of Early Rome and Latium*. London; New York: Routledge.

Johannowsky, W., J.G. Pedley, and M. Torelli. 1983. "Excavations at Paestum 1982." *American Journal of Archaeology* 87, no .3: 293-303.

Jones, D. 2007. "Scandal in Rome: the Capitoline Wolf, an Etruscan or Medieval Masterwork?" *Minerva* 18, no. 4: 22-23.

Lawrence, A. 1996. *Greek Architecture*. Revised by R.A. Tomlinson. New Haven and London: Yale University Press.

Mazzoni, C. 2010. *She-Wolf: The Story of a Roman Icon*. Cambridge; New York: Cambridge University Press, 2010.

Pallottino, M. 1975. *The Etruscans*. Bloomington: Indiana University Press.

Richardson, E.H. 1964. *The Etruscans, Their Art and Civilization*. Chicago: University of Chicago Press.

Serra Ridgway, F. 1998. "Etruscan Bronzes from Tarquinia." *Journal of Roman Archaeology* 11: 404-407.

nith, Christopher John. 1996. *Early Rome and Latium: Economy and Society c. 1000 to 500 BC.* Oxford: Clarendon Press.
awforth, A. 2006. *The Complete Greek temples.* London: Thames & Hudson.
ivey, N.J. 1997. *Etruscan Art.* London: Thames and Hudson.
rong, D.E. and J.B. Ward-Perkins. 1960. "The Round Temple in the Forum Boarium." *Papers of the British School at Rome.* 28: 7-32.
vaddling, J., P. Perkins, and S. Haynes. *Etruscan by Definition: The Cultural, Regional and Personal Identity of the Etruscans: Papers in Honour of Sybille Haynes.* London: British Museum, 2009.
omas, M.L., and G.E. Meyers. 2012. *Monumentality in Etruscan and Early Roman Architecture.* Austin: University of Texas Press.
relli, M. 2000. *The Etruscans.* London: Thames & Hudson.
ck, A. 2006. "The Social and Political Context of the 7th Century Architectural Terracottas from Poggio Civitate (Murlo)". In I. Edlund-Berry, J. F. Kentfield, & G. Greco (eds.), *Deliciae Fictiles III. Architectural Terracottas in Ancient Italy.* 130-135. Oxford: Oxbow Books.
rfa, J.M. and A.G. Steinmayer Jr. 1996. "The Comparative Structure of Greek and Etruscan Monumental Buildings." *Papers of the British School at Rome* 64: 1-39.

hapter IV: Early Republican Rome (500-300 BCE)

mmerman, A.J. 1996. "The Comitium in Rome from the Beginning." *American Journal of Archaeology* 100, no. 1:121-36.
mmerman, A.J. 1990. "On the Origins of the Forum Romanum." *American Journal of Archaeology* 94, no. 4: 627-645.
own, F.E. 1935. "The Regia." *Memoirs of the American Academy in Rome* 12: 67-88.
arelli, F., J.A. Clauss, J.J. Clauss, D.P. Harmon. 2008. *Rome and Environs: An Archaeological Guide.* Berkeley: University of California Press.
avies, H.E.H. 1998. "Designing Roman Roads." *Britannia* 29: 1-16.
owney, S.B. 1995. *Architectural Terracottas from the Regia.* Memoirs of the American Academy in Rome, Vol. 40. Ann Arbor: University of Michigan Press.
antz T.N. 1974. "Lapis Niger. The Tomb of Romulus." *La Parola del Passato* 29. 350-361.
orski, G. and J. Packer. 2014. *The Roman Forum: A Reconstruction and Architectural Guide.* Cambridge: University Press.
rant, M. 1970. *The Roman Forum.* New York: Macmillan.
uidobaldi, P. 1997. *The Roman Forum.* Milan: Mondadori Electa.
umphrey, J.H. 1986. *Roman Circuses: Arenas for Chariot Racing.* Berkeley: University of California Press.
aiser, A. 2011. *Roman Urban Street Networks.* New York; London: Routledge.
alas, G. 2015. *The Restoration of the Roman Forum in Late Antiquity: Transforming Public Space.* Austin: University of Texas Press.
aurence, R. 1999. *The Roads of Roman Italy: Mobility and Cultural Change.* London; New York: Routledge.
acMullen, R. 2011. *The Earliest Romans: A Character Sketch.* Ann Arbor: University of Michigan Press.
eijer, F. 2010. *Chariot Racing in the Roman Empire.* Baltimore: Johns Hopkins University Press.
accioli, R.A. 2003. *Roads of the Romans.* Los Angeles: J. Paul Getty Museum
atkin, D. 2009. *The Roman Forum.* Cambridge, MA.: Harvard University Press

hapter V: The Middle Republic 300-100 BCE

lcock, J.P. 2006. *Food in the Ancient World.* Westport, CT: Greenwood.
eck, H. 2011. *Consuls and Res Publica Holding High Office in the Roman Republic.* Cambridge, New York: Cambridge University Press.
rown, F.E. 1980. *Cosa, the Making of a Roman Town.* Ann Arbor: University of Michigan Press.
urnett, A. 1987. *Coinage in the Roman World.* London: Seaby.
uttrey, T.V. 1989. *Morgantina Studies II: The Coins.* Princeton, NJ: Princeton University Press.
harles-Picard, G. 1970. *Roman Painting.* Greenwich, Conn: New York Graphic Society.
rawford, M.H. 1974. *Roman Republican Coinage.* London: Cambridge University Press.
e Carolis, E. 2001. *Gods and Heroes in Pompeii.* Los Angeles: J. Paul Getty Museum.
ilke, O.A.W. 1971. *The Roman Land Surveyors: an Introduction to the Agrimensores.* Newton Abbot: David and Charles.
entress, E. 2000. "Cosa and the Idea of a City," in Fentress, Elizabeth (ed.) *Romanization and the City: Creation, Transformations, and Failures: Proceedings of a Conference Held at the American Academy in Rome to Celebrate the 50th Anniversary of the Excavations at Cosa, 14-16 May, 1998.* Portsmouth, RI: Journal of Roman Archaeology.
entress, E. 2000. *Romanization and the City: Creations, Transformations, and Failures.* Portsmouth: Journal of Roman Archaeology.
landrin, J.L., M. Montanari, and A. Sonnenfeld. 1999. *Food: A Culinary History from Antiquity to the Present.* New York: Columbia University Press.
arnsey, P. 1999. *Food and Society in Classical Antiquity.* Cambridge, New York: Cambridge University Press.
azda, E.K. 2001. "Cosa's Contribution to the Study of Roman Hydraulic Concrete: An Historiographic Commentary," in N.W. Goldman (ed.), *New Light from Ancient Cosa: Classical Mediterranean Studies in Honor of Cleo Rickman Fitch.* New York: P. Lang.
ianfrotta, P.A. 2011. "Comments Concerning Recent Fieldwork on Roman Maritime Concrete." *International Journal of Nautical Archaeology* 40, no. 1: 188-193.
old, B.K., and John F. Donahue. 2005. *Roman Dining: A Special Issue of American Journal of Philology.* Baltimore, MD: Johns Hopkins University Press.
otti, E., J.P. Oleson, L. Bottalico, C. Brandon, R. Cucitore, and R.L. Hohlfelder. 2008. "A Comparison of the Chemical and Engineering Characteristics of Ancient Roman Hydraulic Concrete with a Modern Reproduction of Vitruvian Hydraulic Concrete." *Archaeometry* 50, no. 4: 576-590.
arl, K.W. 1996. *Coinage in the Roman Economy, 300 B.C. to A.D. 700.* Baltimore: Johns Hopkins University Press.
esse, B., and P. Wapnish. 1985. *Animal Bone Archeology: from Objectives to Analysis.* Washington, DC: Taraxacum.
ollander, D.B. 2007. *Money in the Late Roman Republic.* Leiden: Brill.
olliday, P.J. 2002. *The Origins of Roman Historical Commemoration in the Visual Arts.* Cambridge; New York: Cambridge University Press.
olliday, P.J. 1997. "Roman Triumphal Painting: Its Function, Development, and Reception." *Art Bulletin* 79, no.1: 130-47.
ent, J. 1978. *Roman Coins.* New York: H.N. Abrams.
eppie, L.J.F. 1983. *Colonization and Veteran Settlement in Italy, 47-14 B.C.* London: British School at Rome.
lein, R.G., and K. Cruz-Uribe. 1984. *The Analysis of Animal Bones from Archeological Sites.* Chicago: University of Chicago Press.
aidlaw, A. 1985. *The First Style in Pompeii: Painting and Architecture.* Rome: G. Bretschneider.
ancel, S. 1995. *Carthage: a History.* Oxford: Blackwell.
ing, R. 1991. *Roman Painting.* Cambridge: Cambridge University Press.
alacrino, C.G. 2010. *Constructing the Ancient World: Architectural Techniques of the Greeks and Romans.* Los Angeles, CA: J. Paul Getty Museum.
altby, M. 2006. *Integrating Zooarchaeology.* Oxford: Oxbow.
atalas, A.L. 2001. *The Mediterranean Diet: Constituents and Health Promotion.* Boca Raton, FL: CRC Press.
azzoleni, D., U. Pappalardo and L. Romano. 2004. *Domus: Wall Painting in the Roman House.* Los Angeles: J. Paul Getty Museum.
ouritsen, H. 2011. *Plebs and Politics in the Late Roman Republic.* Cambridge, New York: Cambridge University Press.
leson, J.P., L. Bottalico, C. Brandon, R. Cucitore, E. Gotti, and R.L. Hohlfelder. 2006. "Reproducing a Roman Maritime Structure with Vitruvian Pozzolanic Concrete." *Journal of Roman Archaeology* 19: 29-52.
leson J.P., C.J. Brandon, and R.L. Hohlfelder. 2004. "The Roman Maritime Concrete Study (ROMACONS): Fieldwork at Portus, Anzio, Santa Liberata, Cosa, 2002-2003," *in* F. Maniscalco (ed.), *Mediterraneum. Tutela e Valorizzazione dei beni culturali ed ambientali* 4:185-194.
leson, J.P., C. J. Brandon, S.M. Cramer, R. Cucitore, E. Gotti, and R.L. Hohlfelder. 2004. "The ROMACONS Project: a Contribution to the Historical and Engineering

Analysis of Hydraulic Concrete in Roman Maritime Structures." *International Journal of Nautical Archaeology* 33, no. 2: 199-229.
Oleson, J.P. 1988. "The Technology of Roman Harbours." *International Journal of Nautical Archaeology* 17:117-129.
Pappalardo, U., and D. Mazzoleni. 2009. *The Splendor of Roman Wall Painting.* Los Angeles: J. Paul Getty Museum.
Pietilä-Castrén, L. 1987. *Magnificentia publica: The Victory Monuments of the Roman Generals in the Era of the Punic Wars.* Helsinki: Societas Scientiarum Fennica.
Pollitt, J.J. 1978. "The Impact of Greek Art on Rome." *Transactions of the American Philological Association* 108: 155-174. Johns Hopkins University Press.
Purcell, N.. 2005. "The Way We Used to Eat: Diet, Community, and History at Rome," in Gold, B.K. and J.F. Donahue (ed.), *Roman Dining: A Special Issue of American Journal of Philology.* Baltimore, MD: Johns Hopkins University Press.
Reiter, W. 1998. *Aemilius Paullus, Conqueror of Greece.* London; New York: Croom Helm.
Reitz, E.J., and E.S. Wing. 1999. *Zooarchaeology.* Cambridge: Cambridge University Press.
Salmon, E.T. 1970. *Roman Colonization under the Republic.* Ithaca: Cornell University Press.
Serjeantson, D. and T. Waldron. 1989. *Diet and Crafts in Towns: the Evidence of Animal Remains from the Roman to the Post-medieval Periods.* Oxford: British Archaeological Reports.
Soren, D., A.B.A. Khader, and H. Slim. 1990. *Carthage: Uncovering the Mysteries and Splendors of Ancient Tunisia.* New York: Simon and Schuster.
Southern, P. 2007. *The Roman Army: A Social and Institutional History.* Oxford: University Press.
Sutherland, C.H.V. 1974. *Roman Coins.* New York: Putnam.
Tesse D.S. 2009. *Cult Places and Cultural Change in Republican Italy: A Contextual Approach to Religious Aspects of Rural Society after the Roman Conquest.* Amsterdam: Amsterdam Archaeological Studies 14.
Tuck, S. 2000. "A New Identification for the 'Porticus Aemilia' [in Honour of Bloch]." *Journal of Roman Archaeology* 13, no. 1: 175-182.
VanDerwarker, A.M. and T. M. Peres. 2010. *Integrating Zooarchaeology and Paleoethnobotany: a Consideration of Issues, Methods, and Cases.* New York; London: Springer.
Whittaker, C.R. 1990. "The Consumer City Revisited: the Vicus and the City." *Journal of Roman Archeology* 3: 110-118.

Chapter VI: Rome in the Revolutionary First Century BCE

Adam, J.P. 1994. *Roman Building: Materials and Techniques.* Bloomington: Indiana University Press.
Beacham, R.C. 1991. *The Roman Theatre and its Audience.* London: Routledge.
Bergmann, B., S. De Caro, J.R. Mertens and R. Meyer. 2010. *Roman Frescoes from Boscoreale: The Villa of Publius Fannius Synistor in Reality and Virtual Reality.* New York: Metropolitan Museum of Art.
Bergmann, B. 2010. "New Perspectives on the Villa of Publius Fannius Synistor at Boscoreale." *Metropolitan Museum of Art Bulletin* 67, no. 4: 11-32.
Bieber, M. 1977. *Ancient Copies: Contributions to the History of Greek and Roman Art.* New York: New York University Press.
Billows, R.A. 2009. *Julius Caesar: The Colossus of Rome.* London; New York: Routledge.
Bodel, J. 1997. "Monumental Villas and Villa Monuments." *Journal of Roman Archaeology* 10: 5-35.
Clarke, J.R. 1979. *Roman Black-and-White Figural Mosaics.* New York: Published by New York University Press for the College Art Association of America.
Charles-Picard, G. 1970. *Roman Painting.* Greenwich, Conn: New York Graphic Society.
Cohen, A. 1997. *The Alexander Mosaic: Stories of Victory and Defeat.* Cambridge; New York: Cambridge University Press.
Dando-Collins, S. 2010. *The Ides: Caesar's Murder and the War for Rome.* Hoboken, NJ: Wiley.
D'Arms, J.H. 1970. *Romans on the Bay of Naples: A Social and Cultural Study of the Villas and Their Owners from 150 B.C. to A.D. 400.* Cambridge: Harvard University Press.
De Carolis, E. 2001. *Gods and Heroes in Pompeii.* Los Angeles: J. Paul Getty Museum.
Dunbabin, K.M.D. 1999. *Mosaics of the Greek and Roman World.* Cambridge: Cambridge University Press.
Dyson, S.L. 2003. *The Roman Countryside.* London: Duckworth.
Fields, Nic and Peter Dennis. 2012. *Pompey: Leadership, Strategy, Conflict.* Oxford; Long Island City, NY: Osprey.
Fejfer, J. 2008. *Roman Portraits in Context.* Berlin: Walter de Gruyter.
Fierz-David, L. and N. Hall. 2005. *Dreaming in Red: The Women's Dionysian Initiation Chamber in Pompeii.* Putnam, CT.: Spring Publications.
Fierz-David, L. 1988. *Women's Dionysian Initiation: The Villa of Mysteries in Pompeii.* Dallas, TX: Spring.
Freeman, P. 2008. *Julius Caesar.* New York: Simon & Schuster.
Flower, H.I. 1996. *Ancestor Masks and Aristocratic Power in Roman Culture.* Oxford: Clarendon Press.
Gazda, E.K., C. Hammer, Brenda Longfellow, and Molly Swetnam-Burland. 2000. *The Villa of the Mysteries in Pompeii: Ancient Ritual, Modern Muse.* Ann Arbor: Kelsey Museum of Archaeology and the University of Michigan Museum of Art.
Goldsworthy, H. and M. Zhu. 2009. "Mortar Studies Towards the Replication of Roman Concrete." *Archaeometry* 51, no. 6: 932-946.
Goldsworthy, A.K. 2006. *Caesar: The Life of a Colossus.* London: Weidenfeld & Nicolson.
Grant, M. 2004. "Slavery in Roman Society," in C. Nardo (ed.) *Living in Ancient Rome.* San Diego: Greenhaven Press.
Hearnshaw, V. 1999. "The Dionysiac Cycle in the Villa of the Mysteries: a Re-reading." *Mediterranean Archaeology* 12: 43-50.
Hitchner, R.B. 2002. "Olive Production and the Roman Economy: the Case for Intensive Growth in the Roman Empire," in W. Scheidel and S. Von Reden (ed.), *The Ancient Economy.* Edinburgh: Edinburgh University Press.
Højte, J.M. 2002. *Images of Ancestors.* Aarhus; Oxford: Aarhus University Press.
Jackson, D. 1987. "Verism and the Ancestral Portrait." *Greece and Rome* 34, no. 1: 32-47.
Joshel, S.R. 2010. *Slavery in the Roman World.* New York: Cambridge University Press.
Kamm, A. 2006. *Julius Caesar: A Life.* London; New York: Routledge.
Kleiner, D.E.E. 1992. *Roman Sculpture.* New Haven: Yale University Press.
Kleiner, D.E.E. 1977. *Roman Group Portraiture: The Funerary Reliefs of the Late Republic and Early Empire.* New York: Garland
Lancaster, L., G.S. F. Marra, and G. Ventura. 2011. "Provenancing of Lightweight Volcanic Stones Used in Ancient Roman Concrete Vaulting: Evidence from Rome." *Archaeometry* 53, no. 4: 707-727.
Lancaster, L.C. 2005. *Concrete Vaulted Construction in Imperial Rome: Innovations in Context.* Cambridge: Cambridge University Press.
Leach, E.W. 2004. *The Social Life of Painting in Ancient Rome and on the Bay of Naples.* Cambridge: Cambridge University Press.
Lehmann, P.W. 1953. *Roman Wall Paintings from Boscoreale in the Metropolitan Museum of Art.* Cambridge: Archaeological Institute of America.
Ling, R. 1998. *Ancient Mosaics.* Princeton, N.J.: Princeton University Press.
Ling, R. 1991. *Roman Painting.* Cambridge: Cambridge University Press.
Ling, R. 1977. "Studius and the Beginnings of Roman Landscape Painting." *Journal of Roman Studies* 67: 1-16.
Lydakes, S. *Ancient Greek Painting and Its Echoes in Later Art.* Los Angeles, CA: J. Paul Getty Museum, 2004.
MacDougall, E. 1987. *Ancient Roman Villa Gardens.* Washington DC: Dumbarton Oaks Research Library and Collection.
Malacrino, C.G. 2010. *Constructing the Ancient World: Architectural Techniques of the Greeks and Romans.* Los Angeles, CA: J. Paul Getty Museum.
Manuwald, G. 2011. *Roman Republican Theatre.* Cambridge; New York: Cambridge University Press.
Marzano, A. 2007. *Roman Villas in Central Italy: A Social and Economic History.* Leiden, Boston: Brill.
Mazzoleni, D., U. Pappalardo and L. Romano. 2004. *Domus: Wall Painting in the Roman House.* Los Angeles: J. Paul Getty Museum.
McKay, A.G. 1975. *Houses, Villas, and Palaces in the Roman World.* Ithaca, N.Y.: Cornell University Press.

eyboom, P.G.P. 1994. *The Nile Mosaic of Palestrina: Early Evidence of Egyptian Religion in Italy.* Leiden; New York: E.J. Brill.
oreno, P. 2001. *Apelles: The Alexander Mosaic.* Milano, Italy: Skira.
üller, F.G.J.M. 1994. *The Wall Paintings from the Oecus of the Villa of Publius Fannius Synistor in Boscoreale.* Amsterdam: J.C. Gieben.
rlin, E.M. 1997. *Temples, Religion, and Politics in the Roman Republic.* Leiden: E.J. Brill.
vadiah, A.. 1980. *Geometric and Floral Patterns in Ancient Mosaics: A Study of Their Origin in the Mosaics from the Classical Period to the Age of Augustus.* Roma: L'Erma di Bretschneider
inter, K.S. 1980. *Roman Villas in Italy: Recent Excavations and Research.* London: British Museum [Department of Greek and Roman Antiquities].
ıppalardo, U., and D. Mazzoleni. 2009. *The Splendor of Roman Wall Painting.* Los Angeles: J. Paul Getty Museum.
ercival, J. 1976. *The Roman Villa: An Historical Introduction.* Berkeley: University of California Press.
olinger Foster, K. 2001. "Dionysos and Vesuvius in the Villa of the Mysteries." *Antike Kunst* 44: 37-54.
idgway, B.S. 1984. *Roman Copies of Greek Sculpture: The Problem of the Originals.* Ann Arbor: University of Michigan Press.
ichter, G.M.A. 1955. "The Origin of Verism in Roman Portraits." *Journal of Roman Studies* 45: 39-46.
obertson, M. 1955. "The Boscoreale Figure-Paintings." *Journal of Roman Studies* 45: 58-67.
ossiter, J.J. 1981. "Wine and Oil Processing at Roman Farms in Italy." *The Phoenix* 35, no. 4: 345-61.
ozenberg, S. 1994. *Enchanted Landscapes: Wall Paintings from the Roman Era.* London: Thames and Hudson.
eager, R. 2002. *Pompey the Great: A Political Biography.* 2nd ed. Blackwell Ancient Lives. Malden, MA: Wiley-Blackwell.
ear, F. 2006. *Roman Theatres: an Architectural Study.* Oxford: Oxford University Press.
mith, J.T. 1997. *Roman Villas: A Study in Social Structure.* London; New York: Routledge, 1997.
mith, R.R.R. 1981. "Greeks, Foreigners, and Roman Republican Portraits." *Journal of Roman Studies* 71: 24-38.
tackelberg, K.T V. 2009. *The Roman Garden: Space, Sense, and Society.* London; New York: Routledge.
anner, J. 2000. "Portraits, Power, and Patronage in the Late Roman Republic." *Journal of Roman Studies* 90: 18-50.
aylor, R.M. 2003. *Roman Builders: a Study in Architectural Process.* Cambridge: Cambridge University Press.
Vallace-Hadrill, A. 2008. *Rome's Cultural Revolution.* Cambridge; New York: Cambridge University Press.
Valker, S. 1995. *Greek and Roman Portraits.* London: British Museum Press.
Vestgate, R. 2000. "Pavimenta atque emblemata vermiculata: Regional Styles in Hellenistic Mosaic and the First Mosaics at Pompeii". *American Journal of Archaeology* 104, no. 2: 255-275.

hapter VII: The Age of Augustus

icher, P.J. 1995. *Guide to the Aqueducts of Ancient Rome.* Wauconda, Ill.: Bolchazy-Carducci Publishers.
lexander, C. 1943. *Arretine Relief Ware.* Cambridge, MA: Harvard University Press.
nderson, J.C. 2012. *Roman Architecture in Provence.* Cambridge: Cambridge University Press.
nderson, J.C. 1984. *The Historical Topography of the Imperial Fora.* Bruxelles: Latomus.
nderson, M.L. 1987. "The Portrait Medallions of the Imperial Villa at Boscotrecase." *American Journal of Archaeology* 91, no. 1: 127-35.
ailey, D.M. 1991. "Lamps Metal, Lamps Clay: a Decade of Publication." *Journal of Roman Archaeology* 4: 51-62.
ailey, D.M. and M.O. Miller. 1980. *Roman Lamps Made in Italy.* London: British Museum Publications.
ailey, D.M. 1963. *Greek and Roman Pottery Lamps.* London: Trustees of the British Museum.
ernacchio, N., E. La Rocca, L. Ungaro, and R. Meneghini. 1995. *The Places of Imperial Consensus: The Forum of Augustus, the Forum of Trajan.* Roma: Progetti museali editore.
eiswanger, W.L., P.J. Hatch, L. Stanton, and S.R. Stein. 2001. *Thomas Jefferson's Monticello.* Chapel Hill, NC: The University of North Carolina Press.
illows, R. 1993. "The Religious Procession of the Ara Pacis Augustae: Augustus' *Supplication* in 13 B.C." *Journal of Roman Archaeology* 6: 80-92.
romwich, J. 1993. *The Roman Remains of Southern France: a Guidebook.* London: Routledge.
rulet, R., J.P. and P. Talloen (ed.). 2004. *Early Italian Sigillata: The Chronological Framework and Trade Patterns: Proceedings of the First International ROCT-Congress, Leuven, May 7 and 8, 1999.* Leuven, Peeters.
astriota, D. 1995. *The Ara Pacis Augustae and the Imagery of Abundance in Later Greek and Early Roman Imperial Art.* Princeton, N.J.: Princeton University Press.
leere, H. 2001. *Southern France: An Oxford Archaeological Guide.* Oxford: Oxford University Press.
onlin, D.A. 1997. *The Artists of the Ara Pacis: The Process of Hellenization in Roman Relief Sculpture.* Chapel Hill: University of North Carolina Press.
ooley, A. 2009. *Res Gestae Divi Augusti: Text, Translation, and Commentary.* Cambridge, UK; New York: Cambridge University Press.
Davies, P.J E. 2000. *Death and the Emperor: Roman Imperial Funerary Monuments, from Augustus to Marcus Aurelius.* Cambridge, U.K.; New York: Cambridge University Press.
De Carolis, E. 2001. *Gods and Heroes in Pompeii.* Los Angeles: J. Paul Getty Museum.
De Grummond, N.T. 1990. "Pax Augusta and the Horae on the Ara Pacis Augustae." *American Journal of Archaeology* 94, no. 4: 663-77.
ck, W., D.L. Schneider and S.A. Takács. 2003. *The Age of Augustus.* Malden, MA: Blackwell.
vans, H.B. 1994. *Water Distribution in Ancient Rome: the Evidence of Frontinus.* Ann Arbor: University of Michigan Press.
veritt, A. 2006. *Augustus: The Life of Rome's First Emperor.* New York: Random House.
abre, G. 1992. *The Pont Du Gard: Water and the Roman Town.* Paris: Caisse nationale des Monuments historiques et des sites.
abre, G., J.L. Fiches, and J.L. Paillet. 1991. "Interdisciplinary Research on the Aqueduct of Nimes and the Pont du Gard." *Journal of Roman Archaeology* 4: 63-88.
avro, D.G. 1996. *The Urban Image of Augustan Rome.* Cambridge: Cambridge University Press.
ulle, G. 1997. "The Internal Organization of the Arretine Terra Sigillata Industry: Problems of Evidence and Interpretation." *Journal of Roman Studies* 87: 111-155.
Galinsky, K. 2012. *Augustus: Introduction to the Life of an Emperor.* New York: Cambridge University Press.
Galinsky, K. 2005. *The Cambridge Companion to the Age of Augustus.* Cambridge: Cambridge University Press.
Galinsky, K. 1996. *Augustan Culture: an Interpretive Introduction.* Princeton, NJ: Princeton University Press.
Gambini, Y. and J.G. D'Hoste. 1993. *Pont Du Gard and the Roman Aqueduct from Uzes to Nimes.* Florence: Bonechi.
Geiger, J. 2008. *The First Hall of Fame: A Study of the Statues in the Forum Augustum.* Mnemosyne Supplementa 295. Leiden; Boston: Brill.
Granier, J., R.I. McLaren, and D.J. Kulash. 1990. *Water Supply in Antiquity in Provence and Languedoc: The Pont Du Gard: Aqueducts, Thermal Springs, Sacred Wells, Water Catchment.* Monaco: Sté Ajex, Éditions du Boumian.
Harris, W.V. 1980. "Roman Terracotta Lamps: The Organization of an Industry." *Journal of Roman Studies* 70: 126-45.
Hauck, G.F.W. 1988. *The Aqueduct of Nemausus.* Jefferson, NC: McFarland.
Hodge, A. Trevor. 1992. *Roman Aqueducts & Water Supply.* London: Duckworth.
Holliday, P. 1990. "Time, History and Ritual on the Ara Pacis Augustae." *Art Bulletin* 72, no. 4: 542-557.
Johns, C. 1971. *Arretine and Samian Pottery.* London: British Museum.
Kenrick, P. 1993. "Italian Terra Sigillata: a Sophisticated Roman Industry." *Oxford Journal of Archaeology* 12, no. 2: 235-242.
Kleiner, D.E.E. 1994. *Roman Sculpture.* New Haven, CT.: Yale University Press.
Kleiner, D.E.E. 2005. *Cleopatra and Rome.* Cambridge, Mass.: Belknap Press.
Knauer, E.R. 1993. "Roman Wall Paintings from Boscotrecase: Three Studies in the Relationship between Writing and Painting." *Metropolitan Museum Journal* 28: 13-46.

Lamp, K. 2009. "The Ara Pacis Augustae: Visual Rhetoric in Augustus' Principate." *Rhetoric Society Quarterly* 39, no. 1: 1-24.
Leach, E.W. 2004. *The Social Life of Painting in Ancient Rome and on the Bay of Naples.* Cambridge: Cambridge University Press.
Leach, E.W. 1988. *The Rhetoric of Space: Literary and Artistic Representations of Landscape in Republican and Augustan Rome.* Princeton, N.J.: Princeton University Press
Ling, R. 1991. *Roman Painting.* Cambridge: Cambridge University Press.
Lydakes, S. *Ancient Greek Painting and Its Echoes in Later Art.* Los Angeles, CA.: J. Paul Getty Museum, 2004.
Marabini Moevs, M.M.T. 2006. *Cosa: The Italian Sigillata.* Ann Arbor, MI: Published for the American Academy in Rome by the University of Michigan.
Mazzoleni, D., U. Pappalardo and L. Romano. 2004. *Domus: Wall Painting in the Roman House.* Los Angeles: J. Paul Getty Museum.
Mirti, P., L. Appolonia, and A. Casoli. 1999. "Technological Features of Roman Terra Sigillata from Gallic and Italian Centres of Production." *Journal of Archaeological Science* 26, no. 12: 1427-435.
Pappalardo, U., and D. Mazzoleni. 2009. *The Splendor of Roman Wall Painting.* Los Angeles: J. Paul Getty Museum.
Perlzweig, J. 1961. *Lamps of the Roman Period, First to Seventh Century after Christ.* Princeton, N.J.: American School of Classical Studies at Athens.
Pollini, J. 1995. "The Augustus from Prima Porta and the Transformation of the Polykleitan Heroic Ideal: the Rhetoric of Art," in W.G. Moon (ed.), *Polykleitos, the Doryphoros, and Tradition.* Madison, WI.: University of Wisconsin Press.
Powell, Anton. 1992. *Roman Poetry and Propaganda in the Age of Augustus.* London: Bristol Classical
Raaflaub, K.A., M. Toher, and G.W. Bowersock. 1990. *Between Republic and Empire: Interpretations of Augustus and His Principate.* Berkeley: University of California Press.
Reeder, J.C. 1992. "Typology and Ideology in the Mausoleum of Augustus: Tumulus and Tholos." *Classical Antiquity* 11, no. 2: 265-307.
Rehak, P., and J.G. Younger. 2006. *Imperium and Cosmos: Augustus and the Northern Campus Martius.* Madison: University of Wisconsin Press.
Rickman, G. 1980. *The Corn Supply of Ancient Rome.* Oxford; New York: Clarendon; Oxford University Press.
Ridley, R.T. 2003. *The Emperor's Retrospect: Augustus' Res Gestae in Epigraphy, Historiography and Commentary.* Leuven; Dudley, MA: Peeters.
Rozenberg, S. 1994. *Enchanted Landscapes: Wall Paintings from the Roman Era.* London: Thames and Hudson.
Ruddock, T. 2000. *Masonry Bridges, Viaducts, and Aqueducts.* Aldershot, Hants; Burlington, VT: Ashgate/Variorum, 2000.
Simon, E. 1968. *Ara Pacis Augustae.* Greenwich: New York Graphic Society.
Slane, K.A. 1993. "A New Typology for Italian Sigillata." *Journal of Roman Archaeology* 6: 411-414.
Smith, R.R.R. 1996, "Typology and Diversity in the Portraits of Augustus." *Journal of Roman Archaeology* 9: 30-47.
Soren, D. and N. Soren. 1999. *A Roman Villa and a Late Roman Infant Cemetery: Excavation at Poggio Gramignano, Lugnano in Teverina.* Roma: L'Erma Di Bretschneider.
Stahl, H.P. and E. Fantham. 1998. *Vergil's Aeneid: Augustan Epic and Political Context.* London: Duckworth, in Association with the Classical of Wales.
Thompson, H.A. 1933. "Terracotta Lamps." *Hesperia* 2, no. 2: 195-215.
von Blanckenhagen, P.H. and C. Alexander. 1990. *The Augustan Villa at Boscotrecase.* Mainz am Rhein: P. von Zabern.
von Blanckenhagen, P.H., C. Alexander, and G. Papadopulos. 1962. *The Paintings from Boscotrecase.* Heidelberg: F.H. Kerle.
Wightman, G. 1997. "The Imperial Fora of Rome: Some Design Considerations." *The Journal of the Society of Architectural Historians* 56, no. 1: 64-88.
Woodman, A.J. and D.A. West. 1984. *Poetry and Politics in the Age of Augustus.* Cambridge; New York: Cambridge University Press.
Zanker, P. 1988. *The Power of Images in the Age of Augustus.* Ann Arbor: University of Michigan Press.

Chapter VIII: The Julio-Claudian Successors of Augustus

Ball, L.F. 2003. *The Domus Aurea and the Roman Architectural Revolution.* Cambridge, UK: Cambridge University Press.
Ball, L.F. 1994. "A Reappraisal of Nero's *Domus* Aurea," in Humphrey, J.H (ed.), *Rome papers: the Baths of Trajan Decius, Iside e Serapide nel Palazzo, a late Domus on the Palatine and Nero's Golden House.* Ann Arbor, MI: *Journal of Roman Archaeology* 11, 183-254.
Beacham, R.C. 1999. *Spectacle Entertainments of Early Imperial Rome.* New Haven: Yale University Press.
Biers, W.R., J.C. Biers, D. Soren. 1982. "Excavations at Mirobriga, The 1982 Season," *Muse* 16. 29-43
Biers, W.R. 1988 (et al). *Mirobriga: Investigations at an Iron Age and Roman Site in Southern Portugal by the University of Missouri-Columbia, 1981-1986.* Oxford: British Archaeological Reports.
Boëthius, A. 1960. *The Golden House of Nero: Some Aspects of Roman Architecture.* Ann Arbor: University of Michigan Press.
Carey, S. 2002. "A Tradition of Adventures in the Imperial Grotto." *Greece & Rome* 49, no. 1: 44-61.
Champlin, E. 2003. *Nero.* Cambridge, Mass: Belknap Press.
Coates-Stephens, R. 2004. *Porta Maggiore: Monument and Landscape : Archaeology and Topography of the Southern Esquiline from the Late Republican Period to the Present.* Roma: L'Erma Di Bretschneider.
Dando-Collins, S. 2010. *The Great Fire of Rome: The Fall of the Emperor Nero and His City.* Cambridge, MA: Da Capo.
De Grummond, N.T. and B.S. Ridgway. 2000. *From Pergamon to Sperlonga : Sculpture and Context.* Berkeley: University of California.
Elsner, J. and J. Masters (ed.). 1994. *Reflections of Nero: Culture, History, & Representation.* Chapel Hill: University of North Carolina Press.
Kleiner, F.S. 1985. *The Arch of Nero in Rome: A Study of the Roman Honorary Arch Before and Under Nero.* Roma: G. Bretschneider.
Hope, V.M. 2003. "Trophies and Tombstones: Commemorating the Roman Soldier." *World Archeology* 35, no. 1: 79-97.
Hope, V.M. 2001. *Constructing Identity: The Funerary Monuments of Aquileia, Mainz and Nimes.* BAR International Series, No. 960.
Hope, V.M. 2000. "Inscription and Sculpture: the Construction of Identity in the Military Tombstones of Roman Mainz," in Oliver, G.J. (ed.), *The Epigraphy of Death: Studies in the History and Society of Greece and Rome.* Liverpool: Liverpool University Press, 155-86.
Osgood, J. 2011. *Claudius Caesar: Image and Power in the Early Roman Empire.* Cambridge; New York: Cambridge University Press.
Purcell, N. 2007. "The Enigmatic Porta Maggiore in Its Setting." *Journal of Roman Archaeology* 20: 446.
Rose, C.B. 1997. *Dynastic Art and Ideology in the Julio-Claudian Period.* Cambridge: Cambridge University Press.
Saflund, G. 1972. *The Polyphemus and Scylla Groups at Sperlonga.* Stockholm: Almquist and Wiksell.
Segala, E. and I. Sciortino. 1999. *Domus Aurea.* Milan: Electa.
Shotter, D.C.A. 2005. *Nero.* London: Routledge.
Smith, R.R. R. *Hellenistic Sculpture : A Handbook.* New York, N.Y.: Thames and Hudson, 1991
Solmsen, F. 1979. *Isis Among the Greeks and Romans.* Cambridge, MA: Published for Oberlin College by Harvard University Press.
Soren, D.. 1987. *The Sanctuary of Apollo Hylates at Kourion, Cyprus.* Tucson: University of Arizona.
Soren, D. and J. James. 1988. *Kourion: The Search for a Lost Roman City.* New York: Anchor.
Squire, M. 2003. "Giant Questions: Dining with Polyphemus at Sperlonga and Baiae." *Apollo* 497: 29-37.
Stewart, A.F. 1977. "To Entertain an Emperor: Sperlonga, Laokoon and Tiberius at the Dinnertable." *Journal of Roman Studies* 67: 76-90.
Takács, S.A. 1995. *Isis and Sarapis in the Roman World.* Leiden: E.J. Brill.
Warden, P.G.. 1981. "The Domus Aurea Reconsidered." *The Journal of the Society of Architectural Historians.* 40, no. 4: 271-278.
Weis, A. 1998. "Sperlonga and Hellenistic Sculpture." *Journal of Roman Archaeology* 11: 412-420.
Wilkinson, S. 2005. *Caligula.* London; New York: Routledge.
Winterling, A. 2011. *Caligula: A Biography.* Berkeley: University of California.
Witt, R.E. 1997. *Isis in the Ancient World.* Baltimore: Johns Hopkins University Press.

itt, R.E. 1971. *Isis in the Graeco-Roman World*. Ithaca, N.Y.: Cornell University Press.

hapter IX: The Flavian Emperors

llison, P.M. 2004. *Pompeian Households: an Analysis of Material Culture*. Los Angeles: Cotsen Institute of Archaeology.
nery, C. and B. Curran. 2011. *The Lost World of Pompeii*. London: Frances Lincoln.
acham, R.C. 1999. *Spectacle Entertainments of Early Imperial Rome*. New Haven: Yale University Press.
ard, M. 2008. *The Fires of Vesuvius: Pompeii Lost and Found*. Cambridge, MA: Belknap Press of Harvard University Press.
ard, M. 2008. *Pompeii: the Life of a Roman Town*. London: Profile.
rry, J. 2007. *The Complete Pompeii*. New York: Thames & Hudson.
mgardner, D.L. 2000. *The Story of the Roman Amphitheatre*. London and New York: Routledge.
ssanelli, R., P.L. Ciapparelli, E. Colle, M. David. 2002. *Houses and Monuments of Pompeii: The Works of Fausto and Felice Niccolini*. Los Angeles: J. Paul Getty Museum.
arke, J.R. 1991. *The Houses of Roman Italy, 100 B.C.-A.D. 250: Ritual, Space, and Decoration*. Berkeley: University of California Press.
Coarelli, F., A. Foglia, and P. Foglia. 2002. *Pompeii*. New York: Riverside Book Co.
arelli, F., and A. Gabucci. 2001. *The Colosseum*. Los Angeles: J. Paul Getty Museum
arwall-Smith, R. 1996. *Emperors and Architecture: a Study of Flavian Rome*. Bruxelles: Latomus.
Carolis, E. and G. Patricelli. 2003. *Vesuvius, A.D. 79: The Destruction of Pompeii and Herculaneum*. Los Angeles: J. Paul Getty Museum.
La Bedoyere, G. 2010. *Cities of Roman Italy: Pompeii, Herculaneum and Ostia*. London: Bristol Classical.
Laine, J. 1992. *Roman baths and bathing: proceedings of the First International Conference on Roman Baths, held at Bath, England, 30 March-4 April 1992*. Portsmouth: Journal of Roman Archaeology.
obbins, J.J. and P.W. Foss. 2007. *The World of Pompeii*. London: Routledge.
odge, H. 2011. *Spectacle in the Roman World*. Classical World Series. London and New York: Bristol Classical Press/Bloomsbury Academic.
lis, S.J.R. 2011. *The Making of Pompeii: Studies in the History and Urban Development of an Ancient Town*. Portsmouth, RI: *JRA* Supplementary series 85.
lis, S.P. 2000. *Roman Housing*. London: Duckworth.
tienne, R. 1992. *Pompeii: the Day a City Died*. New York: H.N. Abrams.
agan, G.G. 2001. "The Genesis of the Roman Public Bath: Recent Approaches and Future Directions." *American Journal of Archaeology* 105, no .3: 403-26.
agan, G.G. 1999. *Bathing in Public in the Roman World*. Ann Arbor: University of Michigan Press.
utrell, A. 1997. *Blood in the Arena*. Austin: University of Texas Press.
ardner Coates, V.C., and J.L. Seydl. 2007. *Antiquity Recovered: the Legacy of Pompeii and Herculaneum*. Los Angeles: J. Paul Getty Museum.
azda, E.K., and A.E. Haeckl. 1991. *Roman Art in the Private Sphere: New Perspectives on the Architecture and Decor of the Domus, Villa, and Insula*. Ann Arbor: University of Michigan Press.
rant, M. 2005. *Cities of Vesuvius: Pompeii and Herculaneum*. London: Phoenix Press.Hopkins, Keith and Mary Beard. 2005. *The Colosseum*. Cambridge, MA: Harvard University Press.
ales, S. 2003. *The Roman House and Social Identity*. Cambridge: Cambridge University Press.
nsen, G.C.M., A.O. Koloski-Ostrow, and E.M. Moormann. 2011. *Roman Toilets: Their Archaeology and Cultural History*. Leuven: Peeters.
shemski, W. F. and F. G. Meyer. 2002. *The Natural History of Pompeii*. Cambridge; New York: Cambridge University Press.
ngman, W. 1988. *The Economy and Society of Pompeii*. Amsterdam: J.C. Gieben.
nes, B.W. 1992. *The Emperor Domitian*. London; New York: Routledge.
nes, B.W. 1984. *The Emperor Titus*. London; New York: Croom Helm; St. Martin's.
nes, D. 2004. "Meta Sudans at the Colosseum." *Minerva* 15, no. 6:36-37.
leiner, D.E.E. 1994. *Roman Sculpture*. New Haven: Yale University Press.
öhne, E., C. Ewigleben, and R. Jackson. 2000. *Gladiators and Caesars: the Power of Spectacle in Ancient Rome*. London: British Museum.
osso, C. and A. Scott. 2009. *The Nature and Function of Water, Baths, Bathing, and Hygiene from Antiquity through the Renaissance*. Leiden: Brill.
raus, T. and L. von Matt. 1975. *Pompeii and Herculaneum: the Living Cities of the Dead*. New York: H.N. Abrams.
yle, D.G. 1998. *Spectacles of Death in Ancient Rome*. London: Routledge
aurence, R. and A. Wallace-Hadrill. 1997. *Domestic Space in the Roman World: Pompeii and Beyond*. Portsmouth, RI: Journal of Roman Archaeology.
aurence, R. 1994. *Roman Pompeii: Space and Society*. London: Routledge.
azer, E. 2009. *Resurrecting Pompeii*. London; New York: Routledge.
evick, B. 1999. *Vespasian*. London; New York: Routledge.
ongfellow, B. 2010. "Reflections of Imperialism: The *Meta Sudans* in Rome and the Provinces." *Art Bulletin* 92, no. 4: 275-92.
lattusch, C.C. 2009. *Pompeii and the Roman Villa: Art and Culture around the Bay of Naples*. London: Thames & Hudson.
lau, A. 1982. *Pompeii, its Life and Art*. New Rochelle, NY: Caratzas Brothers.
lcKay, A.G. 1975. *Houses, Villas, and Palaces in the Roman World*. Ithaca, NY: Cornell University Press.
levett, L.C. 2010. *Domestic Space in Classical Antiquity*. New York: Cambridge University Press.
lielsen, I. 1993. *Thermae et Balnea: the Architecture and Cultural History of Roman public Baths*. Aarhus: Aarhus University Press.
arslow, C.C. 1995. *Rediscovering Antiquity: Karl Weber and the Excavation of Herculaneum, Pompeii, and Stabiae*. Cambridge: New York.
lass, P. 1995. *The Game of Death in Ancient Rome: Arena Sport and Political Suicide*. Madison, WI: University of Wisconsin Press.
oehler, E., M. Flohr, K. Cole. 2011. *Pompeii: Art, Industry, and Infrastructure*. Oxford; Oakville, CT: Oxbow.
otter, D.S. and D.J. Mattingly. 1999. *Life, Death, and Entertainment in the Roman Empire*. Ann Arbor: University of Michigan Press.
anieri, M. 2004. *Pompeii: the History, Life and Art of the Buried City*. Vercelli: White Star.
ichardson, L. 1988. *Pompeii: an Architectural History*. Baltimore: Johns Hopkins University Press.
igsby, A.M. 1997. "'Public' and 'Private' in Roman Culture: the Case of the *Cubiculum*." *Journal of Roman Archaeology* 10: 36-56.
outhern, P. 1997. *Domitian: Tragic Tyrant*. London; New York: Routledge.
wift, E. 2009. *Style and Function in Roman Decoration: Living with Objects and Interiors*. Burlington, VT: Ashgate.
Vallace-Hadrill, A. 1994. *Houses and Society in Pompeii and Herculaneum*. Princeton, N.J.: Princeton University Press.
Vard-Perkins, J.B., and A. Claridge. 1978. *Pompeii A.D. 79: Essay and Catalogue*. New York: Knopf.
Velch, K.E. 2007. *The Roman Amphitheatre: from its Origins to the Colosseum*. Cambridge: Cambridge University Press.
Velch, K.E 1991. "Roman Amphitheatres Revived." *Journal of Roman Archaeology* 4: 272-81.
Viedemann, T. 1992. *Emperors and Gladiators*. London: Routledge.
Vilkinson, P. 2004. *Pompeii: the Last Day*. London: BBC
egül, F.K. 1992. *Baths and Bathing in Classical Antiquity*. New York, N.Y.: Architectural History Foundation.
anker, P. 1998. *Pompeii: Public and Private Life*. Cambridge, MA: Harvard University Press.

hapter X: Trajan and Hadrian – The Empire at its Zenith

nderson, J.C. 1984. *The Historical Topography of the Imperial Fora*. Bruxelles: Latomus.

Bakker, J.T. 1999. *The Mills- Bakeries of Ostia: Description and Interpretation.* Amsterdam: J.C. Gieben.
Bennett, J. 1997. *Trajan: Optimus Princeps: A Life and Times.* Bloomington: Indiana University Press.
Bernacchio, N., E. La Rocca, L. Ungaro, and R. Meneghini. 1995. *The Places of Imperial Consensus: the Forum of Augustus, the Forum of Trajan.* Roma: Progetti museali editore.
Birley, A.R. 1997. *Hadrian: The Restless Emperor.* London; New York, N.Y.: Routledge.
Bishop, M.C. 2011. *Handbook to Roman Legionary Fortresses.* South Yorkshire.: Pen & Sword
Blazquez, J.M. 1992. "The Latest Work on the Export of Baetican Olive Oil to Rome and the Army." *Greece & Rome* 39, no. 2: 173-88.
Boatwright, M.T. 2000. *Hadrian and the Cities of the Roman Empire.* Princeton, N.J.: Princeton University Press.
Boatwright, M.T. 1987. *Hadrian and the City of Rome.* Princeton, N.J.: Princeton University Press.
Campbell, D.B. and B. Delf. 2009. *Roman Auxiliary Forts, 27 BC-AD 378.* Oxford: Osprey.
Cichorius, C., F.A. Lepper, and S.S. Frere. 1988. *Trajan's Column: a New Edition of the Cichorius Plates.* Gloucester: Alan Sutton.
Claridge, A. 1993. "Hadrian's Column of Trajan." *Journal of Roman Archaeology* 6: 5-22.
Coarelli, F., P. Zanker, B. Brizzi, C. Conti, R. Meneghini, and C. Rockwell. 2000. *The Column of Trajan.* Rome: Colombo.
Davies, P.J.E. 2000. *Death and the Emperor: Roman Imperial Funerary Monuments, from Augustus to Marcus Aurelius.* Cambridge: Cambridge University Press.
Davies, P.J.E. 1997. "The Politics of Perpetuation: Trajan's Column and the Art of Commemoration." *American Journal of Archaeology* 101, no.1: 41-65.
De Fine Licht, K. 1968. *The Rotunda in Rome. A Study of Hadrian's Pantheon.* Copenhagen: Gyldendal.
Everitt, A. 2009. *Hadrian and the Triumph of Rome.* New York: Random House.
Fleming, S.J. 2001. *Vinum: the Story of Roman Wine.* Glen Mills, Pa.: Art Flair.
Fraser, T.E. 2006. *Hadrian as Builder and Benefactor in the Western Provinces.* Oxford, England: Archaeopress.
Garnsey, P. 1968. "Trajan's Alimenta: Some Problems." *Historia* 17: 367-381.
Hermansen, G. 1981. *Ostia: Aspects of Roman City Life.* Edmonton, Alta: University of Alberta Press.
Jacobson, D.M. 1986. "Hadrianic Architecture and Geometry." *American Journal of Archaeology* 90, no. 1: 69-85.
Jones, M.W. 1993. "One Hundred Feet and a Spiral Stair: the Problem of Designing Trajan's Column." *Journal of Roman Archaeology* 6: 23-38.
Koeppel, G. 2002. "The Column of Trajan: Narrative Technique and the Image of the Emperor," in Stadter, PA and L. Van der Stockt (ed.), *Sage and Emperor: Plutarch Greek*
Intellectuals and Roman Power in the Time of Trajan. Leuven: Leuven University Press, 245-258.
Lancaster, L. 2000. "Building Trajan's Markets 2: The Construction Process". *American Journal of Archaeology* 104, no. 4: 755-785.
Lancaster, L. 1999. "Building Trajan's Column." *American Journal of Archaeology* 103, no. 3: 419-439.
Lancaster, L. 1998. "Building Trajan's Markets." *American Journal of Archaeology* 102, no. 2: 283-308.
MacDonald, W.L. 1976. *The Pantheon: Design, Meaning, and Progeny.* Cambridge, MA: Harvard University Press.
MacDonald, W.L., and J.A. Pinto. 1995. *Hadrian's Villa and its Legacy.* New Haven: Yale University Press.
Mark, R. and P. Hutchinson. 1986. "On the Structure of the Roman Pantheon." *Art Bulletin* 68, no. 1: 24-34.
Meiggs, R. 1997. *Roman Ostia.* Oxford: Clarendon Press.
Moffat, A. 2008. *The Wall: Rome's Greatest Frontier.* Edinburgh: Birlinn.
Opper, T. 2008. *Hadrian.* London: British Museum.
Opper, T. 2008. *Hadrian: Empire and Conflict.* Cambridge, Mass.: Harvard University Press.
Packer, J.E. 2001. *The Forum of Trajan in Rome: A Study of the Monuments in Brief.* Berkeley: University of California Press.
Packer, J.E. 1998. "Trajan's Glorious Forum." *Archaeology* 51, no. 1: 32-41.
Packer, J.E. 1994. "Trajan's Forum Again: the Column and the Temple of Trajan in the Master Plan Attributed to Apollodorus(?)" *Journal of Roman Archaeology* 7: 163-182.
Richardson, A. 2004. *Theoretical Aspects of Roman Camp and Fort Design.* Oxford: John and Erica Hedges.
Rossi, L. 1971. *Trajan's Column and the Dacian Wars.* Ithaca, N.Y.: Cornell University Press.
Soren, D. (editor) 2006, *An Ancient Roman Spa at Mezzomiglio: Chianciano Terme, Tuscany, Vol. 1* (BAR International Series 1548)
Soren, D. and P. Mecchia (editors), *An Ancient Roman Spa at Mezzomiglio: Chianciano Terme, Tuscany, Vol. 2* (BAR International Series 1548)
Thomas, E. 1997. *The Architectural History of the Pantheon in Rome from Agrippa to Septimius Severus via Hadrian.* Lüneburg: Camelion.
Wightman, G. 1997. "The Imperial Fora of Rome: Some Design Considerations." *The Journal of the Society of Architectural Historians* 56, no. 1: 64-88.
Wilmott, T. 2009. *Hadrian's Wall: Archaeological Research by English Heritage 1976-2000.* Swindon, England: English Heritage.

Chapter XI: The Antonine Emperors and the Severans

Beckmann, M. 2011. *The Column of Marcus Aurelius: the Genesis & Meaning of a Roman Imperial Monument.* Chapel Hill: University of North Carolina Press.
Brilliant, R. 1967. *The Arch of Septimius Severus in the Roman Forum.* Rome: American Academy in Rome.
Cyrino, M.S. 2005. *Big Screen Rome.* Malden, MA: Blackwell Pub
De La Bedoyere, G. 2010. *Cities of Roman Italy: Pompeii, Herculaneum and Ostia.* London: Bristol Classical.
DeLaine, J. 1997. *The Baths of Caracalla: A Study in the Design, Construction, and Economics of Large-Scale Building Projects in Imperial Rome.* Portsmouth, R.I.: Journal of Roman Archaeology.
DeLaine, J. 1992. *Roman Baths and Bathing: Proceedings of the First International Conference on Roman Baths, Held at Bath, England, 30 March-4 April 1992.* Portsmouth: Journal of Roman Archaeology.
Elsner, J. and J. Huskinson. 2010. *Life, Death and Representation. Some New Work on Roman Sarcophagi.* New York : De Gruyter.
Elsner, J. 2005. "Sacrifice and Narrative on the Arch of the Argentarii at Rome." *Journal of Roman Archaeology* 18: 83-98.
Fagan, G.G. 1999. *Bathing in Public in the Roman World.* Ann Arbor: University of Michigan Press.
Fejfer, J. 2008. *Roman Portraits in Context.* Berlin: Walter de Gruyter.
Grant, M. 1994. *The Antonines: the Roman Empire in Transition.* London: Routledge.
Hekster, O. 2002. *Commodus: An Emperor at the Crossroads.* Amsterdam: J.C. Gieben.
Joshel, S.R., Margaret Malamud, and Donald T. McGuire. 2001. *Imperial Projections: Ancient Rome in Modern Popular Culture.* Baltimore: Johns Hopkins University Press.
Kleiner, D.E.E. 1992. *Roman Sculpture.* New Haven: Yale University Press.
Koch, G. and K. Wight. 1988. *Roman Funerary Sculpture: Catalogue of the Collections.* Malibu, CA: J. Paul Getty Museum.
Koortbojian, M. 1995. *Myth, Meaning, and Memory on Roman Sarcophagi.* Berkeley: University of California.
Kosso, C. and A. Scott. 2009. *The Nature and Function of Water, Baths, Bathing, and Hygiene from Antiquity Through the Renaissance.* Leiden: Brill.
Packer, James E. 1971. *The Insulae of Imperial Ostia.* Rome: American Academy in Rome.
Provan, D.M.J. 2004. *Architecture and Decoration of the House of the Cascade, Roman Utica, Tunisia.* Tromsø, Norway: University of Tromsø Dissertation.
Solomon, J. 2001. *The Ancient World in the Cinema.* New Haven: Yale University Press.
Strong, D.E.. 1961. *Roman Imperial Sculpture; an Introduction to the Commemorative and Decorative Sculpture of the Roman Empire down to the Death of Constantine.* London: A. Tiranti.
Swain, S., S.J. Harrison, and J. Elsner. 2007. *Severan Culture.* Cambridge: Cambridge University Press.

eodorakopoulos, E. 2010. *Ancient Rome at the Cinema: Story and Spectacle in Hollywood and Rome*. Exeter, UK: Bristol Phoenix.
omas, E. 2007. *Monumentality and the Roman Empire: Architecture in the Antonine Age*. Oxford: Oxford University Press.
rner, E.R. and S.D. Bundrick. 2000. *From Caligula to Constantine: Tyranny & Transformation in Roman Portraiture*. Atlanta: Michael C. Carlos Museum.
alker, S. 1995. *Greek and Roman Portraits*. London: British Museum Press.
inkler, Martin M. 2009. *Cinema and Classical Text: Apollo's New Light*. Cambridge; New York: Cambridge University Press.
inkler, M.M. 2004. *Gladiator: Film and History*. Malden, MA: Blackwell Pub.
inkler, M.M. 2001. *Classical Myth & Culture in the Cinema*. Oxford; New York: Oxford University Press.
inkler, M.M. 1991. *Classics and Cinema*. Lewisburg, PA; London: Bucknell University Press; Associated University Press.
gül, F.K. 1992. *Baths and Bathing in Classical Antiquity*. New York, N.Y.: Architectural History Foundation.

hapter XII: The Third Century CE – Years of Crisis

anchi Bandinelli, R. 1971. *Rome, the Late Empire; Roman Art, A.D. 200-400*. New York: G. Braziller.
anchi Bandinelli, R., E.V. Caffarelli, G. Caputo, and F. Clerici. 1966. *The Buried city: Excavations at Leptis Magna*. New York: F.A. Praeger.
auer, G.C. 1975. *The Age of the Soldier Emperors: Imperial Rome, A.D. 244-284*. Park Ridge, NJ: Noyes.
apizzi, C., F. Galati, A. Ascani and R. Marino. 1990. *Piazza Armerina: The Mosaics of Morgantina*. Bologna, Italy: Italcards.
i Giovanni, G. 1987. *Piazza Armerina: Roman Civilization Through the Mosaics of the Villa del Casale*. Palermo, Sicily: Presso la Tipolitigrafia Priulla.
uncan-Jones, R. 1994. *Money and Government in the Roman Empire*. Cambridge: Cambridge University Press.
ddy, S.K. 1967. *The Minting of Antoniniani A.D. 238-249, and the Smyrna Hoard*. New York: American Numismatic Society.
occhi, N.V., F. Bisconti, and D. Mazzoleni. 1999. *The Christian Catacombs of Rome: History, Decoration, Inscriptions*. Regensburg: Schnell & Steiner.
ejfer, J. 2008. *Roman Portraits in Context*. Berlin: Walter de Gruyter.
entilli, G.V., 1970. *The Imperial Villa at Piazza Armerina*. Rome: Instituto Poligraphico dello Stato, Congleton: Old Vicarage.
oodchild, R G. and Joyce Maire Reynolds. 1976. *Libyan Studies: Select Papers of the Late R.G. Goodchild*. London: P. Elek.
arl, K.W. 1996. *Coinage in the Roman Economy, 300 B.C. to A.D. 700*. Baltimore: Johns Hopkins University Press.
nes, G.D.B and R. Kronenburg. 1988. "The Severan Buildings at Lepcis Magna." *Libyan Studies* 19: 43-53.
leiner, D.E.E. 1994. *Roman Sculpture*. New Haven: Yale University Press.
ouremenos, A., S. Chandrasekaran, R. Rossi and J. Boardman. 2011. *From Pella to Gandhara: Hybridisation and Identity in the Art and Architecture of the Hellenistic East*. Oxford: Archaeopress.
yttelton, M. 1974. *Baroque Architecture in Classical Antiquity*. London: Thames & Hudson.
ancinelli, F. 1994. *The Catacombs of Rome and the Origins of Christianity*. Firenze: Scala.
lattingly, D.J. 1994. *Tripolitania*. Ann Arbor: University of Michigan Press.
ergola, P., Francesca S., and P.M. Barbini. 2000. *Christian Rome: Early Christian Rome: Catacombs and Basilicas*. Roma: Vision.
outhern, P. 2001. *The Roman Empire from Severus to Constantine*. London; New York: Routledge.
pera, L. 2003. "The Christianization of Space Along the Via Appia: Changing Landscape in the Suburbs of Rome." *American Journal of Archaeology* 107, no. 1: 23-43.
tevenson, J. 1978. *The Catacombs: Rediscovered Monuments of Early Christianity*. London: Thames and Hudson.
trong, D.E. 1961. *Roman Imperial Sculpture; an Introduction to the Commemorative and Decorative Sculpture of the Roman Empire down to the Death of Constantine*. London: A. Tiranti.
arner, E.R. and S.D. Bundrick. 2000. *From Caligula to Constantine: Tyranny & Transformation in Roman Portraiture*. Atlanta: Michael C. Carlos Museum.
Vard-Perkins, J.B., B. Jones and R. Ling. 1993. *The Severan Buildings of Lepcis Magna: An Architectural Survey*. London: Published on Behalf of the Dept. of Antiquities, Tripoli by the Society for Libyan Studies.
Vard Perkins, J.B. 1948. "Severan Art and Architecture at Lepcis Magna." *Journal of Roman Studies* 38: 59-80.
Valker, S. 1995. *Greek and Roman Portraits*. London: British Museum Press.
Vilkes, J.J. 1993. *Diocletian's Palace, Split: Residence of a Retired Roman Emperor*. University of Sheffield, England: Ian Sanders Memorial Committee.
Vilson, R.J.A. 2006. "A Life of Luxury in Late Roman Sicily: The Villa of Piazza Armerina." *Minerva* 17, no. 1: 40-43.
Vilson, R.J.A. 1983. *Piazza Armerina*. London; New York: Granada.
Vood, S. 1986. *Roman Portrait Sculpture, 217-260 A.D.: The Transformation of an Artistic Tradition*. Leiden: E.J. Brill.

hapter XIII: Rome in Late Antiquity

omeroy, A.J. 2008. *Then It Was Destroyed by the Volcano: The Ancient World in Film and on Television*. London: Duckworth.
Bannister, T.C. 1968. "The Constantinian Basilica of Saint Peter at Rome." *The Journal of the Society of Architectural Historians* 27, no. 1: 3-32.
Bardill, J. 2011. *Constantine, Divine Emperor of the Christian Golden Age*. Cambridge; New York: Cambridge University Press.
Berenson, B. 1954. *The Arch of Constantine; or, The Decline of Form*. London: Chapman & Hall.
Bianchi Bandinelli, R. 1971. *Rome, the Late Empire; Roman Art, A.D. 200-400*. New York: G. Braziller.
Brandenburg, H. and A. Vescovo. 2005. *Ancient Churches of Rome from the Fourth to the Seventh Century: The Dawn of Christian Architecture in the West*. Turnhout, Belgium: Brepols.
Curran, J.R. 2000. *Pagan City and Christian Capital: Rome in the Fourth Century*. Oxford: Oxford University Press.
Elsner, J. 2000. "From the Culture of Spolia to the Cult of Relics: the Arch of Constantine and the Genesis of Late Antique Forms." *Papers of the British School at Rome* 68: 149-184.
Elsner, J. 1995. *Art and the Roman Viewer: The Transformation of Art from the Pagan World to Christianity*. Cambridge: Cambridge University Press.
Grabar, A. 1969. *Early Christian Art: From the Rise of Christianity to the Death of Theodosius*. New York: Odyssey Press.
Hansen, M.F. 2003. *The Eloquence of Appropriation: Prolegomena to an Understanding of Spolia in Early Christian Rome*. Rome: L'Erma Di Bretschneider.
Hartley, E. 2006. *Constantine the Great: York's Roman Emperor*. Marygate, York: York Museums and Gallery Trust.
Holloway, R. Ross. 2004. *Constantine & Rome*. New Haven: Yale University Press.
Kinney, D. 2001. "Roman Architectural *Spolia*." *Proceedings of the American Philosophical Society* 145, no. 2: 138-61.
L'Orange, H.P. 1965. *Art Forms and Civic Life in the Late Roman Empire*. Princeton, NJ: Princeton University Press.
Lenski, N.E. 2012. *The Cambridge Companion to the Age of Constantine*. Cambridge; New York: Cambridge University Press.
MacCormack, S. 1981. *Art and Ceremony in Late Antiquity*. Berkeley: University of California Press.
McClendon, C.B. 1989. "The History of the Site of St. Peter's Basilica, Rome." *Perspecta* 25: 32-65.
Nasrallah, L.S. 2010. *Christian Responses to Roman Art and Architecture: The Second-century Church amid the Spaces of Empire*. Cambridge; New York: Cambridge University Press.
Painter, K.S. 1977. *The Mildenhall Treasure: Roman Silver from East Anglia*. London: British Museum Publications.
Pergola, P., F. Severini and P.M. Barbini. 2000. *Christian Rome: Early Christian Rome: Catacombs and Basilicas*. Roma: Vision.
Pohlsander, H.A. 1996. *The Emperor Constantine*. London; New York: Routledge
Retief, F. and L. Cilliers. 2004. "Malaria in Graeco-Roman Times." *Classic Acta Classica: Proceedings of the Classical Association of South Africa* 47: 127-37.
Rutledge, S.H. 2012. *Ancient Rome as a Museum: Power, Identity and the Culture of Collecting*. Oxford: Oxford University Press.

Sallares, R. 2002. *Malaria and Rome: A History of Malaria in Ancient Italy*. Oxford; New York: Oxford University Press.
Soren, D. 2003. "Can Archaeologists Excavate Evidence of Malaria?" *World Archaeology* 35, no. 2: 193-209.
White, L.M. 1990. *Building God's House in the Roman world: Architectural Adaptation Among Pagans, Jews, and Christians*. Baltimore, MD: Johns Hopkins University Press.

Chapter XIV: Greece in the Roman Period: The Impact of Incorporation into the Roman Empire on an Ancient Culture

Alcock, S.E., J. Cherry, and J. Elsner. 2001. *Pausanias: Travel and Memory in Roman Greece*. New York: Oxford University Press.
Alcock, S.E. 1993. *Graecia Capta: The Landscapes of Roman Greece*. Cambridge; New York: Cambridge University Press.
Alcock, S.E. 1989. "Roman Imperialism in the Greek Landscape." *Journal of Roman Archaeology* 2: 5-34.
Arafat, K.W. 1996. *Pausanias' Greece: Ancient Artists and Roman Rulers*. Cambridge; New York: Cambridge University Press.
Bookidis, N. and R.S. Stroud. 1997. *The Sanctuary of Demeter and Kore: Topography and Architecture*. Princeton, NJ: American School of Classical Studies at Athen
Camp, J. 2001. *The Archaeology of Athens*. New Haven; London: Yale University Press.
Eckstein, Arthur M. 2008. *Rome Enters the Greek East: From Anarchy to Hierarchy in the Hellenistic Mediterranean, 230-170 BC*. Malden, MA; Oxford: Blackwell
Eilers, C. 2002. *Roman Patrons of Greek Cities*. Oxford; New York: Oxford University Press.
Engels, D.W. 1990. *Roman Corinth: An Alternative Model for the Classical City*. Chicago: University of Chicago Press.
Grammenos, D.V (ed.). 2003. *Roman Thessaloniki*. Athens: Thessaloniki Archaeological Museum.
Gregory, T.E. 1993. *The Corinthia in the Roman Period: Including the Papers given at a Symposium Held at The Ohio State University on 7-9 March, 1991*. Ann Arbo MI: Journal of Roman Archaeology.
Macready, S. and F.H. Thompson. 1987. *Roman Architecture in the Greek World*. London: Society of Antiquaries of London Distributed by Thames and Hudson.
Makaronas, C. 1970. *The Arch of Galerius at Thessaloniki*. Thessaloniki: Institute for Balkan Studies.
Matyszak, P. 2009. *Roman Conquest: Macedonia and Greece*. Barnsley: Pen & Sword Military.
Nasrallah, L.S., C. Bakirtzis and S.J. Friesen. 2010. *From Roman to Early Christian Thessalonike: Studies in Religion and Archaeology*. Cambridge, MA: Harvard University Press.
Newby, Z. 2005. *Greek Athletics in the Roman World: Victory and Virtue*. Oxford; New York: Oxford University Press.
Oliver, J.H. 1983. *The Civic Tradition and Roman Athens*. Baltimore: Johns Hopkins University Press.
Ostenfeld, E.N., K. Blomqvist and L.C. Nevett. 2002. *Greek Romans and Roman Greeks: Studies in Cultural Interaction*. Aarhus; Oakville, CT: Aarhus University Press.
Parry, R.L. 1999. "Excavating the Roman Agora at Thessalonica." *Minerva* 10, no.1 :22-24.
Romano, D.G. 2010. "Romanization in the Corinthia: Urban and Rural Developments," in Rizakis, A.D. and C. Lepenioti (ed.), *Roman Peloponnese III, Society, Economy and Culture under the Roman Empire: Continuity and Innovation*. Athens: National Hellenic Research Foundation, Research Institute for Greek and Roman Antiquity, 155-172.
Romano, D.G. 2005. "Urban and Rural Planning in Roman Corinth," in D.N. Schowalter and S.J. Friesen, (ed.), *Urban Religion in Roman Corinth: Interdisciplinary Approaches*. Cambridge: Harvard Theological Studies, 25-59.
Romano, D.G. 2000. "A tale of two cities: Roman colonies at Corinth," in E. Fentress, (ed.) *Romanization and the City: Creation, Transformations, and Failures: Proceedings of a Conference Held at the American Academy in Rome to Celebrate the 50th Anniversary of the Excavations at Cosa, 14-16 May, 1998*. Portsmouth, RI: Journal of Roman Archaeology.
Rousset, D. 2008. "The City and its Territory in the Province of Achaea and 'Roman Greece'." *Harvard Studies in Classical Philology* 104: 303-337.
Spawforth, A.J.S. 2011. *Greece and the Augustan Cultural Revolution*. Cambridge: Cambridge University Press.
Tobin, J. 1997. *Herodes Attikos and the City of Athens: Patronage and Conflict under the Antonines*. Amsterdam: Gieben.
Walbank, M. 1997. "The Foundation and Planning of Early Roman Corinth." *Journal of Roman Archaeology* 10: 95-130.

Chapter XV: Ephesos– How a City Functioned in the Roman Empire

Ball, W. 2002. *Rome in the East: The Transformation of an Empire*. London and New York: Routledge.
Biguzzi, G. 1998. "Ephesus, Its Artemision, Its Temple to the Flavian Emperors, and Idolatry in Revelation." *Novum Testamentum* 40, no. 3: 276-90.
Emerson, M. 2007. *Greek Sanctuaries: An Introduction*. London: Bristol Classical: Duckworth.
Ferguson, J. 1966. "Roman Algeria." *Greece & Rome* 13, no. 2: 169-87.
Jenkins, I. 2006. *Greek Architecture and Its Sculpture*. Cambridge, MA: Harvard University Press.
Jones, A.H.M. 1971. *The Cities of the Eastern Roman Provinces*. Oxford: Clarendon Press.
Koester, H. 1995. *Ephesos Metropolis of Asia: an Interdisciplinary Approach to Its Archaeology, Religion, and Culture*. Valley Forge, PA: Trinity press international.
Krinzinger, F., A. Ertug, S. Ladstatter, and S. Cormack. 2008. *Ephesos: Architecture, Monuments & Sculpture*. Istanbul: Ertug & Kocabyk.
Laale, H.W. 2011. *Ephesus (Ephesos): An Abbreviated History from Androclus to Constantine XI*. Bloomington, IN: WestBow.
Lawrence, A. 1996. *Greek Architecture*. Revised by R.A. Tomlinson. New Haven and London: Yale University Press.
Lund, H.S. 1992. *Lysimachus: A Study in Early Hellenistic Kingship*. London; New York: Routledge.
Macready, S. and F.H. Thompson. 1987. *Roman Architecture in the Greek World*. London: Society of Antiquaries of London Distributed by Thames and Hudson.
Millar, F. 1993. *The Roman Near East, 31 B.C.-A.D. 337*. Cambridge, MA: Harvard University Press.
Murphy-O'Connor, J. 2008. *St. Paul's Ephesus: Texts and Archaeology*. Collegeville, MN: Liturgical.
Ottaway, P. 2004. *Roman York*. Stroud: Tempus.
Parrish, D. and H. Abbasoglu. 2001. *Urbanism in Western Asia Minor: New Studies on Aphrodisias, Ephesos, Hierapolis, Pergamon, Perge, and Xanthos*. Portsmouth, RI: Journal of Roman Archaeology.
Quatember, U. 2010. "The "Temple of Hadrian" on Curetes Street in Ephesus: New Research into its Building History [Archaeological notes]." *Journal of Roman Archaeology* 23: 376-394.
Raja, R. 2012. *Urban Development and Regional Identity in the Eastern Roman Provinces, 50 BC-AD 250: Aphrodisias, Ephesos, Athens, Gerasa*. Copenhagen: Museum Tusculanum Press.
Richardson, P. 2002. *City and Sanctuary: Religion and Architecture in the Roman Near East*. London: SCM Press.
Rogers, G.M. 1991. *The Sacred Identity of Ephesos: Foundation Myths of a Roman City*. London; New York: Routledge.
Scherrer, P. 2001. "The Historical Topography of Ephesos," in D. Parrish (ed.), *Urbanism in Western Asia Minor: New Studies on Aphrodisias, Ephesos, Hierapolis, Pergamon, Perge, and Xanthos*. Portsmouth, R.I.: Journal of Roman Archaeology.
Segal, A. 1997. *From Function to Monument: Urban Landscapes of Roman Palestine, Syria, and Provincia Arabia*. Oxford; Oakville, CT: Oxbow; David Brown Book Co.
Spawforth, A. 2006. *The Complete Greek Temples*. London: Thames & Hudson.
Trebilco, P.R. 2004. *The Early Christians in Ephesus from Paul to Ignatius*. Tubingen: Mohr Siebeck.
Trell, B.L. 1988. "The Temple of Artemis at Ephesos," in Clayton, Peter A., and Martin J Price (ed.), *The Seven Wonders of the Ancient World*. London; New York: Routledge.
Vermeule, C.C. 1968. *Roman Imperial Art in Greece and Asia Minor*. Cambridge, MA: Belknap Press of Harvard University Press.
Wiplinger, G., G. Wlach and K. Gschwantlerand. 1996. *Ephesus: 100 Years of Austrian Research*. Vienna: Bohlau.
Zimmermann, N., S. Ladstatter and M. Buyukkolanc. 2011. *Wall Painting in Ephesos from the Hellenistic to the Byzantine Period*. Istanbul: Ege Yaynlar.

ppendix I: The Importance of Roman Pottery

nold, D.E. 1985. *Ceramic Theory and Cultural Process.* Cambridge: Cambridge University Press.

iley, D. 1980. *A Catalogue of the Lamps in the British Museum.* London.

tioli, G., and I. Angelini. 2010. *Scientific Methods and Cultural Heritage: an Introduction to the Application of Materials Science to Archaeometry and Conservation Science.* Oxford; New York: Oxford University Press.

nning, E.B. 2002. *The Archaeologist's Laboratory: the Analysis of Archaeological Data.* New York: Kluwer Academic.

nifay, M. and J.C. Treglia. 2007. *LRCW 2: Late Roman Coarse Wares, Cooking Wares and Amphorae in the Mediterranean: Archaeology and Archaeometry.* Oxford: Archaeopress.

wman, A.K., and A. Wilson. 2011. *Settlement, Urbanization, and Population. Oxford Studies on the Roman Economy.* Oxford; New York: Oxford University Press.

wman, A.K., and A. Wilson. 2009. *Quantifying the Roman Economy: Methods and Problems.* Oxford: Oxford University Press.

rragato, F., P. Pensabene and P. Tucci. 2002. *Archaeometry and Classical Heritage.* Rome, Italy: Bardi.

eagh, D.C. and D. Bradley. 2007. *Physical Techniques in the Study of Art, Archaeology and Cultural Heritage.* Amsterdam: Elsevier Science Ltd.

Blois, L., C.E. Lo, O. Hekster, and G. de Kleijn. 2007. *The Impact of the Roman Army (200 BC-AD 476 : Economic, Social, Political, Religious, and Cultural Aspects: Proceedings of the Sixth Workshop of the International Network Impact of Empire (Roman Empire, 200 B.C.-A.D. 476), Capri, March 29-April 2, 2005.* Leiden; Boston: Brill.

menech-Carbo, A., M.T. Domenech, and V. Costa. 2009. *Electrochemical Methods in Archaeometry, Conservation and Restoration.* Berlin; Heidelberg: Springer.

eene, K. 2005. "Roman Pottery: Models, Proxies and Economic Interpretation." *Journal of Roman Archeology* 18: 34-56.

eene, K. 1992. *Roman Pottery.* London: Published for the Trustees of the British Museum by British Museum Press.

rt, E.J.M., I. Garrigos, J. Buxeda, and O.M.A. Cau. 2005. *LRCW I: Late Roman Coarse Wares, Cooking Wares and Amphorae in the Mediterranean: Archaeology and Archaeometry.* Oxford, England: Archaeopress.

yes, J.W. 2008. *Roman Pottery: Fine-ware Imports.* Princeton, NJ: American School of Classical Studies at Athens.

yes, J.W. 1997. *Handbook of Mediterranean Roman Pottery.* Norman: University of Oklahoma Press.

nrick, P.M. 2009. "Understanding the Technical Aspects of Making—and Studying—Ancient Pottery." *Journal of Roman Archaeology* 22: 647-650.

likoglou, V., A. Hein, and Y. Maniatis. 2002. *Modern Trends in Scientific Studies on Ancient Ceramics : Papers Presented at the 5th European Meeting on Ancient Ceramics, Athens, 1999.* Oxford: Archaeopress.

ute, U. 1987. *Archaeometry: An Introduction to Physical Methods in Archaeology and the History of Art.* Weinheim, Germany: Wiley-VCH.

wit, T. 2011. "Dynamics of fineware production and trade: the puzzle of supra-regional exporters." *Journal of Roman Archaeology* 24: 313-332.

illett, M. 1979. *Pottery and the Archaeologist.* London: Institute of Archaeology.

alamidou, V. and J.W. Hedges. 2005. *Roman Pottery in Context: Fine and Coarse Wares from Five Sites in North-eastern Greece.* Oxford: John and Erica Hedges.

artin, Archer. 2000. "Amphorae at Olympia," *Rei Cretariae Romanae Fautorum Acta* 36: 427-433

enchelli, S. 2010. *LRCW3 : Late Roman Coarse Wares, Cooking Wares and Amphorae in the Mediterranean : Archaeology and Archaeometry: Comparison between Western and Eastern Mediterranean.* Oxford: Archaeopress.

in, J. S. and A. D. Franklin. 1982. *Archaeological Ceramics.* Washington, D.C.: Smithsonian Institution.

ton, C., P. Tyers, and A. G. Vince. 1993. *Pottery in Archaeology.* Cambridge: Cambridge University Press.

swald, F. 1964. *Index of Potters' Stamps on Terra Sigillata, Samian Ware.* London: Gregg.

pi, E. and M/ Bonifay. 2007. *Supplying Rome and the Empire: The Proceedings of an International Seminar Held at Siena-Certosa Di Pontignano on May 2-4, 2004, on Rome, the Provinces, Production and Distribution.* Portsmouth, R.I.: Journal of Roman Archaeology.

acock, D.P.S., and D.F. Williams. 1986. *Amphorae and the Roman Economy: an Introductory Guide.* London: Longman.

acock, D.P.S. 1982. *Pottery in the Roman World: an Ethnoarchaeological Approach.* London: Longman.

ña, J.T. 2007. *Roman Pottery in the Archaeological Record.* Cambridge: Cambridge University Press.

uinn, P.S. 2009. *Interpreting Silent Artefacts: Petrographic Approaches to Archaeological Ceramics.* Oxford: Archaeopress.

ice, P.M. 1987. *Pottery Analysis: a Sourcebook.* Chicago: University of Chicago Press.

obinson, Henry. 1959. *The Athenian Agora, Volume V: Pottery of the Roman Period. Chronology.* Princeton University Press.

ye, O.S. 1981. *Pottery Technology: Principles and Reconstruction.* Washington, D.C.: Taraxacum.

carcella, S. 2011. *Archaeological Ceramics: A Review of Current Research.* Oxford, England: Archaeopress.

nopoli, C.M. 1991. *Approaches to Archaeological Ceramics.* New York: Plenum Press.

hackley, M.S. 2011. *X-ray Fluorescence Spectrometry (XRF) in Geoarchaeology.* New York: Springer.

ill, E.L. 1992. "Production, Distribution, and Disposal of Roman Amphoras," in Bey III, George J and Christopher A. Pool (ed.), *Ceramic Production and Distribution: an Integrated Approach.* Boulder: Westview Press.

ppendix II: Excavating a Roman Archaeological Site

itken, M.J. 1990. *Science-based Dating in Archaeology.* London: Longman.

ldenderfer, M.S., and H.D.G. Maschner. 1996. *Anthropology, Space, and Geographic Information Systems.* New York: Oxford University Press.

llen, K.M.S., S.W. Green, and E.B.W. Zubrow. 1990. *Interpreting Space: GIS and Archaeology.* London: Taylor & Francis.

ndresen, J., T. Madsén, and I. Scollar. 1993. *Computing the Past: Computer Applications and Quantitative methods in Archaeology: CAA92.* Aarhus: Aarhus University Press.

aillie, M.G.L. 1995. *A Slice Through Time: Dendrochronology and Precision Dating.* London: Batsford.

anning, E.B. 2002. *Archaeological Survey.* New York: Kluwer Academic/Plenum Publishers.

anning, E.B. 2002. *The Archaeologist's Laboratory:Tthe Analysis of Archaeological Data.* New York: Kluwer Academic.

arker, P. 1993. *Techniques of Archaeological Excavation.* London: Batsford.

arker, P. 1986. *Understanding Archaeological Excavation.* London: B.T. Batsford

arnard, H., and J.W. Eerkens. 2007. *Theory and Practice of Archaeological Residue Analysis.* Oxford: Archaeopress.

intliff, John. 2004. *A Companion to Archaeology.* Oxford: Wiley-Blackwell.

lau, S., and D.H. Ubelaker. 2009. *Handbook of Forensic Anthropology and Archaeology.* Walnut Creek, CA: Left Coast Press.

owman, A. K. and M. Brady (ed.). 2005. *Images and Artefacts of the Ancient World.* Oxford; New York: Oxford University Press.

owman, S. 1990. *Radiocarbon Dating.* London: Published for the Trustees of the British Museum by British Museum Publications.

rothwell, D, R. and A.M. Pollard. 2001. *Handbook of Archaeological Sciences.* Chichester: J. Wiley.

uikstra, J.E. and L. A. Beck. 2006. *Bioarchaeology: the Contextual Analysis of Human Remains.* Amsterdam: Academic Press.

ameron, F. and S. Kenderdine. 2007. *Theorizing Digital Cultural Heritage a Critical Discourse.* Cambridge, MA: MIT Press.

armichael, D.L., R.H. Lafferty and B. Molyneaux. 2003. *Excavation.* Walnut Creek, CA: AltaMira Press.

lark, A.J. 1996. *Seeing Beneath the Soil: Prospecting Methods in Archaeology.* London: B.T. Batsford.

ollins, J.M., and Brian Molyneaux. 2003. *Archaeological Survey.* Walnut Creek, CA: Altamira Press.

ollis, J. 2001. *Digging up the Past: an Introduction to Archaeological Excavation.* Stroud, Gloucestershire: Sutton.

onyers, L.B. 2004. *Ground-penetrating Radar for Archaeology.* Walnut Creek, CA: AltaMira Press.

onyers, L.B., and Dean Goodman. 1997. *Ground-penetrating Radar: An Introduction for Archaeologists.* Walnut Creek, CA: AltaMira Press.

Drewett, P. 1999. *Field Archaeology: an Introduction*. London: UCL Press.
Eckstein, Dieter, M.G.L. Baillie, and H. Egger. 1984. *Dendrochronological Dating*. Strasbourg: European Science Foundation.
Dupras, T.L. 2012. *Forensic Recovery of Human Remains: Archaeological Approaches*. Boca Raton, FL: CRC Press.
Favro, D. 2009. "Assessing Virtual Reality Simulations in Archaeology." *Journal of Roman Archaeology* 22: 621-624.
Fleming, S.J. 1976. *Dating in Archaeology: A Guide to Scientific Techniques*. London: Dent.
Forte, M. 2010. *Cyber-archaeology*. Oxford: Archaeopress.
Forte, M. and P.R. Williams. 2003. *The Reconstruction of Archaeological Landscapes Through Digital Technologies: Proceedings of the 1st Italy-United States Workshop, Boston, Massachusetts, USA, November 1-3, 2001*. Oxford, England: Archaeopress.
Forte, M., J.A. Barceló and D.H. Sanders. 2000. *Virtual Reality in Archaeology: Computer Applications and Quantitative Methods in Archaeology (CAA)*. Oxford: Archaeopress.
Forte, M and A. Siliotti. 1997. *Virtual Archaeology: Re-creating Ancient Worlds*. New York: H.N. Abrams.
Gaffney, C.F., and J. Gater. 2003. *Revealing the Buried Past: Geophysics for Archaeologists*. Stroud: Tempus.
Haglund, W.D., M.H. Sorg and D.L. France. 2002. *Human Remains: Recognition, Documentation, Recovery, and Preservation*. Boca Raton, Fla: CRC.
Harris, E.C. 1989. *Principles of Archaeological Stratigraphy*. London: Academic Press.
Haselberger, L., J.H. Humphrey and D. Abernathy. 2006. *Imaging Ancient Rome: Documentation, Visualization, Imagination: Proceedings of the Third Williams Symposium on Classical Architecture, Held at the American Academy in Rome, the British School at Rome, and the Deutsches Archäologisches Institut, Rome, on May 20-23, 2004*. Portsmouth, RI: Journal of Roman Archaeology.
Hester, T.R., H.J. Shafer, and K.L. Feder. 2008. *Field Methods in Archaeology*. Seventh Edition. Left Coast Press, Incorporated.
Hodder, I. 1999. *The Archaeological Process: an Introduction*. Oxford: Blackwell.
Hodder, I. 1995. *Interpreting Archaeology: Finding Meaning in the Past*. London: Routledge.
Hodder, I. 1986. *Reading the Past: Current approaches to Interpretation in Archaeology*. Cambridge: Cambridge University Press.
Hunter, J. and M. Cox. 2005. *Forensic Archaeology: Advances in Theory and Practice*. London: Routledge.
Ioannides, M. 2010. *Heritage in the Digital Era: International Conference on Virtual Systems and Multimedia*. Brentwood, Essex: Multi-Science Publishing.
Joukowsky, M. 1980. *A Complete Manual of Field Archaeology: Tools and Techniques of Field Work for Archaeologists*. Englewood Cliffs, N.J.: Prentice-Hall.
Keller, D.R., and D.W. Rupp. 1983. *Archaeological Survey in the Mediterranean Area*. Oxford: B.A.R.
Maschner, H. D. G., and C. Chippindale. 2005. *Handbook of Archaeological Methods*. Lanham, MD: AltaMira Press.
Mays, S. 1998. *The Archaeology of Human Bones*. London: Routledge.
McIntosh, J. 1986. *The Practical Archaeologist: How We Know What We Know About the Past*. New York, N.Y.: Facts on File.
Michael, H. N., and Elizabeth K. Ralph. 1971. *Dating Techniques for the Archaeologist*. Cambridge: MIT Press.
Michels, J.W. 1973. *Dating Methods in Archaeology*. New York: Seminar Press.
Mook, W. G., and H.T. Waterbolk. 1985. *Radiocarbon Dating*. Strasbourg: European Science Foundation.
Neumann, T.W.and R.M. Sanford. 2001. *Cultural Resources Archaeology: An Introduction*. Walnut Creek, CA: AltaMira Press.
Neumann, T.W.and R.M. Sanford. 2001. *Practicing Archaeology: a Training Manual for Cultural Resources Archaeology*. Walnut Creek, CA: AltaMira Press.
Orton, C. 2000. *Sampling in Archaeology*. Cambridge: Cambridge University Press.
Roskams, S. 2001. *Excavation*. Cambridge: Cambridge University Press.
Schweingruber, F.H. 1988. *Tree Rings: Basics and Applications of Dendrochronology*. Dordrecht: D. Reidel Pub. Co.
Scollar, I. 1990. *Archaeological Prospecting and Remote Sensing*. Cambridge: Cambridge University Press.
Spence, C. 1990. *Archaeological Site Manual*. London: Dept. of Urban Archaeology, Museum of London.
Taylor, R.E. 1987. *Radiocarbon Dating: An Archaeological Perspective*. Orlando: Academic Press.
Tite, M.S. 1972. *Methods of Physical Examination in Archaeology*. London: Seminar Press.
Waldron, T. 2001. *Shadows in the Soil: Human Bones & Archaeology*. Stroud, Gloucestershire: Tempus.
Watson, P.J. , S.A. LeBlanc, and C.L. Redman. 1971. *Explanation in Archeology: An Explicitly Scientific Approach*. New York: Columbia University Press.
Wien, S. 2004. *Enter the Past: The E-way into the Four Dimensions of Cultural Heritage : CAA 2003, Computer Applications and Quantitative Methods in Archaeology : Proceedings of the 31st Conference, Vienna, Austria, April 2003*. Oxford: Archaeopress.
Zimmerman, L.J. 2003. *Presenting the Past*. Walnut Creek: Altamira Press
Zimmerman, M.R., and J.L. Angel. 1986. *Dating and Age Determination of Biological Materials*. London: Croom Helm.

Some Useful Internet Websites

Ancient World Mapping Center: http://www.unc.edu/awmc/
Archaeological Institute of America: http://www.archaeological.org
Corinth Computer Project: http://corinthcomputerproject.org
De Imperitoribus Romanis ("On the Rulers of Rome"): An Online Encyclopedia of Roman Rulers and Their Families: http://www.roman-emperors.org/
Digital Augustan Rome: http://digitalaugustanrome.org/
Digital Materials on the Geography of the Ancient World: http://pleiades.stoa.org/
Digital Sculpture Project: http://www.digitalsculpture.org/
Forma Urbis Romae : http://formaurbis.stanford.edu/index.html
Lacus Curtius: Into the Roman World: http://penelope.uchicago.edu/thayer/e/roman/home.html
Mapping the Grand Tour: https://republicofletters.stanford.edu/
Maecenas: Images of Ancient Greece and Rome: http://wings.buffalo.edu/AandL/Maecenas/general_contents.html
Pompeii in Pictures: http://pompeiiinpictures.com/pompeiiinpictures/index.htm
The Romans: http://www.the-romans.co.uk
Roman Empire : http://www.livius.org/rome.html
Rome Reborn: http://www.romereborn.virginia.edu/
The Stanford Geospatial Network Model of the Roman World: http://orbis.stanford.edu/
A Virtual Community for Teaching and Learning Classics:http://vroma.org/
Virtual World Heritage Laboratory: http://vwhl.clas.virginia.edu/

Index (pages 1-185 found in Volume I)

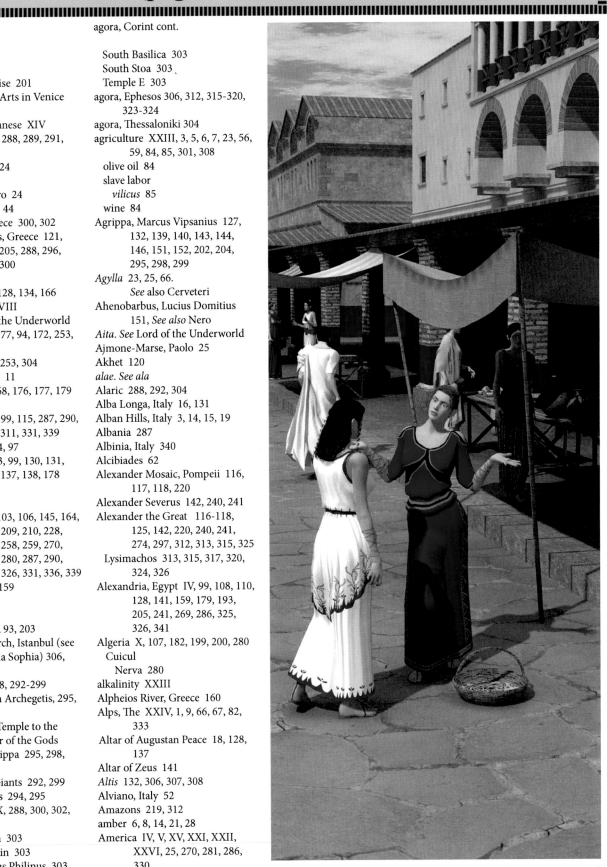

Roman life on the decumanus or main street at Ostia, reconstructed by Angelo Coccettini and Marzia Vinci.

G

Films in this text can be found at:

http://www.

Films in this text can be found at:

http://www.midmar.com/SOREN.html

or send $2 to
Midnight Marquee Press, Inc.
9721 Britinay Lane
Baltimore, MD 21234 for 2 disc set of films

or send $2 via paypal to
mmarquee@aol.com

78596601R00124

Made in the USA
Lexington, KY
11 January 2018